"This well-proportioned book offers an unusually reliable guide to the history and present circumstances of Seventh-day Adventism that should be appreciated equally by Adventists and outsiders. Among its many strengths are a careful account of origins in the 1840s, discriminating treatment of the role of prophet Ellen G. White, full attention to the Adventists' remarkable range of medical and educational institutions, perceptive details about parallels to fundamentalist and evangelical movements, many details for the Adventist communities found in almost every part of the world, and up-to-date coverage on topics like ongoing debate over women in ordained ministry and the effect on Adventist churches in Russia and Ukraine of the war begun in 2022. A judicious denominational history."

—Mark Noll
professor emeritus of history, University of Notre Dame

"This mission-driven history of Seventh-day Adventism traces the denomination's story from a unique perspective—one especially suited for twenty-first-century readers. It not only outlines the history, but wrestles with the challenges faced by a worldwide movement in an ever more complex world. As a result, it deals with issues and ideas that are important both to those inside and outside of Adventism. Campbell and Allen's volume is highly recommended for those who desire to tap into the past and present of a multifaceted religious body whose outreach circles the globe."

—George R. Knight
professor emeritus of church history, Andrews University

"The Seventh-day Adventist movement originated in the 1840s among scattered New Englanders who believed ardently in the imminence of the second coming of Christ; over time, the movement became an elaborately structured global church identified with health reform and educational effort as well as the simple gospel. Michael W. Campbell and Edward Martin Allen have written a stimulating and authoritative account of its development which, with an extensive glossary of technical terms and questions for discussion, will be invaluable for Adventists and non-Adventists alike."

—David Bebbington
professor emeritus of history, University of Stirling

"Campbell and Allen have provided a timely and thoughtful resource that places Adventist history in its rightful worldwide context. This important work fills a needed place in our collective understanding and will be of value to students, scholars, and general readers alike."

—Delbert W. Baker

former vice president of the SDA General Conference,
former vice chancellor of the Adventist University of Africa

A Global History of
SEVENTH-DAY ADVENTISTS

Michael W. Campbell | Edward Martin Allen

WILLIAM B. EERDMANS PUBLISHING COMPANY
GRAND RAPIDS, MICHIGAN

Wm. B. Eerdmans Publishing Co.
2006 44th Street SE, Grand Rapids, MI 49508
www.eerdmans.com

Published 2026
Printed in the United States of America

32 31 30 29 28 27 26 1 2 3 4 5 6 7

ISBN 978-0-8028-7938-7

Library of Congress Cataloging-in-Publication Data

A catalog record for this book is available from the Library of Congress.

Grateful acknowledgment is given to Pacific Press for permission to use material from Michael Campbell, *Pocket Dictionary for Understanding Seventh-day Adventism* (Nampa, ID: Pacific Press, 2020). Photo credits are listed on p. 300.

Contents

Preface

A new introduction to Seventh-day Adventist history has been needed for some time. This became apparent in a survey of Seventh-day Adventist classrooms conducted around 2015. The rather lengthy tome *Light Bearers* was rarely, if ever, being used, and a myriad of small treatises and articles was being used instead. As a result, as we (Ed and Michael) discussed this challenge at the Association of Seventh-day Adventist Historians, we felt the necessity of a new history of the Adventist Church. As we have collectively spent some three decades in the classroom teaching Adventist history, we saw the need for a readable text that would appeal to college students. At the same time, we wanted to create an approachable and useful history, especially for someone unfamiliar with the Adventist tradition.

We have tried to be as fair and balanced as possible. However, we know that we bring our unique interpretative approaches to this project that reflect our unique experiences. One evident approach is the strong missiological outlook of this volume. Ed was raised as a missionary kid in the Philippines, and together, we have spent over a decade of mission service as adults (Michael in the Philippines and Ed in Hong Kong). This cross-cultural experience has been most enriching and certainly informs some of our themes on the global scope of Adventism. Together, we have traveled to well over a hundred countries and have taught and spoken in many of them. In fact, it was in the Philippines that many of these concepts began to take more concrete form, as Michael was teaching and Ed would periodically come to Adventist International Institute of Advanced Studies (AIIAS), located in that country, to teach classes. As plans for the book started to take shape between bird-watching trips, we began to formulate a definite outline incorporating many of our lectures and testing out material with many undergraduate and graduate students. We are deeply grateful to those students who, over the years, have either directly or indirectly enriched our teaching. However, this history ultimately reflects our personal scholarship and perspectives. It doesn't necessarily reflect the views of the organization or leaders with whom we currently work or have worked.

Engagement in the wider academic community, especially through participation at the American Academy of Religion, the Adventist Society for Religious Studies, the Adventist Theological Society, and the American Society of Church History, provided opportunities for continued conversations and plans for this volume. We deeply respect and value the insights and discussions that have shaped this book. As the book began to take shape, Ed met Tom DeVries from Eerdmans on a flight to one of these meetings, which prompted discussions about publishing this volume. We are deeply grateful to Tom, along with Andrew Knapp, Kimberly Benedict, and the rest of their team who have helped to shepherd the editorial process along and get us through the production process.

The production of any book involves a debt of gratitude to many who have provided assistance along the way. The Center for Adventist Research, with Kevin M. Burton and his associate, Katharine Van Arsdale, and their staff, has been especially helpful. We also want to express a deep debt of gratitude to Ashlee Chism and David Trim from the General Conference Archives, Statistics, and Research. Historians who have taken the time to read this manuscript include Brian Strayer, George Knight, George Gibson, Jud Lake, Alden Thompson, Doug Matacio, Douglas Morgan, John Doh, Savonna Greer, Andrew Howe, and Laura Wibberding. Special thanks go to others who have given valuable information and feedback, including Simbarashe Musvosvi, Tom Lemon, Annelise Jacobs, and Robert Burrow. Special thanks to Dale Galusha and Pacific Press for permission to use some excerpts from Michael's *Pocket Dictionary of Seventh-day Adventism* (2020) as a basis for our condensed glossary. Finally, we are deeply grateful to our spouses, Dr. Madalyn Burtoft Allen and Dr. Heidi Olson Campbell, for their love and support, and to our children, who have provided encouragement along the journey. Special thanks to Madalyn for compiling the bibliography! We acknowledge and appreciate the invaluable contributions of all these individuals and institutions.

Introduction

A history of Seventh-day Adventists focused on their global history is long overdue. For over one hundred years, the majority of Adventists have lived outside North America. However, histories of the church have remained centered on North America. Many North Americans are unaware of developments in global Adventism. The predominant population of the church has shifted to Africa, and the intellectual center may be moving to South America. These shifts mark a dramatic turn for a church that began in the late 1840s in upper New England.

From the beginning of the movement in the late 1840s, Adventists were compelled to share their understanding of what they saw as God's new work. At first, they severely limited the scope of their activity to former Millerites. However, a deeper understanding of Scripture and the unexpected spread of their ideas caused them to broaden their activity to include the entire world. Adventists share a conviction that they are called to actively proclaim a unique message to everyone everywhere. They are impatient with waiting and feel called to actively cooperate with God in preparing for Jesus's return.

David Bebbington argues that evangelicals are marked by four characteristics: a focus on the cross as the means of salvation, an emphasis on conversion, biblicism, and activism. As this history of the church will demonstrate, Adventists exhibit all four of these characteristics, but their activism has spread their reach to the whole world. They developed a unique mission and then set out to fulfill it. In what is an intentional interpretive lens, this narrative strives to focus on Adventism as a global phenomenon.

Adventist activity embodies not only theological ideas but also convictions about health and education. This relatively small denomination came to operate one of the largest Protestant educational systems on the planet and one of its largest health-care systems. This is the story of a people committed to actively working to share both the gospel of personal salvation and the gospels of health, education, and freedom for all.

"Telling the truth about history is a moral obligation that requires effort."

—Gary Land

"Human history is the long terrible story of man trying to find something other than God which will make him happy."

—C. S. Lewis

"I think that to a very great extent we are partners with the divine in this enterprise called history. That is an ongoing relationship, and there is absolutely no guarantee that things will automatically work out to our best advantage. We will have to have very serious efforts put into the making of good history in order for us to benefit from it."

—Chaim Potok

CHAPTER 1

Beginnings

The Adventist movement began at the intersection of history and prophecy. William Miller was not the first student of the Bible to find apocalyptic prophecies fulfilled in historical events. Historians have traced that history back to some of the earliest Christian writers in the first centuries of the church. Miller was also aware of some of the Protestant prophetic expositors of his day. He adopted their assumptions and extended their ideas to see fulfillment in his time. However, the dominant view of future events in Protestant America saw the world evolving into a more perfect place. The church was the kingdom of God on Earth, and Christians were to wait patiently while the church flourished during a spiritual millennium. Once the church had conquered the world, Jesus would return to rule as king. In contrast, Miller believed Christ would return in glory before the thousand-year period described in Revelation 20. He also believed that Daniel and Revelation described the history of the kingdoms of the world in advance, a system of prophetic interpretation known as historicism.

Edward Irving

Miller was not alone in his prophetic endeavor. Manuel de Lacunza in South America arrived at similar conclusions. His work influenced Edward Irving in England and inspired Joseph Wolff's travels across central Asia. These men used a method of interpreting the apocalyptic prophecies of Daniel and Revelation that focused on their development in history between the time the prophetic vision was given and the "end of time."

Historicism pointed to actual verifiable historical events fulfilling the prophets' written accounts. In one sense, these interpreters had the Bible in one hand and history books in the other. The underlying assumption of the historicist prophetic interpreters was that God had revealed to the prophet what would take place in the future. The apocalyptic prophecies were not hidden or sealed up forever. The careful student could study the prophecies, compare them to historical records, and point to a correspondence between them. For example, Daniel predicted in the eighth chapter of his book (vv. 20–21) that the empire of the Medes and Persians would overwhelm the Babylonian Empire. In turn, the Medes and Persians would be overthrown by the Greek

The 1826 Albury Park Conference and Joseph Wolff

Joseph Wolff (1795–1862) was born into a Jewish home in Germany. As a young person, he was converted to Christianity while discussing religion with his Christian barber. As a teenager, he was baptized into the Catholic Church, and then, as a student and tutor, he wandered Europe, teaching various languages (especially Hebrew) as he furthered his education. After he was expelled from the Collegio Romano in Rome for questioning the authority of the pope, he began to travel on his own, lecturing on various religious subjects. English businessman Henry Drummond heard the aspiring missionary speak and offered to cover his travel expenses if he would visit him in England.

Joseph Wolff

The first evening after Wolff arrived at Drummond's home in 1826, he met Edward Irving, the founder of the Catholic Apostolic Church and student of Bible prophecy. Wolff and Irving shared many common interests, and together they participated in a weeklong conference about unfulfilled prophecies featuring scholars from across Europe. Wolff's knowledge of Hebrew enhanced the discussions significantly. Their studies convinced them that the antichrist was yet to come. They believed that Christ's return would occur about the year 1847. Wolff traveled across the Middle East to India and then returned to England after traveling through Ethiopia and North Africa, spreading the news about Christ's soon return. Irving and Drummond held five additional prophetic conferences at Drummond's home, Albury Park, hence the name for the Albury Park Prophecy Conferences.

Empire. Prophetic interpreters could point to the historical record to show the fulfillment of this prophecy.

For Miller and his second advent followers, it mattered that historical evidence pointed to the Bible's truthfulness. The Enlightenment's emphasis on reason influenced Miller and others far more than they realized in their day. The evidence in history of prophetic fulfillment was viewed as reasonable proof for the divine origin of the Bible. Since even to this day historians wrestle with the issue of historical evidence, and many question how reliable any historical record is, we need to address the nature of history and its relationship to faith.

What Is History?

History is closely related to identity. Our past is crucial to understanding who we are. Even beyond our personal identity, history applies to how we collectively construct our religious, social, or political identity. This identity involves telling the story of our past. Almost everyone enjoys hearing a good story. So, history is all about discovering identity through the stories shared about those who have gone before.

A historian investigates the past and asks questions about truthfulness and reliability. Leopold von Ranke once remarked that history is to "tell it as it actually happened." History involves curiosity about what happened in the past as well as a critical approach to evaluating the sources those stories are based upon. A critical approach means that historians sort through the often-conflicting records of the past to discover as much as possible what happened based upon the most reliable evidence.

The seventeenth-century historian Paolo Sarpi once warned: "Men are so much in love with their own opinions that they persuade themselves that God favors them as much as they do themselves."[1] The danger in studying history is to only remember the positive and leave aside the negative. Such nostalgia becomes historical shortsightedness. Some people romanticize the people, events, and places from "long ago" and "far away." They dream about the "good old days" when life was simpler and unspoiled. Unfortunately, doing so contributes to a complacent forgetfulness about the dangers and hardships related to past persons and events. The resulting mythology always distorts the truth. The minds of individuals and societies play tricks on them

1. Peter Burke, *Sarpi: History of Benefices and Selections from History of the Council of Trent* (New York: Washington Square Press, 1967), xxxii.

in a psychological process of repression. Adventist historian Gary Land observed that Christians who study history have a moral responsibility to speak the truth as best they can. Because men and women of the past were also fellow creatures made in the image of God, they deserve to be represented as accurately as possible.[2]

Some historians despair at accurately knowing anything about the past. Indeed, it is unlikely that anyone can know past events with the detail and certainty of an eyewitness. It is also true that even eyewitnesses mold their accounts for their own purposes, as do historians who write many years afterward. However, it remains possible to determine, with varying degrees of accuracy, the essential happenings of historical events.

Several factors contribute to how historians weigh the accuracy of an account. These include the number and quality of firsthand accounts remaining, the bias of the reports, and the reactions of others to these earliest reports. For example, many high-quality reports about William Miller's life and activity exist. Most descriptions are highly biased, either strongly for or strongly against him and his ideas. However, both the positive and negative reports generally agree upon the essential events of his life. Numerous contemporary accounts of his life and activity are easily available for anyone to study. Thus, while it is not possible to know everything about William Miller, it is possible with confidence to reach an understanding of who he was and his basic ideas with a high degree of accuracy. This example suggests that while it is not possible to reproduce a complete, accurate, and flawless representation of a past person or event, that does not mean one cannot know anything about it either. The more objective and accurate we strive to be in our history, the better off everyone is when it comes to assessing its accuracy and learning from it. Furthermore, an objective stance contributes to a recognition of the complexity and uncertainty in describing historic events. One must recognize that in the present, as well as the past, there are many narratives and factors that have shaped the stories.

Accurate reflection about the truth of the past also helps educate future generations. Christianity has no place for half-truths or myths. Both individuals and societies must take responsibility for informed and responsible decisions. For Christians, the Bible sets forth the necessary foundation for studying history. Therefore, followers of Christ have a moral responsibility to study and understand the past.

2. Gary Land, *Teaching History: A Seventh-Day Adventist Approach* (Berrien Springs, MI: Andrews University Press, 2000).

Biblical Foundations for Studying History

The Bible affirms that history is essential because only through history is it possible to discern God's actions and involvement with humanity. Furthermore, the Bible describes God's principles and ways of dealing with humanity, specifically through prophetic messengers. Throughout the Scriptures, God shares his redemptive message, culminating in the life and person of Jesus Christ.

The Bible records human successes and failures. While many ancient texts record only accomplishments or victories of people, the Bible is unique in describing not only the successes but also the failings of key leaders in the salvation narrative. Recording such shortcomings informs people about God's perspective. For example, only a loving God would care enough to correct King David after his moral failure with Bathsheba.

One way that God reveals his thoughts to human beings is by informing them about the future through the prophetic gift. Bible writers traced the his-

Tools of the Trade

Historians use a variety of tools to help them reliably reconstruct history. While Christians accept the Bible as divine revelation, in practical terms, historians utilize several methods to determine what happened in the past.

The first is to recognize change. A common mistake is to assume that people today live and act the same as they did in earlier times. After many generations, it is possible to observe how change happens across different customs, cultures, and places. Life today differs from what it looked like many centuries or millennia ago. Historians begin their task by asking, "What has changed?"

The next task requires critical thinking. This means using discernment to recognize the probable truth in the face of conflicting descriptions or arguments. Historians realize that each person possesses a unique point of view. Historians ask: What biases does this person have? An angry or polemical piece of writing against someone is obviously more biased than a more neutral source of evidence, such as a shopping list, which most people would not ordinarily try to change or manipulate. A private letter serves a different purpose than a published record.

Finally, historians pursue the earliest available source. Generally, earlier sources tend to be the most reliable, as memories fade over time. A firsthand witness to an event is usually far more reliable than someone who could not have been present. Numerous firsthand accounts help to determine and create a more accurate depiction of what happened. Historians relentlessly search for the earliest and most reliable evidence.

Historiography Versus Hagiography

The term "historiography" developed during the early modern period across Western civilization as a way to describe the "writing of history." It became "the study of the way history has been and is written—the history of historical writing. . . . When you study 'historiography,' you do not study the events of the past directly, but the changing interpretations of those events in the works of individual historians."[1]

By way of contrast, "hagiography" is an ancient term from the early Christian church that refers to the lives of the saints. Originally, the term described the pure and miraculous lives of martyrs and saints. However, it developed a derogatory tone as a way to describe the gullible and uncritical (often fictitious) historical accounts of these same early Christian figures. Historians use the term to describe an uncritical and reverential acceptance of the past.

1. Conal Furay and Michael J. Salevouris, *The Methods and Skills of History: A Practical Guide*, 2nd ed. (Wheeling, IL: Harlan Davidson, 2009), 223.

torical fulfillment of biblical prophecies, the most important of which was the coming of the Messiah in the person of Jesus Christ (cf. Matt. 1:22–23; 2:5–6, 15, 17–18; 3:3, 14–16; 8:17; 11:10). The pattern of Christ's life and ministry illustrates that there is a greater narrative at work that has existed throughout salvation history. This greater narrative began with the fall of Lucifer in heaven and became tangible on this earth through the entrance of sin with Adam and Eve. All the prophets pointed forward to the life, death, and resurrection of Jesus Christ. Once the plan of salvation was assured through Christ's sacrifice and atonement, the "blessed hope" (Titus 2:11–13) culminates with the second coming of Jesus when God takes his people to their promised heavenly home.

Adventism in Wider Perspective

The Seventh-day Adventist Church arose within a historical context. The success of Adventism is directly related to its sense of prophetic identity. Following the resurrection and ascension of Jesus, the New Testament's most significant prophecies pertain to the second coming of Jesus (see John 14:1–3).[3] It promises that Jesus will return literally in the sky (Matt. 24:30–31;

3. Unless otherwise noted, all Scripture quotations come from the New International Version (2011).

Rev. 1:7). This hope animated the apostolic church; yet by AD 100, all the apostles were gone. Over the next few centuries, the early church wrestled with major controversies as tensions mounted over how to preserve and transmit the faith as new and pressing concerns eclipsed this earlier apocalyptic emphasis.

A crucial topic early Christians faced was how to maintain the pure truth of the gospel (2 Thess. 2:1–4). Paul predicted a "falling away" as a descent into a time of spiritual darkness. As the church aligned itself with the state at the time of Constantine, it also began to lose a sense of the urgent expectancy about the second advent. Christian leaders grew more influential and powerful, which suggested that God was already setting up his kingdom here on Earth through the church. A sense of the need for the Lord's return diminished. Those who rekindled this hope in the advent were deemed subversive. A significant turning point occurred in 538 when the western Roman emperor Justinian decreed that the bishop of Rome was the "head of all the Holy Churches" and corrector of heretics. For the next 1,260 years, the pope claimed authority and primacy that included the authority to interpret Scripture. A natural result was the tendency to rely on tradition and the authority of religious figures to interpret Scripture.

During the medieval era, a variety of reformers brought renewed attention back to the Bible and sought to reform the Christian church. The Waldensians trained young pastors or "barbes" to share the Bible as they traveled from town to town across Europe. Other notable reformers include John Wycliffe

Basic Biases

How do you know if something is true? Several common problems in history making are:

- *Bias by inertia*, in which someone presents outdated information and interpretations.
- *Unconscious falsification*, which emphasizes what is good about one's country.
- *Bias by omission*, which tends to overlook unfavorable facts and interpretations.
- *Bias in the use of language*, in which words that favor one side over another are used.
- *Bias through cumulative implication*, which suggests that one's nation (or group) won all the wars and invented all the new technologies.

(ca. 1330–1384), an Oxford lecturer, who organized a team of individuals to translate the Bible into English. His intention was that even the man in the field would learn about and understand the Scriptures. The increased literacy and accessibility of the Scriptures undermined papal authority and brought the wrath of the papacy down upon him. Jan Hus (ca. 1372–1415), another educator and priest from Bohemia (today the modern Czech Republic), caught wind of Wycliffe's writings and began a religious renewal in his native land. He was tragically burned at the stake at the Council of Constance. Together, these individuals and many more were messengers of a more profound reform to come.

In 1517, the German monk Martin Luther (1483–1546) presented ninety-five protests or theses against the sale of indulgences for public disputation. Those selling indulgences claimed they could grant forgiveness from sin and the release of deceased loved ones from purgatory. Sold across Europe in Luther's time, they were being used to raise funds to build and embellish the grand basilica of St. Peter's in Rome. Luther visited Rome in 1510 but became disenchanted with the widespread corruption of priests and the lack of spirituality by the pope, who was more interested in earthly power and endeavors.

Luther never meant to break with the Roman Catholic Church—he desired to reform it with the hope that other church leaders would join him in a quest for spiritual renewal. However, his attack on indulgences quickly spread throughout Europe, in no small measure due to technological advances made possible through Johann Gutenberg's printing press. It was now possible for an obscure monk on the margins of the Holy Roman Empire to challenge the pope and the Roman Catholic Church in a way that was not possible before. As the full force of the papacy and imperial government arose against him, Luther came to see the papacy as an apostate church. When he attacked the sacramental system and burned the papal decree against him, it became clear that it would not be possible to merely reform the Roman Catholic Church. Consequently, Luther's followers became known as "Protestants" when the German electors banded together to support the work of the Reformation despite ongoing spiritual and political pressure.

Over the next three hundred years, more reforms were launched. Jacob Arminius (1560–1609) rejected the idea that God chooses who will be saved or lost apart from their individual actions because of his divine foreknowledge or will. He instead emphasized the free will or agency of all to respond to the grace that God extends to everyone. John Wesley (1703–1791) experienced a remarkable conversion to Christ in 1738. He emphasized practical Christian holiness, synthesizing some of the best aspects of Calvinism with an Arminian outlook. His followers became known as Methodists for their consistent way of monitoring small groups and their corresponding accountability. They had a profound impact on American Christianity in the late eighteenth and early nineteenth centuries and provided a significant formative influence for early Sabbatarian Adventism.

Within the United States, religion took many creative new forms. The emphasis on democracy allowed ordinary people to study the Bible for themselves and arrive at their own conclusions. George Whitefield (1714–1770) and Jonathan Edwards (1703–1758) focused on conversion as the foundation of renewal and revival. The Great Awakening (1730s to 1740s) extended across New England as a series of revivals began that continued almost unabated (except for the years of the American Revolution) for most of the next two centuries.

The Second Great Awakening (1790s through the 1830s and 1840s) occurred after the American Revolution. Such revivals burned especially hot on the frontier and breathed new life into established churches. As the Second Great Awakening faded, various Methodist and Baptist movements dominated the religious landscape. The emphasis on human choice in salvation encouraged individual people to follow Christ and remained a key ingredient of spiritual renewal and revival. This approach set the stage for the Millerite revival that began when William Miller felt called to preach in 1833. Second advent preachers utilized the same practices that revivalists had used to invite people to make a deliberate choice to come forward and experience an individual conversion in preparation for the end of the world.

Christendom American Style: The Cultural and Religious Context

Two significant revolutions formed the political backdrop to the religious life of America in the early 1800s. The first was the birth of the United States. The creation of this new nation encouraged a friendly separation between church and state. American religion became "democratized" as a free religious marketplace enabled individuals to ascertain truth. During the 1790s, another political revolution overthrew the French monarchy. In 1798, Pope Pius VI was arrested while celebrating the twenty-third anniversary of his coronation. The French general Louis-Alexandre Berthier captured Rome, proclaimed Rome a French republic, and took the pope prisoner. Adventists interpreted this as the papacy being stripped of its secular power after 1,260 years of dominance. This event sparked renewed interest in Bible prophecy, especially among those who believed the papacy had thereby received a "fatal wound" (Dan. 7:25; Rev. 13:3).

In the wake of these changes, other broad social, economic, and political forces set the stage for the advent movement's rise. Democratic liberty spread from the United States and France to Canada, Great Britain, South America, the West Indies, and continental Europe. This was an age of activism as significant reform movements arose. They sought to realize the ideals of freedom and democracy in society and personal life.

The most prominent reform movement focused on the abolition of slavery. It sought to bring freedom to men, women, and children oppressed into bondage. Beginning in 1820, many antislavery periodicals appeared. In some denominations, slavery became a significant point of contention, leading to a division between northern and southern factions. Meanwhile, the concept of religious freedom spread to the local and state levels as the ideals of the American Constitution and specifically the Bill of Rights enshrined freedom of religious practice where previously there had been an established church.

Another significant reform was the push for women's rights. Margaret Fuller and Lucy Stone held a women's rights convention in 1848 in Seneca Falls, New York. American women claimed the same rights of life, liberty, and the pursuit of happiness that men were guaranteed in the US Constitution. The groundswell of support culminated with an amendment to the Constitution that gave women the full right to vote. Adventism would find itself in a unique situation with women preachers at the forefront of the second advent awakening. Many of these same women were involved in the pursuit of equality. All these reform groups utilized freedom of speech and a free press. Newspapers increased rapidly in number, many advocating new reforms, novel religious ideas, or secular ideologies.

The pursuit of democracy increasingly required that the masses be educated. During the first half of the nineteenth century, all levels of education rapidly expanded. Many colleges, seminaries, and universities were established. In 1815, the American Education Society was formed, and by 1850, the United States had over 120 colleges. Educational reform sought to bring freedom from ignorance to the entire population. By the end of the nineteenth century, free public education was the established norm across the nation.

Another major area of reform concerned health and, specifically, temperance, defined primarily as abstinence from alcohol. Sylvester Graham (1794–1851) emphasized a vegetarian diet with whole-ground wheat and rye grains. Edward Hitchcock (1793–1864) stressed complete abstinence from alcohol, tea, coffee, tobacco, and all foods prepared with grease. Tragically, this was a time of medical ignorance and comparatively short life spans compared to today. Yet movements in favor of health and temperance brought freedom from disease and the horrors of alcoholism. New technological inventions, notably the steamship (1807), and the growth of railroads in

America (after 1828) facilitated the westward movement of European Americans across the North American continent. Along with the invention of the telegraph in 1837, these new technologies made the rapid dissemination of information possible.

Setting the Stage

The combination of religious revivals and a renewed interest in Bible prophecy created a profound sense of expectation in some circles, contributing to a sense that something dramatic was about to take place. One of the most famous evangelists of the day was Charles Grandison Finney (1792–1875), who left his profession as a lawyer to plead the Lord's cause. He promoted a system of evangelistic techniques that emphasized human free will and the need to choose salvation. The emotional intensity fostered by these techniques was on full display at "camp meetings" and other similar revival meetings, where large groups gathered to hear preachers speak. At times they might be gathered in a large forest or field, or at other times, revivals might break out at a church or public hall. The Millerite movement adopted and appropriated these techniques as a significant part of the Second Great Awakening.

Those accustomed to studying biblical prophecy saw signs on the earth and in the heavens pointing to the world's end. The dreadful 1755 Lisbon earthquake, felt over much of Europe, spawned a tsunami that reached all the way to the Caribbean islands. Strange lights in the northern United States, today known as the aurora borealis, were seen as another sign of the eschaton. On May 19, 1780, across New England, the day darkened until, by noon, it was so dark that farmers recorded their animals coming to their barns as if it were night. That evening, the moon became as red as blood. Historians now recognize that forest fires in Canada caused these events, but for this time, such environmental changes were seen as a fulfillment of the words that "the sun will be darkened" (Matt. 24:29a) and the moon will become as blood (Rev. 6:12). The dramatic display of the Leonid meteor shower in the dark hours of November 12–13, 1833, suggested a fulfillment of the word that "the stars will fall from the sky" (Matt. 24:29b).

Many claimants to the prophetic gift accompanied the revival of interest in prophetic interpretation. Jemima Wilkinson (1752–1819) believed she was commissioned by God to spread his message. She founded a utopian community on Seneca Lake, New York, that existed from 1776 to 1819. Similarly, Ann Lee (1736–1784) established the Shakers in 1775, a movement that flourished in America during the 1830s and 1840s. Both groups emphasized celibacy, which

Leonid meteor shower, November 12–13, 1833

limited their long-term viability. Somewhat later, Joseph Smith (1805–1844) founded the Church of Jesus Christ of Latter-day Saints. His Book of Mormon (1830) described the story of a lost civilization. Smith's followers, known simply as "Mormons," were led by a series of prophets.

The spread of American society westward, along with the religious fervor that characterized the frontier, laid the groundwork for the reception of a message about the soon coming of Jesus. The advent awakening had its origins in New York and New England. Still, many of its most dedicated followers were from western New York, often dubbed "the Burned-Over District" because of the intense religious fervor that characterized the region. Political, religious, and technological advances facilitated the spread of the advent message from the 1840s onward. Still, the critical motivation for the spread of the Millerite movement was to be found in a deep personal piety based upon God's revelation as found in the Bible. This is clear in the life of William Miller (1782–1849).

CHAPTER 2

The Advent Awakening

The movement prompted by William Miller is typical of the broader American experience and of the dangers of impatience with God. Miller's ancestors settled in New England nearly two centuries before his birth. Many English settlers, including Miller's ancestors, were Puritans, men and women deeply affected by the Protestant Reformation who arrived in America with firm and independent religious convictions. Many were influenced by the Puritan ethos, which held that each church member must have a personal experience with God—yet they continued to practice infant baptism. The result was a crisis as baptized children who grew into adulthood did not experience this conversion experience. The Baptist denomination offered a solution to this difficulty. They called for the end of infant baptism and only baptized adults who could testify to God's work in their lives. Significantly, Miller's maternal grandfather was a Baptist preacher and one of the earliest settlers in what is today the state of Vermont.

In contrast to his mother's family, Miller's father never publicly professed religion, yet he often allowed his home to be a gathering place for friends and neighbors who heard itinerant preachers. However, as Miller grew older, it became increasingly evident that his home was divided about religion. His mother was an early adherent of the local Baptist church, whereas his father never became actively involved in religious matters. Initially, Miller followed his mother's spiritual ideas. Early in his teenage years, he became convicted of sin and decided to remedy his defects by obeying his parents and doing nothing wrong. He also felt he might earn God's favor by sacrificing his most cherished possessions. Yet, he never found peace with God through these means.

Miller's father was part of a late eighteenth-century movement influenced by the European Enlightenment, a period marked by a decreased emphasis on religious piety and church attendance in America. As a teenage boy, Miller attended the local school when work on the farm allowed. His father, initially hesitant about his son's reading habits, later encouraged his love of learning.

Like many contemporary Americans, Miller was primarily self-educated. At twenty-one, he married Lucy Smith, and together they began life in nearby Poultney. In addition to running a small cottage farm, Miller's involvement in civic responsibilities increased. He served as a constable, sheriff, and justice of the peace, each adding new dimensions to his life.

As a young adult, Miller's religious ideas rapidly shifted. He read works by well-known Enlightenment authors such as Voltaire and Hume and their American counterparts, Thomas Paine and Ethan Allen. Miller, persuaded by their ideas, became a Deist. He continued to believe in God but rejected the Bible as a divine revelation or the need for a personal conversion experience. Convinced that the Bible contained errors and superstitions, he made fun of his grandfather and uncle, both Baptist preachers, imitating them before his skeptical friends.

As conflict between the United States and Great Britain erupted in 1812, Miller joined the local militia. He went immediately to work recruiting soldiers to defend his country from attack, especially as his community was less than a hundred miles south of British troops on the Canadian border. Miller had second thoughts about his Deist outlook as he became gravely ill from disease while preparing for battle. Within a short time, both his sister and his father died, a close friend was killed on the battlefield, and Lucy became gravely ill. Miller recognized his own mortality and worried that his children might become orphans. Deism did not offer a clear idea about what happened after death. It also taught that all humans were innately good, yet Miller realized from his interactions with others and his reading of history how capable humans are of great wickedness. When faced with the reality of death, human depravity, and the whole problem of evil in the world, Miller recognized Deism's shortcomings.

Miller was deeply impressed by what he considered a providential intervention that he could not explain rationally or materialistically. Toward the end of the War of 1812, Miller participated in the decisive battle on Lake Champlain. A large British invasion force traveling down the lake attempted to divide the United States with the goal of reaching New York City. The 8,000 British regulars, armed with a contingent of fortified ships, were challenged by an American force of 1,500 regular troops with an additional 2,000 untrained militia and a handful of boats. It appeared that they were doomed to fail. On September 11, 1814, as the Battle of Plattsburgh unfolded, Miller watched from the shoreline as the Americans were victorious and the enemy forces were captured. The outcome, from Miller's viewpoint, was nothing short of miraculous. Miller wondered if perhaps God had intervened in the battle. Such an idea challenged Miller's Deistic assumptions.

After the war, Miller began to attend church sporadically, much to his mother's relief. When asked why he did not attend more often, Miller complained that when the pastor was not present, the person reading the sermon did so rather poorly. His mother suggested that he read the sermon instead. He accepted the challenge and read the sermon when asked.

William Miller

On September 11, 1816, on the second anniversary of the Battle of Plattsburgh, Miller and his fellow American veterans planned a special celebration that included speeches and a gala dance. During a break from the preparations, Miller and some of his associates heard a sermon preached at a local church. The sermon brought such conviction that the celebration and dance were postponed. The following Sunday morning, Miller read the sermon before the local Baptist congregation and became convicted anew by its message about parental duties. Miller wrote, "The character of a Saviour was vividly impressed upon my mind. It seemed that there might be a Being so good and compassionate as to himself atone for our transgressions, and thereby save us from suffering the penalty of sin. I immediately felt how lovely such a Being must be; and imagined that I could cast myself into the arms of, and trust in the mercy of, such an One."[1] Still, Miller resisted full commitment because of his questions about the Bible. As he searched the Scriptures for answers, he was forced to admit that the Scriptures were indeed a divine revelation.

He wrote: "They [the Scriptures] became my delight; and in Jesus I found a friend. The Saviour became to me the chiefest among ten thousand; and the Scriptures, which before were dark and contradictory, now became the lamp to my feet and light to my path. My mind became settled and satisfied. I found the Lord God to be a Rock in the midst of the ocean of life."[2]

1. Sylvester Bliss and Apollos Hale, *Memoirs of William Miller, Generally Known as a Lecturer on the Prophecies, and the Second Coming of Christ* (Boston: J. V. Himes, 1853), 66.

2. Bliss and Hale, *Memoirs of William Miller*, 67.

The Battle of Plattsburgh

Miller laid aside all other reading to devote himself to intensive Bible study. Instead of contradictions, he now found sublime harmony and "a remedy for every disease of the soul."[3] When his Deist friends made fun of his newfound faith, they reminded him about the same arguments he had once used against the Bible. Consequently, Miller sought to harmonize all of the supposed contradictions. He used the simple cross-references in the margin of his Bible along with a concordance. As Miller compared Scripture with Scripture over the next two years, he eventually concluded that the Bible was a "system of revealed truths" anyone could understand.

Still influenced by his earlier Enlightenment ideals, Miller described the Bible as "a feast of reason."[4] Its contradictions and inconsistencies were resolved by a simple internal logic. In this, he approached the Bible using an American pragmatism built on Scottish common sense realism. This approach made the ordinary person the highest priority, arguing that anyone could take the Bible just as it was, with reason and commonly available resources, and come

3. Bliss and Hale, *Memoirs of William Miller*, 67.
4. Bliss and Hale, *Memoirs of William Miller*, 77.

to understand its message without consulting a priest or preacher. Such views dominated America's religious landscape in the years before the Civil War.

A significant focus of Miller's reasoning and Bible study centered on Bible prophecy, especially the visions recorded in the book of Daniel. He reached the startling conclusion that the world was in its last days. The prophecy of the 2,300 days of Daniel 8:14 appeared to suggest that the "time of the end" was indeed at hand. His interpretation was based upon the assumption that a prophetic day represented a year, so that the 2,300 days or years would stretch from 457 BC all the way to 1843, at the time only twenty-five years into the future.

Miller shared his findings with family and friends but was intimidated by the thought that he might be wrong about such an important issue. To be sure that he was correct, he kept studying the prophecies. By 1823, he was confident enough to share his ideas more widely. Some became interested and agreed with him. Others dismissed him as a religious extremist. His experience with his family doctor (see the text box on page 20) helps to illustrate his ideas, reasoning, and even his evangelistic goodwill.

Opportunities to share his discoveries multiplied, but Miller refused to speak publicly. He did not see himself as a preacher. He was afraid that he might mislead others. Yet the conviction grew that he must go and tell the world about his discovery. Agonizing in prayer, he covenanted with God that he would share his ideas if asked. Later that same afternoon, his nephew arrived asking him to speak about what he was learning from the prophecies to a church group at a nearby Baptist congregation in Dresden, New York. Shocked at the rapid turn of events, Miller spent additional time in prayer before accepting the invitation. His message was well received, and soon, others heard about the impact of his message.

Miller shared his ideas across rural New England as speaking invitations multiplied. Miller's primary message was that Christ would return "about the year 1843" or, as the time drew closer, sometime between March 21, 1843, and March 21, 1844. Deeply embedded in the core of his message was an appeal to turn to Jesus as the only hope for eternal life. His Christ-centered message avoided divisive doctrines. It appealed to a broad spectrum of people across various backgrounds and denominations. Some of his most prominent followers came from the Restorationist Movement, which emphasized a return to the New Testament purity of "primitive godliness" and drew upon apocalyptic themes. The wide appeal of Miller's message drew people who were Baptists, Congregationalists, Presbyterians, Methodists, Episcopalians, and adherents of many other religious groups.

Monomania and Miller's Message

Miller's friends reported that his doctor had joked about diagnosing Miller with the disease of "monomania." One day, when the doctor came to his house to treat one of his children, Miller playfully pretended to be ill and asked for the doctor's diagnosis and prescription. The doctor felt his pulse and examined his face but found nothing wrong. He asked Miller what he thought might be the matter. Miller replied that he was worried that he had monomania and wondered if the doctor could tell if a man had it. The doctor replied that he could diagnose the disease if a man were rational on all subjects except one, and when that one subject was brought up, he would become a raving maniac. Miller offered to pay the doctor for a couple of hours of medical consultations so that he might know whether he really had the disease or not. The doctor agreed, and Miller opened his Bible to Daniel 8. He reviewed the prophecies in that chapter and those in Daniel 2 and 7. The doctor knew the Protestant interpretations of these chapters and readily agreed with Miller about the first parts of the prophecies. The doctor was familiar with the prophetic interpretations of Sir Isaac Newton and found that Miller agreed with Newton and his understanding of many of the symbols in the prophecies. Miller asked how long the vision of the empires was to be, and the doctor readily answered, "2,300 days." In mock horror, Miller asked, "They only cover 2,300 literal days?" The doctor replied, "Everyone agrees that those kingdoms are to last 2,300 years." Miller then asked him when the 2,300 years would end. The doctor did not know since he did not know when they began. Miller demonstrated from Daniel 9 that the angel Gabriel had revealed to Daniel the time for the beginning of a seventy-week period, which was to last until the time of the Messiah. He then showed how the 2,300 days included the seventy weeks and how they began at the same time.

Miller, pressing the point, asked when the seventy weeks ended. The doctor answered that the seventy weeks ended in AD 33. Making the connection between Daniel 9 and the 2,300 days in Daniel 8, Miller asked, "Then how far would the 2,300 extend after 33?" The doctor subtracted 490 from 2,300 and replied, "1810. But that is past." Miller pointed out that the starting point was AD 33, so he needed to add 1810. Miller asked him, "In what year would that come to?" The doctor did the calculation and replied, "1843." Startled, shocked, and at a loss for words, he picked up his hat and fled the house in a rage. The next day, however, he returned and confessed to Miller his spiritual need, saying, "I am going to hell." The doctor had spent a sleepless night trying to find another way of interpreting the passage without success. He was convicted of his lost condition and asked Miller for help. Over the next week, Miller led him to the place where he found peace for his soul in Jesus.[1]

1. This text box is based upon Bliss and Hale, *Memoirs of William Miller*, 94–97.

Ultimately, Miller's message appealed to both the heart and the mind. As a result, his message was persuasive not only to his own doctor but to many others. However, Miller and his followers confidently assumed that the "cleansing of the sanctuary" at the end of the 2,300 days of Daniel 8:14 described the cleansing of this earth by fire at the coming of Christ. Underlying this assumption was a profound impatience with life's pain, sorrow, and difficulties, and a desire to escape them. This was particularly poignant in some early second-advent hymns. One example that reveals deep discontent with life here on earth is the song "Here Is No Rest," first published in the *Millennial Harp* in 1843:

> Here o'er the earth as a stranger I roam
> Here is no rest, is no rest
> Here as a pilgrim I wander alone
> Yet I am blest, I am blest,
> For I look forward to that glorious day,
> When sin and sorrow will vanish away.
> My heart doth leap while I hear Jesus say,
> There, there is rest, there is rest.

Subsequent verses describe fierce temptations from surrounding foes who revile and scoff at them, laugh at their weeping, and attempt to shame them. This world is seen as a wilderness where the believer bears the world's hatred. The author hopes to be soon released from the wicked and to lean on Jesus's breast.[5]

The Millerites' impatience for Jesus to come closed their eyes to their error in interpreting Scripture and left them vulnerable to disappointment, despondency, and fanaticism. However, the movement itself remained Christ-centered, generally tried to avoid fanaticism, and brought profound joy to many believers who embraced it. Ellen White described her own involvement in the movement in 1843–1844 as the "happiest year of [her] life."[6]

Miller and others who preached the second-advent message sparked spiritual revival among their listeners by calling for them to make an intentional decision to follow Christ and be ready for his appearing. Miller's extensive

5. James R. Nix, *Early Advent Singing: A Collection of 52 Early Adventist Hymns with Illustrating Stories* (Hagerstown, MD: Review and Herald, 2000), 18–20.

6. Ellen G. White, *Life Sketches of Ellen G. White* (Mountain View, CA: Pacific Press, 1915), 59.

Joshua V. Himes

travels were often at his own expense, showcasing his upward social mobility and the thriftiness of his wife, Lucy, who managed their household and farm while he left on preaching forays across the country. He journeyed as far west as Ohio and as far south as Maryland. He also made numerous forays across New England and into what is today Ontario and Quebec in Canada. Since most Americans lived in rural areas at that time, his message impacted people in many rural villages. Yet his message had not reached the growing cities or attained national prominence. This all changed after Joshua V. Himes (1805–1895) invited Miller to speak at the reform-minded Chardon Street Chapel in Boston, Massachusetts, in December 1839. His arguments persuaded Himes, who, now under conviction, asked Miller what he could do to help spread the message about Christ's imminent return. Miller replied that he was merely a farmer doing what he could. Yet, he also recognized that he needed help.

In January 1840, Himes approached his acquaintances at the local abolitionist press about starting a Millerite periodical called the *Signs of the Times*. Himes soon edited and published a new edition of Miller's lectures. Afterward, other periodicals and pamphlets were quickly printed and distributed by the millions. Himes's detractors dubbed him the "Napoleon of the Press." He even organized a series of Second Advent General Conferences. By 1842, these were supplemented by area camp meetings (an idea earlier popularized by Methodists and other revivalists as part of the Second Great Awakening). Himes recruited many more preachers and laypeople to staff these events. By mid-1842, the Adventists were using the largest freestanding tent in the world, which seated approximately six thousand people. This portable tent could be moved from city to city to facilitate large revival meetings. These activities required extensive funds, which Himes and other preachers raised through their publications and revival meetings.

As a result of the Adventist media blitz, other ministers joined the movement on a much broader scale. One prominent recruit was Josiah Litch (1809–

The Great Millerite Tent

1886), a Methodist minister. A friend shared a copy of Miller's *Lectures*, urging him to read it. Initially opposed to Miller's ideas, he was reluctantly persuaded to study them. Convicted, he joined Himes as the movement's first paid field agent. He proclaimed the advent message far and wide, often utilizing the "great tent." Litch persuaded the Presbyterian minister Charles Fitch (1805–1844) to reconsider his initial prejudice toward Miller's message. Fitch also joined the movement as one of its leading champions. Along with Apollos Hale, Fitch went on to design a large prophetic chart based on the prophecies of Daniel and Revelation. The initial version could be split vertically in half, with brief notes and scriptural references, as a visual aid during sermons or Bible studies. Ministers could take smaller, more portable versions of the chart as they traveled from village to village, holding meetings.

Not to be outdone by their male counterparts, women took a leading role in spreading the second-advent message. These included Lucy Stoddard, Clorinda S. Minor, and Emily Pearson, all of whom were powerful preachers and prolific authors. Martha Spence, a Millerite in Rochester, New York, described the preaching of Lucy Maria Hersey (1824–1888): "Our dear sister Hersey . . . is an able and very interesting lecturer, as much so, I think, as any of our brethren in the field."[7] Other women who joined her at this camp meeting included

7. Martha Spence, "Camp Meeting Near Rochester," *Midnight Cry!*, August 1, 1844, 22.

sisters Mary Seymour (1819–1881) and Emily C. Clemons (1818–1900), who described the crowded and attentive audiences. As the revivals spread, Hersey soon needed the largest auditorium in town so the large crowds could gather to hear her preach. The second-advent message empowered women in an environment of "all hands on deck." This egalitarian message of reform argued that if women were the first to proclaim the Lord's resurrection, they had an equal responsibility to tell of his soon return. Millerite women also founded a periodical to engage and encourage each other entitled the *Advent Message to the Daughters of Zion*.

The initial focus of the movement centered on the year 1843. At the close of that year, speculation focused on March 1844. After that time passed, the movement lost some of its enthusiasm. Miller remained convinced that his basic understanding of Bible prophecy was correct but thought their mistake might be related to a minor miscalculation in the date. At most, he speculated that he could not be off by more than a few months. They were heartened by the message of Habakkuk 2:3: "The vision is yet for an appointed time, . . . though it tarry, wait for it; because it will surely come" (KJV).

They also found additional encouragement in the parable of the virgins, as found in Matthew 25:1–13. The ten virgins went to meet the bridegroom. They waited while he tarried. Based on these texts, Millerites saw themselves living within a "tarrying time" immediately before the end. During that summer, the activist impulse of many Millerites in the fight against slavery, along with mounting tensions from opposition to their egalitarian message, caused many congregations to expel second-advent believers from their congregations. Unsurprisingly, the revivalist and abolitionist Charles Fitch taught that it was time to "come out of Babylon" due to their expulsion because of their egalitarian activist Adventist beliefs. Since the advent message was fused with the message of reform and deeply embedded with the fight against slavery, they felt that the mainstream churches were far too lax about social reforms. George Storrs (1796–1879), a Methodist minister, urged Millerites to leave their churches but not to form a new religious denomination. He argued that this would be tantamount to creating a new Babylon.

A new idea became popular among Millerites in early 1844 and gained widespread acceptance after the Exeter, New Hampshire, camp meeting in August. Samuel S. Snow (1806–1890) was a Millerite advocate who converted from agnosticism in 1839 after reading a copy of Miller's *Lectures*. He advocated a new theory that answered the question of the delay. Snow paralleled the ministry of Jesus to the Jewish calendar of feasts and related activities.

Snow argued that Jesus fulfilled the symbolic types found in the Jewish feasts during the spring of the Jewish calendar. All Christians agreed that Jesus was crucified on Passover day, raised at the beginning of the Feast of Unleavened Bread, and ascended to heaven on Pentecost. Yet, the three feasts that fell during the autumn were not fulfilled at the time of Christ's first coming. In the autumn of the Jewish festal calendar, the Feast of Trumpets was followed by the Day of Atonement, seen as a day of judgment. Immediately afterward came the Feast of Booths, which pointed to the gathering of the holy people in paradise. Snow suggested that the key to finding when Jesus would return lay in the timing of the Day of Atonement. According to Leviticus 23:27, it was to be observed on the tenth day of the seventh month of the Jewish calendar. Snow observed how Jesus perfectly fulfilled the prophecy in the Passover, dying precisely at the time of the sacrificial lamb at three o'clock in the afternoon on the very day predicted. In the same way, he argued, Jesus would return to perfectly fulfill the prophecy found in the Day of Atonement when he would return to judge the earth on the tenth day of the seventh month to take his people home. Using the calculations of the Karaite Jews, he pointed to October 22 as the great day of anticipation when, on the literal Day of Atonement, Jesus would return.

George Storrs

When Snow finished his presentation, the crowd at the camp meeting was deeply moved. They saw in Snow's presentation a biblical answer to the problem of when Christ would return. They accepted it, and the message spread swiftly to the many waiting for Christ's appearance. Snow remained faithful to the movement through the October 22 date, but afterward, his impatience drove him into fanaticism. He declared himself Elijah and demanded that all nations submit to his authority as Christ's prime minister. He died in obscurity in 1890.[8]

Initially unsure about the October 22 date, Miller endorsed it by the second week of October. As the "seventh-month movement" quickly spread across the northern United States and Canada, most Millerites accepted it. As many were now expelled from their churches, they worshiped in homes, barns, or even

8. Kevin Vinicius Felix Oliveira and Clodoaldo Tavares, "Snow, Samuel Sheffield (1806–1890)," in *Encyclopedia of Seventh-day Adventists*, April 7, 2022, https://tinyurl.com/4e77yess.

Firsthand Account of S. S. Snow's Arrival at the Exeter Camp Meeting

The following account comes from J. N. Loughborough, who attended the Exeter, New Hampshire, camp meeting and later wrote several early denominational histories about the Millerite movement and the birth of the Seventh-day Adventist Church.

> On Sunday forenoon, as Elder Bates was preaching of their situation in the tarrying time, . . . a brother minister came riding a horse at a furious pace to the camp. Having hastily provided for his horse, he came into the meeting, and seated himself near the family of Elder John Couch, with whom he was acquainted. Then with open Bible in his hand, in a whisper, he explained to Sister Couch the cause of their [Spring 1844] disappointment, and the midnight cry. As Sister Couch received this light, the mighty power of God came upon her. She at once arose and beckoned to Elder Bates. He said, "Sister, what is it?" So she replied, "What you are saying is all very good, but there is a brother here who has light on the 'midnight cry.'" Elder Bates responded, "Then let him come up on the platform and give to the congregation," and sat down.
>
> Thereupon Elder S. S. Snow, who was the one that had this light, ascended the platform and introduced the matter by asking questions, with responses from the audience, as follows:
>
> "What has been our position as Adventists, since about April 1?"
>
> "We have been in the tarrying time."
>
> "How long was the vision to tarry?"
>
> "Till midnight."
>
> "What is a day in symbolic prophecy?"
>
> "A year."
>
> "Then what would a night be?"
>
> "Half a year."
>
> "Then what would a midnight be?"

outside in small groups. Even their exclusion from their churches was seen as a fulfillment, some believed, of the parable of the bridegroom when, after the delay, the midnight cry was given, "Behold the bridegroom cometh, go ye out to meet Him." This brought a new impetus as people repented of their sins and made wrongs right. Some even sold their farms and all their worldly possessions to raise means to share the advent message in eager anticipation of Christ's soon return. Charles Fitch baptized a large group of new believers in Lake Erie on a cold, windy day in early October. Shortly afterward, he became

"Three months."

Then Elder Snow said, "We have been in the tarrying time of the message just three months. It is not the midnight of the time, and I am here to give you the 'midnight cry.'"

The effect of that statement on the audience was powerful. All eyes were fastened intently on him, and all ears open to know what they should hear. He said:

"We came into the tarrying time because of a mistake in our reckoning of the 2300 days. The first portion of that period was the seventy weeks, cut off from the whole period. This was from the time that the commandment went forth for the restoration and rebuilding of Jerusalem. This was not the beginning of 457 B.C., as we have been reckoning, but from the tenth day of the seventh month of 457, corresponding to October 22 according to our reckoning. So the whole period, instead of terminating near April 1, as we taught, will terminate October 22, 1844. The midnight cry is now due." Then in a strong voice he said, "Behold the Bridegroom cometh on October 22, 1844; *go ye out to meet Him!*"

As he uttered those words, a mighty wave of the power of God swept over the vast audience, prostrating many of them to the earth. That meeting was suddenly turned into a social meeting, in which there were confessions and earnest seeking of the Lord. The meeting thus continued for an hour. At its close Brother Snow was requested to remain and labor in the meeting. His reply was, "You have the message now. I must go on to another place to give the message tonight," and soon his horse bore him at full speed away from the camp. When asked afterward, "Why did you ride the horse so furiously?" his reply was, "I could not hold him in. It seemed that he was impelled by the same power that urged me on to give the message."[1]

1. From J. N. Loughborough, "The Second Advent Movement—No. 4," *Review and Herald*, August 18, 1921, 4–6.

ill and tragically died on October 14, just eight days before the great Day of Anticipation. His wife was so confident in the advent message that she reportedly shed no tears, expecting to be reunited with her husband very soon.

The Day of Anticipation

On Tuesday, October 22, many second-advent believers gathered to await the coming of Christ in the clouds. The sense of anticipation was high. Many prayed, confessed their sins, and sang hymns to encourage one another. Such fervor continued until the clock struck midnight. In an instant, all their hopes and dreams dissolved. Hiram Edson (1806–1882), a Millerite living in Port Gibson, New York, described his advent convictions as the richest and brightest of all his Christian experience. But now, with Christ's failure to appear, he began to doubt everything, questioning whether the Bible was true or if there even was a paradise in heaven. The believers gathered in his home were in tears. But instead of giving up their belief in God and the Bible, Edson called on his advent friends to pray early that morning. Gathered in his barn, they searched their hearts as they prayed for God to give them new light to help them understand their disappointment. It was not long before Edson and those gathered with him felt they had received an answer to their request.

Resources

Barkun, Michael. *Crucible of the Millennium: The Burned-Over District of New York in the 1840s.* Syracuse, NY: Syracuse University Press, 1986.

Bliss, Sylvester, and Apollos Hale. *Memoirs of William Miller, Generally Known as a Lecturer on the Prophecies, and the Second Coming of Christ.* Boston: J. V. Himes, 1853.

Crocombe, Jeff. "'A Feast of Reason': The Roots of William Miller's Biblical Interpretation and Its Influence on the Seventh-day Adventist Church." PhD diss., University of Queensland, 2011.

Knight, George R. *William Miller and the Rise of Adventism.* Nampa, ID: Pacific Press, 2010.

Nichol, Francis D. "The Growth of the Millerite Legend." *Church History* 21, no. 4 (December 1952): 296–313.

———. *The Midnight Cry: A Defense of the Character and Conduct of William Miller and the Millerites, Who Mistakenly Believed That the Second Coming of Christ Would Take Place in the Year 1844.* Washington, DC: Review and Herald, 1944.

Rowe, David L. *God's Strange Work: William Miller and the End of the World.* Grand Rapids: Eerdmans, 2008.

Discussion Questions

1. Which aspects of the Millerite movement were biblical, and which were not?
2. How broadly based was the Millerite movement? What difference did this make?

3. What was the Millerite movement's relationship to basic orthodox Christianity in such matters as salvation through faith in Christ?
4. How were early Millerites activists? How did the Millerite message resonate with early believers concerned about supporting the abolitionist cause and empowering women to preach?
5. How important was date setting to the Millerite movement?

CHAPTER 3

From Millerism to Seventh-day Adventism

As the great Day of Anticipation turned into the Great Disappointment, many Adventists gave up their faith altogether. The main body of Adventists who retained their faith followed the leadership of Joshua V. Himes and were supported by William Miller. They organized themselves into a body in May 1845 at Albany, New York. Publicity about the recent Israel Dammon trial resulted in the Albany Conference excluding Adventists who claimed to have visions or kept the seventh-day Sabbath. However, the Sabbatarian Adventist movement grew rapidly between the Great Disappointment in 1844 and the formation of the Seventh-day Adventist Church in 1863.

For those Millerite Adventists who patiently clung to their hope in Christ's soon return, the "shut door" teaching based upon Christ's parable of the bridegroom (Matt. 25:1–13) became a lens through which they could find biblical guidance as they waited. They expressed their continued faith in Christ's return even though they did not necessarily understand the delay. In the parable, as the ten virgins waited, five were prepared for a delay, and the other five were not. Both groups waited, but only five had enough oil to accompany the bridegroom to the wedding feast. The others had to search for oil, and the door to the feast was closed when they returned from their search. Disappointed Adventists interpreted this parable to mean that they were called to wait patiently. In contrast, those who abandoned their Adventist beliefs would be excluded, since the close of probation, they believed, had occurred on October 22, 1844.

The individuals who formed the core of what would later become the Seventh-day Adventist Church were deeply committed to studying the Scriptures. Some, such as Hiram Edson in Port Gibson, New York, ended the night of October 22/23, 1844, in deep anguish. On that "Black Tuesday," as the clock tolled midnight and Christ did not return, he "wept and wept until the day dawn[ed]."[1] As the morning began, Edson invited the group gathered at his

1. Hiram Edson, "Description of Hiram Edson's Experience in the Cornfield on Octo-

Israel Dammon

A former sea captain, Israel Dammon (1811–1886) was a second-advent preacher who traveled around Maine. On the evening of February 15, 1845, a group of believers gathered at the James Ayer Jr. farm to encourage one another after the disappointment. During that meeting, two visionaries, Dorinda Baker and Ellen Harmon, shared their supernatural experiences. As some Millerites had already drifted into fanaticism, all Millerites were considered suspect, and there was a great deal of opposition to their meetings. After a complaint by an opponent of Adventism, the deputy sheriff, Joseph Moulton, and three others investigated and attempted to arrest Dammon for vagrancy and disturbing the peace, but some of those present prevented his arrest. Eventually, with additional support, they took Dammon into custody. Some witnesses described a bedlam of noise and ecstatic experiences. The sources for this material are biased reports in the local newspaper. Ultimately, Dammon was convicted of the charges and sentenced to ten days in prison, but after an appeal by his attorney, his case was dropped, and he never served any time. Adventist historians have often cited the published accounts to illustrate the dynamic and chaotic time after the Great Disappointment. For her part, Ellen White later reflected on what happened as an illustration of the rampant fanaticism she sought to combat during her early ministry.

home to his grainery to pray. He reported, "We continued in earnest prayer until the witness of the Spirit was given that our prayer was accepted, and that light should be given, our disappointment explained, and made clear and satisfactory."[2] With renewed hope, they went out after breakfast to encourage other disappointed believers.

Avoiding the main roads where he might be derided, Edson took a shortcut through a nearby cornfield, and as he walked Edson saw the work of Christ going on in the heavenly sanctuary. Years later he wrote, "I was stopped about midway" when "heaven seemed open to my view. . . . I saw distinctly and clearly, that instead of our High Priest coming out of the Most Holy of the heavenly sanctuary to come to this earth on the tenth day of the seventh month, at the end of the 2300 days, He, for the first time entered on that day the second apartment of that sanctuary; and that He had a work to perform

ber 23, 1844," Center for Adventist Research, Andrews University, 8, https://tinyurl.com/bdypud74.

2. Edson, "Description," 8–9.

in the most holy before coming to this earth."[3] This new conviction resonated with other believers searching for new light on the nature of Christ's ministry in the heavenly sanctuary. Even before the disappointment, Emily Clemons and a small group of Millerite women began teaching about Christ's two-phase ministry in the heavenly sanctuary.

These early discussions began to crystallize as Edson, with renewed zeal, studied with his friends O. R. L. Crosier (1820–1912) and Dr. F. B. Hahn (1809–1866). They were especially drawn to Revelation 10, which describes a "little book" that, when eaten, was initially sweet but turned bitter. They saw this as a fulfillment of their own bittersweet experience. The chapter concludes with the command to "prophesy again before many peoples, and nations, and tongues, and kings." These advent believers took this text personally to mean they still had a work to do. They expressed their newfound discovery in an article authored by Crosier entitled "The Law of Moses."[4] At the center of their argument was the concept that a literal sanctuary does exist in heaven, just like the Old Testament sanctuary, with two successive phases of Christ's ministry in the Holy Place and the Most Holy Place. They argued that on October 22, 1844, Christ moved from the Holy Place to the Most Holy Place in the heavenly sanctuary. Therefore, ever since 1844, Christ has continued his sanctuary ministry and would return only after he completed this special preparatory work in the second apartment in heaven. This emerging understanding of the heavenly sanctuary became the theological rationale and cornerstone for early Sabbatarian Adventist beliefs. Building on this theological cornerstone along with the continued conviction of Christ's return were three additional developments: the visionary experiences of Ellen Harmon (who became Ellen White) (1827–1915), the seventh-day Sabbath and its apocalyptic significance, and the application of the three angels' messages of Revelation 14 to those following the sanctuary and Sabbath messages. In addition, the pioneers continued to adhere to the belief in soul sleep and rejected any notion of eternal damnation. As they waited, a new set of theological convictions emerged.

Ellen Harmon (White) and the Gift of Prophecy

In December 1844, Ellen Harmon had tuberculosis, so she was staying with another Millerite believer, Elizabeth Haines, who was taking care of her. As

3. Edson, "Description," 10.

4. O. R. L. Crosier, "The Law of Moses," *Day Star Extra* 9 (February 7, 1846), https://tinyurl.com/8tnvkbcj.

Summary of Crosier's Article "The Law of Moses"

1. A literal sanctuary exists in heaven.
2. The Hebrew sanctuary was a complete earthly representation of the plan of salvation modeled after the one in heaven.
3. In the same way that the earthly sanctuary had human priests as part of a two-phase ministry, so, in the heavenly sanctuary, Christ conducts a two-phase ministry. The first phase began in the Holy Place at his ascension. The second phase began on October 22, 1844, when Christ moved from the Holy Place to the Most Holy Place. Thus, the antitypical or heavenly day of atonement began on that date.
4. The first phase of Christ's ministry dealt with forgiving sins. The second phase deals with blotting out sins and cleansing sins in the sanctuary and for individual believers.
5. The cleansing of Daniel 8:14 was a cleansing from sin and was therefore accomplished by blood rather than fire.
6. Christ would return once that second-apartment ministry was completed.[1]

1. Adapted from George R. Knight, *Anticipating the Advent: A Brief History of Seventh-day Adventists* (Boise, ID: Pacific Press, 1993), 23.

they prayed and studied their Bibles together, searching for spiritual guidance, the seventeen-year-old Ellen Harmon reported receiving a vision that brought spiritual encouragement after their disappointment. She later described how she felt that God was near, and then she lost consciousness. After her recovery, she shared an extraordinary experience. The earliest report appeared in a letter in the *Day Star* that was later revised and published as a broadside titled "To the Little Remnant Scattered Abroad."[5] She shared seeing the advent people traveling from this earth to the heavenly city on a narrow path. A bright light behind them at the beginning illuminated their path. What was the bright light? An angel told her that it was the "Midnight Cry," a reference to the name of the movement advocating for October 22, 1844, as the date of Christ's return. An even brighter light came from Jesus, who stood on the other end of the path. Those who kept their eyes fixed on Jesus remained safe and secure on

5. This appears in Ellen G. White, *Early Writings* (Washington, DC: Review and Herald, 1882), 13–20. The following account is taken from these pages.

the path, but those who took their eyes off Jesus or denied their second-advent experience fell into the darkness below.

Other parts of the vision affirmed their literal belief in Christ's soon return. All eyes were drawn to the east, where a small black cloud appeared, about half as large as a man's hand. Jesus approached the earth, raised the dead, and brought the living faithful up to him in the clouds. All traveled to heaven, but the focus of the description quickly shifted to the descent of the new Jerusalem to the earth. When the believers tried to remember their greatest trials, they seemed to fade in comparison to the bright and glorious experience in the earth-made-new. What they experienced was so much greater than they could have imagined that they cried out, "Heaven is cheap enough!"

In the new Jerusalem, there was a table of pure silver. It was many miles long and filled with wonderful food, including the fruit from the Tree of Life. Ellen asked Jesus to let her eat the fruit, but he said, "Not now. Those who eat of this fruit go back to earth no more. But if you are faithful, you will get to eat it in a little while." Then he told her, "You must go back to earth again and tell others what I have revealed to you." An angel bore her gently back to Earth. It seemed dark and dreary and lonely. She closed her report of the vision with these words: "Oh, that I had wings like a dove, then would I fly away and be at rest." Ellen would afterward struggle to put into words this keystone experience that would become the foundation for her spiritual leadership.

Such mystical experiences were not unusual in the nineteenth century. If taken out of context, the description might seem like many other depictions, common in the era, about visiting heaven and returning with a message for humanity. Yet a careful examination of this first vision reveals significant theological meaning for both Ellen Harmon and the fledgling group of disappointed Adventists.

Perhaps most important was the vision's central idea that God had indeed led them through their Millerite experience and the teaching about the Midnight Cry. The vision's most crucial point was directed to those disappointed Adventists searching for spiritual meaning after the Great Disappointment. The message was that God had led them through this experience. If they wished to see the heavenly city, they must not deny their belief in his return. Although the vision did not offer any theological explanation for their disappointment, it did encourage them not to repudiate God's leading in the rise of this movement.

Another significant emphasis in the vision reaffirmed their belief in Jesus's literal return. At one point, Ellen Harmon shared how God let it be known that the day and hour of his return was set. The manner of his return was just as the Millerites expected it to be—a dramatic end-of-the-world event just before the millennium. There was no way that anyone on earth would miss it. While in his sovereignty God knew the day and hour of his return, he would not allow this time to be revealed, as "about that day or hour no one knows" (Matt. 24:36). Thus, although some Adventists would continue to set dates, Ellen Harmon routinely warned against date setting. For some Adventists, this must have been a bitter pill to swallow. Central to the Millerite movement was a message about time. The Midnight Cry was all about a very specific date. Even some of Ellen Harmon's closest associates had great difficulty giving up their penchant for setting dates. Yet, in this initial vision, she starkly warned against this practice.

Another point recorded in this vision was that heaven and the new earth are real places. The flowers there don't fade; the food is recognizable, and individual people can be identified. Believers will be reunited with people who have died, such as Charles Fitch, whom Ellen Harmon reported seeing there. Heaven is not a spiritual or shadowy place but a vastly different place beyond our present comprehension. These ideas might seem ordinary for the time. Still, after the Great Disappointment, one group of Millerites came to believe that they were already living in the heavenly kingdom. Some reportedly took this idea to an extreme. Jesus said they must become like a little child to enter the kingdom of heaven. So, they crawled on their knees, believing they were already in the kingdom. Others spiritualized away the heavenly realm so that men could have spiritual wives as if they already were in paradise. Since they believed they were already perfect, God must bless any impulses they felt. While there is no evidence that this was a widespread practice, the potential for gross immorality, or accusations thereof, was real. In this milieu, Ellen Harmon's vision affirming Jesus's dramatic return and the physical reality of heaven and the new earth combated extreme views and comforted the disappointed believers. Ellen Harmon traveled widely through 1845 and 1846, sharing what she believed the Lord had revealed to her. She countered fanatical and extreme ideas, operating within Millerite circles to disseminate her views. As a result, a small group of those who accepted her visions began to build a new network of faith centered around a new set of core beliefs.

However, the most significant part of Ellen Harmon's vision was the centrality of Jesus Christ throughout her visionary narrative. Jesus was the one depicted as coming on the clouds of glory, speaking from the cloud, and blowing

Early Visionaries

Ecstatic experiences were commonplace, as some fifty individuals in the early 1840s claimed prophetic dreams and visions. Two individuals who interfaced with Ellen Harmon (later White) include William Ellis Foy (1818–1893) and Hazen Little Foss (1819–1893).

The former, Foy, was a black Free Will Baptist minister who married Ann in 1837. The previous year, he founded a religious paper, the *Morning Star*, and became an active revivalist during a series of revivals known as the Second Great Awakening. This era of revivalism encouraged equality, including the preaching of blacks and women, and was eager to share the news about Christ's soon return as part of the Millerite awakening. On January 18, 1842, Foy, while worshiping with other believers at the Twelfth Street Baptist Church in Boston, experienced an event in which his "soul was made happy in the love of God." He later wrote, "I was immediately seized as in the agonies of death, and my breath left me." According to eyewitnesses, he remained in an "inanimate condition" for two and a half hours. In his *Christian Experience*, he detailed his first vision, which included an angelic guide who led him by the bank of a river to sing next to a grape-like fruit tree. In a second vision, on February 4, 1842, he described seeing "innumerable multitudes" from the four corners of the earth. In the vision, Foy enters paradise, accompanied by an angelic being on "chariots," and ultimately, he meets Christ. He witnesses the saints who are transformed while the wicked sink away below. He later had at least one more vision.[1] While he initially shared his experiences with others, he eventually withdrew to northern Maine due to

1. William E. Foy, *The Christian Experience of William E. Foy Together with the Two*

the trumpet announcing his return. He was at the end of the narrow path at the entrance to the heavenly city. Once the group arrived, Jesus placed crowns on the heads of those who entered. He led the way when the new Jerusalem came down from heaven to Earth. Throughout Ellen Harmon's visionary experience, he was her guide, and in the end, he commissioned her to tell others what had been revealed to her. In one account, Ellen Harmon concluded her report, writing, "I could see that Jesus was our only hope and that to Him we can trust everything. He will never leave or forsake us."[6]

6. Ellen G. White, "Faith, Patience, and Hope," *Letters and Manuscripts*, vol. 9 (1894), Manuscript 16, 1894, paragraph 21, https://tinyurl.com/2md254cp.

"persecution." Ellen heard him speak to a group of Millerites at Beethoven Hall, later commenting on his "remarkable" testimony.

Hazen Foss met Ellen Harmon in January 1845 at a meeting in Poland, Maine. Ellen had been invited by her sister Mary to share her first visionary experience. Mary's husband was Samuel Foss, a brother of Hazen. Ellen later remembered Hazen Foss as a "man of fine appearance, pleasing address, and education." He had a vision just before the Great Disappointment about the journey of the advent believers to the city of God. He later had a second vision in which he was warned to be faithful, but if he was not, the responsibility would be taken from him and given to another. Hesitant, he shared how he heard a voice stating he had "grieved away the Spirit of the Lord." Frightened, he tried to share his experience with a group but could not recall the vision. Later, when he heard Ellen Harmon's experience, he requested to meet with her afterward. He warned: "The Lord gave me a message to bear to His people. And I refused after being told the consequences; I was proud; I was unreconciled to the disappointment. . . . I heard you talk last night. I believe the visions are taken away from me, and given to you. Do not refuse to obey God, for it will be at the peril of your soul."[2]

Visions He Received in the Months of Jan. and Feb. 1842 (Portland, ME, 1843). A transcription is accessible at https://tinyurl.com/4m99vmef.

2. This conversation is later recounted by Ellen G. White in a letter to her sister, Mary Foss. See Letter 37, 1890, dated December 22, 1890, Ellen G. White Estate.

In her accounts of the experience, Ellen Harmon focused on issues within her religious community in a thoroughly orthodox manner. She avoided the novel or strange ideas circulating among other contemporary visionaries. She viewed her writings as providing spiritual encouragement, fostering community, and ultimately pointing people to their need to study the Bible for themselves. Even during this formative period, she never indicated that she saw herself as having any significant role in the future, nor did she receive any special revelation that was to be a test for others. She believed her writings would be self-validating by pointing people to Christ and the primacy of Scripture, to which she gave more authority than her writing and by which her writings were to be evaluated.

Joseph Bates and the Seventh-day Sabbath

Joseph Bates

If the sanctuary message is the cornerstone of Seventh-day Adventist theology, then the seventh-day Sabbath, as promulgated by Joseph Bates (1792–1872), became the foundation of Adventist theology. Originally a sea captain, he experienced a conversion after reading a Bible placed in his trunk by his wife, Prudence. After making his fortune and retiring from the sea, he participated in various reforms, from temperance to abolitionism. He became active in the Millerite movement as the ultimate reform and, after the Great Disappointment, accepted the seventh-day Sabbath after he read an article by Thomas M. Preble (1810–1907) on the topic.

Adventist historians generally agree that Preble must have heard about the seventh-day Sabbath from a neighboring Millerite preacher, Frederick Wheeler. The two circuit-riding ministers lived in adjoining towns and certainly knew one another. Wheeler first heard about the seventh-day Sabbath after presiding over a communion service, during which he exhorted the congregation to keep all of God's commandments. After the service, Rachel Oakes, a Seventh Day Baptist, challenged him to follow his own advice by keeping the seventh-day Sabbath. As he studied the Bible on the topic, perhaps with some Seventh Day Baptist literature provided by Mrs. Oakes, he became convicted about the validity of the seventh day. Wheeler, Oakes, and two brothers, Cyrus and William Farnsworth, and

Thomas Preble

their families soon joined them in observing the seventh day as the Sabbath. Wheeler presumably shared his convictions about the Sabbath with Preble, who in turn wrote an article in the February 1845 *Hope of Israel* (that also appeared in tract form) containing material espousing ideas that demonstrate this early Seventh Day Baptist influence.

When Bates read Preble's tract in early 1845, he traveled to Washington, New Hampshire, to share his newfound convictions with second-advent believers with whom he had developed a friendship and previously shared his faith about Christ's second advent. To his surprise, when he arrived, he found they were already keeping the seventh-day Sabbath. They were so delighted as they shared their newfound faith that they stayed up all night. With renewed faith and confidence, he returned home. As he crossed the bridge from New Bedford to Fairhaven, Massachusetts, he met a fellow second-advent believer, James Hall, who asked him, "What's the news, Captain Bates?" He replied immediately: "The news is that the seventh day is the Sabbath of the Lord our God!"

This was indeed news to Hall, who studied the subject and eventually joined Bates in keeping the Sabbath. In the spring of 1846, Bates decided to write a tract advocating his ideas on the Sabbath. Printed by the local abolitionist printer, Benjamin Lindsey, the tract first came out in August 1846. Its presentation of the seventh-day Sabbath was similar to Preble's, but it broke new ground by connecting the Sabbath with the second coming of Jesus. Bates argued that the Sabbath was among the "all things" that must be restored before Jesus returns (Acts 3:21). Restoration of the true Sabbath was required, according to Bates, since both imperial and papal Rome had changed the seventh-day Sabbath to the first day of the week. He also made a more precise and detailed case for the creation origins of the Sabbath than Preble had.

In the summer of 1846, Joseph Bates became acquainted with James White (1821–1881) and had heard of Ellen Harmon's visions. At that point, he did not accept her visions as genuine, nor did the Whites share his convictions about the Sabbath. At the time of their marriage on August 30, 1846, James and Ellen White believed that Bates stressed the idea of the fourth commandment too much. However, during the fall of 1846, they studied Bates's tract on the Sabbath and became convinced of its truth. After observing Ellen White in vision several times, Bates also became convinced of the genuineness of Ellen White's prophetic gift.

Bates revised his tract *The Seventh-day Sabbath, a Perpetual Sign* and published a new edition in January 1847.[7] Now Bates connected the three angels'

7. Joseph Bates, *The Seventh-day Sabbath, a Perpetual Sign* (New Bedford, MA: Benjamin Lindsey, 1847), https://tinyurl.com/37jzpmfr.

James White with a chart of the law of God

messages in Revelation 14:6–13 to the advent people's experience. He argued that the first angel's message about judgment "represents all those who were preaching the second Advent doctrine since 1840."[8] According to Bates, the second angel's call to come out of Babylon represented a call for God's people to depart from the churches that refused to accept the Millerite message. Concerning the third angel's message, Bates argued that it describes two very different groups. One has the mark of the beast, whereas the other keeps the commandments of God and the faith of Jesus. Who is the second group? None other than those who came out of Babylon. According to Bates, this company was not keeping *most* of the commandments but *all* of them. Bates identified this group as those Sabbath-keeping Millerites. He also equated them with the remnant described in Revelation 12:17, those who are "keeping the commandments of God and the testimony of Jesus." At the conclusion of the second edition of his work, Bates wrote that there would be a mighty struggle to restore and keep the seventh-day Sabbath and that this struggle would test every living soul who enters the holy city.

Bates connected the seventh-day Sabbath with the prophecies in Revelation 13 and 14, moving beyond Millerite and Seventh Day Baptist ideas. In the spring of 1847, Bates, James and Ellen White, and many in their circle expected the return of Jesus at any time. In contrast to the idea of Jesus's imminent return, Bates described a crisis immediately before Jesus's return centered on the Sabbath. Bates's idea implied that there was more time before Christ returned and that significant events would precede his coming. That the seventh-day

8. Bates, *The Seventh-day Sabbath*, 58.

Ellen White, William C. White, James White, and J. Edson White, ca. 1865

Sabbath was at the center of this final crisis before the second advent was a radical departure from what other Christians were teaching.

The publication of the second edition of Bates's *The Seventh-day Sabbath, a Perpetual Sign* was followed by Ellen White's report of a vision on April 7, 1847, that connected the sanctuary with the seventh-day Sabbath. She described being ushered into the heavenly temple to the Most Holy Place, where she saw the ark of the covenant and the brightness of God's glory. The ark was opened, and she saw the two tables of the Ten Commandments. The first four commandments were brighter than the last six. The fourth commandment had a halo of glory around it. Ellen White realized that God had not changed the Sabbath. After describing how Sabbath-keeping people would be persecuted, she contrasted them with those who would receive the mark of the beast as depicted in Revelation 13.

By 1847, the delay of the second coming forced Sabbath-keeping Millerites to reevaluate their beliefs. As a result, they eventually developed the unique teachings of Seventh-day Adventists. The doctrine of the sanctuary was connected to the seventh-day Sabbath, which was seen in the context of the three angels' messages. The new understanding of the sanctuary explained the believers' deep disappointment in 1844 and gave them a new purpose, vision, and mission centered on the Sabbath. They came to believe that Jesus entered a new phase of his ministry, and he had entrusted them with a message to prepare a people for his return. They believed that their mission to proclaim the Sabbath came from the ministry of Christ in the holy of holies in the heavenly sanctuary. There, Jesus was exalting his law and preparing a people who valued all his commandments. They would stand firm in allegiance to him in the face of intense opposition. They believed his intercession in the heavenly sanctuary would sustain them, enabling them to be patient to the end.

The Whites and Bates were convinced that their mission was described by the three angels' messages in Revelation 14. The early Sabbath-keeping Adventists adopted "the three angels' messages" as a shorthand way to describe their unique teachings. They understood these messages as part of Revelation 13 with its two terrifying beasts. Following historicist prophetic interpretation, they identified the first beast from the sea as the imperial church, the papacy. It was a church power that used government power to persecute, and it represented the antithesis of the American ideal of religious freedom. Sabbath-keeping Adventists built upon this idea with a startling innovation, identifying the second beast, the persecuting beast from the earth, as the United States. They pointed to slavery and the creedalism of American churches as evidence of the oppressive and imperial-like nature of the United States. They saw themselves as resisting the oppression of the popular churches to enforce Sunday observance. Ultimately, Sabbath keepers would resist this "mark of the beast" (Rev. 13:16–18) and be persecuted for their stalwart convictions. Only those patient saints who kept all the commandments of God and the faith of Jesus (Rev. 14:12) would be ready for him to return. This extraordinary perspective was a direct challenge to the American Christianity of the day.

Most Americans were religious, though no denomination was established as the nation's official church. The First Amendment to the US Constitution forbids religious establishment and infringement on its free exercise. Church and state in the United States were to be separate. While there was no official religion, there was still a consensus among the people and their elected officials that America was a Christian nation. Many of the arguments for the abolition of slavery were Christian arguments. Yet this tiny group of Adventists argued that, in the future, the United States would become a beastly persecuting power. Their ideas marked a more pessimistic assessment in contrast to the widespread Christian consensus of the day. Adventists taught that persecution would come when Christians in America abandoned their basic tradition of religious freedom. Once this happened, only Sabbath-keeping Adventists would uphold true religious freedom while the rest of American Christianity would leave it behind.

The United States depicted as a fierce beast chained to creeds and slavery

Conditional Immortality

Another distinctive teaching that developed among Sabbath-keeping Adventists was the conditional nature of human immortality. In 1840, George Storrs concluded, after three years of careful Bible study, that human beings do not have inherent immortality. Such immortality belongs only to God and then to his people after the resurrection at the second coming. In other words, when people die, they do not go straight to heaven but wait in their graves until the resurrection, when Christ returns. Those who do not accept Christ remain mortal and are subject to death. The ungodly who are present when Christ returns are destroyed by the brightness of his coming (2 Thess. 2:8) and cease to exist after the earth is made new at the end of the millennium (Rev. 20). In 1842, Storrs became a Millerite Adventist, and his views were widely circulated. By 1844, he became a leading advocate of the seventh-month movement focused on October 22, and his ideas were widely discussed and debated among the Millerites. The three founders of Sabbatarian Adventism—Joseph Bates, James White, and Ellen White—accepted this teaching while still Millerites. While not unique to early Sabbatarian Adventist theology, it quickly became adopted as one of its core doctrinal pillars, in no small part due to a theology of wholeness that valued the physical body as God's creation, a concept of wholeness that would later become central to an Adventist theology of health and healing.

Sharing the Message

The earliest Sabbatarian Adventist literature was often printed by abolitionist printers at great expense, bound by hand, and individually mailed out. In this way, Ellen White disseminated her first vision in the spring of 1846, with the funds for the first 250 copies raised by James White and Heman S. Gurney (1818–1896). The following spring, James White compiled these nascent writings, with articles by Joseph Bates and his new wife, Ellen, into a pamphlet entitled *A Word to the "Little Flock"*—their first joint publishing venture. It contained the record of some of Ellen White's earliest visions, testimonials about and endorsements of these visions, and additional articles by James White and Joseph Bates about the last plagues and the second coming of Christ.

Though these publications were relatively brief, they did develop a shared understanding among a group of Millerites who now shared three core ideas: the heavenly sanctuary explanation for the Great Disappointment, the seventh-day Sabbath, and God's supernatural leading through the ministry of Ellen G. White. This group coalesced through Bible Conferences held between 1848 and early 1851. During these meetings, the leaders of the Sabbatarian Adventist movement defined and connected the distinctive beliefs that came to characterize what evolved into the Seventh-day Adventist Church. The five pillar doctrines of the new movement were the sanctuary, the Sabbath, the state of the dead (or the nonimmortality of the soul), the spirit of prophecy, and the second coming. At the Bible Conference held November 18–19, 1848, Ellen White reported divine instruction to begin a periodical. "I have a message for you. You must begin to print a little paper, and send it out to the people. Let it be small at first; but as the people read they will send you means with which to print, and it will be a success from the first. From this small beginning it was shown to me to be like streams of light that went clear around the world."[9] For the estimated two hundred Sabbatarian Adventists at that time, the prospect of making a worldwide impact was unimaginable.

In the summer of 1849, James established the periodical *The Present Truth*. His first issue, published in Middletown, Connecticut, was one thousand

9. Ellen G. White, *Life Sketches of Ellen G. White* (Mountain View, CA: Pacific Press, 1915), 125.

copies of an eight-page paper. A short time later, he started a second periodical, the *Advent Review*, emphasizing God's providential leading through the Millerite movement. By November 1850, both journals were combined into the *Second Advent Review and Sabbath Herald*. Today, known simply as the *Adventist Review* and *Adventist World*, the weekly and monthly versions of these periodicals remain the official voice of the Seventh-day Adventist Church.

Church Organization

The earliest Millerites, many of whom were disfellowshiped from their denominations for their advent belief, were also fiercely anti-organizational. Some, such as George Storrs, warned that "no church can be organized by man's invention but what it becomes Babylon the moment it is organized."[10] This deep suspicion of church organization after the Great Disappointment occurred at a time when early Sabbatarian Adventists were perplexed by their disappointment and too bewildered to even think about organization. Instead, they spent their time in earnest Bible study, building consensus around their distinctive beliefs. The Bible Conferences of 1848 to 1851 were an initial formative step toward organization, along with print publications. Further opportunities refined this consensus as they wrestled with additional beliefs, lifestyle, and polity. For example, an important topic at these early conferences was the literal affirmation of their belief in the second advent through regular celebrations of the Lord's Supper and the literal practice of foot washing. This service celebrated Christ's death and resurrection and promised to do this until he returned. Such "general conference" sessions formed the nucleus for discussions about "church order" or "church organization."

At the same time, the fledgling movement quickly multiplied. The number of believers went from approximately two hundred in 1850 to two thousand by 1852. Much of that growth was due to the work of Joseph Bates, who traveled widely, contacting both Millerite Adventists and Sabbatarians. In Jackson, Michigan, in 1849, Bates encountered a somewhat disinterested Adventist blacksmith, Daniel Palmer (1817–1897), who questioned his recent advent experience after the disappointment. Palmer would not quit his work to listen to Bates, so Bates shared his convictions as he hammered iron and shoed horses. At the end of the day, Palmer was convinced, and soon, an Adventist group in

10. Quoted in John Norton Loughborough, *The Church: Its Organization, Order, and Discipline* (Washington, DC: Review and Herald, 1907), 87.

Jackson became Sabbath keepers. Three years later, Bates returned to Jackson and met M. E. Cornell (1827–1893), a twenty-five-year-old preacher. He taught, along with others, that Christ would establish an earthly kingdom in Palestine at the beginning of the "age to come," a time when people received a second chance at salvation. Cornell and his wife, Cornelia, reluctantly agreed to hear Bates at Palmer's house. Unable to show the error in Bates's beliefs, within two weeks he was taking the message he learned to his in-laws and their neighbor, John P. Kellogg (1807–1881). Kellogg became a pillar of Adventism in Michigan and the father of sixteen children, including Merritt G. Kellogg (1832–1921), John Harvey Kellogg (1852–1943), and Will K. Kellogg (1860–1951), all of whom played influential roles in later Adventist history.

Bates left Jackson in 1852, traveling on railroad cars heading for Indiana, but was impressed to stop at the little village of Battle Creek, Michigan. He went first to the post office, where he asked for "the most honest man in town." The postmaster directed him to the home of David Hewitt (1805–1878), a staunch Presbyterian. Bates knocked on the door early in the morning and announced that he had important truth to share. The Hewitts invited him in for breakfast, and they spent the morning together as Bates explained his understanding of end-time events from Bible prophecy and Jesus's imminent return. In the afternoon, he presented his beliefs about the Sabbath. They accepted Bates's message and became part of a nucleus group of Sabbath-keeping Adventists in Battle Creek.

The Sabbatarian Adventist movement was driven by young men and women who, after they accepted these beliefs, devoted their lives to spreading the Sabbath-keeping Adventist message. J. N. Loughborough (1832–1924) was twenty years old when he reluctantly attended some Adventist meetings, became convinced, and afterward shared his newfound beliefs. Annie Rebekah Smith (1828–1855) was twenty-three when she joined the Whites in Rochester. A talented author and editor, she contributed regular poems, some of which still appear in the *Seventh-day Adventist Hymnal.* Her younger brother Uriah Smith (1832–1903) attended a Sabbath conference in 1852 at age twenty and spent the next three months studying what he learned. He became a Sabbath-keeping Adventist and joined his sister in Rochester. He quickly rose to prominence, eventually becoming the managing editor of the *Review and Herald.* This allowed James and Ellen White to travel and preach more widely. Stephen Haskell (1833–1922) started sharing his second-advent views at age nineteen. In 1853, he went to Canada to meet with a group of believers who had formed due to his preaching. While changing trains in Springfield, Massachusetts, he met William Saxby, another early Sabbath-keeping Adventist. They studied together, and Haskell stayed overnight. On the way to Canada, he read the literature Saxby had given him, and by the time he arrived, he had accepted the new truths.

Stephen N. Haskell

As others joined the Sabbatarian Adventist group during the early 1850s, they increasingly saw themselves less as isolated individuals and more as a cohesive movement. Some early reinforcements came from groups that shared similar core beliefs. For example, R. F. Cottrell (1814–1892) came from a Seventh Day Baptist background. He first heard William Miller preach on the second coming but was not impressed because he felt Miller didn't take seriously the perpetuity of God's law. However, as he read the *Review and Herald* in 1851 at age thirty-seven, he studied its teachings from the Bible, which convinced him they were true. Though he opposed formal church organization through the 1850s, he later accepted the need for organization and became a valuable leader and administrator as the church continued to grow. J. H. Waggoner (1820–1889) was thirty-one and the editor of a political paper in Baraboo, Wisconsin, when he heard some Sabbath-keeping preachers give a one-hour summary of Sabbath-keeping Adventist beliefs. He was intrigued and began to study. Eventually, he left his paper and became an itinerant Sabbath-keeping Adventist evangelist traveling across the American Midwest. His writings became an effective apology for the new movement. John Byington (1798–1887) initially rejected Miller's message but was intrigued by the Sabbath-keeping Adventists' message, which he first heard at age fifty-four (1851). Already an effective religious and community organizer, Byington was known for his abolitionist views, and his home was reportedly a stop on the Underground Railroad. Eventually, he built the first Sabbath-keeping Adventist church building in Bucks Bridge, New York, and became the first president of the organized church.

A common characteristic among these individuals is that none traced their conviction or conversion to James White, Ellen White, or her visionary reports. Instead, through a growing network of believers, they became convinced through careful Bible study and prayer and, in turn, shared their faith with others. Mounting challenges over a lack of finances meant that, by 1855, the group was at a standstill. The twenty staff members at the printing office lived together with the Whites in a single home without even drawing wages. In exchange for their work, they received room and board. James personally owned all the equipment and property in his name. He couldn't continue to keep enough cash flow to maintain operations. After considering a possible move to Vermont, the Whites instead accepted an offer by four men in Michigan who offered to build a print shop and home. These individuals (J. P. Kellogg, Cyrenius Smith, Henry Lyon, and Dan R. Palmer) each pledged $300 to finance the move. The first issue of the *Review and Herald* came off the press in Battle Creek in November 1855; the office and staff moved to Battle Creek and produced their first issue of the *Review and Herald* in December. For the first time, the Whites had their own home. James received a small but regular salary, and the intense pressure of leading the work was off his shoulders. Uriah Smith took over the responsibilities of publishing the weekly *Review and Herald.*

With these new resources, the publishing house soon prospered, and with its prosperity came accusations and jealousy that James had somehow profited from the publishing venture. A committee was appointed to investigate. Ultimately, they discovered that James had instead incurred increasing personal debts on behalf of the printing office and the growing work, so the committee raised additional funds to help pay off those debts.

One issue remained unresolved even after the move. How should they relate to Ellen White's visions? Seeking to solidify the biblical foundation for the Adventist and Sabbatarian messages, James was reluctant to publish anything about her visions in the *Review and Herald.* The frequency of her visionary experiences diminished, and some wondered if such revelations had ceased altogether. She expressed how she often felt they were a burden to her and expressed her preference to relinquish the prophetic role and focus on raising her young children. However, spiritual conditions among the Sabbath-keeping Adventists deteriorated. Believers became lethargic in their religious practices. Fewer converts joined the movement, and things came to a standstill. A general conference was called in late 1855 to meet the crisis. As they met in November 1855, two critical issues arose: when to observe the beginning and end of the weekly Sabbath, and the role and authority of Ellen White's spiritual gift.

Many felt that the question of when to begin the Sabbath was already answered. Joseph Bates, a sea captain who was widely traveled, had taught as early as 1848 that the Sabbath hours began at 6 p.m. every Friday. He knew that in the polar regions, sunset could be very early or late, creating inconsistencies in observance. Others had argued that the beginning of the Sabbath was at midnight. Ellen White reported a vision in which she was told both views were incorrect. Though not explicitly stated, she favored Bates's 6 p.m. time as correct. However, other Sabbath keepers were still not so sure. J. N. Andrews (1829–1883) was tasked with studying the matter in-depth. He concluded that the biblical Sabbath began at sunset and was kept that way throughout biblical times. The conference attendees were convinced and ended the first Sabbath of the conference at sundown.

However, Ellen White and Joseph Bates resisted the consensus. They felt convinced that God endorsed the 6 p.m. time. Ellen shared that she received additional divine revelation that she was wrong and should support this new interpretation instead. She and Bates accepted the message as the group reached a consensus about the biblical evidence presented by Andrews. Later, James used this story as a paradigm to explain how God guides his people. God had not directly revealed the answer to their question but instead wanted them to study the topic for themselves from the Bible. Once they had done this and reached a consensus, they received divine confirmation through the prophetic gift that clarified and affirmed this new understanding.[11] This underlined James White's argument that the Sabbath-keeping Adventist beliefs were grounded in Scripture alone, without referencing the modern gift of prophecy.

At the November 1855 conference, there was a growing sense that a spiritual decline had occurred among the scattered flock of believers. The conference seemed to spark a spiritual revival. It approved a request for a small committee to address the subject of the "gifts" of the church, meaning the spiritual gift of prophecy. In particular, there was a collective conviction that the church had neglected the gift of prophecy through Ellen White, resulting in their sad spiritual decline. The committee, composed of Joseph Bates, J. H. Waggoner, and M. E. Cornell, published their report in the *Review and Herald*. They quoted Acts 2:17, which states that the Spirit poured out in the last days would fall on men and women who would see visions. They believed God had given his people visions in the last days, but they had been inconsistent about how to use and apply them. On the one hand, they claimed to believe they were

11. James White, "Time to Commence the Sabbath," *Review and Herald* 31, no. 11 (February 25, 1868): 168.

messages from God, yet, on the other hand, they treated them on the same level as any human message. The inconsistency was largely due to fear of general prejudices about such claims and a desire to "conciliate the feelings of our opponents." They argued that this was not a wise course to follow. Since they regarded the visions as from God and in harmony with his written word, they argued that they all must acknowledge themselves "under obligation to abide by their teachings, and be corrected by their admonitions." What about those who did not acknowledge Ellen White's visions as from God? The committee counseled tolerance and forbearance so that her writings would not be made a test of fellowship.[12]

The conference was a turning point for the *Review and Herald* and the fledgling movement. Not only did the publication have a new editor in Uriah Smith, but it published an article by Ellen White in January 1856. It shared her anguish at giving visionary messages to people that she was very uncomfortable delivering. In an emotional appeal, uncharacteristic of her writings in general, she described how depressed and discouraged she was to see how little her messages were heeded and what little effect they had. But at the recent conference, she felt God had worked a mighty revival. There was the prospect of God reviving the gifts again so they could live in the church "to encourage the desponding and fainting soul, and to correct and reprove the erring." If the neglect of the gifts brought spiritual lethargy, now accepting the gifts and heeding their instruction brought new consensus and cohesiveness. She wrote, "We need a LIVING faith and then we shall have a living experience." She added that since the conference, she and James had felt the power and blessing of God. He had experienced divine healing but was not yet fully restored. She also reported that, for the previous weeks, their peace had been like a river. Encouraging faith and trust in God, she wrote, "There is a fullness in Jesus. We can partake in His rich grace and abundant salvation."[13] This article demonstrates that the expectation of the early Adventist believers was not that Ellen White's spiritual gift would solve doctrinal issues or give them fantastic new truths, but instead, that her visions would encourage, correct, and reprove so that the church would put their trust fully in Jesus. At this time, her leadership was more pastoral than doctrinal.

As a result of this new appreciation for the prophetic gift in the church,

12. Joseph Bates, J. H. Waggoner, and M. E. Cornell, "Address," *Review and Herald* 7, no. 10 (December 4, 1855): 78–79.

13. E. G. White, "Communication from Sister White," *Review and Herald* 7, no. 15 (January 10, 1856): 118.

the *Review and Herald* began to publish Ellen White's writings more widely, and the body of believers took her counsel more seriously. One area that contributed to the movement's spiritual advancement was organization. In 1852, Ellen White described a vision in which she was told that "order" was needed. She challenged the church to "become established upon gospel order which has been overlooked and neglected." James White continued this rallying cry with a series of articles in the *Review*. He saw that the "scattered flock" needed direction and organization to maintain their faith and expand their witness. To regain their momentum, they needed more than a set of beliefs. "Gospel order" was necessary if they were to work together to share their faith efficiently. Furthermore, the movement needed a way to support its ministers. Without an organized system of support, most ministers resorted to work as farmers or artisans. Some ministers received significant contributions for their ministry, while others received barely anything. J. N. Loughborough and another worker spent all of one summer ministering in New York and Pennsylvania but only received four dollars a week for their labor, which was not enough to support their families. Overwork and poverty contributed to poor health. Some ministers, like J. N. Andrews and Loughborough, gave up full-time ministry, moved to Waukon, Iowa, and returned to farming to support their families. The result was a loss of spiritual fervor and a preoccupation with temporal matters.

The Dash to Waukon

In late December 1855, James and Ellen White became deeply concerned about the spiritual welfare of Sabbatarian Adventist believers who moved to Waukon, Iowa. They were unhappy about not being consulted about the move to Battle Creek and unsure whether the interpretation of the seven messages to the churches in Revelation 2 and 3 pointed to Adventists as lukewarm Laodiceans. The Whites, despite visiting believers in central Illinois, decided to make the three-hundred-mile journey by sleigh to Waukon over snow and ice. Upon reaching the frozen Mississippi River the day before Christmas, they discovered that a recent rain had created a shallow river of water on top of the ice. They debated about whether to proceed. Ellen White felt confident they could make it; others feared the ice might crack. The sleigh driver urged the horses onto the ice and successfully made it across.

Once they arrived in Waukon that Christmas Eve, the Whites announced a meeting for that evening. Few were enthusiastic about the gathering. The Waukon Adventists met with the Whites almost daily for the next week. The sessions were intense, and the results were dramatic. Mary Loughborough was the first to confess her negative attitude toward her husband's long absences. She confessed her willingness for him to return to ministry and urged others to repent and find peace with God. The meetings broke down previous barriers that had stood between the Waukon believers and the Whites. Afterward, Ellen White reported that J. N. Andrews expressed his appreciation for the ministry of the Whites and admitted that he believed the Lord had sent them. The whole experience propelled the Sabbatarian Adventists toward organization as a way to solve the problems of remuneration for ministers, ensure unity, and confirm the spiritual leadership of the Whites.

The challenges in Waukon, Iowa, led to broader discussions about church organization. James White wrote in the *Review*, "We lack system," arguing that a system of organization was not opposed by the Bible and was supported by common sense. Then he named the brethren who opposed such a system:

1. Bro. Overcautious will be frightened and be careful to warn everyone not to go too far.
2. Bro. Confusion will cry out: This looks like Babylon, following the fallen churches.
3. Bro. Do-Little will say: The cause is the Lord's. We can leave it in his hands. He will take care of it.
4. Love-this-world, Selfish, Slothful and Stingy all agree. If God calls men to preach, let them go preach. God will take care of them.
5. Korah, Dathan, and Abiram are ready to rebel against those who really care about souls as those who must give account.[14]

Andrews, Loughborough, and the Whites wanted to know what the Bible said about supporting ministers. Andrews was tasked to study the matter and report the Bible's evidence for a plan for church giving. This new plan, dubbed "Systematic Benevolence," sometimes affectionately known as "Sister Betsy," would provide the financial strength for a growing denomination. The scriptural evidence he gathered and his careful reasoning won the day. Using the example in 1 Corinthians 16:1–2, these early believers committed themselves to lay aside a specific amount each week for the Lord's work. Later, during another economic depression, church leaders reexamined this plan and refined it further into the biblical tithing system (adopted in 1878). Together, these two successive plans provided an increasingly consistent way of gathering

14. James White, "Yearly Meetings," *Review and Herald* 14, no. 9 (July 21, 1859): 68.

Bucks Bridge, New York

and distributing funds across the denomination, finally resolving the issue of ministerial support.

Meanwhile, in the late 1850s, James White advocated for an organization to take ownership of the publishing work. The sticking point was the name of the organization. A general workers meeting was called for Battle Creek in September 1860. Many speeches were made on both sides of the issue.[15] James White wanted a scriptural name and favored the Church of God. Others objected: it sounded too exclusive. Other denominations were already using that name. Soon, a consensus developed around the name Seventh-day Adventist. David Hewitt, dubbed the most honest man in Battle Creek for his honesty in selling goods, first moved to accept this name.

The next step was to incorporate the publishing operations officially. Before this, the press had been owned and operated by James White, who assumed all the liability and risk. It was a major step toward organization when the Seventh-day Adventist Publishing Association was formed and legally incorporated in May 1861. In October 1861, the workers in Michigan gathered and organized the first state conference of Seventh-day Adventists. The organization of the state conference proved highly successful. The new church orga-

15. "Business Proceedings of B.C. Conference," *Review and Herald* 16, no. 21 (October 9, 1860): 161ff.; 16, no. 22 (October 16, 1860): 169ff.; and 16, no. 23 (October 23, 1860): 177ff.

nization adopted Systematic Benevolence, providing financial stability. The workers received a regular weekly salary; despite being small, it enabled greater economic security and more efficient work. James White urged all states to follow Michigan's example and organize similar state conferences. He knew that only when that happened could there be a general organization bringing together all the state conferences. In 1862, other groups of churches organized into state conferences.

In May 1863, twenty delegates from these state conferences gathered to organize a General Conference. James White was initially asked to serve as president, but he declined. He didn't want anyone to say that he had advocated organization so he could seize the top position and force his will upon the entire body. Instead, John Byington was elected president. With the naming of the church and its organization, the stage was set for the rapid expansion of the Seventh-day Adventist Church in increasingly broader ways.

Adventists and the Civil War

With strong abolitionist convictions, most Adventists firmly supported Abraham Lincoln and the Union when the southern American states seceded in 1861. Ellen White wrote that the system of slavery, "and this alone," lay at the foundation of the American Civil War. In Parkville, Michigan, three months before hostilities broke out, she reported seeing that the war would be far more horrific and deadly than generally believed. However, tension developed between the condemnation of slavery and whether Adventists should participate in military combat on the side of the North. In August 1862, the United States government appeared ready to force men to join the army and fight in combat. James White wrote an article entitled "The Nation" in the *Review and Herald* that supported conscripted soldiers fighting for the North. He argued that if conscription were implemented, the government would take responsibility for soldiers' violations of the fourth and sixth commandments. Resistance would be suicidal. In contrast, the Iowa conference had petitioned the state legislature for recognition as pacifists, though their petition was unsuccessful.

Ellen White pushed for a more moderate position. She wrote that her husband's article was based on the best information he had on the subject and that the Iowans had acted out of a lack of faith in God. She favored a stance of noncombatancy yet endorsed the antislavery and pro-Union positions:

> I was shown that God's people, who are His peculiar treasure, cannot engage in this perplexing war, for it is opposed to every principle of their faith. In

> the army they cannot obey the truth and at the same time obey the requirements of their officers. . . . The ten precepts of Jehovah are the foundation of all righteous and good laws. Those who love God's commandments will conform to every good law of the land. But if the requirements of the rulers are such as conflict with the laws of God, the only question to be settled is: Shall we obey God, or man?[16]

Between January 1863, when this testimony was first published, and the summer of 1864, it was possible for conscripted men to buy a substitute for $300. If conscripts could not raise the requisite funds on their own, church members helped raise the money for them. Nonetheless, many Adventist young men enlisted in or were conscripted into the Northern army and served in combat. In July 1864, the United States Congress restricted the option of paying a commutation fee to be exempt from military service. J. N. Andrews secured official government recognition that Seventh-day Adventists were "'a people unanimously loyal and anti-slavery' but unable to shed blood because of their views of the Ten Commandments and the teachings of the New Testament."[17]

The trauma of war brought new meaning to waiting for the end. As the North and South struggled over slavery, church leaders wondered if the end was indeed upon them. As they waited and experienced growing pains as a fledgling denomination, the reality and struggles of war forced them to come to grips with the need for organization. They even debated whether it was morally right to participate in the war effort. Ultimately, they debated these topics, developed consensus as they organized, and created new systems for sharing the Adventist message while they waited.

Resources

Baker, Delbert. *The Unknown Prophet*. Washington, DC: Review and Herald, 1987.

Froom, Le Roy Edwin. *The Conditionalist Faith of Our Fathers: The Conflict of the Ages over the Nature and Destiny of Man*. Washington, DC: Review and Herald, 1966.

16. E. G. White, *Testimonies for the Church*, published as testimony no. 9 in January 1863. Published in *Testimonies for the Church*, vol. 1 (Mountain View, CA: Pacific Press, 1885), 136.

17. Douglas Morgan, "Civil War," in *The Ellen G. White Encyclopedia* (Hagerstown, MD: Review and Herald, 2013), 718–21. Morgan cites J. N. Andrews, "Seventh-day Adventists Recognized as Non-Combatants," *Review and Herald* 24, no. 16 (September 13, 1864): 124.

Knight, George R., and Gerald Wheeler. *Organizing to Beat the Devil: The Development of Adventist Church Structure*. Hagerstown, MD: Review and Herald Publishing Association, 2001.

Mustard, Andrew Gordon. *James White and SDA Organization: Historical Development, 1844–1881*. Berrien Springs, MI: Andrews University Press, 1987.

Timm, Alberto Ronald. "The Sanctuary and the Three Angels' Messages 1844–1863: Integrating Factors in the Development of Seventh-day Adventist Doctrines." PhD diss., Andrews University, 1995. https://dx.doi.org/10.32597/dissertations/155/.

Wheeler, Gerald. *James White: Innovator and Overcomer.* Hagerstown, MD: Review and Herald Publishing Association, 2003.

Discussion Questions

1. How did early Adventists connect the sanctuary, the Sabbath, and the three angels' messages? How significant is this for Adventist identity?
2. Compare and contrast Ellen White's report of her vision with those of Foy and Foss.
3. Ellen Harmon's report of her initial vision did not explain how God could have led the Millerites to focus on a mistaken date. In your opinion, how might God have been leading the Millerites if the main focus of their movement (October 22, 1844) was a mistake?
4. What factors encouraged the Sabbatarian Adventists to organize as the Seventh-day Adventist Church?
5. What is conditional immortality, and what part does it play in Seventh-day Adventist theology?
6. What do the conversion stories of Palmer, Hewitt, Loughborough, Cornell, and Waggoner have in common?

CHAPTER 4

Adventist Expansion, 1863 to 1890

As early as 1855, Adventism shifted westward to Battle Creek. As the denomination organized, a host of related institutions sprung up. The ever-growing need for print caused church leaders to expand the publishing work from a small Washington hand press purchased in 1849 to a modest publishing house in Battle Creek. The continued growth necessitated a name and a more formal organization. Adventist church leaders quickly expanded in the 1860s by developing health and educational institutions. On Christmas Day 1865, Ellen White received a vision in which she challenged the fledgling denomination to start a health institution of their own. The following year the Western Health Reform Institute was established. During its first decade of existence, it would struggle, but when the young and talented Dr. J. H. Kellogg returned from medical school in 1874, he transformed it into the world-famous Battle Creek Sanitarium. By the 1890s the institution was so famous that it was said that a letter simply addressed to "Battle Creek Sanitarium" would be properly delivered from any post office in the world. Similarly, Adventist schools took their first tentative steps in the 1860s with Goodloe Harper Bell (1832–1899), who worked diligently to establish an educational system.

John Harvey Kellogg

CHAPTER 4

George I. Butler

When George I. Butler (1834–1918) was elected president of the Iowa Conference in 1865, he faced a significant challenge. Just before his election, a major split occurred in the Iowa church. Previous conference officers traveled from church to church, sowing doubt and discord. Known as the Marion Party, they left the denomination and eventually took the name Church of God (Seventh-day). Their primary objection to Seventh-day Adventist teaching centered on Ellen White's prophetic role and their denial of some basic Adventist beliefs, such as the three angels' messages. They no longer believed that the beast of Revelation 13 was the United States and claimed that the three angels' messages had been preached before 1844. At age thirty-one, Butler seemed largely unprepared, without any formal training or ministry experience. Butler had been a farmer and a schoolteacher during the three months of the winter season. Would serving as a local church deacon and then as the elder of the Waukon, Iowa, church provide enough leadership experience to succeed?

Butler's journey to leadership in the Iowa Conference was not exactly a straightforward path either. Like some other second- and third-generation Adventists, he initially showed little interest in religion despite growing up in an Adventist home. However, a significant turning point arrived when he was converted at age twenty-two and baptized by J. N. Andrews. This spiritual awakening, coupled with his marriage to Lentha Lockwood (1826–1901) and their settling on a farm, marked a new life chapter. Despite significant misgivings raised by the Marion Party about the leadership of James and Ellen White, Butler's doubts were dispelled when he heard M. E. Cornell speak in defense of Ellen White's testimonies. This newfound conviction led to a surprising turn of events. Butler was elected as the new president of the Iowa Conference even though he was not ordained or even a licensed minister. Undeterred, he embarked on the monumental task of visiting every church member in the territory. This act of personal connection and inspiration prevented further defections to the Marion Party and instilled in the six hundred members a vision of what they could do for God. In Butler's view, the role of the gospel minister was not to pastor a local congregation but to lead new evangelistic efforts, with the local church caring for its own needs and developing young men and women to join in the evangelistic efforts of the fledgling denomination.

Over the next three decades, Butler's commitment to the Seventh-day Adventist Church was tested more than once. Still, his work in Iowa in defense of Ellen White's ministry and his efforts as a pastor and evangelist bore fruit. The defections to the Marion Party faded away. As a result of Butler's example, many of the leaders and missionaries in the third generation of the church came from Iowa. This included A. G. Daniells, Robert M. Kilgore, Henry Nicola, and J. H. Morrison, who all played significant roles in expanding the Seventh-day Adventist message.

Spreading West

As men and women of European heritage moved across the North American continent, the Adventist message spread with them. Capable men and women without formal training shared the Seventh-day Adventist message from town to town across the Midwest and the ever-expanding frontier. A shopkeeper, Solomon Myers, was the first Adventist in the Nebraska Territory. Merritt G. Kellogg, John Harvey Kellogg's older half brother, was the first Adventist to spread the message to California. He was twenty-seven years old when he crossed the central plains of North America in a wagon with his family in 1859. His carpentry skills were in demand in San Francisco, which was rapidly expanding. Both Myers and Kellogg began Bible studies with those they came into contact with, and local churches were soon organized. California was a particularly fertile field. In 1874, James and Ellen White moved to Oakland and began another publishing ministry known as the Pacific Seventh-day Adventist Publishing Association. It circulated the *Signs of the Times* as an evangelistic tool to build camaraderie in the western part of the United States. Soon, a health institute and a college were founded in California, supported by the growing number of Adventists. A similar pattern occurred across the Pacific Northwest region, where the Walla Walla Valley became another Adventist center. By 1900, Walla Walla had become the home of an Adventist college and a health institution.

M. B. Czechowski

Even more remarkable was the global spread of the Seventh-day Adventist message. In 1857, a former Polish Catholic priest, Michal B. Czechowski (1818–1876), accepted the Sabbath-keeping Adventist message. He soon began to share his faith, yet he yearned to return to Europe and requested church leaders to send him. The leaders of the newly organized Seventh-day Adventist denomination were reluctant to sponsor Czechowski. There were concerns about his financial management, willingness to take counsel from the church's leadership, unpredictable temper, and commitment to basic Adventist beliefs. Czechowski turned for support to the Advent Christian Church, another group that descended from the Millerites. They agreed to support his proposed mission to the Waldensians in Italy. After a year in Italy, opposition forced him to relocate to the small Swiss village of Tramelan. There he taught the prophecies of Christ's return and the seventh-day Sabbath. Soon, he had a congregation of sixty members meeting on the Sabbath. He never revealed the existence of his Advent Christian sponsors or the source of the Seventh-day Adventist doctrines that he preached. A member of the congregation, Albert Vuilleumier, accidentally discovered a copy of the *Advent Review and Sabbath Herald* in a room Czechowski had occupied. He knew enough English to understand that an organization in the United States believed the same things as the congregation in Tramelan.

Jacques Ertzberger

When word of this Tramelan group reached denominational leaders in Battle Creek, they invited them to send a delegate to the 1869 General Conference. Though he arrived too late for the conference, twenty-six-year-old Jacques Ertzberger remained in the United States long enough to become fully grounded in Seventh-day Adventist teachings and was ordained to the Adventist ministry. When he returned to Switzerland, he was the first officially ordained Seventh-day Adventist minister outside North America.

At the 1869 General Conference, consideration was given to sending missionaries to other lands. Still, it was not until 1874 that an official action was taken to send J. N. Andrews and his two teenage children to support Ertzberger in Europe. In September of that year, Andrews left, accompanied by Ademar Vuilleumier, a young man from the Swiss group who had studied at the fledgling school run by Goodloe Harper Bell in Battle Creek. Soon, Andrews and his Swiss associates traveled through much of Europe, raising congregations of Seventh-day Adventists in Germany, France, and Italy.

One convert in Italy was an Irish physician, Herbert Ribton, who was based in Naples. By 1879, he had moved to Alexandria in Egypt and translated several Adventist tracts into Arabic. However, anti-European riots broke out in Egypt in 1882, and Ribton and several Italian converts to Adventism were killed, ending the first outreach to the Arabic-speaking world.

An influential mechanism for spreading the Adventist message was the Tract and Missionary societies. The first of these societies was founded in 1869 in the home of Stephen and Mary Haskell in South Lancaster, Massachusetts. Beginning as a lady's prayer meeting for the children of members, it soon broadened to include backsliding Adventists and non-Adventist neighbors. The women in the group wrote letters, visited, and spread Adventist literature far and near. Stephen Haskell saw great potential in this work and guided the group as it was formally organized. Haskell traveled from state to state, organizing similar groups into Tract and Missionary societies. These state societies, coordinated by Maria Huntley, became the foundation for the wide distribution of Adventist literature.

Colporteur George Drew prepared to sell Adventist literature

Adventist literature, scattered on ships, provided early points of contact for Adventist work in Scandinavia, England, South Africa, Australia, and even tiny Pitcairn Island in the South Pacific, all notably dominated by Protestants of European descent.

Adventists adopted a popular media distribution method with the rise of full-time literature evangelists, often referred to simply as "colporteurs." One especially popular book was a 1,600-page volume on home, health, and hygiene by Dr. John Har-

Music in the Seventh-day Adventist Church

Listening to music can be an intensely emotional experience. Therefore, it should be no surprise that changes in musical style and instrumentation arouse strong emotions. Even in the early Christian church, arguments over the use of organs in church created controversy since organs were associated with events in "pagan" coliseums where organ music accompanied violent and immoral activity.

In early American Methodism, organs were considered evidence of worldliness and were not installed in churches until after 1836. That same year, an organ was built in Ellen Harmon (White)'s home church, the Chestnut Street Methodist Church, in Portland, Maine. It was the first organ in a Methodist church. As an eight-year-old, she and her family were undoubtedly aware of its controversial installation.

The Millerite movement was accompanied by much singing, primarily unaccompanied by musical instruments. Joshua V. Himes published the popular *Millennial Harp, or Second Advent Hymns*, as early as 1842. As a Millerite preacher, James White reported beginning a meeting by walking down the central aisle of a church, singing, "You will see your Lord a-coming," keeping time by tapping his Bible. He reported that the crowd of almost one thousand people watched spellbound until he finished the hymn. On another occasion, a group of early Adventists were arrested for disturbing people with their singing. When they appeared before the judge, they sang three thrilling hymns and were set free at once. "If people are disturbed with that kind of singing," remarked the judge, "they ought to be disturbed."

James White was naturally interested in publishing his own hymnal. The first bound book ever produced by Sabbatarian Adventists was *Hymns for God's Peculiar People, That Keep the Commandments of God and the Faith of Jesus*, published in 1849. Most early hymnbooks published just the words or printed the tunes separately to be sung to multiple lyrics. The 1869 edition of this hymnal was the first second-advent hymnal published with tunes in four-part harmony on two staves.

As musical tastes changed, new hymnbooks were published. *Hymns and Tunes* was the most extensive ever produced by the church and released in 1886. An abbreviated version known as *Christ in Song* was released in 1900. Other smaller hymnbooks for camp meetings, temperance gatherings, and youth meetings were also published. *The Church Hymnal* in 1941 would be the next major officially sponsored hymnal, with a new *The Seventh-day Adventist Hymnal* published in 1985.

Ellen White wrote about music, focusing on its purpose to elevate the heart and fill one with gratitude to God. She encouraged instrumental accompaniment to congregational singing but cautioned that it needed to be done skillfully and handled carefully.[1]

1. Ellen G. White, *Testimonies for the Church*, vol. 9 (Mountain View, CA: Pacific Press, 1909), 144.

According to her granddaughter, she loved to sing her favorite hymn, "Jesus, Lover of My Soul."

Her nephew, Frank E. Belden (1858–1945), wrote numerous hymns that appeared in all hymnals from his lifetime onward. Belden would take the preacher's text for the sermon, compose words and a tune while the preacher spoke, and debut the new song at the close of the service. Once his remarkable musical abilities became known, he served as the music editor of *Hymns and Tunes*. Unfortunately, Belden became disenchanted with his aunt, Ellen White, and her son, W. C. White. He was disfellowshiped in 1907 and died a bitter man in 1945.

By the late 1940s, popular gospel songs and choruses spread across radio stations in North America. Many opposed the use of this popular genre, including J. L. McElhany, president of the General Conference. When H. M. S. Richards (1894–1985) utilized Adventist-composed gospel songs sung by the King's Heralds, a male quartet, McElhany threatened to withhold denominational support if the Voice of Prophecy continued to use such songs. Consequently, Richards was forced to fire his musical director, Wayne Hooper (1920–2007), who used the opportunity to complete his BA degree in music at Union College. When W. H. Branson (1887–1961) was elected president in 1950, Richards felt comfortable re-calling Hooper to the Voice of Prophecy and encouraged once again new musical styles. Hooper remained the musical director of the ministry until his retirement.

In 1965, three Southern Missionary College students formed the Wedgwood Trio. It performed folk-style music accompanied by a guitar. They faced significant pushback from older members and administrators. However, years later, they were considered out of date and were popular only among many of the same church members who had opposed them earlier. Max Mace formed another innovative musical group known as the Heritage Singers in 1971. Their gospel music used many of the tropes and techniques of the popular music of their day, earning them the name "Heretic Swingers" from those who did not care for their style.

In the 1980s, in North America and some other places, praise and worship music moved from the charismatic Vineyard churches into evangelical and Adventist churches. It was initially focused on addressing God but evolved under the influence of secular popular music to include almost any kind of contemporary Christian music. It was characteristically led by a "worship band" or "praise team," accompanied by guitars or piano. The words of the songs were projected on a screen behind the singers so the congregation could join in the music. Critics saw the songs as loud and repetitive, but young people appreciated the immersive nature of the experience.

Musical styles and tastes change. There seems to be an inevitable cycle where young people's music becomes traditional and goes out of style as the next generation's music comes onto the scene. Tradition and innovation seem to always remain in conflict.

vey Kellogg, which quickly went through multiple editions and sold hundreds of thousands of copies. At the same time, the Review and Herald Publishing Association combined two books by Uriah Smith on Daniel and Revelation into an attractive volume replete with pictures and available for sale by colporteurs. Eventually, the state Tract and Missionary societies became the local distributors of Adventist literature.

Local conferences sponsored area-wide camp meetings that helped provide fellowship for widely scattered Adventists. Initially, there was some hesitancy lest Adventist camp meetings be associated with more fanatical groups and religious excess. Yet the idea quickly caught on as these gatherings typically lasted five to seven days, with significant meetings scheduled on weekends and often held in new locations to facilitate evangelism. The weekend meetings frequently attracted large numbers of guests. For example, an estimated four thousand people gathered in 1876 at the Groveland, Massachusetts, camp meeting to hear Ellen White speak on the temperance issue. The local Sabbath school became another important motivator of outreach.

Initial efforts to emulate the Sunday-keeping Sabbath schools were weak and poorly directed. However, in the late 1860s, Goodloe Harper Bell began publishing a series of Bible lessons for children and adults. He also organized the Battle Creek Sabbath school into a significant educational enterprise, including a specific curriculum and regular teachers meetings. He began to travel to churches, encouraging them to adopt his methods. By 1877, state Sabbath School Associations had been formed to inspire each church to develop its own Sabbath school. In California and Washington, Sabbath school members began to raise funds for foreign missions, contributing significant sums to the beginning of the work in Australia and South Africa. Fund-raising for missions then became a regular feature of the Sabbath school. The local church members formed the foundation of both the Sabbath school and mission-funding efforts.

As the Adventist church spread across North America and then the world, the vision and hard work of men like Butler, combined with the efforts of local church members, were vital factors in the denomination's growth.

Controversy in Minneapolis

The Seventh-day Adventist Church faced its most important theological test in 1888. The denomination had seldom dealt with basic Christian beliefs in the lead-up to the crucial conference in Minneapolis that fall. It had settled its unique doctrines by 1850, leaving some of the most fundamental Christian beliefs unaddressed. Many leading church members, including James White and Uriah Smith, were resistant and unclear about the three persons of the Godhead and detested the term "Trinity." While this position was never formally spelled out in a doctrinal statement, it was a commonly accepted part of Adventist theology, a situation only challenged in the 1890s. Some Adventists, such as Joseph Bates, held a legalistic approach to understanding salvation. Others merely assumed the message of salvation through faith in Christ and sought to show how Sabbath keeping is not in conflict with it. Since much of their evangelism consisted of convincing other Christians of the necessity of keeping the seventh-day Sabbath, Adventist evangelists rarely addressed the issue of salvation.

One of the early moments when concerns about salvation came to the forefront was when the *Review and Herald* published a book by J. H. Waggoner, a recent convert. One year after becoming a Sabbath-keeping Adventist, he submitted a book, *The Law of God*. The book proclaimed a typical Adventist message that the moral law contained in the Ten Commandments had not been abolished at the cross and continued to be a valid guide to the normal Christian life. However, Waggoner's treatment of the law in the New Testament book of Galatians did not fit the established Adventist understanding. Waggoner stated that the law in Galatians was the moral law of the Ten Commandments. Stephen Pierce (1804–1883) argued that it was much broader and included the ceremonial law. Pierce complained to James White, who called a meeting to discuss the issue. Ellen White was present at the conference, and all agreed that Waggoner's book was in error and should be withdrawn. Ellen White wrote a testimony about the issue and stated that there were incorrect things in Waggoner's book.

J. H. Waggoner accepted the book's withdrawal and continued serving as a successful Seventh-day Adventist evangelist, editor, and finally, as a missionary at the time of his death. He served as editor of the *Signs of the Times* in 1883 when his son Ellet J. Waggoner (1855–1916) was called to serve as his assistant. Shortly afterward, the elder Waggoner was transferred to Battle Creek, and E. J. Waggoner replaced his father as editor.

The younger Waggoner had secured a degree as a physician and briefly practiced medicine at the Rural Health Retreat in Healdsburg, California, according to its archival records. At a camp meeting in Healdsburg, he heard a presentation on the meaning of Christ's sacrifice. For the first time, he saw that Jesus had died for him personally and that his sins were forgiven. It was a profound spiritual experience, leading him to follow in his father's footsteps.

Within a year of his cross-centered conversion, the younger Waggoner was writing for the *Signs of the Times*, and shortly after that, he became its associate editor. He began to explore the book of Galatians and write about it in the *Signs*. In an article published in September 1886, Waggoner made four points in his argument that "the law" in Galatians must be the moral law rather than the ceremonial one. First, he argued, the ceremonial law did not condemn; only the moral law condemned all humanity. Therefore, the offer of redemption must also come to all, not just to those under the ceremonial law. Second, only the moral law could condemn all humanity under the law (Gal. 3:22), since there is nothing in the Levitical law that shows humans to be sinners. Third, if all are under the law until faith comes (Gal. 3:23), then the law cannot be ceremonial since it only governs Jews. The moral law condemns humans and holds them under the law's condemnation until faith comes to them and they believe. Fourth, the law is not a schoolmaster to *point* us to Christ. Nothing in the moral law points to Christ. Instead, Paul's point (Gal. 3:24) is that the moral law *brings* us to Christ. Waggoner wrote: "The moral law does this, by giving the convicted sinner no rest until he flees to Christ."[1]

In response to his Christ-centered teachings, the younger Waggoner received the same opposition as his father. By 1886, President G. I. Butler was solidly opposed to Waggoner's ideas. The issue was explored at the General Conference session in November, but no agreement was reached. At the session's close, Ellen White wrote to Waggoner and his associate editor, A. T. Jones (1850–1923), and to G. I. Butler and Uriah Smith, rebuking each of them for their attitudes at the 1886 session. Jones and Waggoner accepted the rebukes. Butler and Smith also appeared to accept the rebukes but were inwardly resentful and felt that Ellen White had betrayed them and joined forces with their opponents. Ellen White insisted that both sides agree not to publish anything further on the controversial issue until the next General Conference session in 1888. All agreed. Yet Butler broke his promise and published a book entitled *The Law in Galatians*. Waggoner responded in the *Signs* with an article titled "The Gospel in Galatians." Meanwhile, Butler, a strong proponent of Ellen White's prophetic gift, wrote letters requesting her support. He even reminded her about the events of the 1850s concerning the senior Waggoner's stance on the law in Galatians. He asked Ellen White for the testimony she had written on that occasion. She responded that the issue of the law in Galatians was something that needed to be studied more from Scripture. She refused to make

1. [E. J.] W[aggoner], "Comments on Galatians 3. No. 9," *Signs of the Times* 12, no. 34 (September 2, 1886): 534 [7].

a pronouncement on the subject. As for her testimony from the 1850s, she merely stated that it was providential that it had been lost.

A. T. Jones

By the summer of 1888, as battle lines between the two sides intensified, Butler was increasingly frustrated with Mrs. White's position, even as she shared her deep concerns about the legalistic direction of the church leaders. She later wrote that the Adventist people had preached the law until they were as dry as the hills of Gilboa. They had failed to preach Christ in the law, and the church was famishing. She wrote, "We must not trust in our own merits at all, but in the merits of Jesus of Nazareth."[2] Falling ill that summer, she asked that no one pray for her recovery. At sixty years of age, without her husband to support her, she needed rest and was ready to lay down her life if only she could. But many in the church prayed anyway. She recalled the vow she had made to her husband seven years earlier on his deathbed in which she promised to stand by her post of duty. She recommitted herself to move forward by faith since she could not see what the future might hold for her and the church she loved. She eventually recovered from her illness and prepared to move forward.

During the summer before the scheduled meetings, a pastor wrote to Butler describing how Ellen White's son, W. C. White, met with three other individuals in California, including A. T. Jones, to study the matter of the law in Galatians. It seemed to the pastor that Ellen White was part of a conspiracy to advance new and dangerous ideas. Butler wrote Ellen White an angry letter accusing her of betraying him by not backing his position on the law in Galatians. He suggested that she was partly responsible for his broken mental and physical condition. Since Butler was one of her strongest supporters, these false accusations were especially painful to her.

2. E. G. White, "Christ Prayed for Unity Among His Disciples," *Review and Herald* 67, no. 10 (March 11, 1890): 1–2 [145–46].

The General Conference held that autumn occurred in the newly constructed Adventist church building in Minneapolis, Minnesota. As the denomination spread westward, this was a new center of Adventism. The fact that this pivotal meeting was held in Minneapolis was an apparent concession to this shift.

One topic earnestly discussed dealt with the identity of one of the ten barbarian tribes in the prophecy of the ten horns in Daniel 7 that occupied the western Roman Empire. Was it the Huns or the Alemanni (Germans)? Uriah Smith taught it was the Huns, yet during the conference, Jones suggested the alternative. The morning devotional messages by E. J. Waggoner highlighted the righteousness of Christ.

Jones's presentation on the ten barbarian tribes in Daniel 7 was clear and persuasive, putting Uriah Smith on the defensive. He argued that his list of ten tribes was based on the ideas of his Millerite predecessors. Jones impulsively responded, "Elder Smith has told you he does not know anything about this matter. I do; and I don't want you to blame me for what he does not know."[3] Ellen White rebuked Jones for his rashness, but his fighting words provoked a reaction, and soon the delegates were taking sides. Those standing with Uriah Smith took their name from the Huns. Jones and Waggoner's faction took their name from the Alemanni, the tribe that Jones felt should take the place of the Huns. Soon, delegates asked each other, "Are you a Hun or an Alemanni?"

Waggoner's presentations on Romans and Galatians avoided the debated points. Still, they affirmed that the law can only reveal sin and that no one can justify themselves before God by keeping the law. Waggoner pointed to Christ as the remedy for humanity's problem. He affirmed that Christ is eager to give his own righteousness to each person. With that righteousness came the power of victory over sin, according to Waggoner. While Ellen White strongly endorsed the gospel message of Waggoner's presentations, she also noted some aspects of his teaching that she was uncertain about. She did not consider some of his interpretations of Galatians to be correct. However, she used this as an opportunity to counsel tolerance. Just because one might disagree with Waggoner was no reason to consider him dangerous. Some were rejecting Waggoner's entire message because they disagreed with part of it. Ellen White saw that this was wrong. She said she could see "the beauty of truth in the

3. A. T. Robinson, "Did the Seventh-day Adventist Denomination Reject the Doctrine of Righteousness by Faith?" (unpublished manuscript, 1931, 1–2, Ellen G. White Estate, Document File 189, https://tinyurl.com/3rtj74nw); R. J. Wieland and D. K. Short, "An Interview with J. S. Washburn," June 4, 1950.

The ten-horned beast of Daniel 7

presentations of the righteousness of Christ in relation to the law."[4] Since the law had been emphasized since the church's beginning, many found Waggoner's message of righteousness through Christ to be novel and threatening. For others, it was fresh and energizing.

Ellen White spoke at the conference in support of the theme of the righteousness of Christ, urging a deeper study of the Word of God and appealing for a genuine heart conversion to Christ. However, many at the conference were unable to receive her appeals. At the conference's inception, President G. I. Butler had cabled the attendees to "Stand by the Old Landmarks." In response to Butler's appeal, R. M. Kilgore proposed that further discussion of righteousness by faith should be postponed until Butler could be present. Ellen White immediately resisted this proposal. She argued that the Lord's work was not to wait for any one man. At one point, J. H. Morrison, the president of the Iowa Conference, argued that Adventists had always believed and taught justification by faith. So why was there a need to go over it again? While Morrison was technically correct, the subject had become an abstract notion lost in the church's emphasis on the law.

Morrison feared that Waggoner's emphasis on Christ would draw people's attention away from the three angels' messages, which explicitly called people to keep God's commandments. Waggoner and Jones were invited to respond. They read sixteen Scripture passages, one after another, with no comment, directly refuting Morrison's concerns. The application was so direct that the audience was left stunned in their seats.

As Jones and Waggoner's positions were attacked and ridiculed, Ellen White herself was criticized. Some suggested that at sixty-one years of age, she was becoming senile, and that Jones and Waggoner had come to dominate

4. Ellen G. White, *Letters and Manuscripts*, vol. 5 (1887–1888), Manuscript 15, 1888, https://tinyurl.com/cfu6r7m7.

her. There is no doubt that she defended them in the face of unfair criticism, but she was certainly not under their control.

Jones was asked to teach at Battle Creek College, and many saw this as a threat to the orthodoxy of the ministerial students. A motion was made that nothing should be taught at Battle Creek College that had not been taught there before. Ellen White spoke strongly against this motion, urging that it be defeated, but nearly half of the delegates voted for it anyway. She later wrote to one of the men who had voted for the motion, "I stated these things clearly, but STILL you urged that the resolution should be carried into effect. You made it evident that if God was leading me, He was certainly not leading you."[5] Feeling the hostility in the air, contempt, unkindness, and lack of love, Ellen White thought it might be best for her to withdraw. She didn't want to be caught up in the prevailing spirit. But in a vision, an angel told her not to go. God still had work for her to do at the conference, and his grace and power would sustain her. "It is not you that they are despising," the angel said, "but the messengers and the message I sent to My people."[6]

The next morning, October 24, she spoke boldly to the delegates. She expressed her disappointment that the Spirit of God had been shut out and that there had been no turning to the Lord during the conference. She was alarmed at their indifference. She mentioned Kilgore's desire to put off the study of the subject of righteousness by faith until Butler could be present, and she argued that it was unnecessary to wait. Hadn't they all been looking closely at the subject? She spoke of the rebellious spirit at the conference and expressed alarm that it was similar to the satanic rebellion in heaven. She urged them to accept no man's opinion on the subject, neither Butler's nor Waggoner's, but to search the Scriptures on their knees. Only then would they be able to know the truth and give a reason for the hope within them. Throughout the entire controversy, she upheld the authority of Scripture and refused to make a prophetic pronouncement to solve the debated issues.

When it was all over, Ellen White said that never before had she been treated like she was at the Minneapolis conference. She saw it as a terrible experience both for her and for the church, and one of the saddest chapters in its history. Particularly disturbing was how the leading ministers discarded the light that

5. Ellen G. White, Letter 22, 1889, to R. A. Underwood, dated January 18, 1889, published as Manuscript Release # 869 in *Letters and Manuscripts*, vol. 6 (1889–1890), https://tinyurl.com/3d6wsvfy.

6. Ellen G. White, Letter 2a, 1892, to Frank and Hattie Belden, dated November 5, 1892, in *Letters and Manuscripts*, vol. 7 (1891–1892), https://tinyurl.com/mpcxas2s.

had come to them. She wrote, "Had Christ been before them, they would have treated Him in a manner similar to that in which the Jews treated Christ."[7] She even implied that it might have been necessary for a remnant to come out of the Seventh-day Adventist Church just as many of them had once come out of the churches that resisted the message of the seventh-day Sabbath. She couldn't understand how gospel ministers could use unchristian methods to defend Christian orthodoxy. If their doctrines produced a pharisaic spirit, she wanted to be as far from their understanding and interpretations as possible.[8]

As the delegates left the conference, they were divided. Some had followed Butler's counsel and stood by the old landmarks. Others were undecided about the issue of righteousness by faith. It seemed genuine and vital, but at the same time, it had received such strong opposition. However, a group left Minneapolis that November transformed by a new view of salvation. They had wholeheartedly accepted the message of righteousness by faith and left with a renewed and revitalized religious experience. Ellen White's son Willie said that hearing Waggoner's sermons was a turning point in his life. A. O. Tait (1858–1941), a minister in the Illinois Conference, said that he was really converted at the meetings and had rejoiced in the light ever since.

During the spring and summer of 1889, Jones, Waggoner, and Ellen White traveled across the country, often together, speaking at camp meetings on righteousness by faith. Their presentations were persuasive, and many people were convinced and won over to their message. At the Illinois Conference camp meeting in early April 1889, A. T. Jones and Ellen White shared the major addresses. The conference president, R. M. Kilgore, had opposed Jones and Waggoner at Minneapolis, but as Ellen White and Jones spoke, he finally caught the central idea of their message. He came to depend "entirely upon Christ's righteousness and not upon works of merit." Once he had realized this, he telegraphed all the churches in the conference, confessing his wrong attitude at the General Conference session and urging the people to come to the camp meeting and hear the message for themselves.[9]

However, Uriah Smith remained unrepentant for the time being. In an 1889 editorial in the *Review and Herald*, he described Jones and Waggoner's theological position without mentioning them and argued that it would overthrow

7. Ellen G. White, Letter 6, 1896, to Brethren who occupy Responsible Positions in the Work, dated January 16, 1896, in *Letters and Manuscripts*, vol. 11 (1896), https://tinyurl.com/y4hw56uy.

8. Ellen G. White, Letter 83, 1890, to William C. and Mary White, dated March 13–17, 1890, in *Letters and Manuscripts*, vol. 6 (1889–1890).

9. Ellen G. White, Letter 1, 1889, to William C. White, dated April 7, 1889, in *Letters and Manuscripts*, vol. 6 (1889–1890).

the law. He wrote: "The law is the divine standard of righteousness. . . . Perfect obedience to it will develop perfect righteousness, and this is the only way anyone can attain to righteousness."[10] When someone asked Ellen White what she thought of Elder Smith's article, she replied, "He doesn't know what he is talking about; he sees trees as men walking. . . . It is impossible for us to exalt the law of Jehovah unless we take hold of the righteousness of Jesus Christ."[11]

Two years later, Ellen White wrote Smith two letters that contained earnest appeals to his heart. She spoke at the Week of Prayer meetings at the Battle Creek church and called for the church members to truly repent and come to Christ. Smith was moved. A few days later, he requested a personal appointment with Mrs. White. During their time together, he cried tears of regret, making it clear that he had changed his mind and had a different attitude. A few days later, he met with church leaders and confessed his mistaken opposition to the message presented at the 1888 conference. Eventually, Morrison and Butler made similar confessions and reunited in spirit with the rest of the church.

What lessons can be learned from the events at the 1888 General Conference? As recalled by several delegates, a lasting lesson was the need to search the Scriptures for oneself and not to allow others to think for them. Ellen White emphasized how she saw her role as not determining doctrinal issues or defining differences between scriptural interpretations. Instead, she urged that the Bible alone was the standard to study. Once the issue was settled, the church understood that Christ and his righteousness were indeed to be the center of each person's spiritual experience, each minister's preaching, and the church's teachings. If that were the experience of the church, its members would recognize that how they treated each other was more important than the relatively minor disagreements between them. Finally, it is clear that amid this conflict and its aftermath, Ellen White acted like one of the Hebrew prophets, defending truth, rebuking injustice, and pointing to God as the only hope of salvation.

Creeds

Concern about creeds came to the forefront as the church began considering formal organization. As James White urged the community to think about "Gospel Order," he pointed to Paul's statement that God was not the author

10. [Uriah Smith,] "Our Righteousness," *Review and Herald* 66, no. 24 (June 11, 1889): 376.

11. Ellen G. White, "Christ and the Law," Manuscript 5, 1889, dated June 19, 1889, in *Letters and Manuscripts*, vol. 6 (1889–1890).

of confusion but of peace (1 Cor. 14:33). He argued that Paul favored order as a means of preserving "purity, unity, and strength in the body." He urged, "Vigorous efforts should be put forth to restore as fast as possible the order of the gospel. We want no human creed; the Bible is sufficient. The divine order of the New Testament is sufficient to organize the church of Christ."[12]

It seemed to many of the loosely knit Sabbath-keeping Adventists that organization and creeds went hand in hand. In their thinking, a legally organized body must state its beliefs, but to state its beliefs was to create a creed that would inevitably be used as a tool of oppression. The followers of the *Review and Herald* struggled with the fact that the group could legally organize without setting out a statement of beliefs. The reasons early Adventists opposed creeds were on display as the subject was debated in the pages of the *Review*.

Opposition to creeds came from Adventists' experience as Millerites. They advocated for the biblical truth of Jesus's coming, but because this truth was incompatible with their church's creeds, they were expelled. Ellen Harmon's entire family was disfellowshiped from the Methodist church, not for wrong or immoral conduct, defects of character, or doctrinal errors, but for "walking contrary to the rules of the Methodist Church."[13]

Creeds could also become a standard or test of correct beliefs instead of the Bible, thus creating a barrier to accepting new biblical truths such as the Sabbath and the doctrine of the state of the dead. Creeds were of human origin and thus in contradiction with each other. How could an incomplete and fallible creed created by humans become the standard of truth?

Creeds also were a barrier to Christian fellowship. Ellen White wrote that "Christ recognized no distinctions of creed, nationality, or rank."[14] Besides that, intellectual assent to creeds was not the same as holiness of heart. One could consent to all the essential articles in the creed and still be spiritually dead.

Above all these reasons, Sabbath-keeping Adventists opposed creeds not so much for their statements of theology as for the use that was made of them. J. N. Loughborough made a foundational observation in an article on the "image of the beast" in Revelation 13. He argued that the image of the beast was formed through "creedalization," a five-step process that would lead to the formation of the image of the beast. First, a creed is created. Then, creeds are made a rule of faith and a test of fellowship. Third, creeds are used to try unruly members instead of the Bible. The creed becomes the tribunal by which men

12. [James White,] "Gospel Order," *Review and Herald*, 4, no. 22 (December 6, 1853): 173.
13. E. G. White, *Life Sketches of Ellen G. White* (Mountain View, CA: Pacific Press, 1915), 53.
14. Ellen G. White, *Ministry of Health and Healing* (Nampa, ID: Pacific Press, 2004), 12.

Hygienic Cooking

As early Sabbatarian Adventists discovered and adapted new health-reform practices, they had to learn how to prepare new foods for the table. This often meant using more fruits and vegetables and using fewer processed foods with fat, grease, and strong spices. At times, the food could be bland; as Ellen White herself testified, the process of changing one's preferences was difficult. After going hungry for several meals, she told her stomach: "You may wait until you can eat bread." With a little patience, she learned even to eat bread made from graham flour. Such health-reform experiments could generate a less favorable response, as Uriah Smith once commented: "The very name 'hygienic' has come to be a terror to me."

Although somewhat in fits and starts, Adventists would develop their own hygienic cuisine replete with recipe books. The very first was printed in 1874 as *The Hygienic Cookbook* and contained over one hundred recipes with practical tips and advice for learning how to prepare and serve healthful foods. It suggested that changes in diet should be made gradually, using common sense, and should avoid making oneself impoverished by lack of adequate nutrition. At times Ellen White would have to admonish early Adventists for becoming "health deformers" by taking her specific health counsels to an extreme. Instead, she called for a sensible application of vegetarianism, but at the same time she could remind people that it was more important to exercise and eat meat than to be a vegetarian who doesn't exercise! True hygienic cooking was an "art" that took a great deal of skill and practice, and as early Adventists grew in their understanding of how to prepare these foods, they increasingly shared their favorite recipes in church periodicals and letters and, over time, have produced hundreds of cookbooks.

One of the most common recipes featured in early recipe books was for "gems," or soft biscuits, that could be served with fruit or nut butter. Ellen White reportedly relished her gems. The very first Adventist cookbook contained recipes for cornmeal, oatmeal, rye-meal, graham, green corn, buckwheat, rice, and pumpkin gems. Closely related were healthful breads: notably graham, potato, coconut, snow, oatmeal, sweet

are judged. Fourth, all those who do not subscribe to the creed are branded as heretics. And finally, those branded heretics face civil penalties for their heresy. Thus, the image of the beast would be formed when Protestant America used civil penalties to enforce its creedal first-day Sabbath observance.[15]

15. J. N. Loughborough, "Image of the Beast," *Review and Herald* 17, no. 9 (January 15, 1861): 69.

potato, and rye. For those on the road, a variety of leavened and unleavened crackers could be had, especially with fruit sauce or fruit butter.

The largest section of this first Adventist cookbook was reserved for puddings. In addition to the "regular" puddings made out of graham flour or oatmeal, other options included farina, boiled rice, crushed wheat, boiled samp, hominy, tapioca, and rice and apple pudding. On special occasions, a Christmas pudding could be prepared with layers of boiled rice alternating with sliced apples, raisins, chopped dates, and any other favorite fruits.

Another favorite was "Bird's Nest Pudding," which contained a mixture of apples and currants. The more adventurous could add chestnuts, gooseberries, figs, or tomatoes. Fresh and cooked vegetables were encouraged, as were fruit sauces. Drying foods, as well as canning them, became important ways to put aside fruits and vegetables for the cold winter months.

For dessert, there were plenty of pies and dumplings. Apparently, Ellen White had somewhat of a sweet tooth, as her family members testified that she especially relished lemon pie. At least two shopping lists from her home testify that she requested cocoa. Ellen White would caution more than anything else about eating too much sugar. She encouraged her readers to do all things in moderation, but Adventists have always enjoyed their desserts.

In Ellen White's later years, she would have a cook on staff, and according to one family member, some of her favorite recipes came from the cookbook *The Laurel Health Cookery*. Even during her lifetime, some of her followers would develop elaborate rule books of what one should or should not eat. However, her overall emphasis was more on how each person's "constitution" was unique and different. What one could eat another might find positively "injurious." As a case in point, Ellen White loved but could not eat beans. When done well, health reform was meant to be a blessing that contributed to longer and happier lives. More recent research by *National Geographic* about "Blue Zones," or the longest-living people groups on earth, has led to a series of studies that point to Adventists being among some of the longest-living people groups on the planet.

Loughborough clarified that the problem with creeds is not their content but how they are used.

Sabbath-keeping Adventists also opposed creeds because they believed in the continuing ministration of the gifts of the Spirit. At the conference in 1861, which began the process of church organization, James White argued that creeds are in direct opposition to spiritual gifts. If Sabbath-keeping Adventists were to create a detailed creed and state their belief in spiritual gifts, and then the Lord revealed new light through the gifts that did not harmonize with the creed, the creed would be overthrown. Thus, he rejected everything in the form of a human creed. In doing this, he was not rejecting an attempt to *describe* the church's beliefs. Instead, he was rejecting a statement of beliefs that would be used to *prescribe* beliefs. He implied that using a creed to prescribe beliefs would be taking the first steps toward becoming Babylon. At the same time, James White affirmed that Adventists covenant "to keep the commandments of God and the faith of Jesus Christ." This was all the doctrinal content they would require.[16]

James White pointed out that the underlying issue in the conflict between creeds and the gifts is how a church ensures unity. The popular churches use human creeds to achieve unity. In contrast, James White argued that the gifts of the Spirit, according to Paul in Ephesians 4, are "heaven's appointed means to secure the unity of the church." Those who have sought unity based on creeds have failed to find that unity.[17]

When a committee studied the idea of a church manual in 1883, its unanimous report to the General Conference session rejected it. The committee stated that the denomination had always opposed the formation of a creed or manual of discipline. The opposition feared that many would study the creed or manual as their guide instead of studying the Bible and relying on the leading of the Spirit of God. This would hinder genuine religious experience and tend to prevent a knowledge of the mind of the Spirit.[18]

Gradually, over the years leading up to the 1980 General Conference session, the statement of fundamental beliefs became more official and was finally approved in 1980. Even then, a preamble to the statement addressed the concern that it was a creed. The preamble stated that Seventh-day Adventists accept the Bible as their only creed. But in affirming this they do not mean that the Bible is to function as a statement of beliefs. Instead, they mean that the Bible is to be the only authoritative standard by which teaching and practice are to be judged. At the same time, the church could hold that its twenty-seven fundamental beliefs were the teaching of the Holy Scriptures. By prefacing the statement of fundamental beliefs with the affirmation that the Bible was Adventism's only creed, they recognized that the doctrinal statement was not

16. James White, in "DOINGS OF THE BATTLE CREEK CONFERENCE October 5 & 6, 1861," *Review and Herald* 18, no. 19 (October 8, 1861): 148.

17. James White, "Spiritual Gifts," in *Spiritual Gifts*, vol. 3, by E. G. White (Battle Creek, MI: Seventh-day Adventist Publishing Association, 1864), 29.

18. General Conference Proceedings, *Review and Herald* 60, no. 46 (November 20, 1883): 733 (13).

to be used in a creedal way as the authoritative standard by which orthodoxy is judged. That place belonged only to the Bible.[19]

Doctrine of God

Many early Sabbath-keeping Adventists, including James White, Joseph Bates, and Joshua V. Himes, participated in a loosely organized group, the Christian Connexion, that arose in the decade after 1800. Adherents were skeptical of church organization, objected to creeds, and rejected "Trinity" as a term because it had Catholic association. To some extent, the group was influenced by unitarian ideas being widely advocated in New England; they argued that the Trinity was illogical, unbiblical, and pagan. It was illogical since the Father and the Son cannot be the same being. It was unbiblical since the Bible does not explicitly mention the Trinity. It was pagan since many pagan religions had a trinity of gods who ruled the cosmos.

Since the Bible was the only creed and the Bible did not mention the Trinity, the Seventh-day Adventist Church did not address the issue. Opposition to the doctrine of the Trinity began to fracture, starting with the General Conference in 1888. There, E. J. Waggoner spoke of the deity of Jesus. In the following years, Waggoner and Jones spoke more directly to the topic and seemed to affirm the equality of the Son with the Father. However, it was only in 1898, with the publication of Ellen White's book *The Desire of Ages*, that the issue came to a head. There, using words written in 1856 by Scottish Presbyterian John Cummings, she affirmed that in Jesus "was life, original, unborrowed and underived."[20] In the same book, she also wrote that Jesus "announced Himself to be the self-existent One."[21] Without fanfare, this clear statement of Jesus's equality with God slowly made its way through the church.

The mid-twentieth-century Adventist theologian M. L. Andreasen (1876–1962) recalled that when he read the statements in *The Desire of Ages*, he could hardly believe that Ellen White had actually written them herself. He traveled to her home in St. Helena, California, and spent months reading her manuscripts to find these statements in her handwriting. That may have been enough for Andreasen, but as late as 1919, attendees at the Bible Conference still argued

19. The preamble was inserted late in the deliberations, almost as an afterthought. The late insertion suggested to some observers that the committee that created the "statement" was not necessarily made up of "creedal people," but the church that tasked them to write it had, perhaps, become creedal.

20. Ellen G. White, *The Desire of Ages* (Mountain View, CA: Pacific Press, 1898), 530.

21. Ellen G. White, *The Desire of Ages*, 469–70.

that it was possible to believe in the deity of Christ without believing in his eternal existence. By 1931, there was enough consensus among the church leadership that a statement of beliefs was published in the denominational *Yearbook* that affirmed that the "Godhead, or Trinity," consists of the Eternal Father, the Lord Jesus Christ, and the Holy Spirit. It referred to Jesus Christ as "very God, being of the same nature and essence as the Eternal Father."[22]

In 1888, the Seventh-day Adventist Church had existed for only twenty-five years. It was still working out some of its basic positions. Their impatience for Christ's return was evident in their reluctance to embrace a more Christ-centered theology. They feared change and thought to bring Christ's coming through their own activity. Those who accuse the church of being a cult point to the early leaders' denial of the Trinity, the emphasis on the law, and the authority of Ellen White. The 1888 experience and its aftermath show that under Ellen White's influence, each of these early misdirections was corrected. Ellen White recognized the truth of the message of righteousness by faith and championed it. She refused to be an extrabiblical authority and decide the doctrinal issues at stake. Beginning in 1898, she affirmed the divinity of Jesus in such a way that the church moved to accept it and teach a fully Trinitarian theology. Thus, by 1920, the church had affirmed its beliefs in three foundational Christian doctrines: salvation by faith alone, the ultimate authority of the Bible, and the Trinity.

Resources

Beecher, Charles. *The Bible a Sufficient Creed*. Boston, 1846. https://tinyurl.com/5enf5wyy.

Ferch, Arthur J. *Towards Righteousness by Faith: 1888 in Retrospect*. Wahroonga, NSW, Australia: South Pacific Division of Seventh-day Adventists; Warburton, Vic., Australia: Signs Pub. Co., 1989.

Fortin, Denis. *G. I. Butler: An Honest but Misunderstood Church Leader*. Nampa, ID: Pacific Press Publishing Association, 2023.

Knight, George R. *A User-Friendly Guide to the 1888 Message*. Hagerstown, MD: Review and Herald Publishing Association, 1998.

Knight, George R., and Gerald Wheeler. *Organizing to Beat the Devil: The Development of Adventist Church Structure*. Hagerstown, MD: Review and Herald Publishing Association, 2001.

22. *Seventh-day Adventist Yearbook* (Washington, DC: Review and Herald, 1931), 377.

Land, Gary. *Uriah Smith: Apologist and Biblical Commentator*. Hagerstown, MD: Review and Herald Publishing Association, 2014.

Whidden, Woodrow W. *E. J. Waggoner: From the Physician of Good News to the Agent of Division*. Hagerstown, MD: Review and Herald Publishing Association, 2008.

Discussion Questions

1. Describe the transition from an inward-focused denomination to a global church movement. Who contributed to this significant change and why?
2. How did the denomination expand from a loosely affiliated movement into a denomination?
3. On what authority did early Adventists explain their beliefs? What role did Ellen White play in the development of Adventist doctrine?
4. Reflect on the differences between the moral and the ceremonial law in Galatians. How did this issue become such a hot-button topic for church leaders in the 1880s?
5. Adventist leaders had begun to focus on the law until the church had spiritually become as "dry as the hills of Gilboa." In the continuum between gospel and law, what has been your spiritual experience?
6. Why were early Adventists concerned about the Trinity?

CHAPTER 5

Developments in Education and Health

Adventists in the nineteenth century were ardent reformers whose beliefs impacted their view of themselves and the world. Their reforming energy grew from their impatience for Jesus's return and focused especially on health and education. Undergirding this focus was a philosophy of the whole person. Adventists believed God desired to restore biblical truths that extended to every facet of their life. Thus, they became intensely focused on how to live healthier and happier lives. Education enabled them to live more healthily and share their understanding of a healthy lifestyle with others. They developed a theology of wholeness that originated at the beginning of the movement. All the earliest Adventist pioneers believed that the soul was embodied and, therefore, had no existence apart from the body. This concept stressed the value and quality of this mortal life and put a high value on the human body. In contrast, they rejected the Platonic idea that the soul has an existence apart from the body and is thus inherently immortal. Platonism furthermore exalted the immortal disembodied soul and denigrated the material body.

When the idea of an embodied soul is coupled with the restoration of God's law, a broad view of life comes into focus. Obeying God's law also includes keeping and observing all natural laws. This holistic viewpoint was how most Adventists lived out their everyday lives and passed on a sense of mission and purpose to a new generation. Their practices included a vegetarian diet, dress reform, and the use of drugless medicine, all aimed at maintaining health and wholeness.

The early Millerites were ardent reformers, with health reform a significant aspect of their beliefs. William Miller warned that it would be a disgrace if Jesus Christ found his followers drunken when he appeared the second time. Larkin B. Coles (1804–1856) was an abolitionist, a preacher, and, most importantly, a physician who wrote about health reform. His 1848 *Philosophy of Health* was the most comprehensive statement of health reform within the Millerite community. Born in 1804, he graduated from Castleton and Newton Theological Seminary. He then graduated again from Castleton in 1826 with a medical degree. After his marriage to Sarah Dyer, they had four children, and by 1836, he affiliated with William Miller, joining forces in the proclamation of Christ's premillennial return. He would argue that it was "truly a sin to violate one of these [health] laws; as it is to violate one of the ten commandments."[1]

Coles's ideas were similar to those of William A. Alcott (1798–1859), who emphasized the moral obligation to preserve one's health. Coles, for his part, connected the need for fresh air, exercise, a vegetarian diet, avoidance of stimulants, dress reform, sexual purity, and drugless medicine as the secret to health. Critics of Coles complained that not only did they read his books, but they were forced to eat them. The strong connection between Adventism and health reform was obvious. It seemed natural for early Sabbatarian Adventist believers to adopt health-reform measures.

Challenging and Changing Times

Life was difficult in the nineteenth century. The ignorance of good sanitation principles meant the rapid spread of diseases and epidemics. A child born in 1840 had a life expectancy of forty years.[2] By 1855, New York City's population of 629,904 people had use of only 1,361 bathtubs and 10,384 water closets. Medical personnel frequently and indiscriminately prescribed drugs such as quinine, digitalis, and opiates for their overall effect rather than to cure their patients. Even quinine was prescribed more generally rather than as a treatment for malaria. The Civil War showed how infrequently new medical inventions from Europe, notably the thermometer and stethoscope, were used in America at the time. When William Hammond (1828–1900) banned some of the mercury-based drugs given to patients as purgatives, he was court-martialed and condemned by the American Medical Association.[3] (Hammond was ultimately exonerated and became a teacher at Bellevue Hospital in New York during the time John Harvey Kellogg was a student.)

At one point, Charles Eliot (1834–1926), elected president of Harvard in 1869, complained: "The ignorance and general incompetency of the average graduate of American medical schools at the time when he receives the degree

1. L. B. Coles, *Philosophy of Health: Natural Principles of Health and Cure: or, Health and Cure Without Drugs; also, the Moral Bearings of Erroneous Appetites* (Boston: Ticknor, Reed & Fields, 1854), 10.

2. J. David Hacker, "Decennial Life Tables for the White Population of the United States, 1790–1900," National Library of Medicine, April 2010, https://tinyurl.com/awzw5eyw.

3. Henry C. Friend, "Abraham Lincoln and the Court Martial of Surgeon General William A. Hammond," *Commercial Law Journal*, March 1957, 71–78.

which turns him loose upon the community, is something horrible to contemplate. The whole system of medical education in this country needs thorough reformation."[4] It would not be until after the Civil War, in 1871, that Harvard began its first medical laboratory in a professor's attic. It is no wonder that Oliver Wendell Holmes opined: "I firmly believed that if the whole *materia medica* could be sunk to the bottom of the sea it would be all the better for mankind and all the worse for the fishes."[5]

In 1860, George States recalled that as a young boy, Joseph Bates would visit their family. When he arrived, his mother tried to serve him some "nice fresh pork." He recalled how strange that "Father Bates," as he was affectionately known, didn't say much but politely declined.[6] Bates shared his views about Christ's second advent during the heyday of the Millerite revival, participating in camp meetings, holding Bible studies in homes, and even chairing at least one of the early Millerite General Conference gatherings. He captained a series of temperance voyages in which he did not allow anyone to drink alcohol on board. Consequently, it was said that Bates never had sailors sign up for a return voyage. Undeterred, upon his return home, he participated in the organization of the Massachusetts Temperance Society, one of the first temperance organizations in America. During his earlier years, he was enthusiastic about living healthfully and sharing the news about Christ's impending return. Bates, the "apostle of the Sabbath," quickly connected keeping God's moral law with following his natural law.

James and Ellen White were initially reluctant to adopt health reform. When another early Adventist minister, S. N. Haskell, argued against eating pork, the Whites admonished him, stating that if God wanted his people to be health reformers, he would show more than one or two people their duty.[7] James White added a postscript, noting they had just put up a hog for the winter. As for the young visionary Ellen, her attention shifted remarkably after an 1848 vision in which she was shown the perilous evils of tobacco and other addicting drugs, notably coffee and tea. By 1853–1854, during a church struggle in Michigan over church order, the question centered on whether

4. Don Colburn, "So Much to Learn, So Little Time," *Washington Post*, April 15, 1986, https://tinyurl.com/mr4ac3cn

5. This statement is a simplified form of a statement made as part of an address to the annual meeting of the Massachusetts Medical Society on May 30, 1860. It omits Holmes's exceptions, which included opium and anesthetics.

6. George O. States, "Lessons from Past Experiences—No. 22," *Review and Herald* 85, no. 5 (January 30, 1908): 11.

7. Ellen G. White, *Testimonies for the Church*, vol. 1 (Mountain View, CA: Pacific Press, 1885), 206.

James Caleb Jackson (1811–1895)

Jackson was an ardent health reformer from New York. After graduating from Chittenango Polytechnic Institute, he farmed until 1838. In his early life, he was an ardent abolitionist who served as secretary of the Massachusetts Anti-Slavery Society beginning in 1840. From 1844 to 1847, he owned and edited the abolitionist newspaper the *Albany Patriot*, but poor health forced him to quit. In search of restored health, he went to a "water cure" in 1846–1847 that developed within him a passion for hydrotherapy; he afterward studied to become a physician, opening his own institute at Glen Haven by late 1847. In 1858, he took over Our Home Hygienic Institute in Dansville, New York, a health institution that James and Ellen White visited and found extremely helpful in restoring their own health and instructing them in natural ways of treating disease. Jackson operated the institute with his wife, Lucretia, and their adopted daughter, Dr. Harriet Newell Austin, who was not only an influential health reformer but also an advocate for dress reform. The Jacksons strongly opposed harmful drugs, along with tea, coffee, alcohol, tobacco, and other stimulants. They also promoted a vegetarian diet and believed that through controlling one's diet it was possible to cure masturbation. In 1863, Jackson invented the first dry, whole-grain cereal called Granula. At the historical society in Dansville, New York, "the World's Oldest Graham Cracker" is on display, dated 1868. When the Whites visited his establishment in 1865, Jackson felt they were too religious and should participate in popular entertainments such as card playing and dancing. Because of these issues, Ellen White felt it was imperative that the fledgling denomination develop its own health institution.

it was permissible for a minister to use tobacco. The church responded with an emphatic no. Yet, in a pragmatic sense, their own personal health, or lack thereof, necessitated the pursuit of wellness just to survive. During the winter of 1862–1863, two of James and Ellen White's children were sick with pneumonia. It was then that James White stumbled upon an article by Dr. James C. Jackson, an unorthodox but sensible health reformer who proffered new ideas for the treatment of disease: no drugs, hot baths, cooling packs, liquid food, and plenty of fresh air, rest, and care. Instead of calling a physician, they followed these simple treatments, and their children recovered. The Whites experienced the benefits of a pragmatic approach to life.

A tidal shift in the early development of the Seventh-day Adventist Church occurred with Ellen White's far-reaching health-reform vision on June 5, 1863. "It was in the house of A[aron] Hilliard, at Otsego, Michigan . . . that the great subject of health reform was opened before me in vision." Aaron and his wife, Lydia, were Adventists who had relocated from northern New York as part of the westward migration. The Whites were visiting this early community of believers about a day's travel by horse and carriage from Battle Creek, to encourage them for the weekend. Martha Byington, the daughter of the church's first General Conference president, reported the scene:

> Sister White was asked to lead in prayer at family worship. She did so in a most wonderful manner. Elder White was kneeling a short distance from her. While praying, she moved over to him, and laying her hand on his shoulder continued praying for him until she was taken off in vision. She was in vision about forty-five minutes. It was at this time that she was given instruction on the health question which soon after became such a matter of interest to our people. Those present at the time this vision was given will never forget the heavenly influence that filled the room. The cloud passed from the mind of Elder White, and he was full of praise to God.[8]

Ellen White later described a series of "true remedies" that were paramount for the recovery and maintenance of health: pure air, sunlight, abstemiousness (temperance), rest, exercise, proper diet, use of water, and trust in divine power.[9] These health laws mirrored those of other health reformers, some of whom felt threatened by the declining birth rates of the white middle-class population, along with a loss of control and influence. Ellen White rejected such racist assumptions and motivations and instead connected these health laws as essential to both physical and spiritual well-being.[10] In fact, Ellen White would see the emerging understanding of health reform as "the right arm to the third angel's message," or, in other words, as an essential component of Adventist identity. "The health reform, I was shown, is a part of the third angel's message and is just as closely connected with it as are the arm and hand with the human body. I saw that we as a people must make an advance move in this great work."[11] Yet these ideas, as important as they were, took some time to implement in the broader community.

8. Arthur W. Spalding, *Footsteps of the Pioneers* (Washington, DC: Review and Herald, 1947), 173.

9. Ellen G. White, *The Ministry of Healing* (Mountain View, CA: Pacific Press, 1905), 127.

10. Gerald Wheeler, "The Historical Basis of Adventist Standards," *Ministry* 62, no. 11 (October 1989): 10–11.

11. Ellen G. White, *Counsels on Diet and Foods* (Washington, DC: Review and Herald, 1938), 74.

Adventist Invalid Party

James White, during the 1860s, had a series of debilitating strokes. In the summer of 1865, he had a third major stroke, and doctors offered no hope for recovery. Leadership was needed. Church leaders requested J. N. Loughborough to come quickly, but under the strain of the moment, within twenty-four hours, he too was debilitated. Even the youthful Uriah Smith, editor of the church's periodical, was worn down by overwork. Within a short amount of time, most of the critical leaders of the fledgling denomination were incapacitated. James and Ellen White led a group of sick church leaders to Dr. James C. Jackson's Our Home on the Hillside in Dansville, New York, to obtain water-cure treatments and to seek out principles of healthful living.

At his "Home," Dr. Jackson practiced a strict regimen, with patients going to bed by 8:00 p.m., lights out at 8:30, and rising early at 6:00 a.m. The day's schedule included health lectures in the parlor and sporadic treatments, including half baths, sitz baths, plunges between cold and hot water, and dripping hot and cold sheets. Regular exercise and natural remedies proved helpful as patients began to recover. The Whites carefully noted what was valuable and observed where they disagreed with Dr. Jackson. They resisted his warnings that the Whites were too religious, and they opposed his endorsement of card playing and dancing. Furthermore, Ellen was skeptical of Jackson's saltless diet. However, they pragmatically followed what seemed beneficial since they and other early church leaders recovered their health. In fact, J. H. Waggoner noted the following year that Adventists never claimed to originate health-reform principles but instead adopted and appropriated them for their own purposes.[12]

On their return from Dansville, the Whites stopped to visit friends in Rochester, New York. While there, Ellen White reported a vision she experienced on Christmas Day 1865. As a result, she challenged the church to develop a center for advocating health-reform ideas. James and Ellen White also worked to assemble their own views, compiled with some of their favorite writings by health reformers such as Jackson and R. T. Trall (1812–1877), into the first Adventist treatise on the subject, a series of six pamphlets titled *Health; or, How to Live* (1865). Later that year, the fledgling denomination bought a small Battle Creek home, renovating it into the Western Health Reform Institute. The new health institution was staffed by Dr. Horatio S. Lay (1828–1900), who had been impressed by Ellen White's early emphasis on health reform.

12. J. H. Waggoner, "Present Truth," *Review and Herald* 28, no. 10 (August 7, 1866): 77.

Founding Physicians

Horatio Lay was the founding physician at the Health Reform Institute in Battle Creek, Michigan. After his initial training at the Detroit Medical College, he graduated from the medical course at the Western Reserve College in Cleveland, Ohio. Lay settled in Allegan, Michigan, and opened a medical practice. As a result of attending meetings held by M. E. Cornell, Lay and his wife, Julia, joined the Sabbatarian Adventist movement. In 1862, Julia's poor health took the couple to James C. Jackson's Our Home on the Hillside. Horatio joined the medical staff at the institute and remained there for four years, learning hydrotherapy treatments and how to create and serve vegetarian cuisine. In September 1866, Lay was appointed the superintendent of the Health Reform Institute in Battle Creek. Shortly afterward, he founded the journal the *Health Reformer*. Lay resumed his medical practice in Allegan in 1870. After retiring as a physician in 1884, he served as a minister for the Michigan Conference.

Phebe Marietta Lamson (1824–1883) was the first female Adventist physician and a vigorous advocate of Adventist health reform. While not much is known about her early life, she appears to have converted to Adventism with her family while living around Rochester, New York, during the early 1850s. In 1855 she went with her sick father to Dr. James C. Jackson's Our Home on the Hillside in Dansville, New York, where she likely gained knowledge about hydropathic medicine. Lamson became a strong supporter of Adventist founders, James and Ellen White. In 1863 she expressed appreciation for instruction from the "spirit of prophecy" that led her to adopt "reform in habits of diet." She testified to an improvement in health, since "abandoning the use of flesh, . . . spices, and all high-seasoned preparations."

When the Health Reform Institute opened in 1866, Lamson joined Horatio S. Lay as medical personnel at the very first Adventist health institution. During the winter of 1867–1868, she attended R. T. Trall's Hygeio-Therapeutic College in New Jersey in order to secure a medical degree. Lamson believed that people only became sick when they violated "the laws of our being." She wrote, "It is natural to be well and happy if we obey those laws." Lamson was a leading advocate for the early adoption of dress reform within Seventh-day Adventism. She urged that tight-fitting clothes that restrict the circulation of the body be avoided. Lamson was also an innovator who promoted the use of specific health or medical products. She was also a strong believer in evangelism through health work. She had a positive Christian influence on patients and associates and supported a wide variety of church activities with her funds. In 1876, Lamson welcomed young Dr. J. H. Kellogg, who recently graduated from Bellevue Medical College. Lamson was the only physician to work consistently at the Health Reform Institute from the time it opened until Kellogg took over leadership. Lamson died unexpectedly of pneumonia on August 2, 1883, while on a trip to visit her family in New York. After her death, a life-size portrait of Lamson was hung on the third floor of the Battle Creek Sanitarium.

John Harvey Kellogg was the medical innovator who transformed the Health Reform Institute into the famous Battle Creek Sanitarium. He was a physician, surgeon, pioneer in physiotherapy and nutrition, and prolific author.

John Harvey was one of sixteen children in the family of John Preston Kellogg and Ann (Stanley) Kellogg. He was initially interested in a teaching career but was encouraged by James and Ellen White to attend R. T. Trall's Hygeo-Therapeutic College, where Phebe Lamson had been trained. The Whites personally sponsored his medical education.

He fell in love with learning and with the practice of medicine, continuing his studies at the University of Michigan and Bellevue Hospital Medical College in New York.

Having completed his formal studies, at twenty-four years of age, he was appointed the superintendent of the Health Reform Institute in Battle Creek in 1876.

Almost immediately, Kellogg renamed the institution the Battle Creek Sanitarium. He argued that most people did not want to be reformed, but they did want to go where they could learn the new sanitary methods and receive instruction on getting well and staying well. He based the name on institutions he had visited in Europe known as sanatoria. The word comes from a Latin root that means "to heal" or "to make healthy." Kellogg was a dynamic speaker and a whirlwind of action. He attracted patients from far and wide. He became a famed surgeon, specializing in abdominal and gastrointestinal operations. He invented specialized hooks and retractors for these surgeries and pioneered the use of heated operating tables. He honed his operating skills on numerous trips to the best medical institutions in Europe during the 1880s and 1890s.

Kellogg married Ella Eaton, a Seventh Day Baptist, in 1879. Ella was a dietitian who played a significant role in developing dietary reform and vegetarian cooking at the Battle Creek Sanitarium. They adopted seven children. Ella's Seventh Day Baptist pastor encouraged John Harvey to read the latest European books on religion. He became interested in the thought of Herbert Spencer, an influential English philosopher who created an all-encompassing conception of evolution as the progressive development of the physical world, biological organisms, the human mind, and human culture and societies. In this context, Kellogg developed a religious philosophy akin to pantheism. In 1902, he published *The Living Temple* with some of these ideas. At the same time, he successfully resisted the merging of the sanitarium with the Seventh-day Adventist Church. In 1907 he was disfellowshiped from the church but continued to manage the sanitarium until his death in 1943.

Ellen White took a motherly interest in him and carried on an extensive correspondence with him for almost twenty years beginning in 1886. She cautioned him against overwork, counseled him about his spiritual life, and warned him about his tendency to strive for supremacy over others.

The new health institution struggled during its first decade. Within two years of John Harvey Kellogg's return to church headquarters in Battle Creek, patronage at the Battle Creek Sanitarium increased substantially, and the sanitarium expanded to seventy employees. During the first six months of 1866, the Health Reform Institute treated only 76 patients, but in the first six months of 1878, they treated 450 patients. Adventist health reform quickly caught the American public's attention, and the sanitarium became world-renowned by the end of the nineteenth century. Well-known patients eventually included American president William Taft, industrialist Henry Ford, and formerly enslaved activist Sojourner Truth.

In 1883, Kellogg and Dr. Kate Lindsay established the first Adventist nursing school to supply the sanitarium with adequate medical personnel. He also developed a series of short courses with charts that health workers could use to teach proper nutrition, massage, and exercise therapy, along with the broader Adventist health-reform message. In 1895, Kellogg began his own medical school in Chicago. During its fifteen years of existence, it graduated over two hundred physicians who advocated natural remedies over the use of harmful drugs. This medical training was firmly rooted in clinical experience, scientific experimentation, and a deep commitment to a broader humanitarian philosophy. Kellogg also developed a line of health foods. However, his younger brother, Will Keith, developed the products into his own food company. Within a few years, W. K. Kellogg became fabulously wealthy, especially by promoting cornflakes. However, he battled with his brother about his right to sell the products under his name. John Harvey Kellogg also worked with church leaders to establish health institutions that would quickly circle the globe. Though Kellogg left the denomination in 1907 after conflicts with Ellen White and church leaders, he left a legacy of institutions that advocated valuable principles of healthful living.

Sojourner Truth

Discovering Education

Early Adventists wondered if time would last long enough to educate their children. Some even suggested that support for schools was equivalent to denying Christ's soon return. In 1862, a church member asked James White if it was "right and consistent for us who believe with all our hearts in the immediate coming of the Lord, to seek to give our children an education? If so, should we send them to a district or town school, where they learn twice as much evil as good?" He replied: "The fact that Christ is very soon coming is no reason why the mind should not be improved. A well-disciplined and informed mind can best receive and cherish the sublime truths of the Second Advent."[13] Beginning in 1853, several Adventist families in Battle Creek and Bucks Bridge, New York, attempted to employ teachers for their community, but neither lasted for long.

The first permanent Adventist school began in 1867 when Goodloe Harper Bell, a schoolteacher, visited the newly founded Western Health Reform Institute to recover his health. While chopping wood one day, he became acquainted with several young people, including the Whites' son, Edson, and the Kellogg brothers, John and Will. They asked if he would teach them. This small "select school" morphed into an expanding class of pupils under his private tutelage. On June 3, 1872, the first official Seventh-day Adventist school opened with twelve students. The next day, two more joined, and by the end of the term the number had grown to twenty. Bell was offered the use of the top floor of the original *Review* structure (by then a storage building), where he provided special classes in the early morning and evening that could benefit "office hands." It was later observed that there was "an excellent spirit of zeal and hearty good-will" during this first term.[14]

When a small group of believers in Tramelan, Switzerland, heard about the new school, they sent one of their young people, Ademar Vuilleumier, across the ocean so that he could benefit from an Adventist education. When he arrived at the train station, he could only say two words: "James White." So, the first Adventist school began with an ESL (English as a second language) component. Within two weeks, he could share his testimony in somewhat broken English. The impact left a deep impression on early church leaders. If a small company of Swiss believers could see the value of an Adventist edu-

13. "Questions and Answers," *Review and Herald* 21, no. 4 (December 23, 1862): 29.
14. "The S. D. A. School," *Review and Herald* 39, no. 26 (June 11, 1872): 204.

cation, the church needed to invest in that endeavor. James White challenged the denomination to raise $50,000 to build a school to train two hundred young people. At the 1873 General Conference, church leaders voted: "That we regard it as the imperative duty of Seventh-day Adventists to take immediate steps for the formation of an educational society and the establishment of a denominational school."[15]

The following year, the denomination bought a home that was remodeled and expanded into what was dubbed Battle Creek College. The new brick building brought sneers from those who mocked: "Who are these Adventists who believe the Lord will come but just spent $20,000 on a brick building?" Sydney Brownsberger (1845–1930), another educator who had joined Bell at the school, replied: "When the Lord comes, Adventists expect to leave their farms, their businesses, and their homes, but take their brains with them." The *Review* editor, Uriah Smith, served as a Bible teacher at the college, supported the school financially, and housed students in his own home who could not afford the schooling otherwise. He described his optimism: "As the mustard seed among plants, we expect this school will occupy an important place among the agencies in operation for the advance of the truth."[16]

A Philosophy of Adventist Education

In 1872, Ellen White set the tone for a broad philosophy of Adventist education by writing that Adventists should be "reformers" ready to combine formal learning and the practical side of life. "True education," she wrote, "provides a counter influence to the selfish ambition, greed for power, and disregard for the rights and needs of humanity that are the curse of our world."[17] In this comprehensive statement, titled "Proper Education," she described true principles for Adventist education from the standpoint of parent, teacher, and student, which entailed the whole person's physical, mental, spiritual, and vocational aspects.[18] Later educational reformers, notably W. E. Howell

15. "Proceedings of the Eleventh Annual Meeting of the General Conference of S. D. Adventists," *Review and Herald* 41, no. 13 (March 11, 1873): 108.

16. Warren E. Howell, "Progress of Our School Work," *Review and Herald* 96, no. 31 (July 31, 1919): 22.

17. Ellen G. White, *True Education* (Nampa, ID: Pacific Press Publishing Association, 2000), 136.

18. Ellen G. White, *Testimonies for the Church*, vol. 3 (Mountain View, CA: Pacific Press, 1885), 131–60.

Battle Creek College

(1869–1943), observed that even if Ellen White never wrote a single thing about education the rest of her life, she had laid out all the "essentials" of an Adventist philosophy of education in this first treatise.

Ellen White was a pragmatist who noted how existing modes of education were not very effective. She also framed education as connected to the spiritual, leading to character formation in preparation for service in this world and the world to come. She wrote, "True education does not ignore the value of scientific knowledge or literary acquirements; but above information, it values power; above power, goodness; above intellectual acquirements, character."[19]

Adventist education would take some time to be established. Interpersonal conflict between Bell and Brownsberger could not be resolved. Brownsberger's son reportedly pushed Bell down the staircase at school. The conflict was so heated that school officials had to close the school during the 1882–1883 school year. Brownsberger left for Healdsburg College, a fledgling new school in California, and Bell left to help found South Lancaster Academy (later Atlantic Union College). Battle Creek College reopened and continued to grow through the 1880s, but it would not be until 1891 that Adventist education would come fully into its own.

The Harbor Springs Convention

The decisive turning point in Adventist education occurred in the 1891 Harbor Springs Convention. Previously, it had merely replicated other educational models, but after 1891, Adventist educators saw how to implement the broad-based and holistic philosophy of education that Ellen White advocated. In the wake of the 1888 General Conference session emphasizing righteousness by faith, church leaders recognized the need for a comprehensive overhaul of

19. Ellen G. White, *Education* (Mountain View, CA: Pacific Press, 1903), 225.

their educational system. W. W. Prescott (1855–1944) led the planning committee for the education convention at Harbor Springs with several other church leaders and educators, notably A. T. Jones, E. J. Waggoner, E. B. Miller (a professor at Battle Creek College), and G. W. Caviness (from South Lancaster Academy). The educators camped on an open piece of property on the bluffs of Harbor Springs, just adjacent to Little Traverse Bay, in northern Michigan. One person remembered this gathering as a camp meeting for Adventist educators. The speakers, including J. H. Kellogg, J. O. Corliss, and, notably, Ellen G. White, urged participants to go back and carefully consider Adventist education from the ground up. The conference began on July 15 and lasted until August 17, with attendees participating in various devotional meetings and teacher-training exercises.

At the very outset, W. W. Prescott claimed to hear, as if spoken with audible words, a voice that said: "They shall be all taught of God." This motto was adopted and placed prominently in the meeting. "It was the guide," he later wrote, "in the work during those six weeks. We expected to receive, and did receive light from God, not only in the study of the Scriptures, but in our plans for educational work."[20] In its Latin form, *Erunt Omnes Docibiles Dei*, this saying became the motto for the new Union College that Prescott was shepherding into existence that very summer in Lincoln, Nebraska.

Up to 1891, Adventist schools had utilized a classical curriculum, emphasizing ancient languages and memorization. The one exception was an optional Bible class tacked on to other course offerings. What made the Harbor Springs Convention significant was the idea of centering the entire curriculum around the study of the Bible in an integrated and cohesive philosophy of Adventist education. The convention adopted an approach to Bible study that went beyond mere doctrinal formulation to focus on personal spiritual growth. This strong spiritual emphasis meant that the meetings were remembered as a significant turning point for many individuals and for the Adventist community at large. One participant, Percy T. Magan (1867–1947), recalled that during these meetings, the term "Christian education" first entered the Adventist vocabulary and was widely used by Adventist educators. Adventists came to understand that their schools were to be essentially different from their secular counterparts rather than just teaching the same information in a religious setting. Adventist education was to grasp a holistic outlook, grounding its entire

20. W. W. Prescott, "Report of the Educational Secretary," *Review and Herald Extra, Daily Bulletin of the General Conference* 5, no. 15 (February 23, 1893): 349–50.

learning system in a solid spiritual and scriptural framework encompassing all aspects of the curriculum and educational experience.

W. W. Prescott communicated this concept when he reported to the 1893 General Conference session on the Harbor Springs meeting:

> Our minds were impressed there as never before with the idea that the purpose of educational work was to teach us of God in his revealed word and his works, and in his dealings with men, that all education should be planned upon such a basis and carried out in such a way that the result would be a more intimate knowledge of God, not merely as a theory but as an experience. While the general purpose up to that time has been to have a religious element in our schools, yet since that institute, as never before, our work has been *practically* [rather than theoretically] upon that basis, showing itself in course of study and plans of work as it had not previously.[21]

Several influential voices helped shape the themes that emerged at the convention. Two of the speakers were A. T. Jones and E. J. Waggoner, who had captured the denomination's attention, emphasizing the centrality of righteousness by faith at the 1888 General Conference session in Minneapolis. The prophetic voice of Ellen White was also a significant influence at the convention. Previously, she had called for more intentional efforts to incorporate Christian principles into the curriculum and teaching methods. Subsequently, the church's educators began to reframe educational goals in light of their new understanding. They realized the previous focus on studying the "heathen" classics was inadequate. Some teachers, such as Edward A. Sutherland (1865–1955) and Percy Magan, advocated the "elimination of pagan and infidel authors from our schools, the dropping of long courses in the Latin and Greek classics, and the substitution of the teaching of the Bible and the teaching of history from the standpoint of the prophecies."[22] These Adventist educational reformers saw the dual focus of the spiritual with the classical curriculum as inherently conflicted and detrimental to the success of Adventist education. Magan and Sutherland, among other educators, would struggle over the next

21. Prescott, "Report of the Educational Secretary," 350.

22. P. T. Magan, "The Educational Conference and Educational Reform," *Review and Herald* 78, no. 32 (August 6, 1901): 508.

decade to implement these reforms at Battle Creek College and its successor, Emmanuel Missionary College.

Prescott sought to standardize the Adventist educational curriculum following the Harbor Springs Convention but discovered that changes needed to be introduced gradually. However, there was significant resistance. "The Institute," he noted in his 1893 report, "discussed and adopted a Bible course which should be used as far as practicable in all the schools represented there. The basis of this course was determined upon [*sic*] as consisting of four years of Bible study, four years history, an advanced course in English Language, while New Testament Greek was made optional, and Hebrew was suggested as optional."

The foundation for the new curriculum was the Bible, followed by courses in history and English.[23] There would also be studies in healthful living, a course promoted by Dr. J. H. Kellogg.[24] The new curriculum required English grammar and composition classes but no classes in literature. Mathematics and logic rounded out the curriculum. Overall, the emphasis in the curriculum shifted, with biblical study viewed as its integrative core. In contrast to studying the ancient classics, the curriculum retained the study of biblical languages, particularly for aspiring ministers. However, the curriculum did not make this mandatory for all aspiring pastors. A short program of study was an essential objective since the church was impatient for Christ's return.

The new emphasis integrated Adventist education around a new Christ-centered Adventist theology. As Prescott put it, this new approach would study "the Bible as a whole . . . as the gospel of Christ from first to last." Adventist teaching was "simply the gospel of Christ rightly understood."[25] In a letter dated July 28, 1891, Ellen White's son, William, described the meeting in terms of a spiritual revival, stressing spontaneous personal testimonies and noting that each day began with an exposition by A. T. Jones on the book of Romans. Ellen White spoke about the necessity of a personal relationship with Christ, the need for spiritual revival among educators, and the centrality of the Christian message to education.[26] This spiritual revival intended to frame Adventist

23. Prescott, "Report of the Educational Secretary," 350.

24. George R. Knight, "Harbor Springs, Michigan," in *The Ellen G. White Encyclopedia*, ed. Denis Fortin and Jerry Moon (Hagerstown, MD: Review and Herald, 2013), 856.

25. Prescott, "Report of the Educational Secretary," 350.

26. George R. Knight, "Spiritual Revival and Educational Expansion: Between 1890 and 1900 the Number of Church Schools Jumped from 13 to 246. Why?" *Adventist Review* 161, no. 13 (March 29, 1987): 9.

education as distinctly *Christian*, encouraging each student to enter into a personal relationship with Jesus Christ.

Ellen G. White saw the Harbor Springs meeting as an opportunity to advocate the educational ideals she had been reflecting upon since the 1870s. She would continue to refine these ideas and put them into practice later in the 1890s in Australia by establishing the Avondale school. Adventist historian George R. Knight observed that her strong support of the Harbor Springs ideals, coupled with a series of six "powerful, unambiguous articles" afterward, contributed to "new standards" in Adventist education.

New Directions

After Harbor Springs, Adventist education expanded rapidly. As the new educational philosophy was implemented, Adventist education became distinctly different from most other kinds of education. Its emphasis on integrating the spiritual with the physical and intellectual was unique and attractive. Getting this kind of Christian education was seen by many as an important part of preparing for Jesus's return. Students who were impatient for Christ's second advent felt compelled to attend an Adventist school. Thus, the church's educational institutions grew from just a handful to over one thousand within a decade.

After the Harbor Springs Convention, Ellen White went as a missionary to Australia and the South Pacific. She warned that the pattern established in Battle Creek "should not" be the pattern for subsequent schools. "I have been shown that in our educational work, we are not to follow the methods that have been adopted in our older established schools."[27] To implement the new approach to Adventist education, the church in 1894 purchased an estate of 1,450 acres in Cooranbong, New South Wales. Although it was initially viewed unfavorably by many leaders and agricultural experts, Ellen White believed God's providence had led them to the property. Later events suggested she was correct.

Between 1896 and 1899, the Avondale School for Christian Workers was created with early students and staff living in tents. They took breaks between classes to cut down trees and construct the buildings. The school formally opened on April 28, 1897, when the first two structures, Bethel Hall and a

27. Ellen G. White, *Counsels to Parents, Teachers, and Students* (Mountain View, CA: Pacific Press, 1913), 533.

Oakwood

dining hall, were ready for use. There were a total of 10 students and 4 teachers. By the end of the first term, enrollment had increased to 60. By 1898, enrollment stood at 104. And by 1900, it was 158. Ellen White raised much of the funds and took an active role in the school's development, establishing her own home, dubbed "Sunnyside," nearby. She continued to write extensively about an Adventist philosophy of education that emphasized moral character and a spirit of service to others. The goal was for Adventist education to be established on an entirely new foundation.

Another turning point in Adventist education was the birth of a school to educate disenfranchised blacks in the American South during the Reconstruction period. Church leaders located a 360-acre estate about five miles outside Huntsville, Alabama. The former slave plantation was named Oakwood from the giant oak trees spread across the property. When the school opened on November 16, 1896, there were 16 students and four teachers. Like Avondale and following the Harbor Springs model, the emphasis was on a holistic approach to Adventist education. From the beginning, there was a focus on practical education, the student's spiritual life, and the development of missionaries.

The most radical implementation of Adventist education after Harbor Springs occurred under the leadership of E. A. Sutherland, who thoroughly imbibed the spirit of educational reform. One of the significant ideas that he took from the meeting was "that, hand in hand with righteousness by faith, there must also be education by faith." His first assignment after Harbor

Emmanuel Missionary College

Springs was as the principal of a new school in Washington named Walla Walla College. Church leaders noticed his success and asked him in March 1897 to take over the presidency of Battle Creek College. Almost immediately, Sutherland joined forces with Percy Magan to lay plans to reform the school. Their reforms focused on four primary areas: practical missionary training, manual training, the Bible as the focus for all areas of education, and the absence of diplomas or degrees (this latter point Ellen White would caution against).[28]

With Ellen White's encouragement, he sought the complete reorganization and relocation of the school. By September 1900, the board had voted to sell the school, and Sutherland and Magan went on bicycle tours to look for a new school property. In May 1901, they discovered the Garland farm in Berrien Springs, Michigan. When the search committee met, they agreed to purchase the property. Even Ellen White wrote how glad she was to hear about this fresh start for Adventism's first school: "The good hand of the Lord appears to be in this opening."[29] Soon, sixteen boxcars were loaded with the school's furniture and supplies to ship to Berrien Springs. Sutherland and Magan were making good their intention to implement educational reforms. Students worked on the 272-acre property to farm the land and build a new

28. Meredith Jones-Gray, *As We Set Forth: Battle Creek College & Emmanuel Missionary College* (Berrien Springs, MI: Andrews University, 2002).

29. Cited in Jones-Gray, *As We Set Forth*, 90n58.

campus. The initial school offices were set up in Franklin Hall, the old courthouse, and they rented the Hotel Oronoko for student housing. Classes were held in the courthouse, sheriff's house, and a nearby office building. The move was designed to provide the newly named Emmanuel Missionary College with a distinctive Adventist philosophy of education in every facet of the school. However, their approach took educational reform to its extreme and provoked significant opposition.

Sutherland and Magan knew that the church's administrators opposed the extremes they had implemented, so in 1904 they decided to try again to develop a new school in the American South, this time on a firmly self-supporting basis.

Resources

Greenleaf, Floyd. *In Passion for the World: A History of Seventh-day Adventist Education*. Nampa, ID: Pacific Press, 2005.

Jones-Gray, Meredith. *As We Set Forth: Battle Creek College & Emmanuel Missionary College*. Berrien Springs, MI: Andrews University, 2002.

———. *Forward in Faith: Andrews University, 1960–1990*. Berrien Springs, MI: Andrews University, 2024.

Knight, George R. *Early Adventist Educators*. Berrien Springs, MI: Andrews University Press, 1983.

Lindsay, Allan G. "Goodloe Harper Bell: Pioneer Seventh-day Adventist Christian Educator." 1982. Digital Commons @ Andrews University 1982-01-01T08:00:00Z.

Numbers, Ronald L. *Prophetess of Health: A Study of Ellen G. White*. 3rd ed. Grand Rapids: Eerdmans, 2008.

Reid, George W. *A Sound of Trumpets: Americans, Adventists, and Health Reform*. Washington, DC: Review and Herald Publishing Association, 1982.

Wheeler, Gerald. *James White: Innovator and Overcomer*. Hagerstown, MD: Review and Herald Publishing Association, 2003.

Wilson, Brian C. *Dr. John Harvey Kellogg and the Religion of Biologic Living*. Bloomington: Indiana University Press, 2014.

Discussion Questions

1. How did wholeness impact a distinctive Adventist philosophy of health, healing, and education?

2. How were Millerites social reformers? Provide examples of how Millerites valued health reform.
3. Adventists embraced innovation and new methods of health and healing. What did they seek to avoid, and what practices did they learn to adopt?
4. How did Dr. J. H. Kellogg and his medical training impact Adventist health reform? What role did the Health Reform Institute and the Battle Creek Sanitarium play in early Adventism?
5. What is a distinctive philosophy of Adventist education? What role did Ellen White play in the development of Adventist education?
6. Why was the Harbor Springs Convention important for Adventist education? What changed afterward?
7. How did the Avondale School play a role in reforming Adventist education? How did it provide a new model for Adventist education?

CHAPTER 6

The Golden Era of World Missions

Beginning in the early 1870s, Abram La Rue (1822–1903) felt a burden to take the Seventh-day Adventist message to China. He was one of the first Adventists to look beyond a North American and European Protestant Christian perspective. La Rue had been a sailor who had traveled far and wide, including trips across the Pacific Ocean. Setting aside the seafaring life, he settled in San Francisco. When his uninsured buildings burned, he was left without money or income. Urged by a friend to visit Honolulu, La Rue found there "the pearl of Great Price." His conversion was real and deep. Like the apostle Paul, he retreated to a deserted place, the coastal valleys of Northern California, where he herded sheep and chopped wood.

Around 1870, La Rue encountered Adventist literature and was convinced by its message. After eight years of sharing his faith with his neighbors, a remarkable series of events led to the foundation of a twenty-member church in the tiny village of Christine. One new member was William C. Grainger. Shortly after his conversion, he became a teacher at the newly opened Healdsburg College. He encouraged La Rue to come and study the Bible. La Rue asked the General Conference to send him as a missionary to China, but the Mission Board replied that, at sixty years of age, he was too old to go. They suggested that instead he could work on one of the islands in the Pacific. After finishing a six-month training course at Healdsburg College, he worked his way to the Hawaiian Kingdom, where he supported himself by selling literature, dried fruit, and nuts. In 1888, he settled on the island of Hong Kong and began a similar ministry among English-speaking residents and sailors. His burden for the Chinese people led him to arrange for the translation into the Chinese language of three tracts. One was on the judgment,

One of Abram La Rue's first tracts

Front row, left to right: Isaac Dolphijn, George T. Kerr, Dudley Hale, Fred Dolphijn. Back row, left to right: Eva Kerr, Francis Dolphijn (center), George Grant.

based on the prophecies of Daniel 2 and 7, and the others were based on the chapters in Ellen White's *Steps to Christ* entitled "The Love of God" and "The Sinner's Need of Christ." He continued to appeal to the Mission Board for missionaries. In 1902, after fourteen years of waiting, the eighty-year-old La Rue welcomed Jacob and Emma Anderson with their young son, along with Ida Thompson, as the pioneers of the Seventh-day Adventist Mission in China.

However, the first official work for non-Christians began in two places in Africa. Francis Dolphijn, a member of the local Akan people in Ghana, received Adventist literature and was convinced by what he read. He wrote to the International Tract Society in the United States requesting help, saying he had given himself to the faith of the Seventh-day Adventists in 1888.[1] Karl G. Rudolph and Edward L. Sanford were sent in response. The *Review and Herald* noted Rudolph and Sanford's departure in December of 1893 for Ghana, then known as the Gold Coast. It noted that they were the first Adventist expedition to a non-European land.[2] They arrived in Ghana on February 22, 1894.

In South Africa, Stephen Haskell held a series of meetings in October 1894 in Kimberly, where diamonds had been discovered. Richard Moko (1850–1932)

1. Kofi Owusu-Mensa, *Saturday God and Adventism in Ghana* (Ghana: Advent Press, 2023), 81; "By a Letter Just Received," *Home Missionary* 6, no. 5 (May 1894): 110–11.

2. L. C. Chadwick, "West Africa," *Review and Herald* 71, no. 1 (January 2, 1894): 16.

Oxcarts like the ones Richard Moko used for gospel wagon tours

happened to stop and listen. Moko was a teacher who came from a long line of Xhosa chiefs and was likely a descendant of one of the earliest Christian Xhosas, Ntsikana (ca. 1770–1820). Captivated by the message, he stepped into the meeting place and took a seat. He returned to hear more. After he attended a Sabbath service, one of the church members invited him home for lunch. He expressed his sense of sinfulness and, after praying with the church member, said he felt like he was released from prison.[3]

Moko completed a series of Bible studies with Fred Reed and was baptized in 1895, the first native south African to be baptized. He translated *Steps to Christ* into the Xhosa language and began to sell books. With the assistance of missionary Joel Rogers, he founded a night school for African laborers. Licensed to preach in 1897, he was primarily responsible for the early spread of Adventism among the Xhosa people. After founding the Maranatha school for Xhosa speakers, he traveled through the countryside on what he called gospel wagon tours accompanied by missionaries showing glass lantern slides. In 1915, he was the first native African to be ordained.

3. Stephen N. Haskell, "South Africa. A Visit Among the Churches," *Review and Herald* 71, no. 51 (December 25, 1894): 810.

W. H. Anderson's home at Solusi

Richard Moko invited David Kalaka (1844–1904), from the Basotho people, to attend Haskell's meetings in Kimberly in 1894. Kalaka was impressed and later introduced Haskell to the leaders of his people. Kalaka grew up in the Lesotho Evangelical Church, a product of the Huguenot Paris Evangelical Mission Society. He had worked for fifteen years at the Evangelical Church printing press at Morija and participated in translating the entire Bible into the Sesotho language, a project completed in 1878. By the end of his trip with Haskell, Kalaka was ready for baptism. After attending an institute at Kimberly with former General Conference president O. A. Olsen in the summer of 1895, he was baptized and returned to his people. He translated *Steps to Christ* into the Basotho language and founded a school at Kolo. He traveled by oxcart through much of Lesotho, sharing literature and preaching the Adventist faith.

Cecil Rhodes (1853–1902), the founder of Rhodesia (now Zimbabwe), took twelve thousand acres of Matabele land and gave it to the Seventh-day Adventist Church in 1894. It was named Solusi after a local chief. The first Adventist missionaries arrived at the property on July 4, 1894. A year later, W. H. Anderson (1870–1950) and five missionary families moved onto the property and began educational and medical work. Half of the missionary team died within a few short years, but others followed to take their place at Solusi.

One Solusi student was Mainza (sometimes written as Mayenza, 1881–1949), a member of the Tonga tribe who had been captured by

Jim and Nangoye Mainza and children

Matebele warriors in the area now known as Zambia. The British had freed all the enslaved people, so Mainza was free to attend the school at Solusi. The missionaries named him "Jim," and on December 1, 1901, he was the first Solusi student baptized. Years later, he was reunited with his parents in what was then known as Northern Rhodesia. When he first tried selling books, he was jailed for selling without a license. Returning to Solusi in 1909, he begged the missionaries to help him obtain a license, but it was costly, and they were not sure he would persevere. After years of entreaties, Mainza announced that he would sell some of his cows to raise money for the license. On hearing this, the missionaries negotiated with the government officials and arranged for him to have a license at no cost. Mainza was overjoyed and devoted most of his life to selling books and evangelism. At one time, it was said that half the attendees at the camp meeting in Solusi were Mainza's converts.

William A. Spicer

The school founded at Solusi became the center for training workers who staffed

A. G. Daniells and the leaders in the Asiatic Division planning mission strategy. Left to right: H. R. Salisbury, J. H. Johanson, J. E. Fulton, A. G. Daniells, and R. C. Porter.

other mission schools and clinics across southern Africa. The church grew rapidly in this territory, reaching 4,428 members by 1922 and laying the foundation for dramatic growth in the future with ten times that number by 1940. Moko, Kalaka, and Mainza are some of the earliest native African evangelists. Often, missionaries assisted them, but much of the Adventist evangelistic work in southern Africa was done by educated and respected local converts such as these.

Beginning in 1901, Seventh-day Adventist mission work outside North America grew rapidly. Leading the way was A. G. Daniells, who orchestrated a restructuring of the denomination in 1901 that facilitated foreign missions (covered in chapter 7). At the 1901 conference, Daniells was elected the leader of the church, and in 1902 W. A. Spicer (1865–1952) was elected General Conference secretary with the primary responsibility of recruiting missionary personnel for overseas work. Working together, Daniells and Spicer took bold steps to spread the Adventist message worldwide. In contrast to congregationally oriented denominations, the new structure of the Seventh-day Adventist Church encouraged a broad, strategic view of the world and its needs. Since Daniells had served during the 1890s in Australia and Spicer had served in England and India, they were aware of the great needs worldwide. Capitalizing on the new denominational structure, they laid plans to spread the Adventist message worldwide.

O. E. Davis: Missionary to Alaska, British Columbia, and Guiana

Ovid Elbert Davis (1868–1911) became a Seventh-day Adventist near Battle Creek, Michigan. After the Battle Creek Sanitarium burned, he was inspired by Ellen White's counsel to become a missionary and spread the message to new places. After completing the ministerial course at Emmanuel Missionary College, he responded to a call to minister to the indigenous peoples of Alaska and British Columbia. At one point, his enemies threatened to tie him to a stake out on the tidelands, leaving him there to drown. On December 11, 1903, he established the first "Indian church" in the Pacific Northwest. In 1905 he established a church among the native peoples of Port Simpson, British Columbia. In 1906 the General Conference called him to go as a missionary to British Guiana. Before his departure, he married Carrie E. Rosley. His main focus was colporteur work and distributing literature. Over the next several years he established several mission stations on the Demerara River. He ultimately found a tribe in the interior that had never been visited by a white man. They asked for the "God-man" to teach them the message of salvation. Later investigation by missionaries indicated that some interest in Christ and the second advent may have extended all the way back to Millerite literature that had circulated from 1842 to 1844. It had been sent on ships and spread inland. While some ideas had been mixed up with tribal traditions and superstitions, the tribe Davis encountered believed that a teacher would come to tell them more about the coming of Christ. By the time Davis arrived in 1910, it took twenty-nine days by boat and another ten days through dense forest to arrive at Mount Roraima. When he arrived, the chief remembered how his father had been visited by a "shining being" who taught them about the creation of the world, the entrance of sin, the story of the promised Redeemer, the Sabbath, and how to live a healthful life. The angelic being changed the chief's name to Owkwa, meaning "great light," and told him that a man would come with a "black book" as a sign that the missionary from God had arrived. When Davis arrived with his black Bible, he instructed them and taught their sons. As a result, the village of 187 individuals took their stand as Christians and Adventists. When Davis returned for a second time in 1911, he complained about feeling ill. He continued to teach them, but he eventually died in the village from blackwater fever. It took over a decade, after regular requests, for Adventist missionaries to follow up and establish a more permanent mission station.

O. E. Davis

The statistics for Adventist membership in North America show an increase of 25 percent between 1900 and 1910. At the same time, Adventist membership overseas surged by 259 percent. Reports of newly entered territory appeared regularly in the *Review and Herald*. During those ten years, official mission work began in much of Asia and Central and South America. However, official missionaries were often welcomed by someone who had already learned the Adventist message through a colporteur's work or literature sent in advance. Outside of North America, in 1900, Adventists had 112 ordained ministers; 377 laborers, including colporteurs and licensed ministers; and 338 organized churches. Ten years later, outside North America, there were more than twice as many ordained ministers (270), more than four times the number of laborers (1978), and almost three times the number of churches (850).

When compared to the size of Adventist membership in North America, the number of Adventist missionaries is amazing. In 1916 there were 110 foreign missionaries for every 10,000 Adventist Church members. No other American church came close to this ratio. The Church of Jesus Christ of Latter-day Saints and the Church of the Nazarene sent out 30 and 15 missionaries for every 10,000 members, respectively. Between 1906 and 1916, the number of American Adventist missionaries sent overseas increased by 310 percent.[4] In 1916, nearly 9 percent of all American foreign missionaries were Seventh-day Adventists, this coming from a denomination that was .07 percent of the American population.[5] This reflects the church's impatience to fulfill its mission to take the gospel in the form of the three angels' messages to every nation, kindred, tongue, and people (Rev. 14:6). It was an investment of human and financial resources that paid great dividends over the next century.

The Missionary Volunteer Movement

The Student Volunteer Movement for Foreign Missions (SVM) became a significant factor in spurring the involvement of the Adventist Church in world missions. This broad Protestant movement began in the summer of 1886 in Northfield, Massachusetts, under the sponsorship of Dwight L. Moody (1837–1899) and the Young Men's Christian Association (YMCA). The conference,

4. Yael Mabat, *Sacrifice and Regeneration: Seventh-day Adventism and Religious Transformation in the Andes* (Lincoln: University of Nebraska Press, 2022), 89.

5. Mabat, *Sacrifice and Regeneration*, 90. Mabat's source is William C. Hunt and Edwin M. Bliss, *Religious Bodies: 1916* (Washington, DC: Government Printing Office, 1919), https://tinyurl.com/mt7ysxbf.

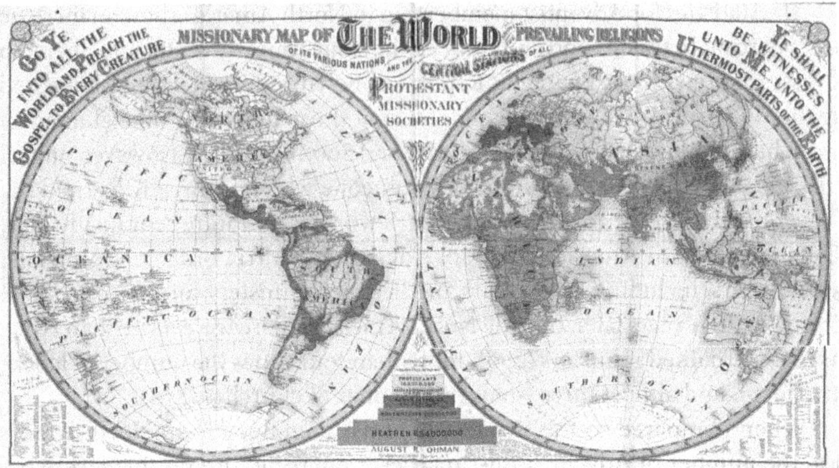

The Missionary Map of the World

with 251 students in attendance, focused on personal evangelism. At the meeting, Robert P. Wilder (1863–1938), the son of a prominent Presbyterian missionary to India, gathered 21 students who were interested in foreign missions. These students asked A. T. Pierson (1837–1911) to address the entire body on missions. His message focused on the idea: "All should go, and go to all."

A week later, 10 students, sons of missionaries and foreign nationals, spoke of the needs in the mission field. Each of the 10 presented the spiritual needs of their country in a three-minute address, each one closing with the words "God is love" spoken in the language of their people. The effect was powerful. A visiting missionary concluded the presentation by saying, "Show, if you can, why you should not obey the last command of Jesus Christ" to go into all the world. One of the delegates deeply affected by this challenge was John R. Mott (1865–1955), a Cornell University student from Iowa. Mott prayed for several days before adding his name to those committed to mission service. By the end of the meeting, 100 of the 241 students had signed a commitment to foreign mission service. A prominent mission scholar, Dana Robert, stated, "The Commitment of the Mt. Hermon 100 changed the course of the history of Christianity."[6] Moving beyond the moment's inspiration, the Mt. Hermon 100 created a way to inspire other students to make the same commitment they had.

6. Dana L. Robert, *Occupy Until I Come* (Grand Rapids: Eerdmans, 2003), 149.

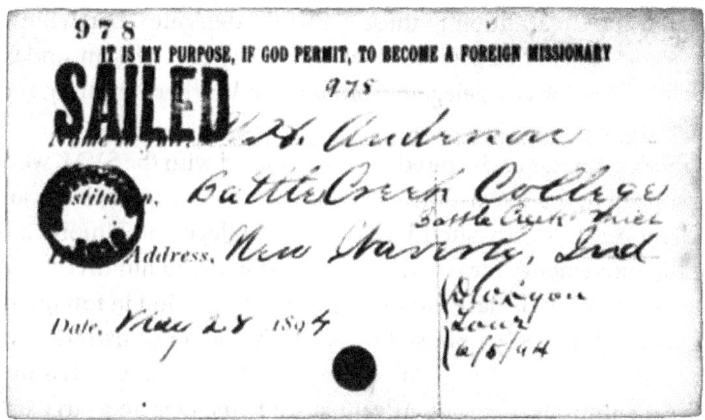
978

IT IS MY PURPOSE, IF GOD PERMIT, TO BECOME A FOREIGN MISSIONARY

SAILED

Battle Creek College

Address.

Date. May 28 1894

W. H. Anderson's SVM commitment card. The date is May 28, 1894. However, documents show he signed another card in August 1890.

In the summer of 1888, John Mott became the de facto leader of the SVM, and his organizational ability expressed itself in the remarkable development of the movement. The motto The Evangelization of the World in This Generation became the watchword of the SVM. During Mott's first year as leader of the movement, he visited colleges and helped organize students into missionary Volunteer Bands. Over the next two years, under Mott's leadership, the movement spread rapidly among students in the United States and Canada. Students were invited to sign a commitment card that read: "It is my purpose, if God permit, to become a foreign missionary." The purpose of the movement was not to create an institution to send missionaries. Rather, its rationale was to motivate students to commit to mission service before they settled down to a career in North America. In the thirty years from 1890 to 1920, at least 20,000 men and women, inspired by the SVM, went overseas in mission service through a wide variety of mission organizations.

The Student Volunteer Movement became a significant factor in motivating Adventist college students to participate in foreign missions. Beginning in the autumn term of 1890, a small group of students at Battle Creek College formed a Mission Band to discuss and pray for foreign missions. The group included William Henry Anderson, who later founded the mission station at Solusi in present-day Zimbabwe. At first, some faculty opposed the group's organization because of its affiliation with the SVM. However, by the spring of 1891, Percy T. Magan and Fred Rossiter (1870–1967) attended the first convention of the SVM in Cleveland, Ohio, along with four representatives of the Battle

Creek Sanitarium. In addition to these Adventist delegates, Uriah Smith's son Leon (1863–1958) was a delegate from the University of Michigan, and Georgia Burrus (1866–1948) was a delegate from a Bible Worker's training school in Oakland, California.

Foreign Mission Bands, inspired by or associated with the SVM, were eventually organized in many Adventist schools across the United States and later worldwide. John R. Mott visited Battle Creek College and Union College to promote the movement's ideals. Mission Bands inspired hundreds of Adventist college students to declare their intention to serve God in foreign mission service. Although initially opposed by teachers and administrators at Battle Creek, Union, and Healdsburg Colleges, the SVM-associated Mission Bands created great enthusiasm among Adventist students. Due, to a large extent, to the SVM-inspired Mission Bands, 13 percent of the graduates of Union College between 1895 and 1906 served in foreign mission fields.[7] Mission Bands remained a potent force on Adventist college campuses through the mid-1920s. Eventually, alums of the bands spread worldwide as Seventh-day Adventist missionaries.

Pioneering Mission Initiatives

After attending the first SVM convention in 1891, Georgia Burrus heard S. N. Haskell describe the need for women to reach other women secluded within *zenanas*, closed households in India. She dedicated her life to that mission and went to Healdsburg College for further training. She was a delegate, as a student at Healdsburg, to the second SVM convention in 1894, where an emphasis on the Holy Spirit inspired her. That summer, she joined a group of missionaries officially appointed by the General Conference to begin work in India. On their way to South Asia, the group sailed first to London. Their leader, Dores Robinson, decided to remain in London for a year. However, Miss Burrus continued alone to begin learning the Bengali language in preparation for her mission to secluded women. Arriving in Calcutta in January 1895, she was India's first official Seventh-day Adventist missionary. Much to her surprise, she was welcomed at the wharf in Calcutta by George and Margaret Masters, Adventists from New Zealand, who had arrived three months earlier as self-supporting missionary colporteurs. A year later, she welcomed the Robinsons. In 1901, Miss Burrus married the mission secretary/treasurer, Luther J. Burgess, in a brief ceremony following the Sabbath worship ser-

7. Mabat, *Sacrifice and Regeneration*, 89.

vice. Mr. Burgess resigned from his administrative positions, and the two of them spent forty years in northern India, pioneering the Adventist work in Uttar Pradesh, Bihar, and Assam. While her male associates in the denomination focused on mission work for English-speaking people, Georgia Burrus Burgess was the first to initiate work in at least four local languages in India: Bengali, Hindi, Urdu, and Khasi.[8]

Georgia Burrus Burgess and Luther Burgess

The Adventist work in Korea began when Lee Eung Hyun chanced upon a sign in Kobe, Japan, that read in Chinese characters, "The Seventh-day Sabbath Christ's Second Coming Church." Lee was an Anglican and, in May of 1904, was waiting for a visa to work in Hawaii. With time on his hands, he decided to find out what the sign meant. Thus, he met a Japanese Adventist evangelist named Hide Kuniya. They began a series of conversations, communicating in written Chinese. Kuniya invited Lee to a Sabbath worship service. He accepted the invitation, bringing his fellow countryman, Son Heung Cho. Kuniya studied the Bible with them, leading to their baptism in June 1904 on the night before they were to leave. However, Son did not receive a visa and was compelled to return to Korea. On his way, he met Im Hyung Joo, a former Methodist evangelist well-known in Korean political and literary

Map of India indicating where Georgia Burrus Burgess served

8. "Luther J. Burgess," *Pacific Union Recorder* 45, no. 48 (July 3, 1946): 6; "Mrs. Georgia Burgess," *Eastern Tidings* 43, no. 20 (October 15, 1948): 6.

Beginnings in the Pacific

As early as the 1840s, Millerite literature reached the "Sandwich Islands," as some outsiders referred to the Hawaiian Kingdom. Literature passed between islands, sparking a revival. Seventh-day Adventists gained a foothold in Hawaii, which became the first westward point of expansion across the Pacific. Once again, Adventist literature helped pave the way. In 1883, S. N. Haskell reported about a Danish carpenter living in Honolulu who received the periodical *Advent Tidende* and then subsequently traveled to Battle Creek, Michigan, to learn more. At the 1883 camp meeting in California, definite "steps were taken" to establish a mission in Hawaii. At a "special meeting" held April 18–28, 1884, church leaders in Oakland, California, voted to send "two laborers" to "commence work" that May. They requested "Brethren L. A. Scott and A. La Rue" to become the first missionaries sponsored by church members in the west to head to these islands. Once in Honolulu, they started a "free reading-room and [book] depository at 189 Nuuanu Avenue." They shared meetings in the local library and held meetings at the YMCA. On December 1, 1885, the General Conference requested William and Clara Healey to go to Hawaii to hold tent evangelistic meetings. They joined forces with Scott and La Rue as thirty to forty persons attended each night. The meetings lasted three months, resulting in a leading businessman closing his business on Saturdays. Eventually, nine were baptized, including one man who left to attend school at Healdsburg College. Scott and La Rue returned to California in 1886, but others continued to follow in building up the work across these islands. Later, on June 15, 1888, A. J. Cudney visited the Hawaiian islands on his way to Pitcairn. He missed the vessel he hoped to take and, while waiting, distributed literature and had the first Adventist tract translated into the Hawaiian language. The interest generated was the catalyst for the attorney general to bring to the legislature a request for religious liberty so that Adventists could worship freely on the seventh-day Sabbath and work on Sunday. Tragically, Cudney left on a missionary vessel that sank, prompting the denomination to sponsor a proper seaworthy vessel later dubbed the *Pitcairn*. The work slowly developed as Hawaii became a frequent rest stop for missionaries traveling across the Pacific.

Pitcairn

circles. Im was so deeply impressed with what he heard from Son that he wrote Kuniya telling him of his decision to dedicate his life to this new cause.

The Adventist message quickly gained a hearing in Korea. Son and Im returned to their hometowns and formed groups of interested people. They recognized their need for further instruction in the Bible. Writing repeatedly to Kuniya, they urged him to come and teach them. Kuniya was ill, did not know Korean, and did not have the finances to make the trip. However, after three or four letters from Korea, he understood it to be a "Macedonian call." On August 9, 1904, Kuniya arrived at Nampo (then known as Chinnampo), fifty kilometers southwest of Pyongyang. He gave the believers that he met further instruction in the three angels' messages. Assisted by Im and Kang Chang Oh, Kuniya visited nearby villages, sharing the Adventist message. The director of the Japan Mission, F. W. Field, joined Kuniya in September. By the time they left Korea, they had baptized seventy-five people and organized four churches. Field and Kuniya also appointed Im and Kang as the leaders of the new Korean Mission. Field felt a resident missionary was needed and asked the General Conference to send one. W. R. Smith (1876–1967) came to support the Korean church in November 1905.[9]

Similar stories of Adventist advances in South America, the Caribbean islands, Africa, and the South Seas could be told. There appears to be a pattern in many of these stories. A self-supporting missionary would arrive, usually selling literature. Finding interest in the message, they would appeal for a full-time missionary to come. The official missionary would arrive, baptize converts, form churches, and organize a mission. Beginning in 1901, within a mere twenty years, the church had developed a presence throughout much of the world.

Advances in Adventist Health Care

From the 1880s through the 1920s, Adventists advocated a way of healthy living that significantly impacted North America and beyond. Beginning with the Battle Creek Sanitarium, the emphasis on natural remedies and exercise as the means to regaining and retaining good health proved successful and attractive to increasing numbers of people in the United States. Its advocacy for a healthier diet introduced cornflakes and granola to breakfast tables worldwide. Hot and cold water treatments became essential to the Sanitarium treatment process. The "Battle Creek Idea" emphasized its rational and scientific methods, focusing on proper diet, exercise, and rest. Up to six thousand people visited the Battle Creek "San" annually as guests. They were attracted to an establishment that sought to be a home, a hotel, a hospital, and a health resort all in

9. Oh Man Kyu, "Korea," in *Light Dawns over Asia*, ed. Gil G. Fernandez (Silang, Cavite, Philippines: AIIAS Publications, 1990), 63–91.

Wu Ting-Fang

Law Keem, ca. 1918

one.[10] At first, there was a significant Adventist atmosphere at the sanitarium. But that changed with Kellogg's theological drift into pantheistic-like ideas. By the time the Battle Creek Sanitarium left its Adventist affiliation, the religious component of the institution was generically Christian.

However, the Battle Creek model spread around the world. Its schools of nursing and medicine and their affiliates encouraged students to consider foreign mission service. By 1900, there were 21 Adventist sanitariums based on the Battle Creek model, including Mexico (1890), Samoa (1895), South Africa (1896), Switzerland (1896), Australia (1896), Denmark (1897), New Zealand (1900), and Germany (1900). When Adventist medical training moved to Loma Linda, California, the name of the new institution, College of Medical Evangelists, emphasized its missionary purpose. The evangelism encouraged at Loma Linda was not generic Protestantism but basic Adventism. By 1922 there were at least 33 Adventist sanitariums in the world, including in the United States (18), Germany (3), Canada (2), England (2), Australia (2), Argentina (1),

10. [John Harvey Kellogg?,] *The Battle Creek Idea* (n.p.: n.d., ca. 1907), https://tinyurl.com/2v799fwu.

China (1), Denmark (1), Norway (1), South Africa (1), and Switzerland (1). Each of these institutions practiced and taught the Battle Creek Idea.

Adventist ideas on health sometimes spread in unusual ways. For example, in 1906, the first Chinese Adventist to return to China, Dr. Law Keem (1867–1919), took a ferry from Hong Kong to Canton (Guangzhou), China. Onboard, he met the distinguished former Chinese ambassador to the United States, Wu Ting-Fang (1842–1922). Learning that Dr. Law was a physician, he began to accuse American doctors of being behind the times. He argued that the best medical care consisted not of medicines but of rational methods, diet, and nature. Unbeknown to Dr. Law, Wu had heard Dr. J. H. Kellogg lecture near Washington, DC, and had adopted his ideas on healthy living, including vegetarianism. As a result, his rheumatism had disappeared. Dr. Law interrupted Wu's attack on American medical practices to assure him that he too was an advocate of Dr. Kellogg's Battle Creek Idea. Wu responded by urging Dr. Law to teach its principles to the people of China. Wu had visited Adventist sanitariums in the United States and had been highly impressed with their methods of treating the sick. His contact with Dr. Kellogg and Adventist ideas of healthy living was part of the reason he was interested in starting a similar work in China. Wu and Dr. Law kept in touch. After the Chinese Revolution in 1911, when Wu became minister of foreign affairs for the South West China Constitutional Government, he helped arrange for Dr. Law to receive financial help to start medical work in Nanning, the capital of Guangxi province.

Advances in Educational Efforts Around the World

During the same era that saw the growth and maturing of Adventist medical work worldwide, a similar effort resulted in the development and spread of Adventist educational work. It also had missions as a central part of its reason for existence. Students attending Adventist schools were trained for and expected to enter denominational service, either in their home country or overseas. Foreign Mission Bands were a regular part of secondary education and college life. In the Mission Bands, students studied an area of the world where they might serve.

Ferdinand (1874–1950) and Ana (1870–1968) Stahl's lives serve as an example of the influence of Adventist education on mission service. In 1902, the young Lutheran couple was befriended by an Adventist book salesman, Nelson Hubbert, who convinced Ferdinand to quit smoking and take Bible studies with Emma Anderson (soon to leave for China with her husband, J. N. Anderson). After the Stahls' baptism, both began the nursing course at the

Missionary Nurses' Training School at the sanitarium in Madison, Wisconsin, but soon transferred to Battle Creek, completing their studies in 1905.

After a successful mission in Cleveland, Ohio, Ferdinand wrote to Ellen White, offering to go to the most challenging mission place in the world. He mentioned Madagascar and the Incas of South America. Ellen White urged him to attend the General Conference session in 1909 in Washington, DC. They packed all their goods into seven trunks and a barrel and, with two children, headed for Washington, DC. There, they met Joseph Westphal, the president of the South American Union. He oversaw the work in Bolivia and Peru and knew where there were many unentered areas. However, there were no funds for their transportation. Ferdinand and Ana were so eager to enter mission service that they agreed to pay their own transportation cost using their personal life savings.

Carmen Vaca

With the Stahls' support, Camacho's educational initiative also empowered women. Under the title "A Girl Pastor Among the Quechuas," W. F. Miller tells in the *Review and Herald* how Carmen Vaca became the first Aymara woman to minister to the Quechua people. Carmen's father had died around 1920 as the result of a fall while working on one of the buildings at the Adventist mission. Her mother was thus a poor widow, owning only a small plot of ground on a steep mountain hillside near the mission in Plateria, Peru. Having completed the schooling available in Plateria, Carmen, who was only sixteen, was asked to teach at one of the mission schools among her Aymara people. At the beginning of the 1924 school term, when she was eighteen, there was a pressing need for teachers among the Quechua tribe. Arriving at the mission in Laro, accompanied by her mother, she discovered that there was an even greater need sixty-four kilometers (forty miles) farther into the mountains. After they settled at the new location, a neighboring teacher died, so the man she was working with left to fill that vacancy. Carmen found herself alone with about seventy students, all the while learning the Quechua language and conducting Sabbath services. In the first six months she prepared more than forty candidates for baptism. She went out on horseback as early as three and four o'clock in the morning to visit and instruct the candidates for baptism.

Carmen Vaca and her mother

After two years in Bolivia selling literature, doing medical work, and ultimately becoming president of the mission, Ferdinand accompanied the Peruvian Mission president on a visit to Plateria, Peru, to consult with Manuel Z. Camacho (b. 1871). Camacho was a veteran of a recent war and a member of the Aymara ethnic group. He was deeply committed to providing educational opportunities for the Aymara and Quechua people in the region around Lake Titicaca. Their medical and educational needs were significant: 95 percent of the people were illiterate, and medical treatment was rarely available. Selling literature to them was thus impossible. Camacho's offer to partner with the Adventist Church created an opportunity for Ferdinand and Ana. They agreed to move to the area to begin medical and educational work. Camacho and Luciano Chambi, another Aymara, had a vision for the education of their people. Camacho and Chambi became the Stahls' indispensable partners, particularly in planting schools in the

A neighbor woman, bitterly opposed to everything Protestant, was suddenly robbed of two hundred sheep and other goods. Her husband was so severely beaten that he could not follow the flock and seek to reclaim them. Carmen visited her the next morning. Having arranged to be absent from the school for the day, she took the larger boys and recovered the sheep from the robbers. When asked why the thieves didn't fight, Carmen answered that she and her boys far outnumbered the thieves. The neighbor woman was very grateful for what Carmen had done and dropped her opposition to the school.

When Carmen was asked to bring the schoolchildren to the town for a festival, the townspeople threw dirt and other things at them and insulted them. When asked to return for another festival, she declined, stating that she was preparing for the end of the school year and pastors were coming to baptize a group of people.

She testified, "The Lord saved us not only from death, but from sickness as well. Thieves prowled about, but we were not harmed. Enemies sought to do violence against us, threatened to kill us, and level down our place, but they never came. I prayed as I had never prayed before, and the Lord heard us. One girl was healed of a severe sickness after we had prayed for her."

The article closed with these comments: "Carmen Vaca was paid just 17 soles a month, which is not over $2 a week, for her services. Does anyone wonder that she often carries her shoes on her back, when she has shoes, to keep them from wearing out so fast?"[1]

1. W. F. Miller, "A Girl Pastor Among the Quechuas," *Review and Herald* 102, no. 16 (April 16, 1925): 13.

towns and villages. As the leader in the educational efforts, Camacho suffered imprisonment and severe persecution over the next ten years.

Ferdinand and Ana faced significant challenges as well. The Aymara and Quechua people were held in virtual serfdom by an alliance of the church, landowners, and judges. The poverty and exploitation were such that the local people seemed unable to do more than rise in periodic rebellions. Working with Camacho, the Stahls helped provide education as another way out of this oppressive system. Beginning in the town of Plateria, they planted schools throughout the Lake Titicaca area. To provide teachers, the best students in the first schools received basic teacher training and were sent to newly constructed schools in the surrounding villages. The Stahls began a formal teacher-training school with the Titicaca Normal School in 1922.

Catholic priests and landowners opposed the formation of schools in the villages, often violently. One school was burned down twice. One town that Ferdinand visited pleaded for a school, but there was no one he could send to staff it. He promised to send a teacher, but the village chief asked how he would know the teacher came from Stahl. Stahl broke a stone in two, giving one half to the chief. Three years later, after considerable communication between the village and Stahl, the new teacher did not need to produce the other half to prove that the Adventist educational system sent him. Stahl's successor, E. H. Wilcox, told how he received twelve requests for a school from indigenous villages in one day. On another occasion, the Stahls found themselves surrounded by an angry mob who had been provided with free alcohol by the local priest. Amid the confrontation, the mob thought they saw an army coming to the rescue of the Stahls. The Stahls thanked God for this providence and quickly escaped.

Despite opposition, the Stahls' perseverance made a world-changing difference. As early as 1918, government officials considered the original Plateria school a model school, calling the Adventist work for the Aymara people extraordinary.[11] The schools that the Stahls planted throughout the Lake Titicaca region had an immediate and far-reaching impact. Ferdinand is the only North American commemorated with a statue in all of Peru. The Stahls could not have accomplished this work without partnering with Camacho, Chambi, and other indigenous men and women. Within a generation of Stahl's arrival, Luciano Chambi's son Ruben received a doctoral degree from the University of Cuzco and was elected to the Peruvian national legislature. In subsequent years, because

11. Fernando Osorio, "In the Inca Union," *Review and Herald* 95, no. 52 (December 26, 1918): 23.

of the work of Camacho, Chambi, and the Stahls, the rigid social separations in Peruvian society became less evident. Echoing Paul's words in Colossians 3:11, there was no more white, *mesti*, or "Indian," but only one Peruvian people.[12]

Similar stories could be told of the rapid growth of the Adventist Church in Ghana, Papua New Guinea, and Jamaica. In Ghana, there was a preexisting respect for the seventh day among the Ashanti, one of the largest tribes of the Akan people. This tipped the balance in favor of Seventh-day Adventists rather than other Christian groups.[13] In Papua New Guinea, Adventist emphasis on education enabled villagers in distant locations to become a part of the broader educated classes. In 2019, James Marape (b. 1971), an Adventist member, was elected prime minister. He was the son of an Adventist minister and a graduate of Kabiufa Adventist Secondary School. His election shows how Adventist education could have a significant political impact. In Jamaica, the Adventist Church provided a similar path to social prominence. In 2024, the governor general, Sir Patrick Allen (b. 1951), and the prime minister, Andrew Holness (b. 1972), were Seventh-day Adventists. Neither Allen nor Holness attended local Adventist schools, but both were active members of vibrant local churches from childhood. Allen attended Andrews University between 1984 and 1998, receiving bachelor's, master's, and doctoral degrees.

Adventist work grew steadily but had less significant social impact in other places. In China, Adventist work began with schools and clinics, baptizing 20,000 members by 1940. While two hundred foreigners were listed in the *Seventh-day Adventist Yearbook* as church workers that year, the frontline work was primarily done by Chinese. Many schools and hospitals were scattered across the country. Reaching every province of China was the explicit goal of denominational officials between 1910 and 1940. By the end of that period, only the far western provinces needed a Seventh-day Adventist presence. Yet the Adventist work in China in 1940 was tiny compared to its population of 511,000,000, equaling 39 Adventists per 1,000,000 population. In Japan, the Adventist work began with W. C. Granger (1844–1899) and T. H. Okohira (1865–1939) in 1896. Yet, like most other Christian efforts in Japan, it grew very slowly. Schools and hospitals contributed to the evangelistic efforts, but by 1940, there were only 1,340 baptized Seventh-day Adventists in Japan

12. Charles Teel Jr., "Revolutionary Missionaries in Peru: Fernando and Ana Stahl," *Spectrum* 18, no. 3 (February 1988): 50–52.

13. Owusu-Mensa, *Saturday God and Adventism in Ghana*; Robert Osei-Bonsu, "Sabbath Observance Among the Akan's of Ghana and Its Impact on the Growth of the Seventh-day Adventist Church in Ghana," *Asia-Africa Journal of Mission and Ministry* 7, no. 3 (2013): 3–26, https://tinyurl.com/4vs529cd.

with a population of 73,000,000, equaling 18.3 Seventh-day Adventists per 1,000,000 population.

North America was not the only source of church workers during this era. Beginning in 1895 with the dispatch of a German missionary to Brazil, other countries started sending missionaries overseas. Missionaries from South Africa headed north on their continent. Scandinavians also became heavily invested in the work in Africa. Australia and New Zealand assumed the responsibility for the islands of the South Seas. Eventually, missionaries from the Fiji Islands came to Papua New Guinea and other islands in the Pacific Ocean. The international nature of Adventist missions became one of its strengths.

The church began the era of foreign missions in 1900, with 83 percent of its membership in North America. The era closed in 1940, at the beginning of World War II, with 63.3 percent of its members outside North America. However, North America remained dominant in the church's governance, creating an issue for the church to wrestle with for the rest of the century.

The Southern Work

Meanwhile, in the early 1890s, a movement arose to begin work in a significant mission field in the United States. After the American Civil War (1861–1865), during the Reconstruction period (1865–1877), formerly enslaved people and their families were often kept in economic slavery as sharecroppers. The white landowner would rent the land to the formerly enslaved people for a share of the crop. The landowner or nearby merchants would often rent tools and machinery to the sharecroppers and sell seeds and food to them on credit. If the crops failed to pay for what the sharecroppers owed, they were left in debt to the landowner. The landowners and merchants often abused the system so the black and white sharecroppers could never be debt-free. Seventy-five percent of African Americans in the American South were sharecroppers in 1900. Almost 45 percent of them were illiterate.[14] Formerly enslaved people could participate in the political process for a short period after the Civil War, but that gain was reversed after Reconstruction ended in 1877. Promises by the Southern states to protect African Americans' civil and political rights were quickly broken, and an era of white supremacy known as "Jim Crow" began.

Millerite Adventists, with their strong support for abolishing slavery, were not welcome in the Southern states. While preaching in Maryland in 1844,

14. "The State of African Americans in the South," Digital History, accessed March 18, 2025, https://tinyurl.com/yn7n6mmh.

Morning Star

Morning Star

Edson and Emma White

Joseph Bates was sent packing when he preached about Christ's soon return and the emancipation it would bring. Seventh-day Adventists continued to support abolition and the policies of Reconstruction that promoted the political rights of formerly enslaved people. Adventist ministers began to visit Southern states in 1871, but their work was almost entirely for the white population. The last states entered were Louisiana in 1883 and South Carolina in 1893.

The work for African Americans was slow to begin. The first African American to join the Adventists in the South was Henry Lowe in 1871 in Tennessee. He was a Baptist preacher who attended the first Seventh-day Adventist meetings in the South. In 1878 Charles M. Kinney (or Kinny) (1855–1951) became a Seventh-day Adventist in Reno, Nevada. He entered the ministry and, in 1889, was the first African American to be ordained. Though he faced many challenges, he built the foundation for the African American Seventh-day Adventist Church. The first church made up entirely of African Americans was not organized until 1886 in Edgefield Junction near Nashville, Tennessee. Despite significant needs, work among African Americans was neglected. Ellen White became aware of the formerly enslaved people's and their descendants' needs when Kinney made an appeal at the General Conference session in Battle Creek. She supported his appeal when she met with church leaders on March 21, 1891, and read to them her own appeal for work among the "colored people." While in prayer, she saw flaming words that stated: "All ye brethren are equal." The appeal was reprinted in a small tract, yet it received only a limited distribution, and no actions were taken in response to it.

Ellen White's son Edson (1849–1928) had drifted away from God and into debt. He was convinced he should reconnect with "the Lord's work" but felt he needed to clear his debts first. After trying for some months, he realized that he would never get out of debt without a resolve to work for God. He surrendered himself to God's will and began to look for what God might want him to do. He attended a meeting where Professor C. C. Lewis (1857–1924) described the needs of African Americans in the southern part of the United States. Edson began to wonder if this was God's calling for him. Shortly after, he reconnected with a friend, Will Palmer, who had experienced a remarkable conversion. They affirmed a shared call to work with "colored people" in the South. They consulted with Dr. J. E. Caldwell (1855–1923), who had recently worked for black people in Knoxville, Tennessee. He referred to Ellen White's message from 1891 but did not have a copy. Edson searched for a copy without success until a man painting the Battle Creek Tabernacle church building directed Edson to some neglected copies on the floor of an upper room in the church.

Ellen White's 1891 message entitled "Our Duty to the Colored People" served as a catalyst to expand the denomination's work in the South. It began with a frank discussion of prejudice against people in her time and place who were seen as "colored." This terminology was commonly used in Ellen White's time but is currently considered disrespectful.

The tract developed a strong argument for the radical equality of all people: Jesus came to save men and women of all nationalities. He died for the colored people as much as for the whites. He is the redeemer of the world. He was poor and sympathizes with the poor, the discarded, and the oppressed. Every insult shown to them is shown to him. Colored people should have as much respect as any other children of God. The God of the white man is the God of the black man. The black man's name is written in the book of life beside the white man's. Prejudice pollutes the soul. Anyone who shows disrespect for a person because of skin color shows disrespect for Christ. All who give themselves to Christ become members of one family.

White then developed a vision for reaching the African Americans in the South. She called on individuals and every church "in our land" to examine their souls. Given the context of formerly enslaving and enslaved people, her words are striking: Whatever their prejudices might be, she said, unless you put on Christ and are led by the Spirit, "you are slaves of sin and of Satan." She furthermore became intensely practical. If a colored brother sits beside you in church, you will not be offended or despise him because you will recognize that you will both be seated at the same table in the kingdom of heaven. When unchristian prejudice is broken down, earnest efforts will be made to do missionary work for the colored people.

She laid down a theological basis for a mission to those of the "African race." God cares no less for their souls than he did for the enslaved Israelites in Egypt. Therefore, he requires far more from the Seventh-day Adventist people in missionary work for the people of the South, "and especially among the colored race." Her case for repairing the damage done to the systems of African American life is compelling: "Who is it that held these people in servitude? Who kept them in ignorance, and pursued a course to debase and brutalize them, forcing them to disregard the law of marriage, breaking up the family relation, tearing wife from husband, and husband from wife? If the race is degraded, if they are repulsive in habit and manners [as some might think], who made them so? Is there not much due to them from the white people? After so great a wrong has been done them, should not an earnest effort be made to lift them up?"[15] She stated that sin rests upon "us as a church" for

15. Ellen G. White, *The Southern Work* (Washington, DC: Review and Herald, 1901), 14.

not making a greater effort to work for the salvation of the colored people. One reason for this lack of action was prejudice. While Ellen White did not prescribe a specific plan for addressing these issues, she was clear about who should act. First, white people should not exclude colored people from places of worship. They should hold membership in the church just as white people do. This was foundational. With this in place, she called for the church to educate colored men to be missionaries for their people. Then, she urged white men and women to qualify for educational work among the colored people and travel to the South as educators. Third, she urged privileged white people to show colored people they are all of one brotherhood. The white people were under obligation to labor for the good of the colored. They need not be wealthy or highly educated to do this work, nor should they all depend on the church structure for support. The whole church needed to be filled with the missionary spirit, and if it were so filled, many would do this work without pay.[16]

Edson White felt called to action as he read his mother's message. No one else had responded to its call. Edson and Will Palmer were already attending a six-month Bible-training course at Battle Creek. They now initiated plans to head south. Dr. Caldwell had warned them that initiating educational work for black people in the South would be difficult. White people would not rent housing or other facilities to them. If they stayed with black people, white hostility would likely result in violence. To meet these challenges, they built a riverboat to serve as a lodging and meeting place. To raise funds for the project, they printed *The Gospel Primer*, a simple book to teach basic reading skills. It would also be helpful for their educational and evangelistic work in the South. Its publication was a success, greatly exceeding their expectations. They arranged for a paddle-wheeled steamboat to be built to their plans. Within five months, the *Morning Star* set sail from Kalamazoo, Michigan, to Vicksburg, Mississippi, arriving in January 1895.

Edson's ministry began by visiting Sunday schools and conducting basic Bible studies. Since many could not read or write, literacy classes were introduced using *The Gospel Primer.* Children attended during the day and adults in the evening. No one raised the topic of the Sabbath until one of the local folks heard the group singing on the *Morning Star.* Asked about the Sabbath, Edson was cautious about answering. After he admitted that his group kept the Sabbath on the seventh day, his inquirers asked to join the group for worship on the *Morning Star* the next Sabbath. The group of new believers grew, as did opposition from the local churches. That necessitated a shift from meetings in churches onshore

16. White, *The Southern Work*, 9–17.

to meeting solely on the boat. It became apparent that a church building was needed, but there seemed to be no sources for funding it. Edson stepped out in faith, began building, and the funds came in. When the church was dedicated in August of 1895, the entire $160 cost for the building was paid in full.

Edson expanded his work in Vicksburg with a medical emphasis. Dr. and Mrs. W. H. Kynett, with their daughter Lydia, a nurse, led this effort at their own cost. The doctor's generous treatment of patients broke down much of the prejudice against the Adventists that had built up over the last year. The literacy meetings offered by the group resumed, with many in attendance. Edson was deeply disappointed by the lack of financial support from the denomination, but he kept moving forward with his mother's encouragement. The church did support Edson's cause by purchasing 360 acres in Huntsville, Alabama, for an industrial school for black students. It eventually became Oakwood University. Once the work in Vicksburg was stabilized and the boat refitted, Edson was eager to sail up the Yazoo River to remote areas with immense needs. By 1900, Edson's work resulted in a thriving work among black people throughout the American South.

The work among the urban black population also began to take hold during the first decades of the twentieth century, principally in Washington, DC, and New York City. Lewis C. Sheafe (1859–1938) was an eloquent Baptist minister when he came to the Battle Creek Sanitarium for treatment in 1896. He became convinced of the truth of the Seventh-day Adventist message and began evangelistic work for the Ohio Conference almost immediately after joining the church. He saw Adventism as an important means of bringing liberation to his oppressed people. In 1902 Sheafe held highly successful evangelistic meetings in Washington, DC. Seventy-five people were baptized at the end of the meetings. But this was only the beginning of Sheafe's influence in Washington.

In December 1903 Sheafe organized the People's Seventh-day Adventist Church. Sheafe's learning, eloquence, and leadership abilities were widely recognized in the wider black community in Washington. During the next four years the General Conference moved to the Washington area. It provided financial support for the white church in the city but failed to provide any financial support for the work among African Americans. After repeated appeals, and after being rebuffed numerous times, Sheafe led the People's Church in breaking its ties with the denomination in 1907. Later that year, he turned in his ministerial credentials. After a brief reconciliation between 1913 and 1915, Sheafe returned to independent status and then to the independent People's church. He and the church eventually affiliated with the Seventh Day Baptist denomination. Nonetheless, his protests at inequality in the church bore fruit in the creation and funding of the Negro Department in 1909 and the appointment of one of his converts, attorney W. H. Green, as the first black director of that department in 1918. The churches that he fostered, the Ephesus Church in Dupont Park and the First Church, became the foundation of the black Seventh-day Adventist community in Washington, DC.[17]

In New York, J. K. Humphrey (1877–1952) began a ministry to the black community in Harlem. Humphrey was a Jamaican Baptist minister who was passing through New York on a planned trip to visit Africa. He stumbled upon an Adventist evangelistic series in Brooklyn and was impressed with the simplicity and clarity of the message. He embraced the Adventist message and began ministry in Harlem just as it was growing into one of the intellectual centers of African American culture. By 1920 Humphrey's church, First Harlem, had a membership of six hundred. By 1928, his congregation had three daughter congregations in the area.

Humphrey was part of a group of leading black Seventh-day Adventists who proposed the creation of regional conferences for African American congregations. The proposal was rejected, and the leaders were told never to bring it up again. As a result, Humphrey became disillusioned with race relations in the church. He began a business venture that would have created a commune called Utopia Park for African Americans outside New York City. When church officials requested information about it, Humphrey refused to give it to them. His ministerial credentials were removed, and his church, which had voted 595 to 5 to support him, was ejected from the local conference. Humphrey created the United Sabbath Day Adventist denomination, which he led until five years before his death in 1952. Though his church and its affiliates had no official ties to the Seventh-day Adventist denomination, in doctrine and practice, its members were Seventh-day Adventists.[18] After Humphrey's death, his denomination fell apart, and most of its members returned to the Seventh-day Adventist Church, which by that time had embraced Humphrey's call for regional conferences.

It is not easy to assess the ministry of Sheafe and Humphrey. Both were immensely talented and effective in evangelism. Both struggled with the authority of Ellen White. Their departure from the official denomination seems unfortunate and probably unnecessary in retrospect. Their impatience with racial injustice seems justified. However, the result of their work outside the

17. Douglas Morgan, "Sheafe, Lewis Charles (1859–1938)," in *Encyclopedia of Seventh-day Adventists*, June 1, 2022, https://tinyurl.com/2p8xaprm.

18. R. Clifford Jones, "James Kemuel Humphrey and the Emergence of the United Sabbath-Day Adventists," *Andrews University Seminary Studies* 41, no. 2 (2003): 255–73.

Seventh-day Adventist denomination did not last. In the end, their protests and departure helped spark movements within the denomination that brought positive changes to issues of racial justice. What if they had been less impatient with the denomination?

The ideals of equality expressed in Ellen White's 1891 message were not easily realized. In 1896, the United States Supreme Court affirmed the legality of "separate but equal" facilities in the case of *Plessy v. Ferguson*. After that, any attempts to integrate black and white people faced legal opposition and mob action. While the races were separated, their facilities and opportunities were never equal. Within twenty years, racial segregation became the rule. Social conditions, often known as "Jim Crow," included legal segregation, white supremacy, and mob lynching. They were not confined to the southern states. Writing in 1909, Ellen White took into account how badly social conditions for black people had deteriorated. Writing about the "color line," her first concern was for an increase in colored laborers in the Adventist cause since white people couldn't work for blacks without suffering violence. She wrote that the Adventist people should create a fund for educating such workers. Great caution would need to be shown in this work because of white prejudice. "We may desire to ignore this prejudice, but we cannot do it," she wrote. She added that the intolerance of white people was growing so harsh that some acted as if slavery had never been abolished. For Ellen White, it was clear that the problem was systemic. She wrote that the people of the United States, their government, and their churches should have done much more for the formerly enslaved people and sustained their help over time.[19] As segregation was imposed by law and mob, it became impossible to ignore the color line. There would need to be separate work and separate churches for black and white people. Nonetheless, as little should be said about the color line as possible. There was to be no political agitation because human lives were at stake. Agitating the color line was not as important as proclaiming the third angel's message to the people of the southern states.[20]

The dangers inherent in the work for African Americans in the South were displayed in Calmar, Mississippi, in 1898. Edson White held meetings near Yazoo City that year, facilitating the conversion of William Casey, the black superintendent at a nearby plantation, and N. W. Olvin, a black sharecropper. A chapel and schoolhouse were then built in Calmar. In February of 1899,

19. E. G. White, *Testimonies for the Church*, vol. 9 (Mountain View, CA: Pacific Press, 1909), 205.

20. White, *Testimonies for the Church*, 9:199–211.

classes began in the school with E. A. Sutherland and Percy Magan as guest lecturers from Battle Creek College, teaching local farmers how to improve agricultural yields. A white planter in attendance vowed to diversify his crops instead of just planting cotton. He also promised to help his sharecroppers get out of debt. Other white planters in the area grew concerned that the social system that supported their dominance was being challenged.

An officer in the Mississippi Volunteer Infantry led a group of white planters to the Adventist mission in Calmar on the evening of May 11, 1899. They forced teacher Dan Stephenson, a white Mississippian, to leave town and tacked a notice on the door of the school warning the Adventists not to return. They then began looking for William Casey, who had become custodian for the school and chapel. Fearing the worst, he successfully hid from the mob. They then found N. W. Olvin at home. He was not as "respectful" as they wanted, so the mob surrounded him, and one man began to beat him with a bullwhip. His wife tried to escape out a window and was shot in the leg. As the violence began to escalate, a voice rang out: "Stop the whipping," but the mob ignored it. In the dark, a man on a horse pulled out his revolver and shot into the air. The men surrounding Olvin raced for their horses and dispersed while the mystery man with the revolver faded into the night. As a result of these events, the school in Calmar was abandoned, and Olvin chose to leave the area and settle in Vicksburg. Shortly afterward, he was falsely accused of murdering a child and was sent to prison for the crime of which he was innocent.[21]

Segregation of churches and church institutions became commonplace. By the 1920s, some white Adventists had become active in the second wave of the Ku Klux Klan, a militant group that terrorized not only black people but also Catholics and Jews. They supported the idea of separate black and white heavens, showing how far some Adventists had moved from the movement's early abolitionist roots.

The movement toward racial equality in the American Seventh-day Adventist Church was sparked when Lucy Byard, a black woman with cancer, was refused treatment at the Washington Sanitarium and Hospital in 1943, even though her husband, James, had made arrangements in writing for her treatment in advance. Given the choice of a room in the basement or treatment at the Freedmen's Hospital, which served African Americans, her husband chose to transfer her. She died at the Freedmen's Hospital shortly afterward.

21. Ron Graybill, *Mission to Black America* (Mountain View, CA: Pacific Press, 1971), 128–32, 138–41. Also, Samuel G. London Jr., *Seventh-day Adventists and the Civil Rights Movement* (Jackson: University Press of Mississippi, 2009), 50–53.

Many black laypeople and ministers were outraged at the injustice. They began to advocate for complete racial equality and desegregation in all aspects of church life. Though the General Conference in the 1930s had opposed the idea of regional conferences organized to serve black churches, it advocated the idea in 1945, and black activists accepted it as the next-best solution. As a result, black voices were heard in church deliberations, often for the first time. The new conferences gave black ministers opportunities for leadership development, and evangelistic work for black audiences became more widespread and effective.

Resources

Damsteegt, P. Gerard. *Foundations of the Seventh-day Adventist Message and Mission*. Grand Rapids: Eerdmans, 1977.

Graybill, Ron. *Mission to Black America*. Mountain View, CA: Pacific Press, 1971.

Mabat, Yael. *Sacrifice and Regeneration: Seventh-day Adventism and Religious Transformation in the Andes*. Lincoln: University of Nebraska Press, 2022.

Morgan, Douglas. *Change Agents: The Lay Movement That Challenged the System and Turned Adventism Toward Racial Justice*. Westlake Village, CA: Oak & Acorn, 2020.

Rock, Calvin B. *Protest and Progress: Black Seventh-day Adventists and the Push for Parity*. Berrien Springs, MI: Andrews University Press, 2018.

Discussion Questions

1. What difference did the reorganization of the Seventh-day Adventist Church make to its missionary activities?
2. What impact did the Student Volunteer Movement have on Adventist college students?
3. In what ways did missionaries support local mission activity in Africa, Asia, and Latin America?
4. What were the elements of the "Battle Creek Idea"? What impact did they have on the Seventh-day Adventist Church and the world at large?
5. How did the Seventh-day Adventist educational work impact Peruvian society?
6. How did Seventh-day Adventists deal with racial issues between 1890 and 1945?

CHAPTER 7

Change and Growth

Two major problems faced the Seventh-day Adventist denomination in 1900: its centralization in Battle Creek and the independence of autonomous structures that arose to support the church, such as the publishing and medical work, the Tract and Missionary Society, and the Sabbath School Association. The denomination had grown from a few thousand members to a membership of 66,547 by 1900. The simple organizational structure of the earlier years needed to be revised. Ellen White increasingly advocated for change during the 1890s. Her nine years in Australia (1891–1900) provided her with firsthand experience of the challenges of frontline mission service: She had to deal with distant administrators who often did not understand the needs of the field and could not respond quickly enough to urgent matters. The Australian experience served as a model for a new way of organizing the church. Beginning in 1894, A. G. Daniells implemented a new system for coordinating the work among the various conferences and ministries of the church. He created the Australasian Union Conference and integrated the different ministries into the Union as departments. While this system varied from the official General Conference policy, it proved successful.

Meanwhile, Ellen White wrote to the General Conference leaders, expressing her concerns about their leadership. At one point, she noted that they were no more competent to lead the church than a child was competent to guide an ocean liner across the Atlantic Ocean. She also called for reorganization. Some anticipated a significant change at the 1897 or 1899 General Conference sessions, but despite the delegates devoting considerable time to studying Ellen White's counsels, they made no substantial changes. The problem was how the church could distribute responsibilities away from Battle Creek while at the same time drawing the independent ministries into a closer connection with the church structure. Dr. John Harvey Kellogg worked hard to keep control of the medical work, and the denominational leadership was unwilling to oppose him. A stalemate between the two prevented any concrete action for change.

When Ellen White concluded her time in Australia and returned to the United States in 1900, she deliberately chose to assert her influence at the General Conference session held in Battle Creek in April of 1901 in the "Dime Tabernacle." This huge Battle Creek church building, constructed in 1878 with seating for 3,200, received its name when believers around the United States contributed dimes (ten-cent pieces) to its construction. Before the session, Ellen White met with church leaders and delivered a one-hour message about the necessity for change. She emphasized that the control of the church by a small group in Battle Creek needed to cease. Decisions needed to be made by those on the ground and in the field rather than those in a distant office. Financial policies were to be more equitable. Leaders were to avoid debt like leprosy. She reiterated that God desired a shift in the approach to the work.

The Dime Tabernacle

Some had been quoting Ellen White's previous writings in an attempt to prevent change from taking place. She said to the gathered ministers, "Do not quote my words again as long as you live until you can obey the Bible. When you make the Bible your food, your meat and your drink, when you make its principles the elements of your character, you will know better how to receive counsel from God. I exalt the precious Word before you today. Do not repeat what I have said, saying, 'Sister White said this,' and 'Sister White said that.' Find out what the Lord God of Israel says, and then do what He commands."[1] Her words had an impact. Daniells's experience in Australia gave church leaders a model. They were now ready to make the necessary changes.

On April 2, 1901, the conference opened under the leadership of President G. A. Irwin. After preliminary remarks, he said, "The Conference is now formally opened. What is your pleasure?" Ellen White, who was sitting in the audience, arose and made her way to the pulpit. She spoke for an hour along

1. Ellen G. White, *Letters and Manuscripts*, vol. 16 (1901), Manuscript 43a, 1901, paragraph 26, https://tinyurl.com/3ewvzb26.

Ellen White speaking from the Dime Tabernacle pulpit at the 1901 General Conference Session

the lines she had shared with the leaders the evening before. One of her themes was the need for a deep personal relationship with God that would be revealed in the lives of his people. At the close of her remarks, the audience was deeply moved. Once more, Irwin asked, "What is your pleasure?" A. G. Daniells came to the pulpit with a plan for organizing the conference and implementing the needed changes.

Four significant changes were implemented after the three weeks of conference meetings. First, local conferences and missions were to be grouped into union conferences and missions. There were two significant differences between a conference and a mission. Conferences were self-supporting, while missions received operating funds from the next higher level of governance. While conference officers were elected by their constituency (delegates from the local churches), mission officers were appointed by the next higher level of governance (the officers of the union). The unions were to be a buffer between the General Conference and the local conferences to ensure that the General Conference could no longer micromanage local conferences and mission work. The unions were to make decisions related to the local field without having to consult the General Conference. Responsibility and authority were now in the hands of those much closer to the actual work.

Second, the General Conference Committee was enlarged to represent many of the church's ministries. It would select its own officers, including its chair, who would be the leader of the church. There would be no more kingly president of the General Conference, only a chair of the Executive Committee. While this policy attempted to prevent "kingly power" from arising again, it proved impractical. At the 1903 General Conference, the delegates voted to change the structure and have the General Conference elect the president and other executive officers in session.

Third, independent organizations were incorporated into the church's structure. This included the publishing work, the Mission Board, and the medical work, including Kellogg's International Medical Missionary and Benevolent Association (IMMBA). While the process of bringing the medical work into close association with the denominational structure began in 1901, it was never completed due to Kellogg's resistance. Thus, the Battle Creek Sanitarium and the IMMBA were never incorporated into the denominational structure.

Fourth, the union conferences became self-governing and self-supporting. Along with the local conferences, the unions were to own and manage the various institutions of the church. However, they also were to aid in spreading the Adventist message around the world. Eventually, the local conferences agreed to give a tithe to the unions, and the unions agreed to give a tithe to the General Conference. Thus, the work of the church around the world received systematic support.[2]

What would the General Conference's role be if the conferences and unions were to manage the institutions? Willie White answered that question at the 1903 General Conference: "The General Conference has to look after the mission fields. . . . Our General Conference is to leave institutional work alone, and let Union Conferences attend to the work of their Union Conference. And the only thing that is left for the General Conference Committee is to do the mission work."[3]

However, the church faced one immense challenge. It needed a solid theological and institutional foundation to advocate for its unique message

2. The list of four major changes comes from Arthur Whitefield Spalding, *Origin and History of Seventh-day Adventists*, vol. 3 (Washington, DC: Review and Herald Publishing Association, 1962), 39–42.

3. William C. White, speaking at a general session on April 9, 1903. *General Conference Bulletin* 5, no. 10 (April 10, 1903): 158.

worldwide. Beginning in 1902, Dr. Kellogg raised significant institutional and theological challenges. His first objection was to the plans for incorporating the church's medical work into the denominational structure. Kellogg had criticized the ministers for not adopting health reform for years. He was unhappy that the ministerial leaders had not made it a more significant issue. Thus, he objected vigorously when those same leaders sought to fold his medical work into the denomination. Since Daniells led the church in the plan to connect the health work with the denomination, Kellogg clashed most directly with him. When they reached an agreement on coordinating the health work with the denominational structure, Kellogg would withdraw from it when the time came to implement it. This happened repeatedly.

In addition to the institutional issues, a theological element entered the conflict. Kellogg had accepted philosophical and theological ideas now known as modernism. In particular, he appreciated the writings of the British philosopher Herbert Spencer, who had developed a theory that used evolution to explain almost everything. Kellogg never explicitly taught evolutionary ideas, but, like other modernist thinkers of the day, he began to speak about God as if he were a principle within all living beings. In 1902, he completed *The Living Temple*, a book published by the Good Health Publishing Association and used as a fund-raiser. However, when church leaders reviewed copies of the manuscript, it became apparent that Kellogg had included unorthodox ideas about God's presence in the world. Church leaders refused to circulate the book, so Kellogg, realizing he could not sell any of the remaining copies of the book, had the problematic pages removed and reissued the book in an amended form.

Cover of *The Living Temple*

In the original edition of *The Living Temple*, Kellogg wrote that if you saw small boots emerging from a larger boot, you would have to conclude that there was a bootmaker in the boot. So, if you see trees producing new trees, you would have to conclude that there was a tree-maker in the tree. Is God in the tree and not a separate personal being? No, Kellogg answered, we human beings need the idea of a personal God to relate to, so there has to be the idea of a personal God. However, a careful reading of Kellogg's ideas suggests that he believed in the concept of a personal God, but the existence of such a God was not necessary for this way of thinking.

Kellogg stoutly denied being a pantheist. Indeed, he was not the typical pantheist who reduced God to a life principle. Today, he might be called a panentheist, believing that God exists within each living being but also outside his creation. Late in the 1880s, Kellogg shared some of his ideas with Ellen White, and she told him that he should keep those ideas to himself. Even after the controversy about *The Living Temple* began, Ellen White chose to remain neutral on the subject. However, when the church leaders gathered for a series of meetings in Berrien Springs, Michigan, in May of 1904, Ellen White spoke directly to the theological problems raised by *The Living Temple*.

She said she was particularly hurt by the assertion that it contained the same things that she herself taught. At first, she didn't even want to read it, but her son persuaded her to listen as he read selected paragraphs. After hearing them, she said they were the same sentiments she had spoken against at the beginning of her public work: "In the *Living Temple* the assertion is made that God is in the flower, in the leaf, in the sinner. . . . God does not abide in the heart of the sinner; it is the enemy who abides there."[4] She then suggested that the denomination's ministers were blind and didn't realize their danger. The young people were also in danger: "'They delighted in the beautiful representations—God in the flower, God in the leaf, God in the trees. But if God be in these things, why not worship them?" Ellen White asked.[5]

She then used a chilling analogy to make the point that the church had to deal with the issue. She described seeing a ship sailing toward an iceberg, a well-known hazard in North Atlantic shipping. Eight years later, in 1912, when the captain of the *Titanic* encountered a similar situation, he commanded the ship to make a sharp turn to avoid the ice. As a result, the *Titanic* scraped the iceberg, slashing almost the entire length of the ship so that it broke apart and sank. However, in Ellen White's story, the captain ordered: "Meet it!" The ship rammed the iceberg with a terrible crash. Unlike the *Titanic*, the vessel in Ellen White's dream was shaken but unharmed.[6] Ellen White applied the story to

4. Ellen G. White, "The Foundation of Our Faith," in *Letters and Manuscripts*, vol. 19 (1904), Manuscript 46, 1904, paragraph 13, dated May 18, 1904, https://tinyurl.com/mpmtdeef.

5. Ellen G. White, "The Foundation of Our Faith," paragraph 19.

6. Ellen G. White, "The Foundation of Our Faith," paragraph 20.

the church. The iceberg that the church was facing was Kellogg's pantheistic-like ideas. Instead of ignoring those ideas, the church had to meet them. The resulting shock would be severe, but the church would recover and survive. Left unsaid was what might happen to the church and its mission if it failed to meet the challenge.

At the same meeting in Berrien Springs, the denominational leadership faced a crisis with the church's educational reformers. E. A. Sutherland and P. T. Magan, who had spearheaded the transfer of Battle Creek College to Berrien Springs, were sympathetic toward Dr. Kellogg.[7] There were rumors that Ellen White opposed their reforms and that Magan had turned against Ellen White.[8] Similar rumors alleged that Kellogg was involved in immorality, that he didn't believe in the foundational doctrines of the church anymore, and that he didn't even believe in Christ.[9] Both Kellogg and the educational reformers denied these rumors and blamed the leading men in the church for starting them.

The educational reformers also distrusted the denominational leaders because of their unwillingness to support Emmanuel Missionary College's program due to its extreme nature. In particular, the leaders opposed Sutherland's scheme of giving free tuition to the children of all Seventh-day Adventist church members and the curriculum that studied only one subject at a time.[10] Thus, the church leaders had reason to suspect the educational reformers of siding with Kellogg and sharing his ideas of independence, institutionalism, and pantheism.[11]

On Friday evening, May 20, in front of all the denominational leaders, W. W. Prescott denounced pantheism, leaving the impression that Kellogg's ideas were the same as classic paganism. Kellogg was incensed. By Monday morning, the stage was set for a marathon eight-hour meeting filled with drama. It began with A. T. Jones hammering away at W. W. Prescott, accusing him of teaching the same things he had denounced on Friday evening. Prescott's defense was that he had changed his mind. Jones kept up the attack

7. This can be seen by the repeated conferences Magan held with Kellogg in early 1904. *The Magan Diary* (copy), the Heritage Room, Andrews University.

8. Ellen G. White, "The Berrien Springs Work," in *Letters and Manuscripts*, vol. 19 (1904), Manuscript 54, 1904, paragraph 5, dated May 23, 1904.

9. Edson Rogers, "Interview with A. T. Jones," dated February 16, 1904, 84.

10. *Magan Diary*, May 15, 1904–June 11, 1904.

11. Emmett K. Vande Vere, *The Wisdom Seekers; The Intriguing Story of the Men and Women Who Made the First Institution for Higher Learning among Seventh-day Adventists* (Nashville: Southern Publishing Association, 1972), 115.

for about three hours, trying to prove that Dr. Kellogg had gotten his ideas from Prescott and other ministers.[12] Then Dr. Kellogg spoke, stating that he had written nothing in *The Living Temple* that was not in harmony with what the denomination taught and Sister White had written. However, his claim did not take into account Ellen White's message given the preceding Wednesday urging the church to meet the errors in his teaching. Next, Sutherland and Magan announced that they could not work with the denominational leaders and, as a result, were resigning from Emmanuel Missionary College. They planned to move to the South to begin a new school. Later that day, Ellen White affirmed the value of their work at Emmanuel Missionary College. She was critical of those who had opposed them. So, the primary effect of her endorsement of the educational reformers was on the denominational leaders who critiqued the methods used in Berrien Springs. They had to recognize that their attitude toward the educational reformers had been wrong.

After the Berrien Springs meeting closed, Ellen White repeatedly called for Kellogg to be reconciled to the church. Still, he remained committed to his ideas and stubborn in his insistence on commanding the medical work. As a result, the church ceased to promote the Battle Creek Sanitarium and Kellogg's American Medical Missionary College (AMMC).

In the end, Kellogg and his faction separated from the church. Kellogg was disfellowshiped in 1907. A. T. Jones, who was allied with Kellogg, developed the idea that all church organization was evil, and he was "cast out" of the church in 1909. The educational reformers left the meeting with Ellen White's endorsement ringing in their ears. She supported their new efforts in Madison, Tennessee. She even moved there for a time. And she encouraged them to repair their relationships with denominational leaders. Over the years, there was significant reconciliation. The denominational leaders were not faultless amid all this drama, but they also continued to have Ellen White's support. The danger of Kellogg's modernist thinking had been met. Emmanuel Missionary College returned to a more solid financial and academic foundation. Sutherland and Magan moderated their educational ideas and later assumed important posts in Adventist education.

In tandem with the needed organizational changes, Ellen White had urged the church to move its major institutions out of Battle Creek. The college had moved to Berrien Springs in the summer of 1901. However, two massive fires in 1902 also prompted talk of moving the other institutions. When the sanitarium building burned down on February 18, Ellen White urged replacing it with a

12. Vande Vere, *The Wisdom Seekers*, 115.

Sanitarium fire of 1902

smaller structure and investing funds in more widespread medical work around the United States. Instead, Dr. Kellogg, who had recently consolidated his control of the sanitarium, built a massive stone structure. On December 30, the Review and Herald building burned in a spectacular fire. This sparked a move to Washington, DC, by the Publishing Association and the General Conference. A college was founded in nearby Takoma Park, Maryland. As these developments occurred in the East, the church also turned to the west to begin medical missionary work anew.

Rebuilt sanitarium

Shifting to Takoma Park

Ellen White expressed her deep sadness when she learned about the destruction of the publishing and sanitarium buildings in Battle Creek in 1902. "I feel very sad as I consider the great loss to the cause," she remarked. "But I was not surprised by the sad news, for in the visions of the night I have seen an angel standing with a sword as of fire stretched over Battle Creek."[1] In the wake of the destruction, she urged church leaders not to amass huge resources in one place. Instead, the church should take this opportunity to become more missional, sending more missionaries and building new institutions. If God's people "were awake to discern the signs of the times" and understood their responsibility, she remarked, many "would leave Battle Creek."[2]

Church leaders began a search process. Their first choice, outside New York City, sold before they could secure it, and some leaders became discouraged. A small group in the spring of 1904 explored a piece of property just north of Washington, DC, called the "Thornton Tract." It was in Takoma Park, Maryland, two blocks from the Baltimore & Ohio Railway station, and had access to plenty of clean water in Sligo Creek. Shortly after the property was purchased, the General Conference secured a temporary location nearby and began to build a new headquarters, publishing house, college, and sanitarium. Takoma Park would become the new headquarters of the denomination. The new location had better access to communication and other resources, which made it easier to send missionaries worldwide. It also had the advantage of distance from the toxic environment that was brewing in Dr. Kellogg's Battle Creek.

1. Ellen G. White, *Testimonies for the Church*, vol. 8 (Mountain View, CA: Pacific Press, 1904), 97. From a letter dated January 3, 1903.

2. Ellen G. White, "Notes of Travel—No. 2," *Review and Herald* 82, no 4 (January 26, 1905): 8.

Work in the West

Once rail lines were built to California, it became fashionable for wealthy people from the eastern United States to travel to California during the winter to escape the snow and ice. As a result, the population in Southern California multiplied. In the late 1880s, large resorts were built, but when the American economy crashed in 1893, many of these resorts were no longer financially viable. Ellen White saw an opportunity for the church. At her direction, beginning in 1905, the church purchased three resort buildings for use as sanitariums. Glendale was near Los Angeles. Paradise Valley was near San Diego. But the largest of the three was in Loma Linda, near San Bernardino. Ellen White took the initiative to ensure that the church secured the Loma Linda property, which she marked out for future educational work. Each purchase included events that showed providential leading.

In the late 1890s, investors had poured over $155,000 into the Loma Linda resort building, but by 1905, they were eager to sell it to the church for $40,000. After making two down payments, church leaders needed $5,000 to make an additional payment on July 15 or they would lose their down payments and the building. However, on the day the money was due, they had nothing. Committee members who opposed the purchase were vocal about how the purchase had been a bad idea. No one had any ideas of where they could get the money. Amid the intense discussion, one committee member described how wise it had been in the past to follow Ellen White's counsel. Since she had initiated this purchase, he expressed confidence that God would also provide in this case. Someone suggested they look at the incoming mail that had just been delivered. An envelope in that mail contained a check for the Loma Linda project for the needed $5,000.

Loma Linda resort building

Once the down payments had been made and the sanitarium in Loma Linda was opened, the remaining indebtedness was paid off within a year. The church began to plan for the training of nurses and physicians at Loma Linda, but Kellogg scoffed at the possibility. He quipped that building a railroad to the moon would be easier than building a new medical school at Loma Linda. However, it was Kellogg's American Medical Missionary College that closed. Loma Linda survived and thrived to become central to Seventh-day Adventist medical work. Its connection to Adventist mission work was in its name: the College of Medical Evangelists. Physicians and nurses who were trained there spread worldwide, founding clinics, sanitariums, and hospitals in many areas that had virtually no access to advanced medical practices. These institutions grew to become models of up-to-date medicine. Some remain today as the premier medical institutions in their region. Others were imitated in local lands, setting the stage for modern medical centers in many countries.

Resources

Ashworth, Warren Sidney. "Edward Alexander Sutherland and Seventh-day Adventist Educational Reform: The Denominational Years, 1890–1904." PhD diss., Andrews University, 1986.

McFarland, Ken, and W. Augustus Cheatham. *Railway to the Moon: The Impossible Dream*. Boise, ID: Pacific Press Publishing Association, 2005.

Oliver, Barry David. *SDA Organizational Structure: Past, Present, and Future*. Berrien Springs, MI: Andrews University Press, 1989.

Discussion Questions

1. How did the reorganization of the General Conference solve the two major problems facing the Seventh-day Adventist Church in 1900?
2. What was the difference between Kellogg's theological beliefs and those of a typical pantheist?
3. What was Ellen White's chief concern with the ideas expressed in Kellogg's *The Living Temple*?
4. Kellogg and the educational reformers, Sutherland and Magan, were allies in 1904 at the Berrien Springs meeting. What made the difference in their future relationship to the Seventh-day Adventist Church?
5. What impact did the medical school in Loma Linda have on the Seventh-day Adventist Church?

CHAPTER 8

War Within and Without

The early twentieth century was a time of significant change. In one sense, it marked the end of an era. Many of the earliest Seventh-day Adventist pioneers passed away in the early twentieth century. The *Review and Herald* publicized the passing of these leaders, sometimes featuring them with a cover photo and life sketch. No pioneer was more deeply mourned by the denomination than its cofounder and prophetic voice, Ellen White. The denomination believed that a living prophet was guiding it, but her death in 1915 brought that to an end. Her passing meant the church had to properly organize and present her writings and define her ongoing prophetic legacy.

A new global conflict enveloped Europe during the last year of Ellen White's life. It was impossible to escape the darkness of "the Great War" or what would later be called World War I (1914–1918). The optimistic hope brought about by technological innovation as a means of solving the world's problems quickly dissipated as individuals discovered more efficient ways to extinguish human life. This war, a global event of unprecedented scale, cast a long shadow over the Seventh-day Adventist denomination and its members, significantly influencing its trajectory.[1]

Meanwhile, another religious and cultural war unfolded among Protestants as some Christians were ready to "do battle royal" to defend their faith. New ways of interpreting the Bible, such as the historical-critical approach, the theory of evolution, and the Social Gospel, influenced mainline Protestants in America to seek accommodation with an ever-changing modern world. The reaction to this movement among conservative Christians created the modernist-fundamentalist controversy. The movement's namesake was a series of pamphlets, *The Fundamentals: A Testimony for the Truth*, published between 1910 and 1915. After 1922, the term "fundamentalists" became a badge of pride among these conservative Protestant leaders who sought to preserve their

1. Norma R. Youngberg and Gerald H. Minchin, *Under Sealed Orders: The Story of Gus Youngberg* (Mountain View, CA: Pacific Press, 1970), 16.

faith based upon the historic foundation of the Bible. Viewing the Scriptures as inerrant and infallible, they militantly defended what they viewed as the historical understanding of the Bible. Many denominations split over these issues. Adventists sided mainly with the fundamentalist camp, with some variation about how far they should go in defending their faith and promoting views of inerrancy. Defining Adventist fundamentalism in reference to Ellen White's writings would become a central feature of the historic 1919 Bible Conference and the era immediately following it.

The Passing of a Prophet

At eighty-two years of age in 1910, Ellen White recognized that she was nearing the end of her life. She began to concentrate her efforts on the custody and translation of her writings rather than producing new work. She created a series of wills that established a board of trustees consisting of church leaders to oversee the custody of her writings. She recognized that her six decades of writing were a permanent legacy that would continue to be a witness to the church and world. She wished to preserve the record of her convictions and revelations so that they might guide the Adventist denomination after her passing. Her driving passion during her last years was translating and promoting her writings. Some of her final works included *The Acts of the Apostles* (1911) and an updated edition of her classic work on Christian history and end-time events, *The Great Controversy* (1911). Yet there was no doubt that her literary output was slowing down. Her assistants worked on a new and updated autobiography, *Life Sketches* (1915). But *Prophets and Kings* (1917), the final volume of her series outlining salvation history, was completed by her assistants just after her death.

As the end drew near, Adventists waited with bated breath for updates about Ellen White's well-being. On February 13, 1915, she suffered an accident when she fell in her home and broke her hip. At such an advanced age, there was nothing anyone could do at the time except to make her comfortable. Friends asked her how she felt. With reference to her death, she replied: "I feel, the sooner the better; all the time that is how I feel—the sooner the better."[2] As her family gathered around to sing hymns and to pray with her, her son reported that his mother's last words, after a season of prayer, could be heard

2. Clarence C. Crisler, "The Death of Sister White," *Pacific Union Recorder* 14, no. 50 (July 22, 1915): 2.

Ellen White graveside service

in a faint whisper: "I know in whom I have believed."[3] Her friends reported that when she breathed her last, it was so quiet that it "was like the burning out of a candle." The end arrived on Friday afternoon, July 16, 1915, at 3:40 p.m. Her "death was not unexpected."[4]

Church leaders were ready with a press release and a series of three funerals—the first one at her Elmshaven home; a second one at the California camp meeting for believers on the West Coast; and a more official funeral held at the Dime Tabernacle in Battle Creek. Church leaders gathered for the most prominent funeral in the denomination's history. Mrs. White was buried in the family plot next to her husband and two of her children. Even her fiercest detractor, D. M. Canright, was reported to have said when walking by her casket, "There is a noble Christian woman gone."[5] Even her neighbors remembered

3. W. C. White to David Lacey, July 20, 1915, Ellen G. White Estate.

4. Crisler, "The Death of Sister White," 1.

5. William A. Spicer, *The Spirit of Prophecy in the Advent Movement* (Washington, DC: Review and Herald, 1937), 127–28.

how she loved to travel around in her buggy with her horse, Belle, going up and down the Napa Valley. She was "the little gray-haired lady from Elmshaven who always spoke so lovingly of Jesus."[6]

The plans Ellen White had for an easy transition of her literary estate came to a quick halt when the judge overseeing the probate of her estate demanded its immediate liquidation. There were substantial debts due to her donations to church and missionary projects. Yet these debts were offset by the value of her ongoing book royalties. The forced liquidation of the estate meant that the General Conference was compelled to buy her literary estate promptly, technically taking ownership of it. However, an independent board of trustees, primarily made up of the same church leaders, was responsible for managing her manuscripts and publications. Ultimately, the church would invest the royalties from her writings in translating her books. The White Estate, as it came to be known, would both be a part of the church and yet serve a somewhat semiautonomous role. Ellen White's son, William Clarence White, was primarily responsible for the work of the White Estate after her death. When her grandson, Arthur White, took over the leadership, the remaining unpublished writings were moved from California to church headquarters in Takoma Park, Maryland. The members of the White Estate Board would continue to appoint life trustees who ensured that her writings were protected and circulated. Over the twentieth century, the White Estate would increasingly be funded by the General Conference and operate as a semiautonomous department of the General Conference.

Perhaps more troubling at the time was whether Ellen White would have a prophetic successor. F. M. Wilcox, editor of the denomination's main periodical, *Review and Herald*, opined, "Since the death of Sister E. G. White, a number have claimed to have the spirit of prophecy and to be appointed to take her place. In different sections of the country, we find some man or some woman who claims to have divine revelations." Wilcox reminded readers that anyone claiming the prophetic mantle must be tested by the Bible, the same way Ellen White was evaluated. "We need to be on our guard," he added. "The Word [the Bible] is our guide."[7]

One sad case was that of Margaret Rowen, a convert from Methodism, who claimed to have received a vision while gathering with a small group of

6. Virgil Robinson, "Ellen G. White: Who Was She? Part 2," *Signs of the Times* 98, no. 11 (November 1971): 32.

7. F. M. Wilcox, "Impressions and Dreams," *Review and Herald* 100, no. 7 (February 15, 1923): 7.

women in Bible study. The story was like Ellen White's early experience, but church leaders approached her claim with extreme caution. They established a committee to review her initial testimonies and speak with her and with witnesses who truly believed she had received Ellen White's prophetic mantle. As time passed, she made increasingly bolder claims about her ancestry and pedigree. She even cited a letter by Ellen White endorsing her ministry, which turned out to be an obvious forgery. She predicted the close of probation, but the predicted events did not occur. Her empire began to crumble when some of her most loyal followers discovered she was stealing from her own organization. When Dr. Bert B. Fullmer, her leading financier, informed her that he was going to expose her theft to church leaders, she tried to murder him. Her initial attempt failed, causing quite a scandal as newspapers covered the story nationwide. After she was convicted of assault and jailed for almost two years in San Quentin prison, she faded from view, much to the relief of denominational leaders.

World War I

While there was conflict within the church, the conflict without quickly captured church members' attention as one more sign of the approaching end of time. World War I changed the geopolitical structure of Europe and the world. More significantly, for Adventist theology, it profoundly changed Adventism. Even as America tried to avoid being drawn into the war, this no longer seemed an option by the time the *Lusitania* sank on May 7, 1915. Warned by radio that the seas ahead were dangerous, the captain had sailed on heedless to the message. When a German U-boat torpedoed the ship without warning, more than one thousand lives were lost. No sooner had it sunk than Adventist evangelists, like many other Christians, began interpreting both the sinking ship and the war in eschatological terms. One Adventist revivalist, Meade MacGuire, stated at a camp meeting: "As the vessel went down without warning—and yet with warning—so this world is hastening on to its doom without heeding, and yet warned."[8]

Adventists were especially interested in the "Eastern Question," the fate of the Ottoman Empire (centered in what came to be known as Turkey). However, the events that took place didn't meet their expectations. Many feared that the war would pit the forces of Russia (the proverbial "king of the North"

8. "Raise Large Sum for Adventists Schools: State Meetings to Come to Close at Park This Evening," *Fresno Morning Republican*, May 9, 1915, 32.

from Daniel 11) against Egypt (the "king of the South"). When Great Britain finally conquered Jerusalem, many were forced to reexamine their interpretations. Daniel 11 had never been a critical aspect of how Adventists interpreted end-time events. However, some had become so enthusiastic in predicting how the end would occur that Britain's capture of Palestine took many by surprise. Adventists were not alone in finding prophetic fulfillment in the events of World War I. Some historians have noted how the Great War was the most important event since the Great Disappointment for reviving interest in America in the premillennial return of Christ.[9] Many conservative Christians attended large prophetic conferences focused on end-time events during the war. The leaders of these conferences become the nucleus of the developing fundamentalist movement.

World War I also raised the problem of required military service, known as conscription. Despite the precedent set by "noncombatant" recognition from the US government during the American Civil War, the denomination lacked a position on military service "that was clearly defined and widely understood and recognized by either the government or the church membership."[10] The massive mobilization of the American economy to support the war effort became a righteous crusade to "make the world safe for democracy." For example, citizens were urged to help by purchasing "liberty bonds" to finance the war. All men between the ages of twenty-one and thirty were required to register for military service. Church leaders struggled with how best to respond. At the April 1917 Spring Council, a "heated debate" occurred over noncombatant military service versus "a more pacifist stance." Ultimately, the council sought to make peace with a position that affirmed loyalty to the government while also requesting that Adventists "be required to serve [their] country only in such a capacity as will not violate [their] conscientious obedience to the law of God as contained in the decalogue, interpreted in the teachings of Christ, and exemplified in His life."[11]

The law drafting men for military service contained an exemption for those who wished to be noncombatants. However, many of the men drafted, many local draft boards, and many military officers were ignorant of this provision. That meant that some Adventist young men faced significant consequences for their

9. Timothy P. Weber, *Living in the Shadow of the Second Coming: American Premillennialism, 1875–1982* (Chicago: University of Chicago Press, 1987), 105.

10. Douglas Morgan, *Adventism and the American Republic: The Public Involvement of a Major Apocalyptic Movement* (Knoxville: University of Tennessee Press, 2001), 90.

11. Quoted in Morgan, *Adventism*, 91.

noncombatant stance, for refusing to work on Sabbath, or both. "Adventists were willing, even eager, to accept other roles defined for them by the government in its effort to mobilize the entire citizenry in support of the total war effort,"[12] and this usually allowed Adventists to find ways to both serve in the military and be true to their conscience. For example, Adventist soldier T. C. Metcalf was court-martialed and sentenced to twenty years in army detention at the United States Disciplinary Barracks at Fort Leavenworth in Kansas, but instead, he was reassigned to the Medical Corp and deployed in that capacity with the troops in Europe.[13] Nonetheless, at least ten Adventists were imprisoned at Fort Leavenworth, and many more faced prejudice, animosity, persecution, and court-martial.

The critical issue for the American-dominated church leadership was patriotic loyalty. This was an awkward moment as the majority of Adventist members were still in North America but other Adventists were on the opposite side of the conflict. Members in America were urged by *Review and Herald* editor F. M. Wilcox to seek "to assist the government in every way possible, aside from the work of actually bearing arms."[14] As in earlier conflicts, records indicate that many Adventists did both bear arms and seek to prove their patriotism during the war. Some historians have estimated that about half of the one thousand American Adventists who served in the military forces chose to bear arms. The denomination remained split on the issue of military service, even if questions of loyalty and patriotism loomed large.

Many denominations that urged pacifism soon found themselves under increased scrutiny. After the war, church leaders shared how government officials came to talk with them. The officials questioned their loyalty, citing Adventist teachings about the role of America as the two-horned beast in Revelation 13. Church leaders were warned not to talk about these controversial and unpatriotic points in their publications, and soon, new editions of censored publications appeared in print. For the first time, widespread government surveillance contributed to a general sense of angst as Adventists sought to meet the dual responsibility of duty to nation and duty to God. American Adventists, at least, would prove patriotic. Like many other American churches, Adventist congregations began to place a United States flag prominently up front near the pulpit. As the war continued, the temptation to interpret it as a sign of the end proved irresistible.

12. Morgan, *Adventism*, 91.

13. Sabrina Riley, "Reconciling Conscience and Patriotism: The History of the Seventh-day Adventist Medical Cadet Corp," chapter 2 (unpublished manuscript).

14. Morgan, *Adventism*, 91.

In Germany, the church split over the very same issues. Germany had required military service from all males long before the war began. Thus, in 1914, it could call upon a vast number of well-trained reservists to increase the number of its soldiers from 808,280 to 3,502,700 men in just twelve days. Adventists in Germany were aware of the church's stance supporting noncombatancy, but the speed with which the conscription happened meant that the German church had only days to create a position. German law had no provision for noncombatants. Conscripted men who refused to fight faced prison and a real possibility of execution by firing squad. Church officials in Germany decided that Adventist men conscripted into the German army could bear arms and render military service to defend their country on the Sabbath. The German Ministry of War was informed of this decision. While this relieved conscripts of the possibility of execution for disobeying orders, it seemed to some in the church to be a denial of the church's historic position of noncombatancy. Some men refused to comply with the conscription orders. Verbal combat erupted in many churches between those who supported the leader's decision and those who opposed it. One man claimed to have received a vision predicting that human probation would close within a year. Several others also made time-setting predictions. L. R. Conradi, the president of the European Division, threatened the dissidents with disfellowshiping. After the war, there were attempts at reconciliation, but the animosity on both sides was too high. The church disfellowshiped about four thousand members. Many of these members became part of the Seventh-day Adventist Reform movement, which continues to remain independent of the official Seventh-day Adventist Church.

Modernist/Fundamentalist Controversy

The hyped-up militarization of American Christianity found a new battlefront at home. The triple threats of religious modernism, the theory of evolution, and the rise of modern science defined the field on which conservative Christians would defend the fundamental basic teachings of what was widely perceived as historic Christianity. Historic Christian truths, such as the traditional inspiration of the Bible with its miracles and an actual atonement by Jesus Christ on Calvary, were perceived as under threat because liberal Christians questioned their veracity. A militant defense of the faith gained traction toward the war's end through the same prophetic conferences that continued to meet across denominational lines.

Milton and Lyman Stewart, the founders of the Standard Oil Company, invested significant portions of their family fortune in various Christian projects.

When they discovered that some of the religion teachers whose salaries they funded were teaching things they viewed as undermining historic Christianity, they were shocked. In some instances, they withdrew their funding and channeled it into new causes that did not contribute to modernist readings of Scripture. One such effort gave the fundamentalist movement its name. Between 1910 and 1915, the Stewarts sponsored the publication of ninety essays in twelve serial volumes named *The Fundamentals: A Testimony for the Truth.* The original essays were written by respected scholars and had much to say that was valuable. However, they laid out the battle lines for a new and combative defense of the historic Christian faith.

Adventists found themselves in an odd situation in relationship to the rise of fundamentalism. They enthusiastically embraced fundamentalism, while the fundamentalists rejected them as legalistic heretics. This odd relationship can be seen in the effort to identify whether Adventists should be included in a list

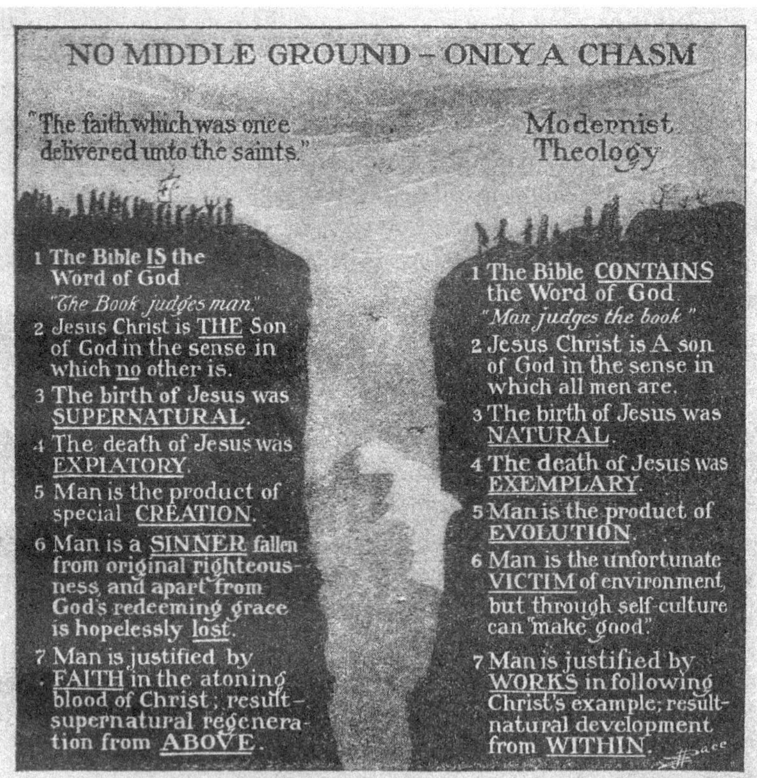

Anti-modernist cartoon

of heterodox or cultic groups. Three essays in *The Fundamentals* dealt with Christian Science, Jehovah's Witnesses, and the Latter-day Saints denominations. They were presented as being outside of orthodox Protestantism. Reuben A. Torrey, the main editor of the fundamentalist pamphlets, had sparred with A. T. Jones and other church leaders during the 1890s. Hence, he was ready to include an essay attacking Seventh-day Adventists as a cult. Lyman Stewart told Torrey to leave the Adventists alone for some unknown reason. Despite fundamentalists' dislike for them, Adventists identified as fundamentalists, and some went so far as to describe themselves as the "true" fundamentalists. W. H. Branson, who later became president of the General Conference, wrote that Adventists were the "fundamentalists of the Fundamentalists."[15] Seventh-day Adventists not only believed in a literal creation but also affirmed the seventh-day Sabbath at creation. Adventists argued that their fundamentalist counterparts had not taken their biblical literalism far enough. If they followed the Bible as it read, they would become Seventh-day Adventists.

Anti-modernist cartoon

Yet this one-sided love affair with fundamentalism profoundly changed Adventism. Adventists had resisted creedalism, stating that their only creed was the Bible; now, they became concerned about defending the historic Christian faith. Earlier attempts by Uriah Smith in 1872 at a declaration of faith now morphed into statements of fundamental beliefs modeled after similar statements by the fundamentalists in the late 1910s. In fact, by 1931, the denomination would officially publish this statement of fundamental beliefs, which was merely the same statements from 1919 onward that F. M. Wilcox and others had published in church publications in response to the rising fundamentalist movement. Like their fundamentalist counterparts, Adventists would resist strict and formal creeds while embracing statements of fundamental beliefs.

15. W. H. Branson, "Loyalty in an Age of Doubt," *Ministry* 6, no. 10 (October 1933): 3.

George McCready Price and Siegfried Horn

The most profound changes to Adventism came in terms of race and gender. Whereas the earliest pioneers of Adventism had been impatient with injustice, socially progressive, and activist in orientation, by the mid-twentieth century, Adventism had largely fallen into the "separate but equal" classification that became normative after the US Supreme Court accepted it in 1896. Even then, "the color line" was a highly contested matter in the church, with many voices, including Ellen White's, against imposing it.

A church building constructed in 1907 near the new headquarters in Takoma Park, Maryland, was typical of the racial separation in American society. The new building became the new white church while the earlier congregation in Washington, DC, which had been integrated for more than a decade, gradually became the black church.

During the first third of the twentieth century, the racial divisions in Adventism deepened so that the American Adventist Church organization divided itself along racial lines in the 1940s. Similarly, early Adventists had been enthusiastic about embracing women within the church. While women had always made up the majority of the church, as characteristic of Christianity in general, the prevalence of women in church leadership positions and as evangelists and pastors decreased significantly during the 1920s until they essentially disappeared. Women were urged to work along domestic lines and, at most, could serve as Bible workers. Some single women chose the freedom of working overseas as missionaries.

One notable exception to the fundamentalist rejection of Adventists was their embrace of George McCready Price (1870–1963). He became well-known among fundamentalists for his ideas of harmonizing geological science with the Bible's accounts of creation and the flood. It appears that Price downplayed his Adventist affiliation, and his books became best sellers during the 1920s. A largely self-educated devotee of Ellen White's writings, he taught in various Adventist institutions. Several historians have noted how his writings contributed to the young-earth creationism of the later twentieth century. His lack of rigorous scientific methods left him open to the charge of anti-intellectualism from those looking on from the outside.

Regarding creationism, its most notable defender was William Jennings Bryan, a three-time Democratic presidential candidate. Bryan was the featured speaker at a lecture on creation and evolution at the Adventist-owned Pacific Press near San Francisco on September 25, 1924. His lecture led to a highly publicized debate in San Francisco on June 13 and 14, 1925, between Dr. Maynard Shipley, who promoted evolution, and Pacific Press editors F. D. Nichol and Alonzo Baker, defending creationism.[16] Pacific Press then published *Creation—Not Evolution* based on Nichol and Baker's presentations.

A month later, Bryan took the lead as prosecutor at the Scopes trial in Dayton, Tennessee (July 10–21, 1925). Bryan invited Price to testify at the trial, but he could not since he was teaching in England at the time. At the trial, Clarence Darrow, the prosecuting attorney, cross-examined Bryan about his biblical beliefs. Darrow's questions highlighted the genuine problems of biblical literalism. He asked about Jonah's three days in the whale, whether the sun stood still at Joshua's command, and whether humans and animals were all descendants from those in Noah's ark. Scopes was convicted of teaching evolution, but the case was dismissed due to a technicality. Bryan died a week after the trial.

Six weeks after the trial, amid worldwide publicity, Price debated Joseph McCabe, a well-known rationalist, in London. Moderated by Bertrand Russell's older brother, Earl Russell, the debate attracted an audience of three thousand.[17] However, the widespread publicity given to the debates and the Scopes

16. Alonzo L. Baker, "The San Francisco Evolution Debates," *Adventist Heritage* 2, no. 2 (Winter 1975): 23–32.

17. George McCready Price and Joseph McCabe, *Is Evolution True? Verbatim Report of*

Is Evolution True?

Creation—Not Evolution

trial tended to mock fundamentalist literalism. As a result, the educated mainstream of the modern world lost respect for fundamentalism. The media no longer covered its ideas; most intellectuals ridiculed and ignored it. However, it remained vibrant and active in much of the country and reemerged into the public's view with Billy Graham's Los Angeles Crusade in 1949. Discarding the name fundamentalist, Graham encouraged the rebranding of conservative Christianity as evangelicalism.

In Adventism, fundamentalism found continued support based on its inerrantist view of inspiration, especially in relation to Ellen White's writings. The fault lines between fundamentalists and those they opposed would be evident for the first time publicly after Ellen White's death at the 1919 Bible Conference.

The 1919 Bible Conference

Adventists were caught in the tension between the past and the ever-changing world at the 1919 Bible Conference. Church leaders had lost a living prophet

---

Debate Between George McCready Price and Joseph McCabe Held at the Queen's Hall, Langham Place, London, W., on September 6, 1925. Rev. by Both Disputants (London: Watts, 1925).

and faced a global war, and now they had renewed reason to believe that the end was near. Adventist leaders had attended the prophetic conferences and were more than a bit jealous that other Christians did so well at proclaiming the world's impending end. Hence, Adventists decided to have a prophecy conference all their own, recruiting sixty-five of their leading theologians and administrators to review their understanding of Bible prophecy in light of the war. If they could only be unified, despite various theories about Daniel 11 and the king of the North, they could follow the example of the fundamentalists in drawing the world's attention to their heartfelt biblical message. Church president A. G. Daniells opened the conference with the hope that it would not only echo what the fundamentalists were doing but would be the beginning of a series of annual meetings that ushered in the second coming of Christ.

Hopes for a united prophetic message were quickly shattered. One Canadian Bible teacher, Clifton L. Taylor, compared its disputes to a boxing match taking place on the Fourth of July 1919, only four days into the Bible Conference. In that match, Jack Dempsey defeated Jess Willard for the heavyweight championship in a brutal performance, knocking him down seven times in the first round and inflicting severe injuries on him. Taylor compared the bravado

1919 Bible Conference

Spicer (center) and Daniells (front row, third from right, in suspenders), pitching the Big Tent for the 1913 General Conference Session

of the disputants to the "big guns" who were "firing broadsides" debating issues early in the Bible Conference.

At least two sides emerged in a debate about interpretative or hermeneutical methods. Both sides believed they were right and laid claim to the prophetic legacy of Ellen G. White. The key questions were how to correctly interpret her writings and how they should relate to the authority of the Bible. The debates became so heated that Daniells forbade controversial topics from being discussed unless he was present. At one point, he became so exasperated with the attention paid to the tiny details about the king of the North in Daniel 11 that he wished he could put the whole matter in a hot air balloon and let it float away. A key question centered on Ellen White's book *The Great Controversy*, with both sides appealing to the authority of her writings to settle differences. Some of those who had worked closely with Ellen White noted how she never claimed to be a historian or a commentator on the Bible. Therefore, it was clear that she

Last Generation Theology

In the late 1910s and 1920s, the Victorious Life movement arose within the wider fundamentalist movement. Its emphasis on perfection had roots in Wesleyan Methodism, the Holiness movement, the teachings of the Keswick conference in England, and Dwight L. Moody's empire. Some Adventists adapted these ideas about perfection to Adventist theology, especially the notion of victory over sin. Adventist authors, including Matilda Andross (1880–1957) and Meade MacGuire (1875–1967), took the ideas a step further by talking about choosing the life that wins—the idea that one must spiritually "win the victory" over sin in order to bring about the second advent of Christ. If God's people achieved perfection, then Jesus would return. "We need victory for Christ's sake . . . evidence that His plan of redemption is a success," wrote MacGuire.[1] At the heart of this "Last Generation Theology" is the idea that God's people vindicate the character of God by their sinless, perfect lives. Their achievement triggers the final events. They stand without a mediator through the final and chaotic times of the end. Such ideas became widely accepted within Adventism. However, the foremost advocate of these teachings was M. L. Andreasen, the leading theologian of the denomination in the first half of the twentieth century. Theologian and church leader W. W. Prescott warned in the 1920s that such teachings were problematic because they focused on a covenant of works rather than the new covenant of grace. This old covenant was any theology that focused on human achievement, especially the idea of not needing the mediatorial work of Christ. Many Adventist theologians in the early twenty-first century see Last Generation Theology as a legalistic distortion of Adventism.

1. Meade MacGuire, "We Need Victory," *Ministry* 1, no. 1 (January 1928): 10.

adhered to a flexible view of inspiration that ruled out inerrancy. As evidence of this, she frequently revised her writings, including *The Great Controversy*.

After the main conference ended, Bible and history teachers stayed for a "roundtable discussion" with church president Daniells. They noted how important it was that the church be educated on these topics. The men and women in the pew needed a more flexible view of inspiration that avoided the rigid inerrancy coming into vogue in fundamentalist circles. This was necessary since some Adventists exalted Ellen White's writings above the Bible. In foreboding words, at least three teachers noted that if they didn't do something now, this problem would only get worse in the future.

While the delegates believed something must be done, no one seemed to agree precisely on what that might look like. Some of the 1919 Bible Conference participants published their presentations, including Daniells, who, before his death, released a book of candid reflections about Ellen White's life and ministry. Still, the church largely forgot about this Bible conference: its records were stored and neglected. Adventist fundamentalism came to dominate the 1920s. Everyone within Adventism believed that modernism was wrong, but the real question was how far in the direction of fundamentalism the church should go in its reaction to modernism. It was along this continuum that Adventists found themselves in a new world. This world was changing, yet they found comfort by reaffirming Adventist fundamentals and advancing the Christian church's global mission.

As a result of comments made at the 1919 conference, Daniells came under intense criticism from the extreme conservative faction of the church. They launched a campaign to oust him from the General Conference presidency. At the 1922 General Conference session, the nominating committee was unable to reach an agreement on the presidency. After days of deliberation, Daniells conceded to W. A. Spicer, and they agreed to trade jobs. Spicer took the presidency, and Daniells became the secretary. Telling his wife about his election, Spicer wrote, "There are no posts of honor, but only of service."

Accreditation

With the successful launch of the College of Medical Evangelists in Loma Linda, California, Seventh-day Adventist education began a series of events that led to a healthy interaction with the world at large and to a higher level of scholarship in all Adventist educational institutions. As the American medical establishment sought to raise the standards in medical schools, it formulated a series of requirements for the accreditation of such schools. The accreditation standards dealt with such matters as curriculum, laboratories, lab instruction, facilities, finances, and libraries. Loma Linda needed to be fully accredited to graduate physicians who could receive credentials from the state medical boards. To be accredited, the American Medical Association required Loma Linda to accept students from accredited premedical courses. At first, the requirement was only two years of instruction, but in 1930 this was expanded to three years of college work at an accredited college.[18]

18. William G. White, "Flirting with the World," *Adventist Heritage* 8, no. 1 (Spring 1983): 40–51. Much of the following material is documented in White's article.

At the same time, there was a growing movement in the United States to require all elementary and secondary schools to meet minimum standards. One of the minimum requirements was for teachers to be state-certified, that is, to have completed their training at an accredited institution. Thus, the push for accreditation came not just from the medical establishment but from educational institutions as well.

At first, the General Conference Education Department strongly opposed accreditation. W. E. Howell, the secretary of the department, likened accreditation to being tied to the tail of a kite and being forced to go wherever the holder of the string might want them to go. The fear was that accreditation would open Adventist schools to the forces of evolution and higher criticism that were eroding trust in the Bible.

A reluctant advocate of accreditation was the educational reformer P. T. Magan. As dean and later president of the College of Medical Evangelists, he knew that accreditation was essential for the medical school to survive. Without the medical school, the unique Adventist medical ministry of sanitariums and hospitals would collapse. Due to his insistence, the General Conference approved the accreditation of all American Seventh-day Adventist colleges in 1931. Because of its proximity to Loma Linda and its well-developed premedical program, Pacific Union College was the first Seventh-day Adventist college to be accredited. Under the leadership of President William Landeen (1891–1982), Walla Walla University received its accreditation in April 1935. Union College and Emmanuel Missionary College had a more challenging time gaining accreditation from their regional authorities. Throughout the process, strident voices opposed accreditation as the beginning of the process of allowing worldly influences into Adventist colleges. Those favoring accreditation argued that the accreditation agencies could not tell the colleges what or how to teach. They were only upholding basic requirements for higher education.

Because of the controversies and difficulties in gaining accreditation, the church's Annual Council in 1935 voted to limit accreditation to only two Adventist colleges: Pacific Union College in California and Emmanuel Missionary College in Berrien Springs, Michigan. However, the boards of all the other colleges chose to ignore this directive and continue the efforts toward accreditation. Walla Walla had already been accredited, and the boards of the other colleges knew there was no going back. Students were no longer willing to attend a college that was not accredited. Soon, all the American Adventist colleges were accredited. The same forces that brought state accreditation to the United States in the 1920s and 1930s brought accreditation to Adventist institutions worldwide in the 1960s.

Adventist Growth Shifts Outside North America

The first third of the twentieth century would find Adventism expanding rapidly around the globe. The Adventist mission was at the forefront of Adventist consciousness. Schools were needed to train workers, and funds were desperately needed to support an ever-expanding missionary program. While some denominations lost their motivation to do mission work in the 1920s, Adventists were even more confident that they must aggressively share their message by sending even more missionaries worldwide. In doing so, Adventism itself was profoundly changed.

One clever way of raising funds was what Adventists called "Harvest Ingathering," though the "harvest" prefix was later dropped. An entrepreneurial businessman, Jasper Wayne, devised an ingenious method to promote missions. Using an edition of the *Signs of the Times*, an Adventist evangelistic magazine, he started sharing copies with friends and neighbors who gave donations for missionary work. Surprisingly, he received $4 for missions on his first day. He ordered more literature and soon developed a system of fund-raising that church leaders gradually adopted. During the first year of its official use, Harvest Ingathering brought in $30,000, providing enough funds to send out twenty-five new missionaries. By the time Wayne passed away in 1920, the denomination had raised over a million dollars for missions. The practice of having annual Ingathering efforts became customary within Adventism for much of the mid-twentieth century.

New funds and church workers were the key ingredients for expanding Adventist missions. The 1921 Statistical Report, for the first time, recorded more members outside North America (99,333) than within it (98,755). Even then, the primary source for funds and personnel remained North American. An excellent example of this expansion can be seen in the development of Adventism in Asia, especially in China. Following Abram La Rue's time in Hawaii (1884) and Hong Kong (1887), the first wave of Adventist missionaries arrived in China in 1902. Another wave of doctors and nurses came two years later, and soon, a publishing house (1905), followed by more intentional efforts for schools and clinics. Adventism rapidly spread across China, forming the Asiatic Division (1909), the Far Eastern Division (1919), and the China Division (1931). During World War I, as Adventist missionary efforts were paralyzed across much of the rest of the world, Adventism invested heavily in

Asia, especially China, which would pay rich dividends through the first half of the twentieth century.

Clarence and Minnie Crisler were one missionary couple who typified the shift of resources from North America to the world field. Both had been trusted confidants and literary assistants of Ellen White. After her death, they needed to find new employment. From the floor of the General Conference session, President A. G. Daniells asked if they were willing to serve as missionaries, even to China. They agreed to go. After their arrival, the duo, with their daughter, quickly fell in love with the people of China, mastering the language and finding ways to adapt the Adventist message to the people. Clarence, for his part, was deeply loved and was remembered by one person for writing Bible promises in Mandarin on the inside of candy wrappers. As someone who had worked closely with Ellen White, he pointed to her example and legacy as a reason for empowering Bible women. Both Clarence and Minnie believed in the power of print, with Minnie translating and editing Adventist periodicals and tracts and Clarence developing a network of colporteurs and expanding the Adventist publishing enterprise across Asia. Tragically, Clarence died during one of his missionary adventures on his way to Tibet, but his legacy inspired many others to follow in his footsteps.

Resources

Knight, George R. *A Search for Identity: The Development of Seventh-day Adventist Beliefs*. Hagerstown, MD: Review and Herald Publishing Association, 2000.

Marsden, George M. *Fundamentalism and American Culture*. 2nd ed. Oxford: Oxford University Press, 2006.

Numbers, Ronald L. *The Creationists*. Berkeley: University of California Press, 1992.

"Report of the 1919 Bible Conference." Office of Archives, Statistics, and Research. Accessed March 18, 2025. https://tinyurl.com/yc2twt7n.

Ruud, Niq. "George McCready Price and Seventh-day Adventism's Influence on the Rise of Modern Creationism." *Church History and Religious Culture* 104, no. 1 (2024): 118–30. doi: https://doi.org/10.1163/18712428-bja10066.

Discussion Questions

1. How did early Seventh-day Adventists deal without a living prophet? How did her death impact the denomination? If you had been alive back then, how would you have responded to the news that Ellen White had died?

2. How did World War I impact Adventism? How did Adventists respond to the war? How did Christianity become militarized?
3. Explain fundamentalism and modernism. How did they impact Christianity? Why did Adventists identify with the fundamentalist movement?
4. How did discussions at the 1919 Bible Conference impact how individuals interpreted the writings of Ellen G. White?
5. Why were Adventists in the 1920s and 1930s concerned about accreditation, and how did the church respond to changing standards in education?
6. The 1920s witnessed a pivotal shift as Adventist membership increased outside North America. In what ways would this change impact Adventism?

CHAPTER 9

Movements Toward Unity

Between September and November 1929, the New York Stock Exchange crashed, losing more than half of its value. Panic set in on October 24, 1929, when it lost 12 percent, or nearly $14,000,000,000, in the valuations of its stocks. As prices gyrated, Adventists reminded anyone who listened to lay up treasure in heaven. One writer, Merlin L. Neff, interpreted the billions of dollars wiped out as a sign of the soon return of Christ. At the end of time, he wrote, "the stock markets will then have completely collapsed, for we read this description of that day: 'They shall cast their silver in the streets, and their gold shall be as an unclean thing' (Ez. 7:19)."[1]

The steep decline in stock market values placed pressure on the ever-expanding world church with its strong missionary focus. The 1930 Autumn Council tried to find resources to supply the far-flung mission fields. Despite the "time of depression," they listened to the "heart-rending" appeals for help. "After every possible source of supply was drawn upon," church officials turned in any surplus funds they could spare. According to Vice President W. H. Branson, they made up 94 percent of the requested funds. He commented, "To us it seems nothing short of a miracle of grace, that in such a time of depression as this the Advent people can thus keep up a constant and nearly uniform flow of means to the great mission lands of earth."[2] Church leaders were too impatient for Jesus to return to let economic contractions force them to pull back from supporting a global network of missionaries and missionary projects, even though they had to tighten their belts. In 1928, the denomination received $6,400,000 in tithe revenue; by 1933, this amount declined to $4,500,000. This loss in revenue came at a time when the church was expanding by 100,000 members, with growth outside North America at 175 percent greater than in

1. Merlin L. Neff, "CRASH! Crash! Goes the Stock Market," *Signs of the Times* 56, no. 48 (December 3, 1929): 2.

2. W. H. Branson, "A Great Forward Movement," *Review and Herald* 107, no. 59 (November 27, 1930): 4.

North America. This crisis happened as the percentage of giving from North America for mission work declined from 67 percent to 60 percent, effectively causing hardships as the work of the church around the globe continued to grow.[3]

By 1933, W. H. Williams, General Conference undertreasurer, described how the Depression prevented them from adding institutions or making large expenditures for equipment. "We have not stopped our evangelistic advance, and never had God worked so mightily for His people in foreign lands, and thousands are being born into this truth." He added: "It may be this thing which we call depression is God's way of readjusting the purpose and spirit of His people to new levels of devotion and sacrificial service. God is shaping events in the mission fields. The developments which are taking place can be explained on no other grounds than that God has set His hand to the finishing of the work. Our great concern at this time is to *hold our mission lines and let God work*. This should be our watchword, and become a household phrase in every Seventh-day Adventist home."[4]

The following year, *Review* editor F. D. Nichol (1897–1966) urged Adventists not "to become discouraged over the demoralized condition of the world—the chaos of international relations, the difficulty in maintaining budgets in view of the depression," which he characterized as a denial of one's faith. "Our belief calls for us to gather courage from catastrophe and richness of faith from the bankruptcy of the world."[5] Church leader M. E. Kern (1875–1961) added, "Neither the great War, which engulfed the whole world twenty years ago, nor the great depression, which followed after, has stopped the onward march of the Advent message in its saving mission for a lost world."[6]

During the 1930s, the Adventist missionary effort advanced worldwide in new and creative ways. One example of creative mission work is found in the life of Leo and Jessie Halliwell, who arrived in Brazil in 1921 and spent the next thirty-seven years in missionary work there.

3. Richard W. Schwarz and General Conference of Seventh-day Adventists Department of Education, *Light Bearers to the Remnant: Denominational History Textbook for Seventh-day Adventist College Classes* (Mountain View, CA: Pacific Press Publishing Association, 1979), 405.

4. W. H. Williams, "Hold Our Mission Lines—This Our Watchword," *Review and Herald* 110, no. 25 (June 22, 1933): 1.

5. F. D. Nichol, "For Such a Time as This," *Review and Herald* 111, no. 27 (July 5, 1934): 4.

6. M. E. Kern, "The Secretary's Report," *Review and Herald* 115, no. 24 (May 31, 1936): 59–61.

South America

Adventism began in Brazil under the most unlikely circumstances. A young man named Borchardt committed a crime and ran away from his hometown, finding a job on a ship. He met some Adventist missionaries who asked for the address of someone to whom they could send literature. He gave them the address of his stepfather. A few years later, his stepfather received a package with Adventist literature. Initially he was fearful about receiving a package he might have to pay a delivery fee for. Eventually a drunk man named Dressler offered to pay the delivery fees for the magazine. He sold the literature that he received from the International Tract Society of Battle Creek, using the profits to buy rum. Eventually some of the literature fell into the hands of Wilhelm (Guilherme) Belz (1835–1912).[7] Despite opposition from his family, "Father" Belz began to keep the Sabbath alone in the woods. Eventually a whole company of family and neighbors joined him. When Frank Westphal arrived in 1894, he baptized and organized these believers into Brazil's first Seventh-day Adventist congregation.[8]

Adventist work in Brazil rapidly expanded between the late 1890s and the early 1930s with the founding of schools, publishing houses, and missionary centers. The Halliwells' most significant work began seven years after they arrived in Brazil. In December 1928, they were called to serve in the Amazon jungle. Before their arrival, colporteurs selling literature had gone ahead as an "advance guard" preparing the way. During their 1930–1931 furlough, at the height of the Depression, they raised $5,400 to build a 33-feet-by-10-feet (10 meters by 3 meters) boat. Leo, who had trained to be an engineer, went to a primitive boatyard to personally supervise the construction. On July 4, 1931, they dedicated and launched their first missionary boat, the *Luzeiro*. As they traveled up and down the Amazon and its tributaries, they watched for the telltale white flag that alerted them to the sick who needed medical assistance.

The Halliwells' ministry marked a new kind of creative evangelism. Jessie, who had trained as a nurse, conducted health clinics as they went along. At times, this meant quinine injections to fight malaria or, on other occasions, vaccination clinics to inoculate against smallpox. At other times, they held

7. Brazilian White Center–UNASP, "Belz, Guilherme (Wilhelm) (1835–1912)," in *Encyclopedia of Seventh-day Adventists*, January 29, 2020, https://tinyurl.com/3mjmnw2r.

8. F. W. Spies, "Brazilian Union Conference," *Review and Herald* 97, no. 39 (September 23, 1920): 12. Spies's story is quite different from the narrative of the article cited in the previous note.

evangelistic meetings on the river. As smaller boats tied up to their larger boat, Leo set up his lantern slide projector, the Amazonian version of the drive-up movie theater. Jessie delivered thousands of babies during their time in the jungle. This creative form of health evangelism was incredibly effective. Before they left Brazil for their home in the United States, they had support from the Brazilian government and a fleet of thirty-seven vessels.

Their missionary philosophy is worth examining in detail:

> Although we were officially missionaries, we saw at once the diseases rampant on the Amazon and we knew that we had first to concentrate on making these people well before we could hope to convert them to any meaningful religion. We had not come to impose by force or fear our ideas or culture or dogmas; we had come to help other human beings. This was our assignment. To do this we had to become a part of the ways and the lives of these people. We learned their language and customs and traditions; we became truly Brazilian. We thought, spoke, even dreamed in Portuguese.[9]

This "blend of medicine and faith" advanced the best of both modern medicine and the Adventist message. It enabled Adventism to become enculturated into the local people's lives. They rejected colonialist assumptions about "civilization," noting that such assumptions were, at best, "a matter of comparison and definition."[10] As their work grew, they sought to empower the local people and train them to take over and provide leadership.

Economic Downturn

Before 1885, most Adventist work in the United States had been in rural areas. As American cities expanded, Adventists began City Missions that sought to bring their message to urban America. The City Mission often housed colporteurs, evangelists, and health-care workers in a building with a meeting room. City life was noisy, polluted, busy, and somewhat dangerous. The ideal situation coupled the City Mission with a retreat center in a more rural setting. In Chicago, under J. H. Kellogg's inspiration, the Lifeboat Mission ministered to people without homes in the inner city, while the outpost health retreat was

9. Leo B. Halliwell and Jessie Halliwell, *Light in the Jungle: The Story of Leo and Jessie Halliwell's Mission Along the Amazon*, abridged ed. (Mountain View, CA: Pacific Press Publishing Association, 1959), 10–11.

10. Halliwell and Halliwell, *Light in the Jungle*, 87, 102.

in suburban Hinsdale. Similar institutions were founded around the world. City living was never the ideal. Those involved in City Missions never intended to live in the city and raise their families there. By the 1920s, most Adventists lived in rural or suburban areas. However, the bleak economic realities of the 1930s drew Adventists back to the cities. In Germany, as early as 1926, the Rhineland Conference opened a Welfare Department. The phrase "welfare work" became extremely popular in Adventist literature from 1930 onward.[11] Dorcas Societies were formed in local churches to do welfare work. The president of the European Central Division, H. F. Schuberth (1868–1961), stated that these societies enabled the church to "bring the rich into closer contact with the poor, as they receive the clothing and food given by the benevolent and disperse them among the needy and the unfortunate."[12]

The General Conference Minority Committee recommended that "welfare work" be "fostered by the Home Missionary Departments of the General, union and local conferences." Their report came to the 1931 Autumn Council, which voted to create a Seventh-day Adventist Welfare Society with chapters in local churches and conferences. These societies were to "render temporary aid to families in real need, along the lines of furnishing clothing, bedding, fuel, and food." They also connected families with housing and financial assistance. Within a year, 311 such societies sprang up, "bringing relief to many in distress."

Some of the most active work was done under the auspices of the Negro Department, which reported that black Adventists were some of the most active in conducting relief work. Some had opened health clinics and searched for other opportunities to meet the needs of those around them.

Rise of Nationalism

War reparations and the Great Depression left Germany vulnerable to extremism. It was difficult for people to obtain food, clothing, and employment. There was a great need for hope and change. This need was filled by a young and charismatic nationalist, Adolf Hitler (1889–1945), who quickly rose to power as the leader of the Nazi Party. He became chancellor in 1933 and took the title of Führer und Reichskanzler in 1934.

11. Ashlee Chism, "Adventists and the City/Country Living," in *Encyclopedia of Seventh-day Adventists*, January 3, 2024, https://tinyurl.com/9nmdttrf.

12. H. F. Schuberth, "Central European Division," *Review and Herald* 107, no. 28 (June 5, 1930): 104–5.

In the following years, some Adventist leaders in Germany began to advocate for Hitler as a friendly voice whom Adventists should trust. H. F. Schuberth attended the 1933 Annual Council and shared with his fellow church leaders his unabashed support for Hitler: "It is marvelous what changes this new German government has created in seven months."[13] He described how much help Hitler had given to Adventists by allowing them to continue their nursing and welfare work independently when other churches that had refused offers to consolidate under the Nazi plan were shut down. Repeating Nazi propaganda, he noted that, thanks to the new government, "improper magazines and atheistic books" were "banned or burned," and "a religious wave has swept the country." Continuing to give voice to the Nazi viewpoint, he added that he had not seen any persecution of the Jews and that such stories were from people trying to misrepresent Germany. "Something had to be done to free Germany from the Jewish influence," he added.[14] From a later perspective, such observations were shortsighted, repulsive, racist, and ugly.

Hulda Jost, leader of the Adventist welfare work in Germany, developed a plan to cooperate with the German Welfare Department, and the West German Union adopted her plan. By mid-1934, she had organized a network across Germany with support from all three German unions. She then petitioned to be recognized by the Nazi government, allowing her to solicit donations and assimilate freed prisoners upon their return to society. She persuaded the seven thousand Adventist members in Germany to mend clothes, hand out raincoats, and provide basic medical care. She obtained a property south of Berlin as a halfway house and hostel. During its first full year, forty-three thousand Germans received a place to sleep and a warm meal.

The rise of the Nazi Party at first seemed to be a setback for the church as it banned all private schools. However, it was not long before the Seventh-day Adventist Church became a constituent member of the National Socialist People's Welfare program. Yet even this initial support wasn't enough. The Nazis began to require government employees to work on Saturday and banned independent publications as they tightened their grip upon the country. G. W. Schubert noticed that when a Methodist bishop in America praised the Nazis, the Methodists in Germany were granted more privileges.[15] Hulda Jost would be just such an Adventist evangelist. She made her case for supporting Hitler

13. "Praise Bestowed on Hitler's Rule," *Battle Creek Enquirer,* October 22, 1933, 5.

14. "Praise Bestowed," 5.

15. For Methodist reactions to the Nazi regime, see Mark Tooley, *Methodism and Politics in the Twentieth Century* (Fort Valley, GA: Bristol House, 2012), and Joe Loconte, *The End of Illusions: Religious Leaders Confront Hitler's Gathering Storm* (Lanham, MD: Rowman & Littlefield, 2004).

on her lengthy journey across America to the 1936 General Conference session held in San Francisco. She spoke some 140 times, accompanied by her interpreter, Louise Kleuser.

At first, things appeared to be going well. However, when Jost and Kleuser reached Chicago, the German consul organized a meeting with the "Friends of the New Germany." Attendees had to sign a statement with a swastika at its head, declaring, "I acknowledge the leadership principle according to which the league is being directed." This "leadership principle" was effectively a personal pledge of loyalty to Hitler. Signers declared that they were not part of any secret society, were of Aryan descent, and had no Jewish or African blood. Jost's participation and speaking at this event was a strong political statement. As she told the Associated Press: "Hitler has devoted his whole strength and power to the reconstruction of Germany. . . . He wants peace with all nations, but also wants to return unto Germany and the German people the mantle of self-respect which they lost at the close of the World War. The German people have implicit faith in their leader."[16] When pressed about rumors of Jewish persecution, she replied: "Communism more than anything else is to blame for the condition of Jews in Germany today."[17]

Adventist reports emphasized Jost's welfare work; public newspapers stressed her support of Hitler. Her interpreter, Louise Kleuser, wrote to church president J. L. McElhany that these speeches were increasingly becoming political rallies. When Jost came to speak at the Boulder Sanitarium, an administrator asked her just to share the gospel and leave Hitler out of it. But she was unable to do so. In a report she sent back to Hitler, she boasted that in response to queries about potential war and whether Adventists were outlawed: "It is to me a very great pleasure that in every case I was able to stand up for Germany's honor, justice for Germany, and German interests."[18] Unbeknownst to her, while she was in America, the German government began to crack down on Adventists. When she returned, Hitler refused to meet with her. Then, the Propaganda Ministry blamed an anonymous letter published in the *Washington Post* on Adventists and used it as a reason to crack down further on Adventists. Jost did win some concessions. When the Gestapo was about to crack down on Adventist nurses, she convinced the Propaganda Ministry that Adventist nurses should be left alone. The German church narrowly avoided

16. "Meeting Hears Hitler Praised," *Detroit Free Press*, April 11, 1936, 5, https://tinyurl.com/34ehj385.

17. "Flashes of Oregon Events," *Roseburg (OR) News Review*, April 30, 1936, 1.

18. Hulda Jost, letter dated April 30, 1936, and addressed to "My Dear Herr Fuehrer." Quoted in full in Roland Blaich, "Selling Nazi Germany Abroad: The Case of Hulda Jost," *Journal of Church and State* 35, no. 4 (Autumn 1993): 813–14.

being banned by the Gestapo. The Adventists in Germany saw themselves walking a dangerous and narrow path fighting for their very existence.

Jost's interpreter believed she was playing with fire. She wrote to McElhany, "I feel she may bring to us in the future far more embarrassment than we can trust our brethren right close up to the problem in Europe to now see."[19] She was also concerned that Jost was far too preoccupied with justifying Hitler's actions, especially about the Jews, stating that they only got what they deserved, a somewhat ironic twist for a woman who started her church service in welfare ministry. Jost was the most visible of the Adventist leaders who promoted Hitler, but she was typical of the approach Adventists took in Germany at the time. Jost died in her forties in March of 1938 while on a goodwill tour to Scandinavia, still working on a plan to meet with Hitler to seek tolerance for Adventists. She never lived "to see the true face of Nazism."

Hulda Jost

Jost's relationship to the Nazi state was part of the German Adventist Church's adaptation to the "new order." Adaptation was followed by explicit support for the Nazi government and collaboration with it. The German Adventist Church removed offensive literature, including *The Great Controversy*, from the shelves of church libraries. They even persuaded the General Conference in Washington, DC, to adopt a policy against publishing anything critical of Nazism or fascism. By 1943, church leaders were urging their members to support Germany's total war effort even if it required them to do their "duty" on the Sabbath. After the war, church leaders defended their actions as the only way to preserve the church, but what they meant by "the church" was the denominational structure. With the hindsight of seventy years, it appears that the church leaders chose to preserve the institutional structure at the expense of their loyalty to God.[20]

Theological Education

The need for a more organized ministry led to the development of the Ministerial Department and efforts to make the Adventist ministry more professional.

19. Blaich, "Selling Nazi Germany Abroad," 825.

20. Roland Blaich, "Render unto Caesar: German Adventists and the Nazi State," *Adventist Today* 33, no. 1 (Winter 2025): 8–11.

Such efforts led the 1932 Autumn Council to vote to start a graduate program in theology at one of the North American colleges. The graduate program entailed one year of advanced study supplemented by five or six months of field evangelism. The summer of 1934 witnessed the birth of the graduate program, starting with a series of summer sessions held at Pacific Union College. The classes were to be taught in the summers on a rotation basis at other Adventist college campuses. Students included academy and college teachers and a few ministers and editors. The faculty for this venture came from Adventist colleges.

Forty students began classes in June 1934. M. E. Kern, General Conference secretary, served as acting dean. Other faculty included George McCready Price, well-known for his views on science and religion, and historian William Landeen. Summer sessions at Pacific Union College continued over three years. At that point, the General Conference Committee voted to organize a theological seminary in Takoma Park, Maryland, which was easily within the reach of the General Conference officers. The original program featured thirty hours of classes and a choice of two majors and three minors (including options for biblical languages), a research component or thesis, and practical training. Students had to pass a written qualifying exam early in their program and a comprehensive oral examination before graduating.

The new seminary held classes in the old Review and Herald cafeteria. Four years later, they dedicated a new building with space for 150 students. When D. E. Rebok (1897–1983), a returned missionary and veteran administrator, became president of the seminary in 1943, it added a division of Missions and Christian Leadership. Many more classes were offered in various languages, especially after the outbreak of World War II, to help train missionaries for foreign service. Theological education would become a significant aspect of professionalizing and broadening a global church throughout the twentieth century.

New Methods of Evangelism

Another significant turning point was determining how Adventists should share their faith with others. The rapid changes after World War I meant that Adventists were confronted with new methods of communication, including the way people spent their leisure time. Most disconcerting was the rise of the radio, which many Adventists warned was positively dangerous. Motion pictures and theaters were seen as equally harmful. Over time, church leaders would find these methods less threatening as they discovered that they brought with them new opportunities for sharing one's faith.

Mobilizing Young People for Mission

Some of the earliest Sabbath-keeping Adventist publications were youth oriented. *The Youth's Instructor* and a hymnal designed for young people were each created in the 1850s. Organized youth work began when two teenagers, Luther Warren (1864–1940) and Harry E. Fenner (1862–1940), were walking along a country road in 1879. They talked about how they could mobilize the youth in their church in Hazelton, Michigan, to share their faith. They held weekly meetings to distribute tracts and papers, wrote missionary letters, and encouraged people to sign the temperance pledge (against the consumption of alcohol). Soon, girls were invited to join their missionary society.

The Student Volunteer Movement formed in the late 1800s and soon spread across Adventist college campuses. By 1900, nearly every Adventist school had a "band" or "chapter" that encouraged mission service both at home and abroad. Many members became missionaries themselves to different parts of the world. By 1907, these groups organized more formally as the Missionary Volunteers (often abbreviated simply as MV).

Under the leadership of Milton E. Kern, the Missionary Volunteer program was officially sanctioned. Kern also started a Junior Missionary Volunteer (JMV) program specifically for "active" youth aged ten to fifteen. Official work began with youth leaders in Colorado in 1909. The MV program adapted the watchword of the Student Volunteer Movement for Adventists: "The Advent Message to All the World in This Generation."

The Boy Scouts, begun in 1910, were another formative influence upon Adventist youth programs. By 1911, several Seventh-day Adventists started Scout-like clubs, including the Takoma Indians and the Woodland Clan (from Maryland). In 1919, Arthur W. Spalding formed the Mission Scouts for his own and his neighbor's children. The program became official when Harriet Holt (1891–1972) directed the Missionary Volunteer program in 1920. She was the first to introduce the Friend and Companion JMV classes and Comrade and Master Comrade for MV classes.

In 1928, C. Lester Bond (1888–1971) replaced Holt, and during his tenure he developed more levels and systematized the program. As early as 1928, an investiture ceremony took place, and Bond developed early manuals for these classes, announcing the first sixteen honors in 1928. During the 1920s, the idea of summer camps began. The earliest documented camp occurred in Australia in 1925. After a summer camp held at Idyllwild in the San Bernardino Mountains of California, church leaders purchased approximately fifteen acres for a permanent youth camp. Dubbed the "JMV Pathfinder Camp," it was later replaced by Pine Springs Ranch. In 1927–1928 John McKim (1890–1944), a Scoutmaster and a counselor at an early summer camp in Julian,

California, along with Willa S. Steen (1891–1964) and Guy E. Mann (1894–1978), youth director of the Southeastern California Conference, decided something should be done for the youth at the Anaheim church. McKim had a Boy Scout troop and now wanted to adapt these ideas to the Missionary Volunteer program, with its spiritual emphasis, to create a new kind of club. This first local "club" called themselves Pathfinders. Nearby, in Santa Ana, two other families, the Martins and Johnsons, started another Pathfinder club at the Santa Ana church. Some Santa Ana church members worried that they were "bringing the world into the church." They feared that activities such as crafts, games, nature studies, cycling, and field trips might distract young people. At one point, the church board requested that the Martins and Johnsons disband their club. However, the idea of Pathfinder clubs persevered, giving rise to the modern Pathfinder movement.

In the 1930s and 1940s, the preferred term for clubs was still JMV, with a strong emphasis on youth evangelism and missions. John H. Hancock (1917–2001) founded a Pathfinder club at the Riverside, California, church with the assistance of a La Sierra College student who directed the club. Unaware of a General Conference prohibition that youth clubs could only be named JMV and *not* Pathfinders, he designed a sleeve emblem that featured a triangle with the three sides representing the spiritual, physical, and social aspects of life. A shield in the center symbolized faith in Jesus, and a sword on top represented the Word of God.

After 1948, church leaders made a concerted effort to multiply Pathfinder clubs across North America. Henry T. Bergh (1918–2011) promoted Pathfinder clubs as a great way to reach young people in the local church and neighborhood. The slogan was "A Pathfinder club in every church!" Clubs spread worldwide and became particularly important in the South American Division.

The Boy Scouts began holding large international gatherings called jamborees in 1937. Smaller localized gatherings of Pathfinders and Missionary Volunteer groups held localized jamborees in the 1930s. The first weekend Pathfinder Jamboree was held for Fresno-area Pathfinders on October 15–16, 1949, at Camp Wawona. By 1950, the term "Comrade," which was increasingly associated with atheistic communists, was replaced with "Guide," with the highest level now referred to as the "Master Guide." Adventists adapted the jamboree to their own unique Pathfinder context, creating events with a strong spiritual focus. They also adapted the name and dubbed it a "camporee." The very first Pathfinder Camporee for all the Pathfinder clubs in a conference was held at Camp Winnekeag, Massachusetts, October 9–11, 1953. Attendees remembered listening to Adventist heritage stories around the campfire. Increasingly larger camporees have been held ever since, with about 60,000 attendees at the 2024 camporee in Gillette, Wyoming.

The 1920s witnessed a few experiments with the radio. The first Adventist to produce a radio broadcast was Bertram M. Heald (1884–1963), who in 1924 broadcast thirteen *Healthograms* from Boston on American Radio and Research Corporation station WGI. This program was also shared from New York City on WSAP. Subjects included "Will-Power," "Think," "Courage," "Nerves," "Worry," and "Faith." Heald wrote: "Our message is being broadcast from several points, and I believe there is nothing today that is more effective in hastening the kingdom. . . . Our responsibility is great in broadcasting. The air at once becomes saturated with the message. The audience may number into the millions. There is a great future in the radio in furthering the third angel's message. This should be the main reason for our becoming interested in it, for it would seem that of all our modern inventions for hastening the coming of Christ, this is one of the greatest."[21]

The first Adventist radio station was KFGZ, called "the Radio Lighthouse," in Berrien Springs, Michigan. Broadcasting began on October 8, 1924, with a musical program and inspirational lecture. One listener reportedly stated after listening to the songs and sermons: "How is it you people keep the seventh day? Your good sermons and the gospel songs have aroused my interest, and I am curious to know more about your beliefs."[22] As Adventists took their message to the airwaves, the potential for evangelism broke down the initial objections to the medium. From late 1924 through early 1925, Charles T. Everson (1874–1956) broadcast a series of evangelistic meetings in a temporary "tabernacle" in Portland, Oregon, becoming the first Adventist to "broadcast" an evangelistic series.

H. M. S. Richards (1894–1985) became Adventism's most famous radio "voice," making his initial debut in 1929 on KNX in Los Angeles. His *Tabernacle of the Air* included a daily religious broadcast carried live from his tabernacle to KMPC in Beverly Hills and KGER in Long Beach. In the 1930s, the name of the broadcast changed to the *Voice of Prophecy*, which also became the name of his ministry. Initially, church leaders were reticent to support such innovative measures, yet as a new generation of evangelists embraced the medium of radio during the 1930s and 1940s, the way Adventists did outreach began to change radically.

The age of tent evangelism was giving way to the airwaves, and even traditional evangelism was supplemented by new advertising methods to attract

21. B. M. Heald, "Radio Possibilities," *Review and Herald* 101, no. 36 (September 4, 1924): 13.
22. "The Message by Radio," *Review and Herald* 101, no. 48 (November 27, 1924): 19.

potential believers. John Ford, for example, brought in over 100 converts from a campaign in California and another 360 in another series in Arizona. In 1935, he became the General Conference's first officially sponsored radio speaker. John L. Shuler, Fordyce Detamore, and R. Allan Anderson also developed innovative forms of evangelism that took advantage of portable tabernacles or large evangelistic meeting halls. Shuler, in particular, encouraged listeners to make simple public decisions leading to progressive points of faith rather than waiting until the end of the meetings to make a total commitment. He pioneered the first Evangelistic Field School and authored a textbook on evangelism. Detamore reinforced his public meetings with a *Bible Auditorium of the Air*, a supplemental radio broadcast featuring a correspondence Bible school, merging traditional evangelism with the airwaves.

H. M. S. Richards

Adventist evangelists increasingly turned to the cities to evangelize immigrant groups. Adventists had successfully worked in the Midwest's large German and Scandinavian populations, most of whom were Protestants. Beginning in the early twentieth century, many immigrants were Catholic, coming from southern and eastern Europe. These newcomers primarily lived in the large cities of the Northeast, and Adventists had neglected them. Now, the church sought to make progress among the Poles and Italians, for example, in New York City. As the work of the Foreign Department for earlier immigrant groups declined, renewed efforts were made to conduct city evangelism with these recent immigrant groups. By 1941, the largest Italian-speaking Adventist congregation in the world was based in Chicago. Other significant areas of growth included Spanish-speaking Adventists, especially in the American Southwest, with accompanying educational programs. Over the twentieth century, the Spanish-speaking population grew significantly in North America. Similarly, in the 1930s, Adventists began to develop ministries among the various native peoples who had long preexisted immigrant settlers.

Global Conflict

The constant conflict and uncertainty about Japan's intentions in China ultimately led to the outbreak of war in 1937 when the Japanese sought to conquer China. As transportation facilities were attacked in air raids, travel became both uncertain and dangerous. Many missionaries lost all their belongings. Much of the educational work in China pivoted to Hong Kong. By mid-1939, the denomination lost properties and churches in China worth an estimated $400,000.[23] Church giving dropped dramatically, and occupying forces confiscated significant funds.

As formal hostilities in Europe erupted with the German invasion of Poland on September 1, 1939, Adventists had to confront the reality of military service again. The Medical Cadet Corp (MCC) began in the 1930s in anticipation of the outbreak of hostilities to provide noncombatant roles for Adventist youth. The training included drills, first aid, military courtesies, defense against chemical weapons, and basic knowledge of anatomy and physiology. It was offered at nearly every Adventist secondary school and college.

Adventists again found themselves on both sides of World War II. Many missionaries were left stranded, and not a few were interned for part or most of the war. Many missionaries in POW camps faced starvation, and despite heroic efforts, some died. Rapid inflation occurred as resources were allocated for the war effort. As the war ended, General Conference leaders estimated it would take more than three to eight times the US$2,700,000 invested initially to build denominational properties across China and the Far East. Among complete losses were the division headquarters in Singapore, the college in Nanking, the Shanghai publishing house, and several academies. More significant losses were incurred in Europe, with church properties and human lives lost during the conflict.

During the war, the Japanese treatment of Adventists varied as they expanded throughout Southeast Asia, through the Philippines and the islands of the South Pacific. Kata Ragoso (1902–1964) directed efforts to rescue Allied personnel, even at the risk of his own life. As the Allied leaders retreated, officials ordered the mission launch *Portal* to be burned. Instead, Solomon Island church members hauled the boat into a small creek, where they camouflaged it. The engine was completely dismantled, and pieces were scattered among believers for safekeeping. When the missionaries returned several years later, they were amazed to find the *Portal* entirely back together, seaworthy, and

23. Schwarz, *Light Bearers*, 375.

Desmond Doss

Desmond Doss (1919–2006) represented the highest ideals of a noncombatant soldier in a combat situation.

Born in Lynchburg, Virginia, to an Adventist mother and an alcoholic father, Doss witnessed an event that changed his life. His father pointed a gun at his uncle. His mother, Bertha, stepped in front of the gun and demanded it from his father. She then handed it to Desmond and told him to hide it. After the incident, he decided that he would never touch a gun again. Under his mother's influence, he developed a close relationship with God and became deeply committed to the Ten Commandments and the Seventh-day Adventist Church.

Doss could have avoided military service as a shipyard worker with his Sabbaths off. Instead, he chose to enlist as a conscientious objector. However, he would often state that he was a conscientious cooperator. Because of his refusal to handle weapons and his commitment to the Sabbath, he was ridiculed and persecuted by his fellow soldiers and commanding officers. Deployed to the Pacific theater, he served as a medic with the Second Platoon, Company B, First Battalion, 307th Infantry Regiment, Seventy-Seventh Division. He distinguished himself in the battles of Guam and Leyte, receiving medals for his courage in caring for his fellow soldiers.

Desmond Doss

When his division was deployed in Okinawa, it received orders to attack the Maeda Escarpment, known to American soldiers as "Hacksaw Ridge." In 2016, well-known Hollywood actor Mel Gibson directed a movie on Doss's story with that name. After a week of intense fighting, Doss's company attacked the enemy on the ridge again on Sabbath, May 5, 1944. An enemy counterattack that day left most of the company dead or wounded. Doss was still on the ridge, seeking to save his buddies. He began to lower wounded soldiers forty feet off the ridge one by one. After lowering a soldier to safety, he returned to the battlefield to find "just one more." At the end of the day, it was estimated that he saved at least seventy-five men. While treating American soldiers, Doss encountered wounded Japanese soldiers, whom he also treated.

A week later, Doss was back on the ridge rescuing wounded men when he took a blast from a grenade to his leg. He began to crawl to safety, treating himself and many wounded soldiers he encountered. Nearing safety, he was shot in the arm by a sniper. He was evacuated from the battle on May 21.

Having received the praise of the soldiers in the Seventy-Seventh Division, "from generals to privates," Doss was awarded the highest honor that a United States soldier can receive: the Congressional Medal of Honor. He was invited to the White House and received his award personally from President Truman.

with a working motor. When Japanese officials ordered that Ragoso be shot for insubordination, with the firing squad in place, the officer was unable to utter the command to fire. Placed in prison, Ragoso and a companion were mysteriously delivered in circumstances described as miraculous. Ragoso returned to his village and continued efforts to save downed Allied aviators. In all, they rescued twenty-seven American pilots and 187 Australian and New Zealand soldiers.

In Europe, the conquest of Poland by Germany quickly led to the conquest in 1940 of Denmark, Norway, the Netherlands, Belgium, and France. The Balkans came under German control as Hitler prepared to attack Russia in 1941. As early as 1939, Nazi pressures led to the closing of 90 percent of Adventist churches in Romania. Before the war's end, some three thousand Romanian Adventists were jailed, serving twenty-five-year sentences. Dozens of Adventist families, seeking to avoid trouble, escaped ahead of the occupation. This was especially true in Belgium and France, where many still remembered the Great War of 1914–1918. So rapid was the German advance that Adventist churches and institutions only encountered minor destruction from occupying forces. The one notable exception was Poland, which faced significant destruction.

During the war, church members faced many hardships. Food and basic necessities were rationed. Dutch Adventists found that food rations were often distributed on the Sabbath, making it difficult to obtain assistance. Many church leaders were removed to labor or concentration camps. The cessation of war in Europe in May 1945 meant that in the ensuing economic crisis, Adventist workers often went hungry as they tried to reestablish the church's work, especially in Europe.

To help meet postwar needs, Adventists in North America gave liberally of both money and clothing. Special depots were established in New York and San Francisco, and some 2,800,000 pounds of clothing were shipped, and an additional $2,000,000 was raised for relief work during the 1940s. In 1946, a special Rehabilitation Offering brought in $1,000,000 to help replace lost mission launches, churches, schools, and publishing houses. This was an addition to over $4,000,000 set aside by the General Conference during the war for rebuilding efforts. The economic depression in Europe after World War II served as a catalyst for Adventists realizing the need for systematic relief efforts.

Captivity and Survival

At the 1946 General Conference session, church leaders reported that during the war years there had been "a greater loss of property, greater suffering, and more deaths than at any other point" in our church's history. The church in Asia especially "suffered much loss." In addition to the buildings, those caught in the war were unable to flee and found themselves "interned in the prison camps."[24]

Gus (1888–1944) and Norma (1896–1984) Youngberg were missionaries to Asia beginning in 1919. They spent significant amounts of time in Singapore and Borneo building up schools and the church's work, pioneering the work among the people of Sarawak. In 1940, they returned to the United States on furlough. While there, Gus received an urgent call to return, deciding that since the embassy would not issue visas for women and children, he would have to go by himself. Recognizing the danger, he wrote to the General Conference, who told him they could not advise him one way or the other. Ultimately, Gus prayed about it and chose to accept whatever fate resulted from his visa application. His visa was approved, but shortly after he arrived in British North Borneo, the Japanese invaded and placed him and other foreigners in the prison at Tanjong Aru army barracks. Soon, Gus and other prisoners were shipped to the infamous Kuching Japanese prison camp. While there, he became sick and died.

Gus Youngberg

John (1892–1959) and Olga (1897–1977) Oss were missionaries in China similarly trapped by war. The General Conference had evacuated most foreign missionaries from Shanghai in November of 1940, but the Osses chose to remain. Once the war began, the Osses were at first placed under house arrest by the occupying Japanese forces. Later, when they were put in a prison camp, Olga recalled being placed in groups of two hundred, with the men separated

24. Arthur W. Spalding, *Christ's Last Legion* (Washington, DC: Review and Herald, 1949), 614–16. Spalding notes, for example, the capture of eighty-seven Adventist missionaries in the Philippines during World War II, which included twenty-seven children.

from the women and children. At first, she was placed on latrine duty but later became the receptionist for the camp. While interned, the Osses shared their faith and held meetings. They reported how some of their Japanese captors had even become interested in their message. As the war drew to a close, their captors reduced the food they ate to only a handful of rice, without salt, three times a day. They were also allowed a cup of tea without sugar or milk. When they asked for salt, their captors gave it out in abundance and cut off the water supply to make the prisoners thirsty, offering them water to drink from the urinals. At the end of their time, John became sick, and they thought he would die. He was removed from the camp, and Olga had no idea where he was taken or if he was alive. After the war, she discovered him in a Shanghai hospital, nearly dead. Olga and her Chinese friends in Shanghai prayed for his healing, and he recovered.[25]

The time after the war was a new world. So much had changed. For many impacted by the horrors of the conflict, the postwar years were challenging times as people sought to rebuild or start anew. Despite the difficult times, the church participated in relief efforts and continued its evangelism. In America, which was largely unaffected by physical destruction, the postwar years became a time of expansion and economic prosperity. The church in America prospered and expanded along with the rest of the country. Many were glad to forget the horrors of the war years and focus on religious and theological issues, some of which brought significant tensions to the church.

Resources

Blaich, Roland. "Selling Nazi Germany Abroad: The Case of Hulda Jost." *Journal of Church and State* 35, no. 4 (Autumn 1993): 807–30.

Doukhan, J. B., ed. *Thinking in the Shadow of Hell: The Impact of the Holocaust on Theology and Jewish-Christian Relations*. Berrien Springs, MI: Andrews University Press, 2002.

Greenleaf, Floyd. *A Land of Hope: The Growth of the Seventh-day Adventist Church in South America*. Tatuí, Brazil: Casa Publicadora Brasileira, 2011.

Moskala, Jiří, and John Peckham, eds. *God's Character and the Last Generation*. Nampa, ID: Pacific Press Publishing Association, 2018.

25. Transcripts of 1946 General Conference Audio Recordings, https://tinyurl.com/4uxud9ms (1:38 and onward) and https://tinyurl.com/4y6zu5kb (1:26 and onward).

Discussion Questions

1. What were some of the effects on the Seventh-day Adventist Church of the stock market collapse in 1929?
2. What was unique about Jessie and Leo Halliwell's ministry in the Amazon?
3. Why did Seventh-day Adventists in Germany develop an alliance with the Nazi government?
4. What were some of the new developments in Adventist evangelism between 1920 and 1945?
5. What challenges did the Seventh-day Adventist Church face during World War II?

CHAPTER 10

Doctrinal Refinements and Controversies

During the post–World War II era, the denomination continued the relief efforts that had begun during the Great Depression. This set the stage for organizing the Seventh-day Adventist Welfare Service (SAWS) in 1956. It also was a time for further refining Adventist beliefs, initiating new projects to educate the church and the wider public, and sometimes dealing with controversy. The era witnessed a remarkable global expansion of the church. Between 1945 and 1960, the denomination's membership increased from 576,378 to 1,200,000 members, doubling its size. As the church grew much more quickly around the globe, the proportion in North America diminished from 36 percent to 26 percent even as it remained the critical economic powerhouse behind the denomination. In 1945, 58.58 percent of tithe originated from North America, versus 55.6 percent in 1960.

Television Ministry

Initially, conservative Christians, including Adventists, were skeptical about new forms of communication and entertainment. However, Adventist evangelism moved beyond radio to embrace television in the post–World War II era. On May 21, 1950, Adventist pastor William A. Fagal stated that he was "downright scared" when the stage lights glared in his face for the first time. With hardly any funding, this local church pastor could not even pay for either actors or scripts, so he appealed to his own local church members to volunteer on set. The stress was so great that during the first three months, Fagal reportedly lost forty pounds. Sixty-six people responded during the first month of programming requesting Bible studies, and a correspondence Bible school was formed. During the first three months, thirteen telecasts were broadcast over WJZ-TV at 9:30 a.m. each Sunday. Fagal used a "parable" format, with a story presenting an everyday problem with the Bible's solution. After "considerable discussion," General Conference leaders opted to underwrite the program for six months, with Fagal eventually devoting himself full time to the project.

William and Virginia Fagal on the set of *Faith for Today*, 1960

On December 3, 1950, *Faith for Today* became the first regularly scheduled television program sponsored by a religious denomination, originating from New York's American Broadcasting Company's studios.[1] At the end of the trial period, General Conference leaders decided to continue their support.

Another Adventist pastor, George Vandeman, laid plans to put together an Adventist television broadcast in color. His first attempt in the late 1940s failed. Without adequate financial support, the project stalled, yet he persisted. He named the program *It Is Written*, a reference to the phrase used by Jesus when tempted in the wilderness. It finally hit the airwaves across thirteen stations on March 25, 1956. Vandeman began to air programs several weeks ahead of evangelistic meetings. In 1958, he conducted evangelistic series in Fresno, California, and Washington, DC, to follow up on contacts made through his programming. Combining the traditional evangelistic series with television and targeting large urban areas bore significant numbers of converts. Such successes meant that the broadcast soon grew internationally, becoming (in 1991) the first regularly scheduled American religious broadcast on Soviet television.

1. Donald W. McKay, "Two Decades of TV Progress: *Faith for Today* Celebrates Its Twentieth Birthday on May 21," *Ministry* 43, no. 5 (May 1970): 3–6.

During its heyday in the 1970s, the broadcast was ranked in the top fifteen of the nation's religious broadcasts.[2]

The 1952 Bible Conference

After World War II, the denomination's leaders held another major Bible Conference in 1952, just as in 1919 after World War I. It was described as a "great spiritual feast." The twenty-five speakers gave eighty-two presentations at the Sligo Seventh-day Adventist Church in Takoma Park, Maryland, September 1–13, 1952. This gathering was unique because it was the first major event to discuss Adventist theology after World War II, with 450 delegates representing every division of the worldwide church. Church president W. H. Branson (1873–1961) stated that the meetings were some "of the most important meetings in our history."[3] LeRoy Edwin Froom (1890–1974), noted Adventist author and educator, added that these meetings "would unquestionably go down in our history as a conspicuous landmark, a turning point in the onward sweep of the message."[4] Yet, unlike the 1919 Bible Conference, this meeting had no open discussion; everything was directed by the organizers. Thus, it seemed to be remarkably homogenous and uncontroversial, though there were a few exceptions.

The focus of the 1952 Bible Conference was the interpretation and application of Bible prophecy. As early as 1943, seminary teachers and other Bible teachers had participated in an informal Bible Study Fellowship that circulated papers for discussion, primarily on disputed prophetic topics. They shared their ideas and obtained feedback from other participants. Some specific concerns that arose during World War II were the identity of the king of the North in Daniel 11 and the nature of the final battle of Armageddon. The General Conference became suspicious of the Fellowship and shut it down in 1951. At the same time, the General Conference leadership saw the need for a more formal discussion of biblical themes.

Church leaders also felt threatened by questions about the historicity of Genesis and scientific proofs for the Bible. The broader fundamentalist move-

2. David Kelley, "George Vandeman; TV Evangelist Made Pioneering Broadcasts to Soviet Union," *Los Angeles Times*, November 4, 2000, https://tinyurl.com/yc57htb8.

3. General Conference of Seventh-day Adventists, *Our Firm Foundation; A Report of the Seventh-day Adventist Bible Conference Held September 1–13, 1952, in the Sligo Seventh-day Adventist Church, Takoma Park, Maryland* (Washington, DC: Review and Herald Publishing Association, 1953), 18.

4. LeRoy Edwin Froom, "Our Earliest and Latest Bible Conference," *Ministry* 25, no. 10 (October 1952): 4.

Adventist Snack Cakes

The early twentieth century saw a variety of innovators who created baked goods, notably cookies and other snack cakes. The most successful were Oather Dorris McKee (1905–1995) and Ruth McKee (1906–1989). The couple met while students at Southern Junior College. After marrying, O. D. McKee's energy and creativity kept them moving around. He was a natural salesman, while his wife, Ruth, had a good knack for business even though she was more soft-spoken and methodical. Together they were ambitious. For a time, he sold cars, worked as a farm manager, and delivered cakes; Ruth was a teacher. After the stock market crash in 1929, they, like many others, lost just about everything and had to start over. They invested in a small shop, Jack's Cookie Company, in Chattanooga, Tennessee, just trying to survive the Great Depression. Ruth devised a plan to put cream between the cookies, making the cookies softer and chewier. The couple sold the business to start over, relocating to Charlotte, North Carolina. After a short time, they sold their business and moved back to Chattanooga to be closer to their family.

In 1960, the McKees bought back the bakery in Chattanooga; in 1962 they renamed it McKee Baking Company. Shortly afterward, they named a product after their four-year-old granddaughter, Debbie. The bakery developed a strong foothold in the American South during the 1960s after the Little Debbie line was introduced. In 1991 the company became McKee Foods Corporation. The McKee family became major benefactors of Adventist philanthropic projects, heavily investing in Southern Missionary College (today Southern Adventist University). They supported the institution as it built and renovated its campus. The family endowed faculty positions and provided jobs at their factory for students looking to work their way through school. In the 1990s the McKee family sponsored the "Net '95" global evangelistic initiative that used new technology in outreach efforts for the denomination.

ment split soon after World War II. The more moderate group, formed under the leadership of Billy Graham, became known as evangelicals. In contrast, the fundamentalists continued to interpret the Bible very literally and tended to be more strict, intolerant, and judgmental. This divide would be mirrored within the Seventh-day Adventist Church. However, in the 1950s, the leadership of Adventism sought active dialogues with the more moderate evangelical leaders even though they had historically identified with the fundamentalist movement during the 1920s and 1930s.

Review editor F. D. Nichol believed that the denomination must take archaeology seriously to combat the threat of skeptical biblical scholarship. He wrote that Adventists "should do enough digging so that our doctrine of Bible

Francis D. Nichol

inspiration will be solidly planted on immovable foundations." At the 1952 conference, delegates discussed the "archaeological evidence for Bible inspiration" as well as "the relation of science to Adventist faith."[5] One of the presenters was Siegfried H. Horn (1908–1993), who had graduated the year before with a PhD in archaeology from the University of Chicago. In the face of skeptical biblical critics, his presentations affirmed that recent archaeological discoveries "have given us evidence which reveal the accuracy of the historical events narrated in the Bible." He concluded that the Bible must, therefore, be reliable.[6] Horn was eager to share with those at the 1952 Bible Conference the recently discovered Dead Sea Scrolls that "unmistakably prove that the Hebrew Bible of the days of Jesus was, without any variations, the Masoretic text."[7] Horn was a rising star within Adventism and would play a significant role in helping Adventism achieve respectability within the wider Christian world.

The topic that received the most attention was the sanctuary doctrine.

5. F. D. Nichol, "The Bible Conference," *Review and Herald* 129, no. 35 (August 28, 1952): 14.

6. S. H. Horn, "The Basic Date of the 2300-Year Period Confirmed by New Discoveries," *Review and Herald* 130, no. 18 (April 30, 1953): 8–9.

7. Siegfried H. Horn, "The Old Testament Text in Antiquity," *Ministry* 60, no. 11 (November 1987): 5.

This was in response to ongoing challenges to this doctrine through much of the first half of the twentieth century. The challenges came especially during the 1930s from A. F. Ballenger, L. R. Conradi, and other dissidents who left the denomination. The next most widely discussed topic pertained to signs of Christ's return. W. E. Read, General Conference field secretary, spoke about Armageddon, arguing that Armageddon wasn't a physical place but a time when spiritual forces fought one another. T. H. Jemison portrayed the final joy of the 144,000 with a strong perfectionist slant advocating what later became known as Last Generation Theology. The intense focus on the apocalyptic amounted to an updating and streamlining of how Adventists would understand end-time events after World War II. In many ways, this articulation of Adventist eschatology became normative into the twenty-first century.

Another important topic discussed in 1952 was the significance of preaching and evangelism. M. K. Eckenroth (1914–1975), a theological seminary professor and an evangelist for the General Conference Ministerial Association, gave three presentations entitled "Christ the Center of All True Preaching," affirming that Adventist preaching must always remain evangelistic in focus. Walter Schubert (1896–1980), secretary of the South American Division's Ministerial Association, shared insights about how to share the Adventist faith diplomatically in Roman Catholic contexts. He advocated cultural sensitivity, meaning that Adventists "must adapt the presentation of the truth in its form and substance to the Catholic mind and even to that of those who do not profess any religion at all." He encouraged Adventist evangelists to make favorable allusions to the "blessed Virgin Mary" and not to make the congregation sing hymns. A "lack of tact," he urged, "can ruin" the "success of meetings." He furthermore encouraged people to think of points they had in common with Roman Catholics, referencing Ellen White's quotation in *The Ministry of Healing*, which says that "Christ's method alone" would bring true success.[8] The Adventist message was beginning to be contextualized in new ways as Adventism continued to expand in new regions.

According to several participants, the most hotly debated topic centered on the presentations given by Edward Heppenstall (1901–1994), a young professor at La Sierra College. His series on law and gospel challenged participants to

8. Walter Schubert, "Addresses Given at the S. D. A. Bible Conference, Takoma Park, Maryland, September 11, 12, 1952: Evangelization of Apostolic Roman Catholics," trans. from Spanish by Leona Running (Washington, DC: Ministerial Association, 1952). Ellen White's quotation appears on p. 143 of *The Ministry of Healing* (Mountain View, CA: Pacific Press, 1905).

think in new ways about how Adventists understood the atonement and sanctification. Many Christians in the broader evangelical/fundamentalist world had become enamored with a dispensationalist view of the covenants (i.e., the "old covenant" belonging to the "Old Testament"). Now Heppenstall argued that both the old and new covenants belonged to an everlasting covenant, nudging the denomination away from the more legalistic and perfectionistic approach of Last Generation Theology. Initially, some found Heppenstall's talks startling, but he revised his material to make it more palatable, and his talks were eventually published with the rest of the conference proceedings.

The conference was also notable because of a presentation by Dr. John L. Trever (1916–2006), representing the National Council of Churches (NCC). He encouraged Adventists to take advantage of the newly released Revised Standard Version. Adventists would never join the NCC but remained in touch and sent observers to keep communication open with other denominations. Perhaps the most significant legacy of the 1952 conference was that denominational leaders recognized the need to embrace Bible scholarship and archaeology by providing credible resources from an Adventist perspective. In this vein, the most substantial and lasting contribution was the initiative to create a *Seventh-day Adventist Bible Commentary* (1954–1957). Under the leadership of the *Review and Herald* editor, F. D. Nichol, the Review and Herald Publishing Association assembled a team that included Julia Neuffer (1907–1998), Raymond F. Cottrell (1911–2003), and Don F. Neufeld (1914–1979), all of whom had advanced degrees in history or biblical studies.

The publication of the seven-volume commentary marked an important milestone in Adventist biblical interpretation. Most Adventist biblical studies in previous years had used a prooftext approach, most clearly evident in *Bible Readings for the Home Circle*, a popular book sold by colporteurs that contained topical Bible studies from an Adventist perspective. While this method provided a simple, biblical approach to various subjects in the Bible, it often ignored both the context of the individual verses and the broader theological meaning in the text. In reaction to this approach, modernism used the historical-critical method, which emphasized the historical and cultural background of the Bible but tended to ignore the spiritual and theological meaning of the text.

The *Seventh-day Adventist Bible Commentary* chose to use a grammatical-historical method of interpretation, which emphasized the meaning of the text in its historical setting. Its editorial policy often described various interpretations of the biblical material without stating the editor's preferences. It also chose not to contradict any of Ellen White's writings. The denomination's best scholars contributed to the commentary. Its publication was a defining moment for Adventism, showing it could confront the modern world and redefine itself by engaging with contemporary scholarship.

Overall, the 1952 meetings and new initiatives that came from them projected confidence in a world of doubt. After shutting down the Bible Study Fellowship, church leaders came to recognize the value of Adventist scholarship. As a result of the 1952 meetings, church leaders formalized ties between the church and scholars by creating the Office of Bible Research led by Walter E. Read (1883–1976).

Leroy Edwin Froom

Evangelical Dialogues

A series of discussions between Adventist and evangelical church leaders began when T. E. Unruh (1894–1982), president of the East Pennsylvania Conference, wrote to Dr. Donald Grey Barnhouse (1895–1960), the editor of *Eternity* magazine. He commended him for his radio sermons on righteousness by faith based upon the book of Romans. Barnhouse replied in astonishment that an Adventist minister would write such a letter "since, in his opinion, it was a well-known fact that Seventh-day Adventists believed in righteousness by works."[9] Since his boyhood, he had known Adventists, he added, so he believed their views about the nature and work of Christ were dangerous. He concluded his letter by inviting this unusual Adventist to lunch with him.

More formal discussions developed when Barnhouse commissioned Walter R. Martin (1928–1989), a consulting editor for *Eternity* magazine, to write a book about Adventists. Martin had already written books critical of Jehovah's Witnesses and the Christian Science Church. Barnhouse encouraged Martin to contact Unruh in order to communicate with the appropriate Adventist Church

9. T. E. Unruh, "The Seventh-day Adventist Evangelical Conferences of 1955–1956," *Adventist Heritage* 4, no. 2 (Winter 1977): 35.

officials. Unruh introduced Martin to Leroy Edwin Froom because Froom had recently published the four-volume apologetic *Prophetic Faith of Our Fathers*.

The first meeting occurred on March 8, 1955, in the General Conference headquarters in Takoma Park, adjacent to Washington, DC. Martin invited George E. Cannon to join them as a resource person for biblical exegesis. Cannon was a New Testament professor at Nyack Missionary College in New York. Froom invited Walter E. Read, a field secretary for the General Conference, whom church leaders had appointed to head up its Office of Bible Research. The two-day session resulted in the Adventists correcting many of Martin's misunderstandings. At the beginning of the second day, Martin expressed his new understanding of Adventists by dramatically extending his hand in fellowship to the Adventists. Those who participated agreed that the meetings needed to continue.

Additional meetings included Barnhouse; his son, Donald Grey Barnhouse Jr.; and Russell Hitt (Barnhouse's publishing associate). On the Adventist side, Froom and Read invited Roy Allan Anderson (1895–1985), editor of *Ministry*, the Adventist periodical for its clergy. At various points, additional Adventist Theological Seminary faculty members joined as the discussions continued through 1956. Unruh kept General Conference leaders closely informed about developments, and General Conference president R. R. Figuhr, despite initial hesitation, ultimately warmed to the initiative. Adventist leaders recognized that they needed to be more proactive in disarming and dissuading the wider public concerning their prejudices about Adventism.

In September 1956, Barnhouse published his revised assessment about Seventh-day Adventists in *Eternity* in an article titled "Are Seventh-day Adventists Christians?" He regretted that they had been "a much-maligned group of sincere believers" and now acknowledged them as "redeemed brethren and members of the body of Christ." Fellow Christians should not consider them as "utter heretics" like Jehovah's Witnesses, Mormons, or Christian Scientists. Martin followed up on this assessment with his own article a few weeks later, a twelve-page article titled "Seventh-day Adventism Today" published in *Our Hope*. He then wrote a more extended three-part report in *Eternity*. He reworked the material and published it in book form in 1960 under the title *The Truth About Seventh-day Adventism*.

This more positive appraisal shocked many evangelicals. Barnhouse estimated that he almost immediately lost one-quarter of the subscribers to *Eternity* magazine (although subscriptions returned to their previous level within a year). Still others, notably Louis Talbot, president of the fundamentalist Bible Institute of Los Angeles (BIOLA), believed that Barnhouse and Martin were "utterly wrong" and encouraged his fellow evangelicals to condemn Adventism.

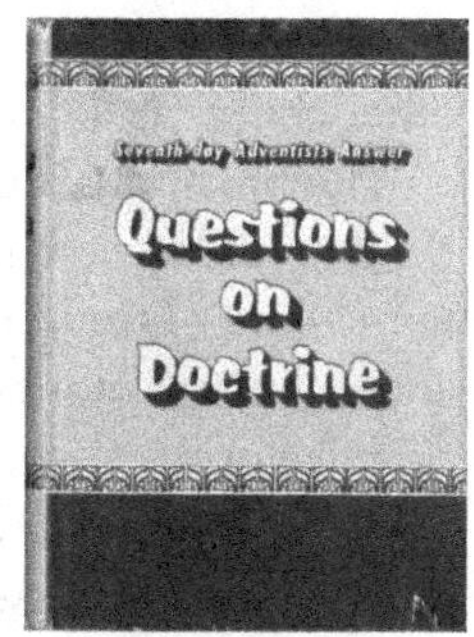

Questions on Doctrine

During the latter part of 1955, Froom, Read, and Anderson met with General Conference leaders about a proposal for a new publication that would express Adventist beliefs in language that the wider Christian public could easily understand. The goal was to use the 1931 Statement of Fundamental Beliefs as the basis for explaining Adventist doctrines. During their August 1955 discussions at Barnhouse's home, both parties agreed to publish books about Adventism that reflected their new understanding of one another. Adventists specifically would design their book to respond to forty-eight questions by evangelical leaders. By October 1956, the General Conference "heartily approved" the plan, and Froom, Read, and Anderson went to work. Through a careful review process, the manuscript was sent to 225 church leaders, teachers, and editors for constructive criticism. The 720-page book *Seventh-day Adventists Answer Questions on Doctrine* (often known as *QOD*) was released in November 1957. The forty-eight chapters were organized into ten categories, with three appendices of Ellen White's writings primarily concerned with the atonement and Christology. The world church would widely distribute the book as an authoritative explanation of Adventist beliefs. Additional questions raised by Martin's book *The Truth About Seventh-day Adventism* resulted in a further series of sixteen articles by various Adventist scholars in *Ministry* (subsequently published in book form as *Doctrinal Discussions*). In one of the articles, Edward Heppenstall pushed past exegetical criticisms to reframe the investigative judgment as a vindication of God before the universe rather than a human-centered judgment of behavior.[10]

The reports by Barnhouse and Martin of their meetings with Adventist leaders polarized evangelical opinion about Adventists. Within Adventism, the reaction to *QOD* was just as polarizing. Even as the meetings unfolded, Froom notified Figuhr that the topic of the sinful human nature of Christ was of particular concern. The evangelical leaders found early Adventist explanations on the subject, at best, inadequate and, at worst, heretical. Controversy on this topic within the denomination was not new. In 1949, church leaders revised

10. For a helpful overview, see Gilbert M. Valentine, "Adventist-Evangelical Conferences, 1955–1956," in *Encyclopedia of Seventh-day Adventists*, December 4, 2023, https://tinyurl.com/5pxjead8.

problematic aspects of *Bible Readings for the Home Circle* on the subject, and other church leaders similarly agreed to modify their writings.

The most vigorous opposition toward *Questions on Doctrine* came from M. L. Andreasen, who viewed a teaching of Christ's sinlessness as tantamount to a sellout of the very soul of Adventism. Andreasen alleged that statements about Christ's atonement at the cross being a "complete, perfect and final" sacrifice undermined Christ's priestly ministry in the Most Holy Place of the heavenly sanctuary, a teaching in place since 1844. Historians have demonstrated how Andreasen misunderstood and misquoted Froom, but Andreasen refused to back down and fanned the flames of opposition. Andreasen's theological system taught that the last generation must achieve sinless perfection. In this system, Christ needed a sinful human nature to be a role model for the last generation to overcome sin and thus accomplish a vindication of God's character and the plan of salvation before the universe. Such a human-centered stance placed Adventists at the center of the plan of salvation. For his part, Andreasen launched an aggressive program to undermine confidence in church leadership, ultimately losing his ministerial credentials (although they were restored posthumously).

Those loyal to Andreasen and his theology developed into a separate movement within Adventism, creating "prolonged alienation" and "two permanently warring factions."[11] Others, notably Robert Brinsmead (1933–), developed these views of perfectionism, sparking vigorous opposition from Heppenstall and Desmond Ford (1929–2019), who challenged Andreasen's perfectionistic theology. Another theologian attributed most of the "dissident" or "independent groups" that arose within Adventism in the last half of the twentieth century to the controversy concerning the atonement and the nature of Christ sparked by *Questions on Doctrine*.[12] Such controversies prevented the book from being translated. Once the initial printing had sold out, opponents blocked it from being reprinted.

Adventist Scholarship Matures

Many scholars involved with the 1952 Bible Conference and *Questions on Doctrine* played a significant role in the *Seventh-day Adventist Bible Commentary*

11. G. R. Knight, "Viewpoints," in *Seventh-day Adventists Answer Questions on Doctrine*, annotated ed. (Berrien Springs, MI: Andrews University Press, 2003), v.

12. As quoted in the Fiftieth Anniversary Conference, November 30, 2023, at Andrews University.

M. L. Andreasen

and *Seventh-day Adventist Bible Dictionary*. These reference works featured numerous recent archaeological discoveries from the early 1950s highlighted by Adventist scholars who worked under the influence of William Foxwell Albright (1891–1971), the "father of American biblical archaeology."[13] Alger Johns (1918–1972), Seigfried Schwantes (1915–2008), Wilson Bishai (1923–2008), and Leona G. Running (1916–2014) obtained doctoral degrees under Albright.

Raymond Cottrell, Donald Neufeld, and Julia Neuffer were the leading commentary editors, working under the direction of Francis D. Nichol. Nichol was the first Adventist to publish a scholarly article in *Church History* debunking claims about Millerite ascension robes. His work helped denominational leaders see the value of academic research for educating church members and the public.

The most significant archaeologist of this period was the brilliant Siegfried H. Horn, who was prolific both within and outside the church, showcasing some of the latest archaeological techniques and discoveries. As a German national serving as a missionary in the Dutch East Indies (Indonesia), Horn had been interned during World War II in Dutch and British prisoner-of-war

13. For background, see Lawrence T. Geraty, "Adventists and Archaeology," in *The Oxford Handbook of Seventh-day Adventism* (New York: Oxford University Press, 2024), 337–51.

camps. The camp authorities allowed the prisoners to request books. Horn's wife, Jeanne, a British national, sent him seventy-five scholarly works. He learned Hebrew, Greek, Latin, and French during his internment. He also wrote four books, read the Greek New Testament twenty-one times, and read the Hebrew Bible two and a half times. After the war, Horn studied at the Seventh-day Adventist Theological Seminary in the United States. He then earned a PhD from the University of Chicago and, beginning in 1951, taught and later served as dean of the Seventh-day Adventist Theological Seminary. During this time, he authored 433 articles and nine books.

Perhaps Horn's most significant contribution was to initiate and direct the Tall Ḥisbān archaeological site in Jordan. With support from Roger Boras (1926–2014) and Richard Hammill (1913–1997), he conducted the first Adventist-led archaeological dig in 1968. The site was chosen because it was thought to be the Heshbon mentioned in the exodus account as the first site in Transjordan taken by the Israelites (Num. 21:25–30). Horn continued leading excavations there in 1971 and 1973 and later served as senior adviser (1974, 1976), paving the way for other future archaeological digs and research, making the Seventh-day Adventist Church a significant player in modern archaeology through the early twenty-first century.

Such scholarly research meant that the denomination needed to create more opportunities for theological education. This necessitated a better-trained and better-equipped theological seminary, which continued to grow and expand through the 1950s. Beginning in 1957, the seminary expanded its offerings to include education, history, and speech courses. Under the name Potomac University, it was located on the campus of what was then Washington Missionary College (WMC). It quickly became apparent that the WMC campus could not accommodate expansion. In 1962, the seminary was moved to the campus of Emmanuel Missionary College in Michigan, and the combined institution was named Andrews University after J. N. Andrews, the first official Seventh-day Adventist overseas worker.

Also, in 1957, Philippine Union College became the first non-American Adventist institution under the General Conference to offer master's degrees. Church leadership also created the Geoscience Research Institute in 1957 to foster research into issues concerning science and religion and to seek academics interested in evidence for a literal creation.

In the United States, military personnel returning from World War II and the Korean War received money for education from the GI Bill. Young men who had not previously considered going to college due to financial constraints found they could receive a college education paid for by the US government.

Many veterans took advantage of this program. Their advanced training facilitated the growth of the middle class in the United States.

As life normalized after the war, Adventist veterans flooded Adventist college campuses. New standards necessitated a professionalization of Adventist pastors and teachers, creating the need for higher education and more graduate faculty. Adventist biblical scholars now featured research that drew the attention of scholars outside the denomination. Evangelical scholars wished to know more about what Adventists believed, prompting, at times, controversial, poignant conversations about Adventist identity. The Adventist denomination was maturing and changing at the same time.

Resources

General Conference of Seventh-day Adventists. *Our Firm Foundation; A Report of the Seventh-day Adventist Bible Conference Held September 1–13, 1952, in the Sligo Seventh-day Adventist Church, Takoma Park, Maryland.* Washington, DC: Review and Herald Publishing Association, 1953.

Nam, Juhyeok. "Reactions to the Seventh-day Adventist Evangelical Conferences and Questions on Doctrine 1955–1971." PhD diss., Andrews University, 2005.

Unruh, T. E. "The Seventh-day Adventist Evangelical Conferences of 1955–1956." *Adventist Heritage* 4, no. 2 (Winter 1977): 35–46.

Weeks, Howard B. *Adventist Evangelism in the Twentieth Century.* Washington, DC: Review & Herald Publishing Association, 1969.

Discussion Questions

1. What does the development of Seventh-day Adventist television ministries tell you about the church's relationship to popular communication media?
2. What were some of the most significant developments in the church that became evident at the 1952 Bible Conference?
3. What do you think? Were the evangelical dialogues of the late 1950s a positive development or were they problematic?
4. What effects might be expected in the church from the maturing of Adventist scholarship?

CHAPTER 11

Institutions in the Late Twentieth Century

Institutions dominated the resources, time, and energy of the Adventist Church after 1960. The administrative structure of the church represented a significant institution in itself, but the church included publishing, educational, and medical institutions. One of the best examples of this institutional focus is the content of the *Mission Quarterly*, which began in 1912, and the *Mission Spotlight* programs from the 1970s and 1980s.[1] Each aimed to highlight the needs of institutions in a specific area of the world. At the end of each quarter's study lessons, the Thirteenth Sabbath special offering was taken to support institutions in the chosen geographic area. The promotional material described schools, clinics, and hospitals worldwide and urged church members to give to meet their needs. Sometimes, there was a personal story connected to the institution, but often, the need for new buildings was the central focus of the material.

As the church multiplied in the last half of the twentieth century, the most significant growth happened outside North America, a testament to the global impact of the Adventist Church. This growth was not just a result of foreign missionaries but was a collective effort of local leaders and members who were actively involved in outreach and took the reins of leadership. Impatience for the coming of Jesus was often an explicit motivator for growth.

Emphasizing the role of local leaders and members made them feel empowered and essential to the church's mission. Public and personal evangelism were primarily responsible for growth, but the supportive role of publications and schools remained crucial. Medical institutions were also a significant factor, though more indirectly. In Africa, Latin America, and other areas of high growth, the education of the children of new members took a high priority. The administrative institutions in each area took the lead in the founding of elementary schools, high schools (academies), colleges, and universities. Students

1. *Mission Spotlight* continues as a video production. Its recent programs often focus on personal and local church stories. See https://tinyurl.com/5d8a5e9y.

in the lower levels were encouraged to continue their education at the higher levels. Academies became feeder schools for colleges and universities.

With each new institution, the need for administrative oversight grew, posing a significant challenge for consistency and accountability throughout the world church. As the number of institutions increased, administrators found their time dominated by overseeing the institutions in their area of responsibility. This shifting focus was, at best, challenging, and many administrators struggled with the new responsibilities. Some resisted this trend, but their success was limited. In North America, the role of conference presidents underwent a significant transformation. Many of them, who were once known as the church's chief evangelists, now found their time dominated by administrative decisions as they chaired the boards of hospitals, schools, and publishing houses, a testament to the growing administrative oversight required by the expanding church. In addition, conference leaders were often caught between cultural expectations and sometimes even between various cultural groups within a constituency.

Changes in Education

The Seventh-day Adventist Church created a worldwide system of schools. This global system became second only to that of the Roman Catholic Church. Although some Protestant groups have significant concentrations of schools in individual countries, the global nature of the Adventist educational system at the beginning of the twenty-first century was unparalleled within Protestantism. One observer suggested that Seventh-day Adventism was an educational system with a church attached to it.

Furthermore, the nature of education at the system's upper levels changed as Adventist education focused on professional development. In the early formative stages of developing schools, colleges were founded to train preachers and teachers for the evangelistic outreach of the church and to staff the schools at the lower levels. Scientific and medical training were also highlighted to support the medical work in the school's area. Other study courses were added to train clerical and laboratory workers at Adventist schools. As the number of lower-level schools grew, the demand for teachers and the institutions that trained them likewise grew. As preachers were trained and sent out to evangelize, more people came into the church, and the need for more preachers increased. However, this cycle continued only as long as the message and mission of the church were seen as vibrant and relevant. As the colleges matured and some became universities, their mission expanded from training "workers for the cause" to training students for professional careers outside the denomination.

After the success of the GI Bill to support veterans' college education, the United States government created loan programs in 1958 to support students in higher education. As a result of these programs, many Adventist young people, and even some who were not church members, sought to improve their earning power by attending an Adventist college. Many students coming to Adventist colleges in the USA had no desire to be church workers after graduation. Consequently, these colleges (and later universities) needed to expand their offerings of courses and degrees and change their focus on preparing graduates for jobs and careers with vastly different expectations.

A similar transformation occurred in Adventist schools of higher education around the world. In Chile, the Adventist University's professional training was so much superior to what was available locally, that by 2025 only one-third of the students were Seventh-day Adventists. Almost all the Adventist colleges and universities shifted their focus from training teachers, preachers, and church workers to training students for much broader needs in the workplace of their country. In some places, such as Korea, Papua New Guinea, Nigeria, Kenya, and Peru, the Adventist institutions of higher learning became some of the most academically advanced schools in the nation. As a result, students who had no affiliation with Adventism were attracted to these schools. As they were admitted and educated, the education itself shifted from assuming students had an Adventist worldview to assuming they did not.

As schools expanded, the need for specially trained teachers also grew. Often, there was no Adventist available to teach, so teachers who were not Seventh-day Adventists were hired. Some schools limited the number of students and teachers not of the Seventh-day Adventist faith, while others saw an evangelistic opportunity and avoided such limits. The schools facing these challenges included the University of East Africa at Baraton in Kenya; Valley View University in Ghana; Babcock University in Nigeria; Pacific Adventist University, Papua New Guinea; Peruvian Union University; and Dominican Adventist University. Some schools in these situations succeeded in retaining an Adventist atmosphere on campus, while others did not. Colleges and universities in North America were not immune to the trend toward more students and teachers without a Seventh-day Adventist background.

In some areas, government policy included financial support for religious schools operated by religious organizations. While Adventists in America generally resisted any direct government financial involvement in education, Adventists in other countries found themselves operating government-supported

Adventist International Institute of Advanced Studies (AIIAS)

As early as 1956, the theological seminary in Washington, DC, held the first extension course for theological training on the campus of Philippine Union College (PUC). In 1965, PUC added degrees in religious education, and in 1971, an MA in theology. On March 21, 1972, the Far Eastern Division approved using the name Seventh-day Adventist Theological Seminary, Far East to create a division-wide seminary. Six years later, in January 1978, the seminary and graduate school was established at PUC offering various graduate programs. When the school moved from Baesa to the PUC campus in Cavite, the seminary became an institution of the Far Eastern Division, with the division supporting its graduate programs and providing decision-making authority. Officially, the Philippines government issued Presidential Decree 2021, establishing the Adventist International Institute for Advanced Studies (AIIAS) on July 31, 1986. While it began as a graduate school of Philippine Union College (which later became the Adventist University of the Philippines), AIIAS was separated from it due to internal political issues.

AIIAS was founded to counter the trend of international students sent for training in North America declining to return to the fields that sponsored them. AIIAS was to be an advanced university-level graduate school that would provide an alternate location for leadership training rather than the United States.

The institution consisted of a seminary and a graduate school (begun in 1988), which offered degrees in public health, education, and business. AIIAS produced its first graduates in March 1991, establishing its current campus in Silang, Cavite, that same year. When the Asia-Pacific Division was divided in 1996, the institution came under the administrative control of the General Conference, becoming the first GC educational institution outside North America.

AIIAS became an affordable alternative for theological and graduate training for students in Asia and other developing parts of the world, with the hope that they would return to their respective countries. Despite this hope, recent research suggests that many international students and faculty leveraged international networks to emigrate to Western countries. Since the 1990s, other schools in South America, the Caribbean, and Africa have expanded and begun offering advanced degrees in many areas. The need to send students to America, and even to AIIAS, for graduate education diminished significantly. Serious discussions continued about training workers in various countries who would remain in their territories to minister to their own people.

schools as evangelistic enterprises. Sometimes they served as feeder schools for the local Adventist college, and sometimes they were required by the government to teach matters incompatible with Adventist education, such as the evolutionary theory of human origins. Even Adventist schools in North America came under increasing scrutiny to comply with government regulations as students received loans and grants from the government. In a way, Adventist higher education, while still small and denominationally oriented, was comparable to large state colleges and universities, as all these institutions faced rapidly changing standards in higher education and expectations of student job prospects after graduation.

A further challenge facing Adventist education was its cost, which in North America increased more rapidly than the general cost of living. Even with grants and loans available to lower-income families, the cost of four years of undergraduate education expanded beyond the means of many Adventists. Some Adventist schools, such as those in the Philippines, retained significant work-study programs where students could earn a portion of their costs by working on campus. However, these programs were largely phased out of many North American schools because students were reluctant to participate in them in their pursuit of professional careers. Thus, many Adventist students chose to attend lower-cost public institutions instead of Adventist colleges and universities. At one time, it was estimated that approximately 70 percent of church members sent their children to Adventist colleges. This gradually reversed so that by the 1980s, approximately 70 percent of church members no longer enrolled their children in an Adventist school. The growth of Adventist education worldwide, with its continued global expansion, often masked this decline in Adventist education in the place of its birth.

Changes in Administrative Leadership

In the last half of the twentieth century, Adventism in North America did not experience significant changes in leadership or administrative structures. However, three dramatic changes occurred in other areas of the world. First, administrative structures were adjusted to account for new geopolitical and demographic changes in Europe and Africa. Second, the leadership of all institutions shifted from foreign missionaries to local leaders. Finally, the structure of the local levels of administration shifted from foreign financial support to local financing.

The late 1950s and the 1960s saw the end of colonial rule in Africa. Before this time, the Adventist church structure had connected the church in Africa to its colonial rulers in Europe. Ethiopia and former colonies in West Africa were part of the Northern European Division. The Southern European Division included much of the rest of northwest Africa, Mozambique, and Madagascar. The remaining parts of Africa, including South Africa and East Africa, were part of the Southern African Division with headquarters in Salisbury, Rhodesia, now Harare, Zimbabwe. In 1960, all division personnel overseeing Africa were Europeans or Americans. In practice, the European divisions were responsible for staffing the missions in colonial African territories, while the General Conference and the North American Division were in charge of staffing the Southern African Division and those places not affiliated with old colonial empire structures.

As colonial rule ended in the mid-twentieth century, so did European and American leadership of the African churches. The educational level of church leaders increased, and, as a result, they assumed greater leadership responsibilities. Nonetheless, Europeans and Americans were reticent, at first, to relinquish church leadership to Africans. The transition began with a reorganization of the administrative levels of the church in 1980 with the separation of most of the African fields from the European divisions. With the creation of the Africa–Indian Ocean Division and the Trans-African Division, all African fields were self-contained within African divisions, except Angola, Mozambique, Morocco, and North Africa, which remained mission territories attached to the Euro-Africa Division. Angola and Mozambique were incorporated into the Southern Africa–Indian Ocean Division in 2002, while Morocco and North Africa became part of a detached field that came to be known as the Middle East and North Africa Union Mission (MENA). Thus, by 2002 the detachment of African territories from traditional colonial structures was complete.

As the changes in administrative structures in Africa happened, leadership in most institutions shifted from foreign missionaries to local people. This was in line with the thought of Anglican mission theorist Henry Venn (1796–1873) and American missionary leader Rufus Anderson (1796–1880), who encouraged missionaries to see themselves as temporary workers building an indigenous church.[2] Their idea was that each national church should became self-supporting, self-governing, and self-extending. The goal of the missionary enterprise was not a permanent foreign mission presence. Instead, the missionary was to work himself out of a job by training local leaders to

2. W. R. Shenk, "Rufus Anderson and Henry Venn: A Special Relationship?," *International Bulletin of Missionary Research* 5, no. 4 (October 1981): 168–72, https://tinyurl.com/27rr8wyy.

take over the administration of the church in each place. Venn and Anderson's ideas took some time to implement, partly because people of European descent assumed they were superior to other races. Racism was challenged by the nonviolent civil rights movement in the United States in the late 1950s and early 1960s. It took some time for the Seventh-day Adventist Church to integrate these ideas into its mission program, but by the mid-1960s, the shift was well under way.

In the Philippines, during World War II, Pedro Diaz was the only Filipino in leadership in a local mission. He successfully negotiated with the Japanese general commanding the occupation of the Philippines for the continued work of the Seventh-day Adventist Church, independent of a combined Protestant church organization. He was then chosen as the president of the Philippine Union Mission during the Japanese occupation. Still, when American forces defeated the Japanese army, the leadership of the Philippine Union Mission reverted to a foreigner. This might seem to be a step backward, but there were immense needs in the Philippines, China, and other locations affected by World War II. Often, the people most experienced in meeting those needs were foreign missionaries. Local leaders were glad to have the additional help and resources experienced foreign workers brought.

In 1951, the Philippine Union was split into the North Philippine Union Mission and the South Philippine Union Mission. Overseas missionaries continued to lead the northern union, but Gil de Guzman, a Filipino, was appointed to lead the southern union. By 1975, all church leadership positions in the Philippines were filled by Filipinos. Similar movements took place around the world. By 1981, in the African divisions, 22 percent of the positions at the division level were filled by Africans, as were 33 percent of the seats on division executive committees. Forty years later, in 2021, virtually all these positions were filled by Africans.

The move toward local leadership was challenging. Choosing leaders became difficult when tribal loyalties were considered. Sometimes the newly elected personnel needed to be more experienced, becoming either dictatorial or lax. There were instances of cronyism, rebellion, corruption, nepotism, and immorality. In some areas, the local members wanted an overseas missionary to fill critical positions when different factions could not mediate their differences, especially regarding the treasurer's position. They knew a local leader would come under unbearable pressure to aid his family from the church's funds. However, moving toward local leadership usually resulted in better outreach and a more vital church. The growth of the church in South America, Inter-America, and Africa attests to the wisdom of adopting local leadership.

At the same time, local leaders began filling administrative posts, and a

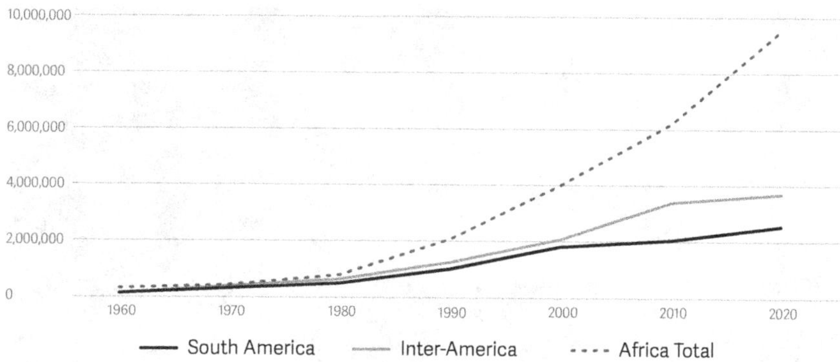

Growth comparison of South American, Inter-American, and combined African totals

transition occurred in the administration of many mission fields. As described in chapter 7, when the church started work in a new part of the world, it was organized as a mission instead of a conference. The executive committee of the next higher administrative level appoints the administrators of a mission. So, the union missions appoint leaders for the local missions, and the divisions appoint the union mission leaders. Local and union missions also receive financial support from the next higher level of church governance.

When an entity reached self-supporting status and no longer needed financial subsidies, it was organized as a conference or union conference. That meant a constituency meeting was called, and delegates from the local churches elected their leaders. In diverse settings with tribal issues involved, conflict could reach a high level at such meetings. Sometimes, mission leaders preferred to remain at the mission level even though they qualified for conference status because they would rather answer to the three union leaders than to the many constituents. In one newly organized conference, the constituency voted for an entirely new conference leadership. None of the previous administrators were reelected, and none of the new administrators had any experience. The new conference experienced some difficult times in the following years. By 2023, there was a mix of missions and conferences at the local and union levels in Africa, Asia, Oceania, and Latin America.

Transitions in the Medical Work

Adventist hospitals founded before 1960 were often the only modern medical facilities in an area or country. Overseas missionary doctors brought a level of sophisticated care unknown to the local population. Wealthy residents were

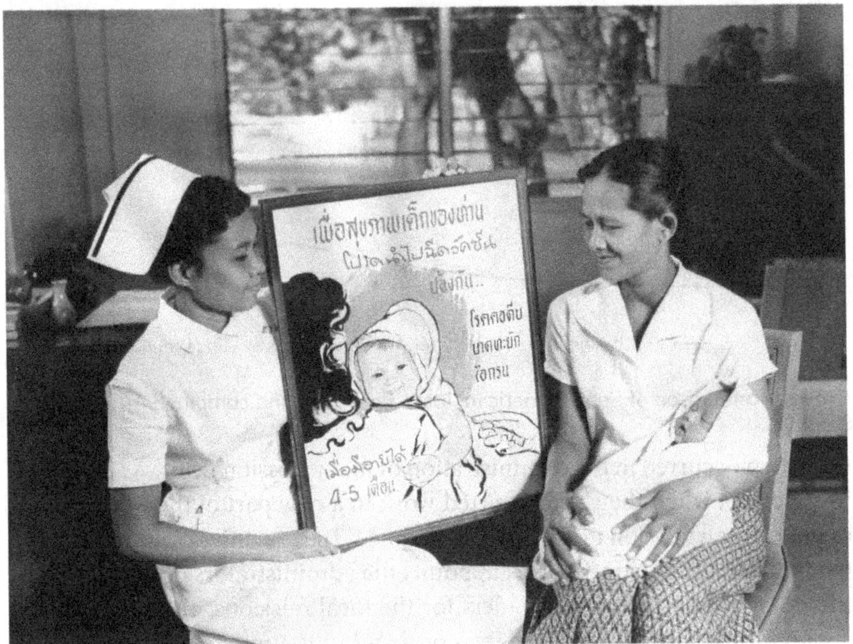

Nurse instructs mother in the midwifery section of the Bangkok Sanitarium and Hospital

glad to pay for the expert medical care offered. Hospitals used funds from paying patients to provide free medical care for people experiencing poverty. At Bangkok's Mission Hospital, Gertrude Green founded a school of midwifery and delivered babies without cost to anyone who came to the hospital for a delivery. At the same time, the foreign doctors at the hospital were on call whenever a foreign dignitary visited Thailand in case of a medical emergency.

After 1970, governments often took the lead in building new health-care facilities that were better equipped and better financed than the church-operated hospitals. Government hospitals provided free care but were usually crowded and required long waits for services. As national wealth increased, private corporations also founded high-quality hospitals. Competition for clients increased, leaving many Adventist hospitals in danger of collapse. Local governments took over some Adventist hospitals, and others were closed. Those that remained usually continued as an alternative to the government facilities, often for the middle or upper classes that could afford them. However, securing up-to-date equipment and maintaining financial viability became a challenge.

A modest attempt from Loma Linda University (LLU) to support these hospitals grew into a significant effort in the twenty-five years between 1998 and 2023. This effort, known as Adventist Health International (AHI), was not another layer of administration. Instead, it provided management, technical advice, and equipment for health-care facilities, primarily in developing countries. Staffed mainly by volunteers, this effort began in 1997 when the local government in Ethiopia gave the Adventist Church one year to upgrade the facilities of Gimbie Adventist Hospital. The hospital appealed to the General Conference and Loma Linda University for help. A group gathered at Loma Linda to consider the request and came to recognize that many other Adventist health-care facilities were in similarly difficult situations.

The greatest needs were not for money, personnel, or equipment. Instead, the real issues were more complex: developing leaders, having solid accounting practices, and creating a steady stream of volunteers. An on-site visit to Ethiopia revealed the need for a new hospital building. The visitors also saw a need to revitalize the staff and regional health-care centers nationwide. Volunteers from LLU and elsewhere came to Gimbie's assistance, built a new hospital, and provided encouragement for good management and accounting. The hospital's debts were paid off, and it began operating with a small surplus.

By 2023, AHI was supporting forty-five hospitals and 100 clinics across the globe. With its emphasis on best practices in medical care, management, and financing, AHI's influence has spread across its service areas like ripples across a quiet lake. Richard Hart, one of the founders of AHI and later president of LLU, said that one of the most gratifying impacts of AHI was on the young professionals at Loma Linda. They have seen what is happening worldwide and want to get involved. Many who have taken short-term appointments, raised money, and provided equipment later committed to long-term service. AHI became an invaluable link between Adventism's flagship medical center and its neediest health-care facilities in some of the most remote regions on earth.

The nineteenth-century idea of a sanitarium was to provide a resort-like setting where clients could retreat to learn healthy living and disease prevention. By the late twentieth century, this idea had faded into the background. Instead, Adventist medical facilities became modern hospitals. For a while, many medical institutions retained the name "Sanitarium and Hospital." Still, by 2021, only 9 out of 227 (4 percent) Adventist medical facilities retained "Sanitarium" in their official name, though little of the sanitarium ideal may have been left.

In North America, health care and the insurance that is paid for it became increasingly more expensive and complex. Adventist hospitals faced significant financial pressures, causing many to explore alliances with other Adventist hospitals. By 1980, four regional Adventist health systems were operating. These corporations helped leverage lower purchasing costs, provided significant efficiencies, and enabled expansion into new areas. In 1982, the four regional systems sought to work under a national corporation, but it failed to provide sufficient benefits to justify its existence. Those Adventist health institutions that did not adopt new programs like Medicare, and new methods for billing insurance, quickly found that their funding had dried up. The New England Sanitarium and Medical Center refused to adopt such measures and eventually went bankrupt. While some Adventist health institutions thrived in a new environment leveraged by large health networks, those who refused to change found their doors closed.

By 2024, there were three major regional systems and three smaller health-care corporations in North America: AdventHealth oversaw fifty-one hospital campuses from its flagship Florida Hospital in Orlando. A separate system known as Adventist Health coordinated medical work among twenty-seven acute-care hospitals in the western United States. Kettering Health developed a system of fourteen hospitals and clinics in central Ohio. Three more localized systems included Loma Linda and two regional systems in the northeastern United States. Together, these health networks served as a catalyst for change as some of the best and brightest students in Adventist colleges and universities were attracted to lucrative health-care careers. Many church administrators on health-care boards envied the significant financial resources available, even as these same health institutions reinvested money, often sponsoring endowed faculty positions and building new buildings on Adventist college and university campuses. The significant financial resources of AdventHealth, for example, allowed Adventism to hit the popular mainstream when the system partnered with Trackhouse Entertainment Group to field the No. 1 AdventHealth Chevrolet Camaro with driver Ross Chastain for six NASCAR races, including the season-opening Daytona 500 on February 20, 2020. It also sponsors the AdventHealth 400 race.

The Dominance of North America Challenged

Influences in the world at large had an unavoidable impact on the Adventist Church. In the last half of the twentieth century, the end of colonialism, the fading of racist ideas and Western notions of superiority, and the growth in population, education, and wealth in every country brought significant changes. Due to these external influences, Adventist Church membership grew more rapidly outside North America, Europe, and Australasia than within those areas.

The result of all these influences was the end of North American dominance in the world church. At the end of 2023, church membership was reported at 22,785,195, with 1,257,884 (4 percent) in North America. Beginning in the 1980s, North America began to suffer from the same secularizing trends already affecting Europe and Australasia. Fewer people were involved with or even interested in religion, so traditional Adventist evangelism that focused on convincing people of Bible truths caught the attention of a much smaller audience. Fewer new members were baptized, and church membership began to plateau. At the same time, significant shifts in population affected the church in North America. Like the population at large, many Adventists moved from rural areas to cities, resulting in the rapid loss of students in boarding academies and significant membership loss for rural churches. Some academies and many rural churches closed. Many new congregations formed in the 1960s in suburban areas, but that growth lessened and nearly ceased by 2000. Another significant demographic factor was age. The 2022 Statistical Report shows that the divisions with the smallest percentage of members in the twenty-one-to-thirty-five age group were the Trans-European Division (13.78 percent), the Inter-European Division (13.86 percent), and the North American Division (14.89 percent). Some voices suggested that the church in North America had lost its vitality.

While the same forces had some effect on the church outside of North America, some areas continued to experience a high degree of vitality. One of these areas was South America. Once the Roman Catholic Church ceased to be a significant political force in the area, Protestant, charismatic, and Adventist churches began to grow. As long as the Catholic Church remained the dominant religious force in most South American countries, Adventist evangelism could count on a Christian population open to Adventism's biblically based appeal. A continual influx of new members meant that their connections to people outside the church remained fresh. The church also retained its youth, primarily through the Pathfinder program. In Brazil, Ecuador, and Paraguay, in 2019, every church had an organized Pathfinder club. Across the South American Division, there were 333,650 Pathfinders in 12,173 clubs and 168,468 Adventurers in 7,662 clubs. These clubs created a culture that inspired young people to be involved in active learning and service. The top divisions with the highest numbers of members in the twenty-one-to-thirty-five age group were the West-Central Africa Division (35.64 percent), the Southern Asia–Pacific Division (28.65 percent), the Inter-American Division (27.67 percent), with the South American Division coming in fourth (25.57 percent). As a result of the factors noted above, the South American Division, and Brazil, in particular, became a significant force in overseas missionary activity. In 2021, seventy missionary families from the South American Division served outside the division as paid full-time missionaries, second only to the North American Division. At the same time, eighty-two volunteer short-term missionaries were sent from South America.

Many of the most successful missionaries in the 2010s in the challenging fields of the Middle East and Asia came from South America. Some were students at local universities whose main work was outreach to the population.

Others took long-term jobs in specialized fields in Middle Eastern countries. These missionaries, known as tentmakers after the apostle Paul, sought to mingle and interact with the local population, seeking opportunities for evangelism. Much of this work was done in secret because of strict rules against evangelism and conversion in Muslim areas.

From 1980 to 2020, the number of overseas missionaries sent from North America dropped significantly. The 1980 Statistical Report shows 1,388 International Service Employees serving in mission fields. By 2022, there were only 556, less than half. As local people assumed administrative leadership in lands around the world, there was less need for North Americans in those places. Eventually, the greatest need for North Americans in the overseas fields was for accountants to do auditing services. People within their own divisions performed most pastoral, evangelistic, publishing, and administrative functions. Thus, when the church gathered for its General Conference sessions from 1980 onward, most delegates were from outside North America, Europe, or Australasia.

Social Activism

Irene Morgan was a civil rights pioneer and a Seventh-day Adventist from Baltimore, Maryland. She had traveled by bus to Gloucester, Virginia, to visit her family. Public spaces and transportation were segregated in the American South at that time. On July 16, 1944, the twenty-seven-year-old woman was returning to Baltimore by bus when the bus seats reserved for white people filled. The bus driver ordered Irene to give up her seat to a white person. Upset at the injustice of the request, she refused, and the bus stopped at the courthouse in the next town. The driver got off and reported her to the local sheriff, who sent two deputies to remove her. She resisted their attempts and was arrested and jailed. She pleaded guilty to resisting arrest but challenged the Virginia law that required her to give up her seat. The National Association for the Advancement of Colored People (NAACP) took her case and appealed it to the United States Supreme Court. Thurgood Marshall, later a Supreme Court justice, argued her case. The Court ruled in her favor, decreeing that it was against the US Constitution to enforce segregation on interstate transport. The historical marker commemorating this event in Hayes, Virginia, notes that it occurred eleven years before Rosa Parks kept her seat in Montgomery, Alabama.

In the years between 1900 and 1960, African Americans couldn't avoid segregation in the United States. While the hand of "Jim Crow" was heaviest in the southern states, there were significant obstacles to African Americans everywhere. Partly to avoid racial discrimination in church employment, African

Americans organized regional conferences beginning in 1944. These remained substantial engines of growth and leadership development among African American Adventists through the beginning of the twenty-first century. Voices within and outside the regional conferences saw them as racist, segregationist, and unchristian. However, those in the regional conference administration strongly supported their existence as an opportunity to resist discrimination and forge leaders within the African American community. No regional conferences were formed in the Pacific Union or the North Pacific Union. Though there was considerable debate, the majority held that the racial climate there was sufficiently different that the work among black and other racial/ethnic minorities could thrive best without separate conferences.

Many Adventist pastors in the regional conferences became involved with the civil rights movement in the 1950s and 1960s, often with significant opposition from white leadership. Charles Edward Dudley Sr. (1927–2010) began service in 1962 as the president of the regional South Central Conference, overseeing churches in Alabama, Kentucky, Louisiana, Mississippi, Tennessee, and part of Arkansas. He remained in that post for thirty-one years, a record time for administrators of a local conference. Shortly after Dr. Martin Luther King Jr. was assassinated in 1968, Dudley participated in the Poor People's Campaign in Washington, DC, which King had planned. Dudley arranged for a medical van from the South Central Conference to provide health care at the Poor People's encampment on the National Mall known as Resurrection City. Television pictures of the van, with the South Central Conference of Seventh-day Adventists displayed prominently on its side, were broadcast nationally. Some church members complained to the Southern Union. Dudley and Earl Moore (1925–2018), a pastor, were ordered to appear before the Southern Union executive committee. They flew from Washington to Atlanta and were grilled about why they and their van were involved in the Poor People's Campaign. Some white leaders suggested that the black conferences were no longer helpful to the denomination because of how they were using their money and power. Dudley defended his involvement and his authorization to use the conference van. The rumor was that the black brethren had lost their way by becoming involved in the Social Gospel. Dudley argued that they had not lost their way but found it. Moore had raised the money for the van from black churches nationwide. He argued that there was no "white money" in the van and that the regional conference could use the van to support the poor people in Mississippi as well as the poor people encamped in Washington, DC.

Many black Adventist pastors played a role in local civil rights efforts. Charles Joseph (1936–2024), the pastor of the Greenwood, Mississippi, Seventh-

E. E. Cleveland

day Adventist church, allowed civil rights groups to use his church for meetings and rallies. Some white Adventist leaders were alarmed at Joseph's activities and demanded that he cease them. However, Dudley and the South Central Conference defended him from these attacks. As he was driving one day, a car pulled up alongside his car, and someone from the other car took a shot at him. It missed Joseph but shattered his windshield. When he got home, he received an anonymous phone call saying that while their shot had missed him, they still intended to get him. He moved to Jackson, Mississippi, and bought a home next to the house of civil rights activist Charles Evers (1922–2020), brother of Medgar Evers. Arriving home one evening, he discovered that someone had taken numerous shots at his home and Evers's home while he was away. The homes were occupied at the time, but miraculously no one was hurt.

Warren Banfield Jr. (1922–2006) pastored the Mt. Calvary Adventist Church in Tampa, Florida, from 1956 to 1962. Banfield became involved in several civil rights organizations. When the president of the Tampa NAACP resigned, he assisted in the search for a replacement. While he was away at an Adventist workers meeting, he was elected president. He was reluctant to take on the responsibility and asked some ministerial colleagues about it. They counseled him not to accept the position because it would jeopardize the church's well-being and go against a long-standing belief that involvement in sociopoliti-

C. E. Bradford

cal activities was improper. He was not persuaded by this reasoning and accepted the position. White Adventists protested his involvement and wrote letters of complaint to Reuben Figuhr, the General Conference president. Figuhr sent the letters to John Wagner, the president of the regional South Atlantic Conference, attaching a note that said, "Go down there and see what you can do with that young man Banfield." Wagner sent the entire set of letters to Banfield with a note that read, "Keep up the good work!" Banfield was deeply moved by his president's support and said that it was one of the factors that kept him in the Adventist ministry.

The South Central Conference's action in support of civil rights and the South Atlantic Conference president's support of Banfield demonstrated the effectiveness of separate conferences in advancing the interests of black Adventists. Their actions strongly countered the objections that regional conferences were racist, somehow instruments of control, and segregationist. Thereafter, most of the opposition among black Adventists to the regional conferences dissipated when they saw what black conferences could achieve. In the 1970s, Banfield suggested that the church set up an office to address social problems. Adventist leaders agreed and created the Office of Human Relations for the North American Division. Banfield was appointed its first director.

The successful creation of regional conferences for African Americans suggested the need for a regional Union Conference. Calvin Rock (b. 1930), the president of Oakwood College, and E. E. Cleveland (1921–2009), an associate in the General Conference ministerial department, urged the creation of a Union of regional Conferences. Their agitation found opponents within and without the black community. Still, in the end, their activism pushed the church in North America toward greater diversity at all levels of church administration.

Rising through the ranks of regional conferences in the 1950s and 1960s, Charles E. Bradford (1925–2021) began service in the General Conference in 1970. On January 11, 1979, he was elected General Conference vice president for the North American Division (NAD). However, the NAD had little autonomy. Bradford's impressive leadership abilities enabled him to successfully advocate for the creation of an autonomous North American Division.

As the church continued to grow in other parts of the world, church leaders recognized that there were unique challenges and needs in North America. For example, when the General Conference gave the division the same autonomy the other divisions had, it was tasked with coming up with strategies for being more inclusive of women, particularly women in ministry.

In 1985, with Bradford as its first president, the North American Division was permitted to develop its own budget and appoint departmental directors for the first time. Alfred C. McClure (1931–2006), who served as division president from 1990 to 2000, continued this autonomous and empowering trajectory. He was strongly focused on mission while simultaneously supporting the work of the world church. McClure was especially notable for developing a series of "Net" satellite evangelistic meetings, which were first launched in 1995. It featured numerous evangelistic downlink sites across the United States and was soon followed by similar events around the world.

Thus, institutions could help spread the Adventist message. They could also create obstacles. When an institution and its policies became the dominant concern in decision making, institutionalism took over. The challenge the church faced at the end of the twentieth century was whether institutionalism would distract the church from its mission and message and blind it to the human need for salvation, justice, and compassion.

The Challenge of Modernity

The growth in Adventist educational institutions outlined above required teachers with advanced degrees. Meeting that need by hiring teachers trained at some of the best Western universities brought the church into direct contact with the forces of modernity already dominant in Western educational institutions. Modernity emphasized science and reason. It ruled out anything supernatural. As a result, modern society has become focused on the individual's subjective experience. Thus, religious and theological studies done from the perspective of modernity emphasized the historical and scientific backgrounds of the Scriptures and left the impression that the Bible was the product solely of human minds. Many of the studies done from this perspective were valuable. However, the overall effect of modernity decreases confidence in the trustworthiness of the Scriptures and puts human perspectives and interpretations at the forefront. The conflict about modernity in the Adventist Church came to a head, first at the Seventh-day Adventist Theological Seminary and then at Loma Linda University.

R. R. Figuhr greets Anna Knight, the first female Black missionary to India

With the expansion of collegiate education in the 1950s and the corresponding need for teachers with advanced degrees in Adventist colleges in North America, Adventist students began to seek academic careers through doctoral studies at some of the best universities in the United States and Europe. This was not a new development. J. N. Anderson, the first official missionary to China, received a bachelor of divinity (the equivalent of a modern master of divinity) from the University of Chicago in 1901, and B. G. Wilkinson received a PhD in history in 1908 from George Washington University. However, the growing need for teachers with advanced degrees in the 1960s increased the number of Adventists pursuing academic careers in Adventist education.

Among those completing doctoral degrees were Siegfried Horn, Richard Hammill, Sakae Kubo (b. 1926), and Mervyn Maxwell (1925–1999) from the University of Chicago; Earle Hilgert (1923–2020) from the University of Basel; and Roy Branson (1938–2015) and Lawrence Geraty (b. 1940) from Harvard University. Edward Vick (1929–2024) studied at London University, Vanderbilt University, and Oxford. Gerhard Hasel (1935–1994) also studied at Vanderbilt. All of these scholars, in their own way, participated in the church's struggle with modernism, underscoring the importance of their work.

As General Conference president between 1954 and 1966, Reuben Figuhr oversaw two significant transitions in Adventist education. First was the already-mentioned merger of Potomac University and Emmanuel Missionary College, forming Andrews University. The second was the transfer of clinical teaching from the White Memorial Hospital to the Loma Linda campus of the College of Medical Evangelists and its renaming as Loma Linda University. The institution had already granted the first Adventist PhD in the medical sciences in 1958.

Figuhr graduated from Walla Walla College with a BA in history, having been inspired by William Landeen, who had done studies toward a doctorate at the University of Pennsylvania and the University of Michigan. Figuhr spent most of his career in the Philippines and South America, serving as the president of the South American Division before moving to the General Conference as a vice president in 1950.

Because of his college education, Figuhr was familiar with scholarship and could hold his own in discussions about biblical and historical subjects. He was not intimidated by criticism and could provide strong leadership in complex issues. The move of the seminary to Michigan is one example. When the General Conference Annual Council in 1958 voted for the move to Michigan and the merger with Emmanuel Missionary College, it encountered stiff opposition from the administration and faculty in Washington, DC. Figuhr, with his unwavering belief in the wisdom of the move, led the way, and the merger was complete by the summer of 1960, a testament to his resilience and leadership.

When Figuhr stepped down as General Conference president in 1966, his successor was Robert H. Pierson (1911–1989). In contrast to Figuhr, Pierson only had a two-year ministerial degree from Southern Junior College, which later became Southern Adventist University. After graduating in 1933, he spent two years in pastoral and leadership positions in America. He was then called to serve in India, then Inter-America, and in 1958 to be president of the Trans-Africa Division.

Pierson's strengths were in personal and public evangelism. Leading the Trans-Africa Division during a time of decolonization, he began the effort to move leadership into the hands of local people. However, his theological perspective remained that of 1920s Adventist fundamentalism. Once elected president of the General Conference, he almost immediately received reports of alleged modernism at the seminary at Andrews University. Pierson felt he had to take action. He raised the allegations with seminary dean W. G. C. Murdoch and university president Richard Hammill. The undercurrent for the allegation was that teachers at the seminary no longer saw Ellen White as authoritative in issues ranging from the authorship of the book of Hebrews to the age of the earth. Murdoch and Hammill responded with detailed rebuttals, but the allegations kept coming. Seminary and university professors began to feel that their positions were in jeopardy.

By October of 1968, Pierson felt he had enough information to call a General Conference committee to consider what should be done. He was concerned with jewelry, drama clubs, and student politics on the Andrews University campus. But even more, he was worried about the spread of what he called "liberalism." By this, he meant intellectualism and issues related to academic freedom and secularism. The pressure for change was evident, and Hammill felt he had to make some changes. First, he moved Sakae Kubo from the New Testament department at the seminary to the James White Library as the seminary librarian. He then chose not to reinstate Edward Vick at the seminary. Earle Hilgert was disturbed by the atmosphere of criticism and suspicion on the Andrews campus, so he decided to leave. After studying for a graduate degree in library sciences, he began working for McCormick Theological Seminary in Chicago. Harold Weiss took a teaching post at St. Mary's College in South Bend, Indiana. Other seminary professors under suspicion either defended themselves or kept quiet. Many of the professors accused of liberalism were far from being advocates for a historical-critical method of Bible study. In academic circles outside of the Seventh-day Adventist Church, most of them would have been classified as conservative. However, in a climate still heavily influenced by fundamentalism, even the study of ideas that seemed to question the Bible or the spirit of prophecy led to accusations of liberalism.

Twice in the 1970s, statements were drawn up to test the seminary faculty's beliefs. Both included statements affirming the earth's six-thousand-year age. In the earliest attempt at imposing this kind of creedal statement, Siegfried Horn, the denomination's most widely respected scholar, let it be known that he could not support a statement that mentioned the six thousand years of Earth's history. The attempt to use this creedal formula was dropped. Later, in 1976, a similar statement was proposed, but North American Division president Neal Wilson (1920–2010) objected before it was implemented. Wilson stated in a forum with all the seminary and undergraduate teachers, including the science teachers, that he had lived too long in Egypt and had learned too much about its ancient history to support the six-thousand-year date. Once again, the attempt to impose a creedal statement failed.

Nonetheless, the controversies and agitation inspired by Pierson's inquiries had a long-term effect on the church. Issues related to modernism became part of hiring discussions. Potential teachers not in harmony with the church's perspectives on revelation, inspiration, biblical studies, and science chose not to seek church employment. Pierson firmly believed in the approaching end of time. He felt the need for a strong evangelistic focus and an emphasis on achieving Christian perfection. As a result, he allocated retirement funds toward Adventist evangelism rather than retaining them to pay retired church

Bible Conferences of 1974

In 1974, church leaders gathered to discuss biblical hermeneutics and inspiration. During the late 1960s, several Adventist scholars requested that a conference on inspiration be held. Concrete plans surfaced at the 1972 Annual Council, and the council authorized three consecutive Bible Conferences to be held in the North American Division in 1974. Meetings were held at Southern Missionary College (May 13–21), then at Andrews University (June 3–11), and finally at Pacific Union College (June 17–25). Kenneth Wood Jr. (1917–2008) stated that since all three meetings were so similar, "the three were, in reality, one." While all three Bible Conferences were held in North America, every division of the world church sent representatives. Altogether, some two thousand individuals participated in the three gatherings.

Pierson opened each conference using the words of King Zedekiah as a theme for his keynote address: "Is there any word from the Lord?" He described his perspective on how accrediting bodies, modern science, and liberal theologians embattled the church. Any view of the Bible that emphasized human reasoning was "poles apart" from a Seventh-day Adventist understanding of inspiration. "Anything that weakens faith in the Word of God, the commandments of God, the divinity and humanity of Christ, in His last-day message, the Spirit of Prophecy, is not God speaking. It may be materialism, secularism, humanism, modernism, liberalism, syncretism, but it is *not* Adventism. It is not God speaking."[1] He believed a high regard for the Bible's divine inspiration was the key to revival and reformation and a new emphasis on personal holiness, character development, and experiencing victorious living. Quoting Ellen White, he argued that "perfection of character" that God requires can only be attained "by becoming familiar with His Word."[2]

Alden Thompson described the 1974 Bible Conferences as characteristic of the "more conservative stance" of denominational leaders during the 1970s. "The crux of the issue," he added, "was whether or not Adventist scholars could use the so-called

1. Robert H. Pierson, "Is There Any Word from the Lord?," *Review and Herald* 151, no. 33 (August 15, 1974): 7.

2. Pierson, "Is There Any Word?," 8. The quote is from Ellen G. White, *God's Amazing Grace* (Washington, DC: Review and Herald, 1973), 61.

employees. While this was not illegal at the time, it did ruin the finances of the traditional Adventist retirement plan, requiring the denomination to embrace a new defined-benefits plan instead. In this case, an impatient application of Adventist beliefs about the nearness of Christ's coming had very practical con-

historical-critical method in any form."[3] Such terminology anticipated adopting the term "historical-grammatical method" as an approach that affirmed biblical scholarship while rejecting naturalistic presuppositions and methods. The focus of the meetings on hermeneutics meant that the Biblical Research Committee emphasized the need to identify "correct methodology" to arrive "at doctrinal positions."

Although all of the major Bible Conferences within the Seventh-day Adventist Church during the twentieth century (i.e., 1919 and 1952) largely focused on hermeneutics, this particular series of Bible Conferences was the most directly focused on this topic. By the time of the 1974 Bible Conferences, there was a continuum of perspectives that ranged from a more progressive view that valued the historical-critical method to others that leaned toward the verbal inerrancy of conservative evangelicals. Neither side fully championed a rigid embrace of the historical-critical method or inerrancy. The Adventist perspective generally fell somewhere on a continuum between these extremes.

Some, such as Siegfried H. Horn and R. F. Cottrell, pushed for a more open approach to Adventist hermeneutics that sought to embrace the best of the historical-critical method. At the same time, others, notably Gerhard Hasel and Gordon M. Hyde, pushed for a more literalistic and conservative methodology. Their perspective repudiated the historical-critical method and leaned toward inerrancy and verbal inspiration. Still others advocated for a more moderate perspective, notably Raoul Dederen (1925–2016), Hans K. LaRondelle (1929–2011), and Kenneth A. Strand (1927–1997), who sought a more irenic stance. Also of note, Kenneth H. Wood and Herbert E. Douglass (1927–2014), both strong advocates of Last Generation Theology, would make a strong push for their views to be heard at the conclusion of the 1974 Bible Conferences. These various hermeneutical approaches and issues, which have ebbed and flowed through the twentieth century, formed the boundaries for new areas of discussion and debate within Seventh-day Adventist theology. In doing so, they took earlier hermeneutical issues raised at the 1919 and 1952 Bible Conferences and showcased the longevity of hermeneutical debates that shaped Seventh-day Adventism.[4]

3. Alden Thompson, *Inspiration: Hard Questions, Honest Answers* (Hagerstown, MD: Review and Herald, 1991), 270.

4. Michael W. Campbell, "Bible Conferences of 1974," in *Encyclopedia of Seventh-day Adventists*, February 21, 2024, https://tinyurl.com/mr24nttb.

Left to right: Neal C. Wilson, Willis J. Hackett, and Robert H. Pierson

sequences in how the denomination spent its resources.

Pierson resigned from the church presidency during the Annual Council meetings in 1978 due to health concerns raised by his physicians. Elected in his place was Neal C. Wilson. Wilson's parents had served overseas in Indonesia, Africa, southern Asia, and the South Pacific. Wilson had grown up exposed to the global work of the church. His father's last position was general vice president of the world church. Wilson himself spent fourteen years in Egypt before serving as a church administrator in California and Maryland. He was appointed vice president of the General Conference for North America in 1966.

Church leadership became concerned about the theological leadership of the seminary, appointing Gerhard Hasel as the dean. Implicit in his appointment was an expectation that he would watch over the orthodoxy of pastors. In his seven-year term, from 1981 to 1988, he steered the school in a more conservative direction. His leadership contributed to polarization among Adventist theologians after pushing out those whom he felt were not conservative enough. Tragically, he died an untimely death in a car accident, which led to the interim leadership, and then appointment, of the irenic Raoul Dederen. His most lasting legacy was his support of the development of the Adventist Theological Society as a mechanism to support and encourage conservative Adventist scholarship within the denomination.

Meanwhile, at Loma Linda University, the accusations of liberalism took a different turn. The focus was on Graham Maxwell (1921–2010) and Jack Provonsha (1920–2004). They were accused of teaching existentialism and situation ethics. Both denied it and pushed back vigorously. Maxwell's theology emphasized the moral influence theory of the atonement and the benevolent character of God. Provonsha emphasized the concept of whole-person care, the teaching of bioethics from a Christian perspective, and the priority of the living human being in discussions of complex ethical issues. At the time, religion classes were required, but the classes were not graded and were not counted toward degree completion. Students could ignore the courses. Other controversies erupted at Loma Linda that eclipsed the concerns about theological liberalism. These included adjusting the pay scale for physicians and serving meat to hospital patients. Then, an earthquake devastated a nearby Veterans Affairs (VA) hospital, and the university sought to have it rebuilt next to its Loma Linda campus. After serious pushback from some who opposed having the VA hospital that close, the university gave the US Department of Veterans Affairs a large plot of land one mile from the university campus so that students could receive valuable training there while keeping the influence of the government hospital at a safe distance.

The concerns about what was being taught at Loma Linda eventually brought changes in the religion program. The university organized the religion faculty into a separate school. Its classes were required, graded, and counted toward degree completion. When Oral Roberts University Medical School closed in 1990, the university agreed to accept its orphaned students and train them through graduation. At the same time, President Lynn Behrens implemented policies that embraced the university's Adventist and Christian character. Its admissions and hiring tactics prioritized teachers and students from Adventist and evangelical Christian backgrounds. After a few years of moving in this direction, Loma Linda began attracting conservative Christian students from a broad spectrum of denominations through its reputation as one of the few medical schools with a Christian perspective.

Adelia Patten Van Horn, the fifth treasurer of the General Conference and the first woman to serve as a General Conference officer

Women in Church Leadership

Historically, women have had significant leadership positions in the Seventh-day Adventist Church. While never a part of the church's administrative structure, Ellen White provided significant leadership throughout her lifetime. Like most denominations founded by women, the church struggled with empowering later generations of women within the denomination.

From the time of the Millerite awakening, women played a significant role in the movement in both the printed page and the spoken word. The majority of missionaries in the first century of Adventism were women, many of whom served as pioneer missionaries alone or with their husbands. These included Anna Stahl, Olga Oss, and Jessie Halliwell, whose ministry was as important as their husbands'. Women serving alone included Ida Thompson and Mrs. B. Miller in China, as well as Georgia Burrus and Della Burroway in India. In the 1870s, two of the earliest treasurers of the General Conference were Adelia Van Horn and Frederika House. By the 1880s and 1890s, some of the most influential evangelists in Adventism were women, including Sarah Lindsey and Ellen Lane.

Yet, due to financial pressures arising from the Great Depression, and changing expectations, not least of which was the influence of fundamentalism, very few women remained in pastoral or administrative positions in North America after 1935. If there were theological reasons for this shift, very few, if any, were raised in the literature at the time.

At the 1881 General Conference session, the Committee on Resolutions put forward the following item: "*Resolved*, That females possessing the necessary qualifications to fill that position, may, with perfect propriety, be set apart by ordination to the work of the Christian ministry." The record states that the resolution was debated and referred to the General Conference Committee. This likely meant that it was indirectly adopted and referred to that committee for implementation.[3] At the time, quite a few women served as pastors and evangelists.[4] Beginning in 1910, the General Conference submitted informa-

3. Kevin M. Burton, "God's Last Choice: Overcoming Ellen White's Gender and Women in Ministry During the Fundamentalist Era," *Spectrum* 45, no. 2 (Summer 2017): 148–76.

4. In appendix C of E. G. White, *Daughters of God* (Hagerstown, MD: Review and Herald Publishing Association, 1998), 249–50, the following list of women licensed to preach during Ellen White's lifetime is given, having been gathered from the General Conference Archives and the *Seventh-day Adventist Yearbook*: 1878—Anna Fulton, Minnesota; Ellen S. Lane, Michigan; Julia Owen, Kentucky-Tennessee; 1879—Libbie Collins, Minnesota; Hattie Enoch, Kansas; Libbie Fulton, Minnesota; Lizzie Post, Minnesota; 1880—Anna Johnson, Minnesota; 1881—Ida W. Ballenger, Illinois; Helen L. Morse, Illinois; 1884—Ruie Hill, Kansas; 1886—Ida W. Hibben, Illinois; 1887—Mrs. S. E. Pierce, Vermont; 1893—Flora Plummer, Iowa; 1894—Margaret Caro, New Zealand; 1895—Mrs. S. A. Lindsay, New York; 1898—Sarepta Irish Henry, Gen. Conf.; Lulu Wightman, New York; 1899—Edith Bartlett, British Conf.; 1900—Hetty Haskell, Gen. Conf.; Mina Robinson, British Conf.; 1901—Carrie V. Hansen, Utah; Emma Hawkins, Iowa; Mrs. E. R. Williams, Michigan; 1902—Mrs. S. N. Haskell, Greater New York; Minnie Sype, Oklahoma; 1904—Alma Bjugg, Finland Mission;

tional material to the US government that affirmed that the Adventist Church ministry was "open to both sexes, although there are very few female ministers."[5] One woman who served in a ministerial capacity was Lulu Wightman (1872–1940). As Mrs. S. J. Wightman, she is listed in the 1908 *Yearbook* as a minister along with all the ordained ministers in the California Conference. However, there are no existing records of a woman receiving ordination to the ministry before 1930.

When the General Conference was reorganized in 1901, the issue of ordination was not placed in the hands of either the local church or the local conference/mission. Instead, it was given to the union conference/mission. The General Conference did not have that responsibility. The fact that ordination was a matter dealt with on the union level reflected the reality that the church was neither congregational nor hierarchical but connectional. Ordination was too important to be left to the local church or the conference/mission level since those ordained served the church as a whole. The union and its constituents were to make that decision for the church. That meant that decisions related to ordination were not to be made by the few who occupied central administrative positions in the General Conference or by the General Conference in session, since they were too far removed from the field and the candidates.

While the issue of the ordination of women was first raised in 1881, it was raised a second time by the Finland Union at the General Conference in 1968. The Finnish context is essential to understanding why the issue was raised. In 1906, Finland was the first European country to grant women the right to vote. The first Adventist preacher in Finland was Alma Bjugg, a former Salvation Army commander. Since the Salvation Army ordained women, she had likely been ordained. When she became an Adventist preacher, she was listed in the *Yearbooks* for 1904 and 1905 as having ministerial credentials, indicating the status of an ordained minister. However, her status in the 1908 *Yearbook* was downgraded to Bible worker. Nonetheless, the work in Finland had a significant number of female workers throughout its history. During World War II, almost all the men in Finland served in the armed forces. Pastoral work was done almost exclusively by women. The experience they gained during that time propelled them to prominence in the postwar years. From the late 1950s into the mid-1960s, Elsa Luukkanen and Aino Lehtoluoto were among the most prominent evangelists in Finland. Thus, the Finland Union wrote to the

Mrs. J. E. Bond, Arizona; Bertha E. Jorgensen, South Dakota; 1910—Pearl Field, Nebraska; Mrs. Ura Spring, Nebraska.

5. Burton, "God's Last Choice."

General Conference before the 1968 General Conference session inquiring about the possibility of ordaining such women.[6]

The item was discussed at the 1968 session, but no decision was made. The question prompted a conference on the subject at Camp Mohaven in Ohio in 1973. At that meeting, the church's leading scholars issued a report concluding that no scriptural evidence forbade ordination to women. Over the next fifteen years, the place of women in the Adventist ministry was widely discussed. The General Conference approved the ordination of women as local church elders and deaconesses. The status of a commissioned minister was created, providing women with virtually the same privileges and responsibilities as an ordained minister but without using the word "ordained."

A commission meeting in 1989 recommended two items to the 1990 General Conference in session in Indianapolis, Indiana. First, it unanimously affirmed "a significant, wide-ranging, and continued ministry for women"[7] according to the spiritual gifts they had received from the Holy Spirit. At the same time, the commission did not have a consensus "as to whether or not the Scriptures and the writings of Ellen White explicitly advocate or deny the ordination of women to pastoral ministry." The commission's second recommendation was that the church "not approve ordination of women to the gospel ministry." The reasons given were pragmatic: There was a widespread lack of support for it in the world church, and a decision to approve women's ordination created "the possible risk of disunity, dissension, and diversion from the mission of the Church." While the commission had looked at a wide variety of theological issues concerning ordination and women in ministry, the actual decision of the church contained no theological content. The delegates voted to accept the commission's recommendations by a vote of 1173 to 377.

The issue was raised again at the 1995 General Conference session in Utrecht, Holland. The North American Division had proposed that "a division may authorize the ordination of qualified individuals without regard to gender" if the division executive committee approves it. This proposal was defeated at the session with 673 votes in favor but 1481 opposed. Once again, the session did not address the theological issues of ordination and women's ministry in this vote. However, neither the 1990 nor 1995 decisions settled the matter. The subject continued to agitate the church. It took up this issue again in the second decade of the twenty-first century.

6. Hannele Ottschofski, "The Problem of Women's Ordination, Part 1: The Church in Finland Led the Way," *Adventist Today*, December 1, 2019, https://tinyurl.com/nh49rhfv.

7. All quotations from this paragraph are from the General Conference Action of July 11, 1990, https://tinyurl.com/2p8y3kze.

Resources

Campbell, Heidi. "Women in Adventist History." In *The Oxford Handbook of Seventh-day Adventism*, edited by Michael W. Campbell, Christie Chui-Shan Chow, David F. Holland, Denis Kaiser, and Nicholas Patrick Miller, 493–509. New York: Oxford University Press, 2024.

Jones-Gray, Meredith. *Forward in Faith: Andrews University, 1960–1990*. Berrien Springs, MI: Andrews University, 2024.

Questions for Discussion

1. What is the difference between operating institutions and institutionalism? How can the church avoid the dangers of institutionalism?
2. How have government policies affected Adventist education? What problems have arisen as a result of government policies? What might be some ways of addressing these problems?
3. What were some of the barriers to the growth of indigenous leadership in the Seventh-day Adventist Church? What have been some of the results of the shift to indigenous leadership?
4. What changes have occurred in the Adventist medical work since 1950? Do you see these changes as positive, negative, or neutral?
5. During the civil rights era in the United States, many black Seventh-day Adventist ministers became involved in social activism. How did this affect the church as a whole?
6. How did the Seventh-day Adventist Church leadership deal with allegations of modernity? Are issues related to modernity still a concern today? If so, how? If not, why not?
7. What has been the historical practice of the Seventh-day Adventist Church in relation to women's involvement in ministry and ordination?

CHAPTER 12

The Quest for Unity amid Diversity

An element of openness to diversity was implanted in the original DNA of Adventism. The legacy of individualism and independence left by puritanism in New England meant that any group of people in the United States would contain a wide variety of personalities with strong convictions and a readiness to express them. Americans wanted no dictatorial kings in any area of life. In addition, there was a strong commitment to religious liberty in the context of an Arminian religious atmosphere that exalted the human ability to choose. The result was an American religious climate that encouraged loosely based group organizations that embraced both a diversity of peoples and ideas. *New York Times* editorials editor Jyoti Thottam wrote, "Having a robust public debate, where many points of view are heard, is crucial to the functioning of a healthy democracy."[1] In the American church, robust debate is not just seen as crucial but is seen as a powerful tool that enables members to shape the future of their faith. Diversity and debate are not new ideas. They are part of the original ethos for America, the American church, and Adventism, and they continue to be the driving force behind its growth. This is why a core value of Adventism has always remained centered on the idea of "present truth" so that new ideas and change can be scrutinized and debated in light of already existing truth.

The issues that early Adventists dealt with continued to foster a wide variety of opinions throughout the life of the church, including personal religion, the relationship of faith and works, the place of the law, organization, biblical prophetic interpretation, and the application and interpretation of Ellen White's writings. Containing a broad spectrum of beliefs while yet retaining unity requires a commitment to some core principles, thereby embracing the sometimes lengthy process of reaching a consensus understanding of biblical truths. Adventism's commitment to biblical truth sets it apart from those trends in Western culture that would deny the possibility of objective truth, seeing truth as solely subjective, internal, and personal. This commitment to objective truth

1. Jyoti Thottam, "Opinion Today," *New York Times*, January 22, 2024, https://tinyurl.com/3hj6e4y7.

Robert Brinsmead, ca. 1966, in the Philippines. Note many of his themes on the blackboard behind him.

also means that the church must embrace the messy and often inconclusive process of agreeing on what is true. The Adventist movement has always had to discern the boundary where dissent moves toward opposition and discord.

The conflict in the late 1950s around the ideas of M. L. Andreasen, provoked by the publication of *Questions on Doctrine*, produced a group in Australia that supported the persuasive and charismatic Robert Brinsmead. Brinsmead's family had been part of the Seventh-day Adventist Reform movement but had joined the official Seventh-day Adventist Church in 1943 when Robert was ten. He studied at Avondale College in 1955 and developed a reputation as a good student who had a strong ideological perspective.

For Brinsmead, the sanctuary doctrine was the central message of the Seventh-day Adventist Church. From that basis, he developed ideas championed by M. L. Andreasen, who taught the necessity of the perfection of the saints before the second coming of Jesus. He reasoned that the sanctuary of the Old Testament and the heavenly sanctuary alluded to in the book of Hebrews were mirrored in the believer's life, each believer becoming a sanctuary of the living God. Satan's charge against God is that human beings cannot keep God's law. According to Brinsmead, the final answer to this charge is the group of believers who have become perfect at the end of time, flawlessly obeying God's law. Jesus had indeed entered the Most Holy Place of their minds, Brinsmead taught, and blotted out whatever conscious or unconscious sin he found there. This final group of saints, and only this group, were ready for Jesus to return.

Because his Avondale instructors and the church at large did not accept his interpretations of the sanctuary as he applied them to the believers, he began to attack the church. He taught that the church was involved in a "Holy Place" ministry when Jesus was calling for them to be involved in a "Most Holy Place" ministry. The church was in apostasy until it entered the open door into the second apartment of the sanctuary and fully embraced Brinsmead's ideas.

Brinsmead's last year at Avondale was filled with conflict, and he was refused readmission to the college in 1958. However, his persuasive presentations continued to be in demand. When his critical attitude toward the church led his home church to disfellowship him in 1961, he began to travel the world, spreading his ideas through the Sanctuary Awakening Fellowship. He remained in touch with some of his fellow students at Avondale, including Desmond Ford, who became the foremost champion of the mainstream church's position. As the two continued their theological dialogue, Brinsmead began to see the light in Ford's critique of his theology based upon the Reformation teaching on justification by faith alone.

By 1970, Brinsmead shifted from advocating an extreme form of perfectionism to preaching an extreme form of justification by faith. For him, justification was entirely forensic, objective, and external to the believer. He barely touched on sanctification and was openly critical of any theological discussion of subjective experience, identifying subjectivity with Pentecostalism. His criticism of the Adventist Church also shifted to an accusation that Adventists had adopted a Roman Catholic understanding of salvation by combining justification and sanctification. He abandoned his previous support of Ellen White's writings, dismissing her as a spiritual mother that he no longer needed. In quick succession, he questioned and then rejected the idea of an investigative judgment, the 2,300-day prophecy's reach to 1844 (in 1979), and then the Sabbath (in 1981). Brinsmead read widely in scholarly literature and became something of a self-taught New Testament scholar. He came to adopt a historical-critical perspective and rejected the divinity of Christ. Many of his followers abandoned his leadership when he rejected the Sabbath, and his influence virtually disappeared after he rejected a divine Christ. He settled on his farm and developed the Tropical Fruit World near Brisbane, Australia. He became concerned about environmental issues and got involved in local politics. He informed a visitor in the early 1990s that he had become agnostic in his religious beliefs.

Controversy over Ellen White

In the early 1960s, Ellen White was revered as a prophet whose writings were inerrant and infallible and needed little, if any, historical context or interpretation. What she had written was considered relevant for everyone, everywhere, and for all times. Few in the church knew how her books were written, revised, and sourced. The Ellen G. White Estate, directed by the prophet's grandson, Arthur White, carefully curated her papers and memory. This was a time when Ellen White was regarded as more than a prophet; she was believed to be a century ahead of her time, with compilations from her writings taken as authoritative in every aspect of life.

Walter Rea (1922–2014), a California minister, was a devotee of Ellen White. He subscribed to an inerrant and infallible view of her writings, often using her writings as a lens through which to interpret the Bible. He compiled enormous collections of Ellen White's comments on Bible characters and other topics. Having heard that Ellen White had used books on the life of Christ published in her day as she wrote *The Desire of Ages*, Rea began to read books by John Harris, Frederick Farrer, and other nineteenth-century authors. To his shock, he discovered passages very similar to what was written in *The Desire of Ages*. The more he read, the more he found. Clearly, the text of Ellen White's book was informed by and drawn from many nineteenth-century authors. Rea's devotion to Ellen White evaporated as his findings contradicted his prior belief that every word of her writings was inspired, having come as from a pipeline revealed to her by God in vision. He now saw how her writings depended on other human authors' words. Abandoning his view that she was inspired, he published a book entitled *The White Lie* in 1982, summarizing his findings. In it, he accused Ellen White of being a literary thief, lying about it, and blatantly stealing 80 to 90 percent of her writings from other authors. He claimed that she and her husband, James, exploited a "captive audience" for financial gain.

Rea's literary findings were news to most Adventists in the late twentieth century. However, the charge that Ellen White was guilty of plagiarism went back at least to D. M. Canright (1840–1919) in the 1880s. It was a topic at the 1919 Bible Conference, but the memory of that event quickly faded during subsequent controversies of the 1920s. When the 1919 Bible Conference records resurfaced in 1975, the subsequent publication in *Spectrum* in 1979 caused deep consternation. Church leaders were surprised that some two generations earlier, many church leaders, notably A. G. Daniells, W. W. Prescott, and Ellen White's son W. C. White, were open about historical errors and sources used in Ellen White's writings. These Adventist leaders did not seem to be bothered that *The Great Controversy* had been revised in 1911 to correct the mistakes in the 1888 edition. They did not see her writings as authoritative upon historical facts, and she clearly adhered to a more flexible and open view of inspiration than what had become familiar in the twentieth century, showcasing the lasting influence of fundamentalist notions of inerrancy within Adventist thought through the twentieth century.

William Peterson and Donald McAdams at Andrews University had already raised issues of Ellen White's use of sources in the late 1960s. Their studies revealed that Ellen White had used biased and inaccurate historians and was almost entirely dependent on them for her historical material. Subsequently, it was discovered that she had copied practically all of the borrowed historical material from Uriah Smith's writings. The Ellen G. White Estate scrambled to respond to this controversy.

The General Conference stepped in to do a thorough investigation of the matter. They sponsored a major scholarly investigation of the sources found in *The Desire of Ages* led by Adventist textual scholar Fred Veltman. They also hired a secular law firm specializing in plagiarism to examine the charges from a legal framework. Veltman's careful study compared *The Desire of Ages* to more than five hundred nineteenth-century books on the life of Christ and measured dependence on a scale of one to seven. It revealed significant borrowing in some chapters of *The Desire of Ages*. The reliance on other sources was more pervasive than expected. But the average level of dependence was that of a loose paraphrase, about 3.3 on Veltman's 7-point scale. There were very few strictly verbatim passages. At the same time, the charge that the entire book was copied from other sources was debunked since only 31 percent of the material showed any marks of dependence. The church had to admit that there was considerably more borrowing than they had previously recognized.[2] This was devastating for those who thought Ellen White's writings were dictated by God word for word. The church's leaders and members had to come to terms with the reality of the source of Ellen White's work, how her books had been compiled, and how to view her authority.

The legal case concerning literary piracy and copyright infringement was handled by the firm of Diller, Ramik, and Wight, with Vincent Ramik as the lead attorney. After reading the material that was critical of Ellen White's use of sources, he was inclined to believe that the charges were valid. However, he then read Ellen White's writings for himself. He described being moved by what he read. He found that Ellen White's use of sources was well within the

2. Fred Veltman, "The *Desire of Ages* Project: The Data," *Ministry* 63, no. 10 (October 1990): 4–7; "The *Desire of Ages* Project: The Conclusions," *Ministry* 63, no. 12 (December 1990): 11–15.

legal boundaries of "fair use" and that she was not guilty of either literary theft or copyright infringement.[3]

Church members who became aware of the controversy reacted in two contrasting ways. For many who had a strict view of Ellen White's originality and inerrancy, the evidence against these ideas was too strong. Instead of changing their minds about the nature of inspiration and adopting a more flexible thought-inspiration model, they rejected Ellen White's prophetic status altogether, or if they chose to remain in the church, chose a form of cognitive dissonance in which they ignored her.

In contrast, the discoveries about her writings brought other Adventists to a more realistic understanding of the process of inspiration. That process went like this: Instead of dictating words, God revealed himself and his ways directly to a fallible human being. He then sent his Spirit to guide that person in communicating what he had shown so that the revelation of him and his ways was accurate. God's revelation always comes in the context of human personality, religion, culture, and science. The person recording the revelation cannot escape these elements of humanity. God ensures that the revelation of him and his ways is true, but he does not miraculously preserve the record of the revelation from errors in history, cosmology, or science.

Thus, Ellen White wrote about God and his ways from within her personality, religious ideals, and cultural norms evident within nineteenth-century American culture and the scientific understanding of her day. These inescapably affected her writings. Those interpreting and applying them in the twenty-first century saw that they must consider the context of her writings. Thus, the church accepted a new understanding of what Ellen White wrote. No longer were her writings deemed inerrant in matters of history and science. From this more realistic perspective, they are accepted as God's revelation to Ellen White about himself and his ways. They are best interpreted and applied with their historical and literary context in mind. Ultimately, when their meaning is taken seriously, they point to God and his love and how humans can embody that love to others.

Controversy over the Sanctuary

Conflicts concerning the sanctuary, perfection, and the authority of Ellen White came to a climax in the person of Dr. Desmond Ford and his appearance at the 1980 Glacier View Conference. A distant relative introduced Ford to the Adventist faith, and he was baptized at seventeen years of age in 1946.

3. Vincent Ramik, "There Simply Is No Case," interview with Vincent Ramik, *Adventist Review* 158, no. 38 (September 9, 1981): 4–6.

1976 Palmdale Conference Wrestles with Theological Issue

The central question of the 1976 Palmdale Conference was the relationship between justification and sanctification. Twenty scholars from Australia and the United States gathered for discussions on the topic in Palmdale, California, April 23–30, 1976. The meeting came about at the request of the Australasian Division after a similar conference met in February of that year to discuss theological issues at Avondale College. A group self-described as the Concerned Brethren (CB) agitated against the theological position of certain teachers at Avondale, arguing that they were teaching a form of antinomianism (against the law) that was not compatible with official church teachings.

Conferees included General Conference president Robert Pierson, two scholars from Andrews University, editors from the *Review*, General Conference administrators, and nine scholars and church administrators from Australia, including Desmond Ford. The discussions focused on the biblical meaning of righteousness and righteousness by faith. They also dealt with the human nature of Christ. Pastor and former Avondale professor A. P. Salom argued that in Scripture righteousness is "essentially a matter of right status in the sight of God." He suggested that including the idea "to make righteous" in the meaning of righteousness was a Catholic interpretation. At the end of the conference, a concluding statement was issued, but it was explicitly not an official pronouncement from the church. Rather, it was a consensus statement that expressed what the group could agree upon.

The following year, he left his job writing for a newspaper and began studies at Avondale College, graduating in 1950. After completing a BA degree at Avondale, Ford was sent to America in 1958. In rapid succession, he earned an MA from the seminary in Washington, DC, and a PhD from Michigan State University with a dissertation featuring a rhetorical analysis of the Pauline epistles as written sermons. He returned to Australia in 1960 to teach at Avondale. He was among the foremost theological opponents of Robert Brinsmead during the 1960s, though he retained a personal dialogue with him. That dialogue bore fruit in Brinsmead's theological shift toward justification by faith.

Both Brinsmead and Ford opposed the theological perfectionism of the 1940s and '50s, which they believed left Adventists with no way of knowing how to be ready for the dreaded judgment day except to "try harder by God's grace" and hope that the judgment was in the distant future.[4] Brinsmead argued for an eschatological perfection with a present assurance in Christ, while Ford denied the

4. Robert D. Brinsmead, "A Review of the Awakening Message, Part 1," Current Theological Issues Reviewed (Fallbrook, CA: Present Truth, 1972), 4.

The first paragraph endorsed Ford and Salom's perspective. It stated, "We agree that when the words righteousness and faith are connected . . . in Scripture, reference is to the experience of justification by faith. God, the righteous Judge, declares righteous the person who believes in Jesus and repents. Sinful though he may be, he is regarded as righteous because in Christ he has come into a righteous relationship with God. This is the gift of God through Christ." In contrast to this perspective, three paragraphs later, the statement also affirmed, "Seventh-day Adventists have often used the phrase 'righteousness by faith' theologically to include both justification and sanctification." Both sides claimed that the consensus statement supported their position.

The consensus statement did not articulate a clear understanding of the Adventist doctrine of salvation and the issues of Christian assurance and perfection. Afterward, the church continued to be divided on these topics. Some feared that an emphasis on righteousness by faith would lead to cheap grace, a relaxed attitude toward the moral law, and the lowering of Christian standards. Others feared legalism, an emphasis on human performance, and inclusion of good works in salvation. The lack of consensus on the topic of salvation is at the root of many of the discussions in the 2020s on perfection and Last Generation Theology.[1]

1. Gil Valentine, "Palmdale Conference (1976)," in *Encyclopedia of Seventh-day Adventists*, January 29, 2020, https://tinyurl.com/2mm8b8ka.

need for personal perfection, seeing perfection as wholly in Christ. However, in the 1970s, neither Brinsmead nor Ford articulated an integrated theology of justification and sanctification. Brinsmead's 1970s emphasis on objective forensic justification left it completely separate from sanctification. For Ford, the most critical issue was justification by faith, which gives the Christian assurance of salvation. Sanctification was the inevitable fruit of the life of faith, according to Ford.

During the late 1960s, Ford experienced tragedy in his personal life. His wife, Gwen, was diagnosed with cancer, suffered for years, and then died in 1970. Ford took a study leave after Gwen's death and began studies toward his PhD in New Testament at the University of Manchester with the well-known scholar F. F. Bruce. Bruce was a conservative to whom evangelicals entrusted some of their most brilliant minds, but when these doctoral students returned to their respective denominations, they sparked major theological controversies.[5] Ford returned to teach at Avondale in 1973, completing his dissertation

5. Brian Stanley, *The Global Diffusion of Evangelicalism: The Age of Billy Graham and John Stott* (Downers Grove, IL: IVP Academic, 2013), 54.

on the "Abomination of Desolation" in Mark 13. Over the next four years, complaints about his teaching on righteousness by faith, the sanctuary, and the authority of Ellen White troubled Australian administrators. They arranged for him to take a temporary appointment at Pacific Union College (PUC), hoping the theological controversies would disappear. Ford's message and unusual charisma attracted renewed attention at PUC. They sparked significant conflict within the Religion Department, with teachers, including Ford, sharing conflicting theological perspectives in their classes. An initial attempt to resolve some of these issues was made at a conference in Palmdale, California, in 1976. (See text box on pages 230–31.) However, the controversy continued.

In this already-contentious atmosphere, Ford gave a presentation to the Angwin Adventist Forum about the investigative judgment on October 27, 1979. He argued that the traditional interpretation of the "cleansing of the sanctuary" and the investigative judgment was erroneous. In addition to questioning significant points of prophetic and exegetical interpretation, he said the doctrine of the investigative judgment robbed the Christian of an assurance of salvation. Ellen White was an important voice, but her inspiration was more "devotional" in nature than authoritative. With many on the PUC campus already upset with theological conflict, reports of the presentation struck like a lightning bolt.

Because Ford was an interdivision worker, the General Conference was quickly drawn into the controversy. His status as one of the leading theologians in the Australian church meant he couldn't merely be ignored or easily dismissed. The General Conference arranged for him to receive a study leave, write a document explaining his ideas, and present his position before church leaders and scholars gathered at the Colorado youth camp, Glacier View Ranch.

Before the gathering took place on August 10–15, 1980, attendees were provided with Dr. Ford's 991-page defense and various other documents written by Adventist scholars. The meeting lasted for five days, during which Ford presented his ideas and defended them from critiques. Ford's basic idea was that Christ had begun his ministry in the Most Holy Place immediately after his ascension in AD 31, not in 1844. One of the significant points of discussion had to do with Ellen White's authority in doctrinal matters. Ford insisted that Ellen White should not be an authority in doctrinal conflicts, but rather, her writings were only pastoral in nature. At the end of the conference, a statement of theological consensus was issued.[6] It included a critique of Ford and

6. "Consensus Statement: Christ in the Heavenly Sanctuary," *Ministry* 53, no. 10 (October 1980): 16–19.

a defense of the traditional teaching on the year 1844. It affirmed the biblical basis for the church's sanctuary teaching. It addressed the issue of Ellen White's authority by stating that "the writings of Ellen White provide confirmation of our doctrine of Christ in the heavenly sanctuary and supplement our understanding of it." However, it also broke new ground by stating that "in Daniel 8:14 it is evident that the word *nisdaq* (cleansed, justify, vindicate, restore) denotes the reversal of the evil caused by the power symbolized by the 'little horn,' and hence probably should be translated 'restore.'"

Ford expressed willingness to work within the "Consensus" document, but it was another ten-point document formulated through a separate administrative process in the Australasian Division that he could not accept. As a result, his ministerial credentials were revoked and his employment was terminated. This ignited a trans-Pacific firestorm, inflaming his supporters in Australia and America. The theological "Consensus," which saw light in some of Ford's ideas, was mostly ignored.[7]

Ford was not a revolutionary and did very little to stoke the flames of dissent, but his partisans soon adopted Walter Rea's and Robert Brinsmead's critiques of Ellen White. Some followed Brinsmead into unorthodox Christianity and agnosticism. Others moved outside of Adventism to other denominations and movements. Hundreds of ministers and teachers left denominational employment due to the turmoil caused by Rea, Brinsmead, and Ford. Some felt that Ford had been poorly dealt with, that his questions were begging for answers, and that the officials' responses were inadequate, but they remained in the church and stayed quiet. Dr. Ford founded an independent ministry and rarely spoke about the Adventist Church. When Brinsmead published his rejection of the Sabbath, Ford published a defense of the Sabbath. Ford's influence in the church faded within a few years of Glacier View.

The exegetical questions raised about the investigative judgment in Daniel remain unresolved in Adventism. In contrast to the perfectionist ideas that both Brinsmead and Ford rejected, recent interpretations emphasize that Jesus's judgment is *in favor* of the saints (Dan. 7:22). Rather than expecting flawless perfection, Jesus will declare that God's grace has saved them through faith; he will vindicate them in the face of their adversary (Satan). From this perspective, the believer can rest confident in the assurance of present salvation without the overconfidence of "once saved always saved." Other interpreters have emphasized that the adversary opposes God and slanders his

7. Trevor Lloyd, "The Untold Story of Glacier View," *Spectrum*, March 25, 2023, https://tinyurl.com/zwp4paje.

character. They suggest that the investigative judgment is ultimately about God and his willingness and ability to save sinful humans. The investigation is not so much about human performance as about the fairness of God's work with all human beings and whether the followers of Jesus are "safe to save." From this perspective, the judgment concerns whether believers' faith in God's justifying and sanctifying work has transformed their lives so they will not reintroduce sin into God's perfect new earth. It reveals how God has been just in his dealings with every human being.

Since Glacier View, the church has avoided further prophetic controversies, though some of the unresolved issues of prophetic interpretation and the authority of Ellen White remain. Some have sought to restore the "historic Adventist" position in opposition to the Trinity. But the church has moved on. By 2024, church members seemed less interested in doctrinal issues and more interested in personal spirituality and mental health. There were fewer attempts to defend traditional Adventist teachings on prophecy and more concern about living a loving, Christian life. For many church members, issues related to the sanctuary faded in significance while righteousness by faith and the relevance of Adventism in an ever-changing world became more prominent. Some suggested that the Adventist message is most compelling when Jesus's work in the sanctuary is presented in the context of righteousness by faith and integrated with the good news of how to live a flourishing Christian life.

Science and Religion

For many mid-twentieth-century Adventists, finding "the Truth" meant accepting the Seventh-day Adventist message and being baptized into the Seventh-day Adventist Church. The doctrines were sometimes referred to as "the Truth," such as "the Truth about the Sabbath" or "the Truth about the State of the Dead." Adventists often present themselves as the true church. The terminology of truth contains some inherent assumptions. These include the ideas that there is an objective truth, that one can distinguish between truth and error, and that one makes that distinction based on evidence. As we will see, these assumptions can be challenged, but they are crucial in discussions concerning science and religion.

Adventism arose at a time when Enlightenment ideas concerning the authority of reason ruled the culture of the Western world. Rejecting the authority of church, superstition, and tradition, the rationalists of the eighteenth-century Enlightenment saw reason as the way to avoid the horrendous religious wars of the sixteenth and seventeenth centuries. Reason decided on truth based on the weight of evidence rather than superstition, inclination, or tradition. Religious people, particularly in Protestant lands, readily embraced this thinking.

John Wesley, the founder of Methodism, had no problem aligning his religious movement with the Enlightenment emphasis on reason. In the eighteenth century, Wesley and the Evangelicals in Britain did not embrace the radical Enlightenment rejection of religion. Still, they shared with more moderate Enlightenment figures a belief that reason could help guide them to what was true.[8] Much of the religious environment of England was carried over the Atlantic to America. Thus, in the first half of the nineteenth century, American religion was characterized by evidentialism, the belief that one can know something is true based on the evidence.[9]

Consistent with American evidentialism, Adventists presented the evidence for the truth of the Sabbath, the state of the dead, the millennium, and other doctrines. The source of the evidence they offered was the Bible. The implications were that if the weight of evidence was on the side of one set of ideas, one should follow reason and the evidence and accept the Truth. In the late nineteenth century, one of Adventists' most effective evangelistic strategies was to debate preachers of other faiths, confident they could convince the hearers with the evidence they presented.

Science also grew from Enlightenment roots and produced incredible technological breakthroughs in the nineteenth century. Both science and religion accepted the Enlightenment's commitment to reason and evidence. However, they diverged when Charles Darwin raised the question of the origins of life with the theory of evolution. Scientists claimed that the evidence showed that life evolved from simple to more complex forms and that humanity evolved from simpler hominoid animals. Creationists, such as George McCready Price, disputed this evidence. The theory of the evolutionary origins of life won the battle for public opinion and has been little challenged since.

From the beginning of Adventist education, science has been taught in Adventist schools. The basic facts of chemistry, physics, and biology were not questioned. Adventists accept the technological advances that emerge from scientific inquiry. They affirm that the way to know truth is to explore the evidence in both the natural and religious worlds. What is remarkable about

8. David Bebbington, *The Evangelical Quadrilateral*, vol. 1 (Waco, TX: Baylor University Press, 2021), 11.

9. E. Brooks Holifield, *Theology in America: Christian Thought from the Age of the Puritans to the Civil War* (New Haven: Yale University Press, 2003), 5–8.

the Adventists of the mid-twentieth century is that they did not pretend that evolutionary ideas didn't exist. Instead, they sought scientific evidence to support their creationist perspective.

Concerns about scientific discoveries in paleontology, archaeology, and geology arose during Reuben Figuhr's presidency (1954–1966). These discoveries challenged the biblical record of creation, the flood, and ancient history. In 1958, a Committee on Teaching Paleontology and Geology was set up at Emmanuel Missionary College (later Andrews University). It took more official status as the Geoscience Research Institute (GRI) in 1962, remaining at Andrews University until its move to Loma Linda in 1980.

The GRI hired three scientists as staff. However, it soon became apparent that there were significant differences among them. Frank Marsh (1899–1982), a biologist, supported a six-day creation week, a recent creation of the earth, and a global flood. The other scientists were Richard Ritland (1925–2019), a biologist with a degree in comparative anatomy from Harvard, and Edgar Hare (1933–2006), a geochemist studying at the California Institute of Technology. Ritland and Hare thought that the scientific evidence for lengthy geologic ages was compelling. In 1964, Marsh returned to teaching, and Hare was released from the GRI appointment. Ritland became the director of the Institute, and Ariel Roth (b. 1927), newly appointed to help lead the PhD program in biology at Loma Linda, became a part-time appointee to the GRI. Three additional staff were appointed: Harold Coffin (1929–2015, PhD in biology), Harold James (PhD in geology), and Edward Lugenbeal (PhD in anthropology).

The divergence of opinions among the scientists at the GRI continued, with Ritland, James, and Lugenbeal seeking to accommodate lengthy periods of geologic time while Roth and Coffin supported a worldwide flood and a short chronology for life on Earth. The GRI sponsored a field trip in the summer of 1968 where church leaders heard presentations on both sides of the issue and viewed evidence in Yellowstone National Park and its surroundings. Robert H. Pierson, elected General Conference president in 1966, was present at these meetings and was shocked to hear GRI staff members advocate ideas counter to what he saw as the purpose of the GRI. By 1971, Ritland had returned to teaching biology at Andrews University, and Robert Brown, president of Union College, was appointed to lead the GRI. He had a PhD in physics and was more interested in addressing the larger issues of the relationship between science and religion than in solving the problems of chronology, life on the earth, and human origins.

In 1974, the GRI began publishing a scientific journal named *Origins* that became a leading advocate for understanding creationism from a scientific perspective. When Brown retired in 1980, he continued to do research while Roth became the director of the Institute. Brown's research uncovered carbon-14 at an unexpected geological level, supporting creationism by questioning the assumed age of geological layers.

In 1980, the Institute transferred to the campus of Loma Linda University to be nearer to other Adventist scientists and a more ample scientific library. The Institute continued to promote research supporting recent creation and flood geology. Creation scientists from other faiths came to respect the GRI's research for its scientific rigor and credibility in scientific circles. Contrary to most other creationists, Adventists had no problem accepting the idea that the creation of the universe took place a significant amount of time before the creation of the earth.[10]

George McCready Price had initially advocated the position that the creation of the universe had occurred at the same time as that of the earth. However, in the 1950s, he became aware of discoveries in astrophysics that dealt with extremely distant objects in space. Given the constant that light travels at the speed of 186,000 miles per second and the fact that light shifts colors according to the direction of an object in relationship to the observer (shifting toward blue for approaching objects and toward red for receding objects), it became apparent that the universe was of immense age, measured in billions of years. Price accepted these discoveries and modified his position, much to the consternation of some of his followers. Price was willing to accept hard scientific findings that were counter to his literal understanding of the Bible, and thus was willing to modify his understanding of the teaching of the Bible based on science. Therefore, Price and other Adventist scientists came to accept that Genesis 1:1–3 describes the creation of the cosmos, including the earth, at an unknown time in the far distant past. In contrast, Genesis 1:4–31 describes the forming and filling of the earth. Adventists do not have a uniform understanding of the process or timing of creation. Still, the shift in Price's thinking suggests a viable model for affirming both God's revelation in Scripture and his revelation in nature. Biblical interpretation and scientific interpretation may clash, but conclusive evidence from nature can guide biblical interpretation to more accurate views of the world. Just as the Roman Catholic Church resisted Galileo's discoveries but later accepted them as the basis for a new scientific paradigm and new ways of understanding the scriptural evidence, present-day scientific discoveries can help clarify biblical teachings.

10. Ariel A. Roth and L. James Gibson, "Geoscience Research Institute," in *Encyclopedia of Seventh-day Adventists*, May 10, 2022, https://tinyurl.com/3w644z6b.

Church Leadership Changes

At the 1990 General Conference session in Indianapolis, Indiana, Robert Folkenberg (1941–2015) was elected president in place of Neal C. Wilson. Folkenberg had most recently served as president of the Carolina Conference in North America, where he had managed some very creative projects, including an insurance program to self-insure the conference and save money. He was born in Puerto Rico to missionary parents, who also served in Cuba. He served many years as a pastor and administrator in the Inter-American Division. Folkenberg's presidency was marked by significant mission outreach. He went on extensive tours worldwide focused on global mission initiatives, working constantly on innovation. He started a weekly newsletter sent digitally to church members around the world. Tragically, his leadership was marred by unwise personal financial dealings that led to his resignation on February 8, 1999.

Jan Paulsen (b. 1935), a General Conference vice president, was elected president in Folkenberg's place. Paulsen, a native of Norway, had served as a teacher and administrator in Africa and Europe before moving to the General Conference. In 1972, he earned a doctorate at Tübingen University, where he wrote his dissertation on the coming of Methodism to West Nigeria. Paulsen, as a young theologian, had participated in the Glacier View meetings but felt that the church had not handled the situation very well. As a General Conference vice president, he had overseen the integration of segregated conferences in South Africa in the early 1990s. As church president, Paulsen brought a stabilizing influence and credibility after Folkenberg's unfortunate resignation. He was easily reelected in 2000, and again in 2005, but lost in a bid to one of his vice presidents in 2010. His presidency was characterized by a thoughtful and irenic style. He hosted a series of live talks with young people and encouraged open dialogue about issues within the denomination. His leadership was noted for its unifying elements. Even though he took a position favoring women's ordination, he did not push the denomination to adopt his stance.

Neal Wilson's son, "Ted" N. C. Wilson (b. 1950), was elected as General Conference president in 2010 with a desire to return Adventism to its roots. When elected, he expressed concerns about the teaching of evolution in Adventist schools and the need to purify the church from corrupt influences, especially the historical-critical method of interpretation, which Wilson believed both weakened and threatened the historical stances of the denomination. Wilson, for his part, had earned a doctorate in religious education from New York University while serving as the assistant director and then

Jan Paulsen

director of Metropolitan Ministries in the Greater New York Conference (1976–1981). His doctoral dissertation was a study of Ellen White's theory of urban religious work in New York City, largely drawn from Ellen White's writings. He distinguished himself early on for taking a literal approach in which he accepted Ellen White's writings, with little regard for historical context, as "totally correct and usable" for the present day. He then served as an administrator in Africa and for the General Conference, and then as the president of the Euro-Asia Division and the Review and Herald Publishing Association. From 2000 to 2010 he was a General Conference vice president.

Ted Wilson's administration was characterized by a more conservative stance toward matters of change, particularly regarding women's ordination. However, it found itself challenged during the recent culture wars by those self-described conservatives who accused it of not taking a stronger stance on issues such as vaccine mandates. He was reelected to the presidency in 2015 and 2022, and in 2025 was replaced by Erton C. Köhler, making him the second-longest serving president of the church in its history.

Adventists and Postmodernism

Reason, evidence, science, and Enlightenment thinking combined to create a modernist sensibility. The denial of these basic viewpoints brought postmodern thinking. Though postmodernist thinking has roots in the nineteenth century, it began to flower in the middle of the twentieth century with the French philosophers Jacques Derrida and Michel Foucault. Postmodernists deny that there is any objective reality. They argue that the human understanding of reality is a "construct" of practices and language. It is entirely internal to each person. Thus, there is no such thing as objective truth. Human reason and knowledge are fallible, so truth is unknowable. Some postmodernists say science, technology, reason, and logic are oppressive and destructive. Therefore, it is necessary to "deconstruct" the dominant general theories (metanarratives) because they impose conformity, marginalize people, and create totalitarian systems.

Adventist Footnote Wars

Adventist historiography rapidly changed beginning in the 1970s. Various new publications provided a new venue for Adventist historians to share their research, notably *Adventist Heritage* magazine, launched in 1974. A young cadre of historians interested in the topic began to share their ideas and scrutinize the past. While some focused on social history and more obscure topics, others began to reanalyze their own denomination's history and challenge long-established myths and hagiographical patterns.

The research of Ronald L. Numbers (1942–2023) with his 1976 book, *Prophetess of Health*, was the most important of these studies. In it, he demonstrated that many of Ellen White's health-reform ideas were not unique to her, showing how she drew from the writings of various health reformers in her day. The publication of his work created an immediate crisis. The White Estate responded with a meticulous critique. They noted all of the book's minor historical errors and typos but failed to respond in any substantive way to Numbers's central argument. Today, most Adventist historians recognize the importance of his research. Due to pressure from some church leaders, Numbers lost his denominational employment. Through these events and some personal difficulties, he lost his faith and became agnostic. However, he secured a tenured position as a professor at the University of Wisconsin–Madison, and had a distinguished career as a historian of medicine. In 1999, he was elected the president of the American Society of Church History. Before his recent passing, he had placed all his personal papers at the Center for Adventist Research at Andrews University.

As a young historian, Donald McAdams wrote a paper on his research about Ellen White's use of sources in *The Great Controversy*. It was privately circulated, but after examining it, the White Estate asked him not to publish it. When the minutes of the 1919 Bible Conference were discovered in 1974, discussion of Ellen White's historical material broadened even though this material was not widely known until *Spectrum* published excerpts in 1979. The 1919 Conference transcripts showed that church leaders, soon after Ellen White's death, recognized a more flexible view of her inspiration. The leaders in 1919 knew that she never claimed to be infallible regarding all historical details. An increasing number of historians, including Gary Land, Ben McArthur, and Paul Landa, found camaraderie by organizing regular meetings in conjunction with the

In his critique of postmodernism, James Sire suggests that there are some valuable insights to be gained from its perspective.[11] Postmodernism opposes modernism's optimistic view that reason and knowledge can arrive at truth. Since humans are fallible, their reason and knowledge are fallible, and absolute

11. James W. Sire, *The Universe Next Door: A Basic Worldview Catalog*, 5th ed. (Downers Grove, IL: InterVarsity Press, 2009), see chapter 9.

annual meetings of the American Historical Association. These gatherings ultimately resulted in the Association of Seventh-day Adventist Historians (ASDAH).

In the early 1980s, controversies over Ellen White's inspiration were sparked by the plagiarism allegations of Walter Rea. As a result, a series of in-depth research studies were initiated to investigate just how much she borrowed. Fred Veltman's "Life of Christ" project demonstrated that her literary dependence was not as widespread as critics alleged, and the opinion of a legal firm argued that she was within fair use of her day. Still, church leaders looked for new historiographical paths forward. One young educator, George R. Knight, established himself as an influential voice in the denomination with the publication of *Myths in Adventism* (1985). In this book, he examined a variety of myths. His careful historical research, placing situations in their context, proffered a more mediating position for many people. He showed a more credible approach that benefited from critical historical study but had a more constructive approach to Adventist history.

In 1979, Richard W. Schwarz wrote a rather expansive and thorough treatment of Adventist history as a textbook titled *Light Bearers to the Remnant*; by 2000, Floyd Greenleaf had updated this book into a new revision titled simply *Light Bearers*. Several Adventist historians from the 1990s onward have produced various historiographical narratives. Adventist historians became increasingly comfortable discussing Adventist history in the twentieth century as time progressed. In 2007, a group of historians gathered at Andrews University to reflect upon the meaning of *Questions on Doctrine* for a fiftieth-anniversary conference. During the 2010s a series of annual sessions about Ellen White and Adventist history became a regular feature at major professional conferences such as the American Society of Church History. Today, the debates over how to interpret Adventist history continue. Examining who cites who in their footnotes or endnotes reveals a lot about a historian's perspective. Apologetic or hagiographical approaches reflect only familiar sources that support the author's views. New and creative ways of educating the church about Adventist history continue with the latest podcasts, notably the *Adventist History Podcast*, *Adventist Pilgrimage Podcast*, and the *Ellen White Podcast*. The popularity of such podcasts showcases scholarly and popular interest by church members in the Adventist past.

truth is beyond human understanding. With postmodernists, it is valuable to remember that language and story are usually associated with power. It is also helpful to remember how social and cultural conditions affect how we understand the world. We do well to recognize that we have a limited perspective as finite creatures. At the same time, Sire suggests that postmodernism fails to provide a viable worldview. Its rejection of general theories is a general theory itself. Thus, postmodernism critiques its basic ideas and defeats itself.

In addition, its claim that we have no access to reality, that all we know is an internal construct, is itself a claim about reality. Is it true that we can never come to what is real and true? Finally, its critique of the autonomy and sufficiency of human reason is itself a product of autonomous and sufficient human reasoning. If reason cannot be trusted to bring real knowledge, then how can reason be used to make this critique?

All worldviews have consequences in the material world. The technology of the Enlightenment brought significant advances to human comfort and ease of transportation, but it also brought the horrors of modern war. No wonder there are those eager to escape the cold rationalism of the modern worldview! However, postmodernism's subjectivity has brought the world to a place where a video game is as real as the threatened environment. Postmodernism offers no way to prioritize the importance of the two. One person's facts are opposed by another person's alternative facts. For postmodernism, there is no way to judge between the two since there is no external and objective truth. One person's use of language is just as valid as the other person's, and both use words to assert their power.

Postmodernism has permeated global popular culture since the beginning of the twenty-first century. Religion is dismissed as a general theory that imposes conformity, marginalizes those outside its boundaries, and encourages totalitarianism. The world's cities are filled with men and women who live for the moment but often find themselves isolated and lonely. God is the ultimate general theory, so God's existence is dismissed. Truth is unobtainable; personal knowledge of another person is impossible; and commitment is just a language game. People are left by themselves, lost in a world without meaning.

Adventists seeking to minister in this environment face significant challenges but also have distinct advantages. Seeking to use modernity's techniques to appeal to postmodern people does not work. How can you convince someone of the truth of your teachings if they do not believe there is such a thing as objective truth? How can someone be convinced of the existence of God when they think that god-talk is just a construct of language and culture? However, Adventists can align with postmodern people because their understanding of knowledge and truth takes into account human limitations and fallibility. Adventists affirm that language is often used to assert power. Adventists have always critiqued empire builders' attempts to crush dissent, use people to enrich the elite, and promote materialist idol-ology. The best Adventist outreach to people in postmodern cities affirms these postmodern truths while affirming what is right and true about the Bible's teachings and ethics.

Beginning in the 1960s, European culture was deeply influenced by postmodernism, while its effects in North America began in the 1980s. By 2021, nearly 30 percent of people in the United States had no religious affiliation, up from 16 percent in 2007.[12] Church membership in the United States had fallen from 70 percent in 2000 to 47 percent in 2020. This drop in membership occurred in all major subgroups.[13] These trends have also affected the Adventist Church. Distaste for organized religion, resistance to authority, and sensitivity to issues of injustice are increasingly characteristic of young Adventists in North America and worldwide.

One example of an Adventist church reaching postmodern urbanites was found in the Zero Church in Madrid, Spain. Abigail Contero, one of the church's founders, explained the name by saying, "You have to start from zero when you work with secular people who don't believe in anything." Its point of contact with people was community outreach: visiting children in the hospital, feeding people who are without housing, and taking city children on outings. After building relationships during these activities, church members invited their new friends to their homes for small-group discussions. Bible studies were then offered at the church. Between 2015, when the church started, and 2023, several community folks were baptized, and a significant group of young Adventists returned to worship with the church. According to Kleber Gonçalves, director of the Global Mission Center for Secular and Post-Christian Mission, sixty-seven postmodern-sensitive congregations have been formed in South America during the same period.[14]

The Seventh-day Adventist Church adapted to the widespread changes in worldview and communication. However, it also found that it would be wise to do so thoughtfully and with its eyes open to unexpected implications. Any attempts at change based upon fear and timidity would keep it cemented in the past and make it impossible to adjust to changing norms and expectations. Adventism was founded as a dynamic movement, but as it became institutionalized, the question remained whether it could retain its truths as present truth. At the same time, some recognized that there was also a danger with adaptation. Some Adventists minimized the unique and distinctive teachings of Adventism, and some of these left the denomination. The denomination became more diverse and complex as new relationships and ways of forming community sought to maintain their connection with the mission and message of the Adventist movement.

12. "About Three-in-Ten U.S. Adults Are Now Religiously Unaffiliated," Pew Research Center, December 14, 2021, https://tinyurl.com/yfknjurf.

13. Jeffrey M. Jones, "U.S. Church Membership Falls Below Majority for First Time," Gallup, March 29, 2021, https://tinyurl.com/mr3d5j7u.

14. Andrew McChesney, "Cero Church," *Mission 360°* 11, no. 4 (January 2024): 13.

Resources

Anderson, Eric, ed. *Reclaiming the Prophet.* Nampa, ID: Pacific Press, 2025.

Davidson, Richard. "The Meaning of Nisdaq in Daniel 8:14." *Journal of the Adventist Theological Society* 7, no. 1 (Spring 1996): 107–19.

Ramik, Vincent. "The Ramik Report: Memorandum of Law Literary Property Rights 1790–1915." Ellen G. White Estate, August 14, 1981. https://tinyurl.com/8sc5rn4x.

Valentine, Gilbert M. *Ostriches and Canaries.* Westlake Village, CA: Oak & Acorn, 2022.

Veltman, Fred. "Life of Christ Research Project." Office of Archives, Statistics, and Research. Accessed March 18, 2025. https://tinyurl.com/bdcwr7w4.

Questions for Discussion

1. What lessons can be learned from the story of Robert Brinsmead?
2. What were the issues related to Ellen White that surfaced in the 1980s? Based on the material in this chapter, describe how you would resolve these issues.
3. What is the relationship between justification and sanctification? Is sanctification the inevitable fruit of the life of faith?
4. What were the issues related to the sanctuary that surfaced with Desmond Ford in 1980? How should the church resolve theological conflict?
5. If the writings of Ellen White are no longer seen to be inerrant in matters of history and science, then what about her writing about a young earth creation?
6. What is postmodernism? How has the church dealt with issues related to postmodernism?

CHAPTER 13

Formation of a Global Church

How did the Seventh-day Adventist Church become one of the planet's most widespread, inclusive, and integrated organizations? The seeds were planted in its earliest years as the unique mission and message of the church were developed. They were planted in fertile locations, and their sprouts were tended by skilled workers who ensured a continued commitment to the mission. The planting and nurture of the seeds were adapted to each local situation, showcasing the church's impressive adaptability. Thus, the church in Papua New Guinea emphasized the importance of peacemaking while putting comparatively little emphasis on eschatology. On the other hand, the church in North America tended to emphasize eschatology while giving little attention to peacemaking. The church in Africa emphasized deliverance from evil, while the church in China emphasized prayer and healing.

With but few exceptions, statistics indicate that the church continues to grow steadily worldwide. Some places, like North America, Europe, and Australia, have seen their rates of growth decline since 1970. Others, such as Central and South America, Africa, Korea, and the Philippines, have seen rapid growth during the same time. Much of the difference between these areas can be attributed to forces at work in the worldview and culture of each area. For the last seventy years, secularism has dominated the cultures of the Global North. In other areas, such as Central and South America and the Philippines, Christianity has, so far, remained dominant. In much of the world, Christianity has become a significant force for reform, renewal, and democracy despite its minority status. At the same time, secular and postmodern perspectives have spread around the globe and have impacted all societies, especially in the cities.

The West (North America, Europe, Australia, and New Zealand)

Unprecedented advances in science and technology fueled the colonial expansion of European culture between 1492 and 1950. As a result, European languages, Europe's Christianity, and its new and powerful technology had a

Adventist Development and Relief Agency International

As early as World War I, the Adventist denomination began to mobilize resources, often working with the Red Cross to provide relief supplies to devastated areas. With continued natural disasters, such as widespread floods and famines in China in the 1920s, the denomination continued to raise relief funds and contribute supplies. In 1956, the denomination officially launched the Seventh-day Adventist Welfare Service (SAWS) program, which began supplying relief shipments to 22 countries during its first year. Over time, the organization has shifted from being a welfare agency to looking at long-term development initiatives, resulting in a change of name in 1973 to the Seventh-day Adventist World Agency. As sustainable community development grew, the program reorganized a second time in 1984 as the Adventist Development and Relief Agency (ADRA). In 1997, ADRA achieved the general consultative status designation from the United Nations, the highest degree a nonprofit organization can be accredited. This allowed ADRA to work with increasingly marginalized populations around the world. Today, ADRA has over five thousand employees and seven thousand volunteers serving in over 120 countries. Apart from supporting communities in long-term humanitarian crises and conflicts, ADRA responds to an average of two disasters per week with country offices across different continents around the globe. ADRA is funded by private individuals, corporations, foundations, and other entities. It also receives funding and commodities from governmental and intergovernmental organizations, such as United States Agency for International Development and the United Nations. In June 2025, changes made by the new American administration forced ADRA to announce reductions of its workforce by 50 percent around the world.

profound impact on almost every land. Protestant missions and, ultimately, Adventist missions were influenced by these changes. Vibrant evangelical Christianity in Europe and North America created vibrant local churches in much of the world. Yet the challenge of modernism began to erode European, Australian, Canadian, and American Christianity. As a result, Christianity faded from cultural dominance in those places. One of the serious questions facing the church in 2025 is the spread of modernism and secularism in every society.

Both world wars were fought in Europe primarily by supposedly Christian nations. Christianity was unable to provide people in Europe with their most basic needs: peace, safety, and security. Christianity moved from being the organizing principle of society to being a relic of the past with little influence on society. In the initial years after World War II, Adventist churches grew in Europe. Still, the growth leveled off by 1965, and after that, the church retained its membership levels only as Adventist immigrants arrived from Africa, Asia, and the Americas. Secular Europeans had little interest in the Adventist message.

In the United States, the influence of secularism seemed limited to the well-educated elite. Compared to Europe, Canada, and Australia, Christianity in the United States seemed to thrive until about 1990. Then, for a complex set of reasons, the level of religious involvement began a significant decline.[1] People raised in religious homes who stopped engaging with religion cited two main reasons for leaving. One was a loss of faith, often due to challenges from scientific ideas. Second was disaffection with organized religion, often due to clergy financial and sex-abuse scandals.[2] Other factors cited were age, gender, education, politics, geography, religious intermarriage, as well as patterns of religious transmission, migration, and fertility.[3] Nonetheless, by 2025, the United States remained unique among wealthy Western countries with a relatively high level of religiosity.[4]

While the religious environment in the United States continues to change, it is still more hospitable to religion than other developed countries. Membership in the Seventh-day Adventist Church in North America continues to climb, but at a reduced rate. One factor in that growth is the high rate of expansion among Hispanic Adventists, primarily due to immigration and the conversion of first-generation immigrants. Other immigrant populations have also surged. Since 1980, African immigration to America has fostered many African churches. In 2024, it was estimated that nearly half of the Seventh-day Adventist members in the Minnesota Conference were African or of recent African descent.

One of the most significant facts about Seventh-day Adventists in the United States is their racial diversity. In comparison to other religious groups, Adventists are the most racially diverse religious group in the United States.[5] Immigration accounts for at least some of Adventism's rich diversity, with

1. "In U.S., Decline of Christianity Continues at Rapid Pace," Pew Research Center, October 17, 2019, https://tinyurl.com/ypxk9m4z.

2. Michael Lipka, "Why America's 'Nones' Left Religion Behind," Pew Research Center, August 24, 2016, https://tinyurl.com/mv2msydh.

3. "Modeling the Future of Religion in America: Methodology," Pew Research Center, September 13, 2022, https://tinyurl.com/3ec5bdfw.

4. Joey Marshall, "The World's Most Committed Christians Live in Africa, Latin America—and the U.S.," Pew Research Center, August 22, 2018, https://tinyurl.com/bdcm7ffv.

5. Michael Lipka, "The Most and Least Racially Diverse U.S. Religious Groups," Pew Research Center, July 27, 2015, https://tinyurl.com/4whhndan.

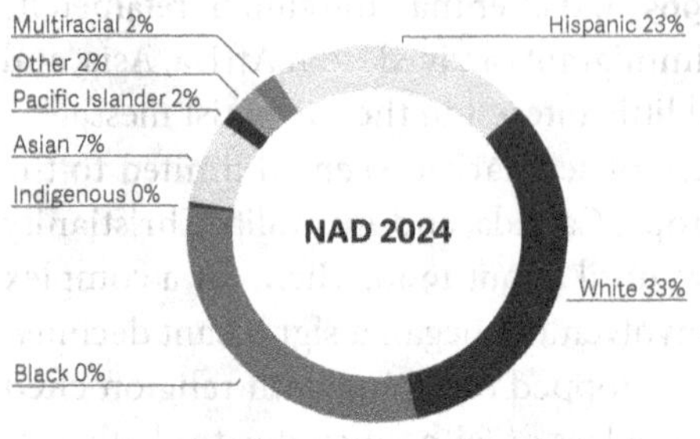

North American Seventh-day Adventist membership by ethnicity, 2024

significant patterns of migration from the Global South to North America. Evangelism among Hispanic immigrants is another factor. American Adventism's vibrant African American churches are a third reason for American Adventism's diversity. When the African American regional conferences were formed, advocates argued that they would be more successful in evangelism among African Americans. That assertion proved true. By 2024, there was no racial majority within the North American Division, with the fastest-growing demographic (30 percent) being the Hispanic and Asian constituencies, with steep declines among white and black church members.

Under communism, some of the Eastern European churches experienced growth. The communist governments sought to repress Christianity, but some were more friendly to Protestant Christians than to the dominant Catholic or Orthodox churches because the Protestants were seen as a counterweight to the influence of the traditional churches. Between 1950 and 1989, the church grew modestly in Bulgaria, Czechoslovakia, and Poland. During the same period, it grew significantly in Romania and Yugoslavia. Still, it lost mem-

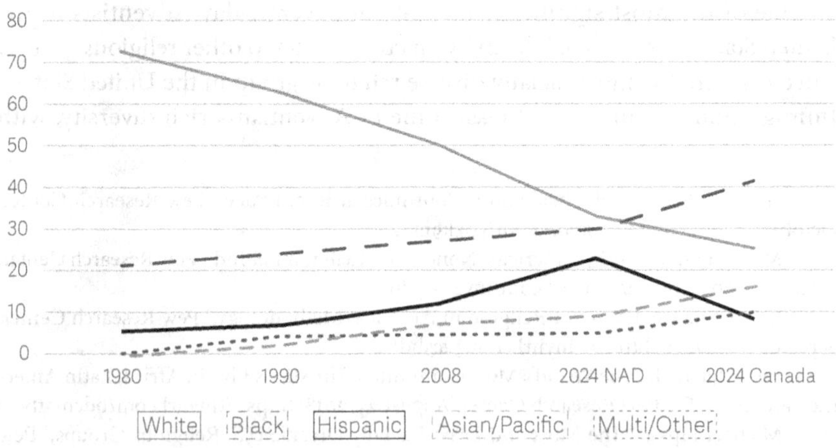

North American Seventh-day Adventist Demographics, 1980–2024

bers in Hungary due to a schism when a group of Hungarian pastors and laypeople left to protest the collaboration of church leaders with a communist-sponsored Protestant Council. For five years after the fall of communism in 1989, the church grew in all these countries, but recently growth has declined. In Romania, growth has leveled off partly because of significant emigration to other parts of the world. For example, there are noteworthy Romanian churches in Israel, England, and the United States, with an estimated six thousand Romanian members residing in Spain in 2008.[6]

Zaoksky Seminary, Russia

In Russia, the Communist repression of religion began to wane in the 1980s. The government allowed the Russian Adventist Church to build a seminary for pastoral training on the foundations of an old school building about seventy-five miles outside of Moscow at Zaoksky. The church members in the Soviet Union were so excited about the possibilities of the new building that 1,500 members volunteered their services for the construction. Most of the work on the building was done by hand since the builders lacked modern construction equipment to raise the four-story building. Those unable to volunteer gave financially, raising 1,500,000 rubles to cover the cost. It was the first Protestant seminary built in Russia. General Conference president Neal Wilson and many local and national government officials attended the dedication ceremony for the building on December 2, 1988. In addition to the seminary, the property also housed the headquarters of the church in Russia and its publishing work. In 2002, the school expanded from its roots as a theological seminary as it began to offer bachelor's degrees. By 2020, it was one of the largest Protestant schools in Russia, offering a full-fledged university program.

With the fall of the Soviet Union and the end of religious repression, Russia

6. Karel Nowak and ANN Staff, "Spain: Romanian President Attends Adventist Church in Madrid," Adventist News Network, October 27, 2008, https://tinyurl.com/e4pur74m.

The 1980 Statement of Fundamental Beliefs

Early second-advent believers borrowed the widely used Protestant statement that the Bible was their only creed. Their primary objection to creeds came not from the statements of belief themselves but from how they were used to enforce uniformity and exclude individuals with supposed heretical ideas.

However, even the earliest Sabbath-keeping Adventists had a strong sense of what they believed. Under the masthead of the *Review and Herald* for the first five months in 1854 appeared a list of "Leading Doctrines." It included "The Bible, and the Bible alone, the rule of faith and duty." Further doctrines included the law of God, the personal advent of Christ, the earth restored to Edenic perfection as the inheritance of the saints, and immortality alone through Christ.

Uriah Smith developed a more comprehensive statement in 1872, which was widely used in Adventist circles. A new statement of belief based upon Smith's statement appeared in 1919, partly in response to the rise of the fundamentalist movement. As Adventist missionaries interacted with colonial government officials and missionaries from other denominations, they wrote to the General Conference requesting a clear statement of beliefs to counter prejudices and misconceptions. After the new statement appeared, several subsequent variations were made.

This process led to the publication of a statement of belief in the 1931 *Yearbook*. Later, in light of the 1950s Evangelical Conferences that resulted in the publication of *Questions on Doctrine*, church leaders saw a new opportunity to explain their beliefs.

was flooded with foreign evangelists. Numerous Adventists held evangelistic meetings across the nation. Many people who knew nothing about God and the Bible were converted and baptized, and joined the Adventist Church. The flood of new members was too much for the newly liberated church to handle, and nearly three-fourths of them faded away. Nonetheless, church membership grew dramatically from 33,530 in the old USSR in 1990, with 7,067 in Russia, to 102,829 in the Euro-Asia Division in 2021, with about 40,000 in Russia. The Ukrainian church grew from almost 15,000 members to 43,000 during the same time.

The Russian attack on Ukraine, which began on February 24, 2022, created considerable difficulties for the Euro-Asia Division. With transportation and communication cut between the two countries, the division's viability seemed questionable since there were more members in Ukraine (43,307) than in Russia (40,864). The division's computer servers were in Ukraine for secu-

Further discussions about righteousness by faith in the early 1970s prompted church leaders to seek further clarity.

In late 1978, the General Conference appointed an administrative committee to work on a revision of the 1931 doctrinal statement. The first draft of the statement was completed in August 1979, and the following month, reviewed by a select group of seminary professors. They agreed that the proposed draft could be improved in style, organization, and content. Twelve professors quickly went to work and, within a reasonably short time, came up with a new draft. Working late one evening, they completed an entire rewriting of the document just in time for a meeting with General Conference officials the following day. Their document's style, organization, and content became the basis for all further revisions. After some minor changes, the document was distributed to union and division officials worldwide. It was eventually published in the *Adventist Review* (February 21, 1980). After collecting responses and suggestions, the document was revised and presented to the General Conference session on April 16, 1980.

General Conference Session, 1980

rity reasons, while the headquarters of the division were at Moscow in Russia, creating a digital nightmare. The interim solution was to reassign Ukraine to be administered directly from the General Conference, leaving Russia and the rest of the division intact. The division office was moved to Turkey on an interim basis. In Ukraine, ADRA provided relief to close to two million refugees and internally displaced people.

Central and South America

One of the most significant factors in advancing the Adventist Church in Central and South America has been educational work. Between 1980 and 2020, many small ministerial and teacher-training schools expanded into relatively large universities. These institutions did not depend on foreign sources for teachers or funding, sustaining themselves on tuition and local subsidies. The influence of students graduating from these institutions multiplied across the entire local church. Since universities focus on a broad range of subjects, graduates enter society in widely different careers. Among the notable schools impacting their countries' national life are universities in the Dominican Republic, Mexico, Jamaica, Trinidad, Brazil, Argentina, and Peru. As of 2023, the Inter-American Division had a total of 3,679,938 members, with the largest membership in Mexico (726,921 members, 0.56 percent of the population), Haiti (496,542 members, 4.3 percent of the population), Jamaica (336,513 members, 11.9 percent of the population), and the Dominican Republic (321,725 members, 2.9 percent of the population). In 2023, the South American Division had a total membership of 2,612,639. Its largest country, Brazil, has the second-largest Christian population in the world (185,000,000) after the United States. The eight unions in Brazil account for 1,764,770 members (0.8 percent of the population), the largest number of Adventists in any single country.

Both the Inter-American and South American Divisions have become almost entirely self-supporting. Much of this resulted from the social uplift provided by Adventist education. This effect is expected to continue since the educational work has expanded rapidly. The church opened medical schools in Mexico in 1975, Argentina in 1994, and Peru in 2012.

Africa

Since 1970, Christianity's fastest-growing region has been sub-Saharan Africa. "From 1970 to 2015, the region's Christian population grew from 47.5 percent (134,000,000) of the total population to 58.7 percent (565,000,000), an average annual growth rate of 3.2 percent," according to Gina Zurlo, a Christian statistician.[7] In other words, while the region's total population more than tripled over forty-five years, from 293,900,000 to 962,000,000, its Christian population grew even more quickly, more than quadrupling over the same period. Adventist membership growth was even more extraordinary: Total Adventist Church membership for sub-Saharan Africa in 1970 was 437,237, compared to 7,027,749 in 2015. For example, the General Conference Statistical Report shows that the 74,066 Adventist members in Kenya in 1970 grew to

7. Gina A. Zurlo, "A Demographic Profile of Christianity in Sub-Saharan Africa," in *Christianity in Sub-Saharan Africa*, ed. Kenneth R. Ross, J. Kwabena Asamoah-Gyadu, and Todd M. Johnson (Edinburgh: Edinburgh University Press, 2017), 1:3–18, https://tinyurl.com/37skt2t9.

824,185 in 2015, a multiple of 11.1 times. The 20,876 members in Zambia grew to 1,006,957 in 2015, for a multiple of 48.2 times. During this same period, there was a transition in leadership from overseas workers to local people. The local leaders had better rapport with the church members, and the church members took responsibility for the work. These factors certainly encourage church growth.

However, the statistical report for 2022 reveals another startling fact about the African church. In 1970, there were about twice as many Sabbath school members as there were church members: 880,534 to 437,153. In 2022, the figures were more than reversed: 9,906,091 church members, with a Sabbath school attendance average of 4,209,061. While statistical reports are subject to wide variations for multiple reasons, the 1970 statistics suggest a vibrant and attractive church, with many people attending for some time before becoming baptized. The 2022 statistics suggest that the church in Africa may have a majority of people listed as members who are actually inactive or that the reporting of Sabbath school attendance is incomplete, as it certainly is in the North American Division. However, the comparison of church membership to Sabbath school average attendance in Africa may reveal a high rate of attrition and a failure of discipleship.

When similar discrepancies developed in the Inter-American Division and the Southern Asia Division, there was a wholesale "cleaning of the books" in 2018 and 2019. Those listed as members who were found to be deceased, apostatized, or missing were removed from the rolls, bringing the numbers closer to reality. An adjustment to African statistics may be expected. Nonetheless, if we take the Sabbath school attendance average as the number of active Adventists in Africa, it is still remarkable. It suggests that there were almost ten times as many active African Adventists in 2022 as in 1970.

If you were to ask an African church member who graduated from an Adventist university in Africa what has changed in the African Adventist Church since 1980, you would hear both joy and concern. There is joy at the rapid growth in church membership and the institutions serving the church. There is a celebration of the transition from missionary leadership to local leadership. There would be rightful pride in the fact that there are Africans in the General Conference leadership. Alongside these joys, there are concerns. The emigration of many white South Africans has left a void that is hard to fill. The end of segregated conferences in South Africa brought some turmoil. The creation of Adventist universities has had a profound impact. In 2024, there were thirteen Adventist universities in Africa, in addition to other institutions of higher learning, more than on any other continent. The church created new medical schools in 2012 at the Adventist University of Central Africa in Rwanda and at Babcock University in Nigeria. The table listing Adventist universities below reveals how widespread they are across the continent and, thus, how influential Adventist education has become. At all these universities, many of the faculty and students are not members of the Adventist Church. This widens the influence of Adventist education but also creates a deep concern about the spiritual atmosphere on campus and the future Adventist nature of the institutions. However, the availability of advanced ministerial training has raised the level of education among the ministers in the entire continent.

Seventh-day Adventist Universities in Africa

Adventist University of Africa	Kenya
Adventist University of Central Africa	Rwanda
Babcock University	Nigeria
Solusi University	Zimbabwe
University of Arusha	Tanzania
Malawi Adventist University	Malawi
Helderberg College of Higher Ed	South Africa
Adventist University of Lukanga	Democratic Rep. of Congo
Clifford University	Nigeria
Bugema University	Uganda
Cosendai University	Cameroon
Valley View University	Ghana
Goma Adventist University	Democratic Rep. of Congo
University of Eastern Africa, Baraton	Kenya

The church in Africa also faces issues that seem to be shared elsewhere. There is a stark difference between conservative rural congregations and congregations consisting of educated and affluent people in the cities. In some places, there is also a contrast between conservative congregations in the less wealthy areas of a city and those in the more affluent areas. The conservative churches emphasize lifestyle issues such as dress, adornment, and Sabbath-keeping rules. Some continue to worship in one of the vernacular languages and use old hymnals such as *Christ in Song.* The educated urban churches in Africa are more attuned to the concerns and values of Europe or North America.

Growing in Christ

By His death on the cross Jesus triumphed over the forces of evil. He who subjugated the demonic spirits during His earthly ministry has broken their power and made certain their ultimate doom. Jesus' victory gives us victory over the evil forces that still seek to control us, as we walk with Him in peace, joy, and assurance of His love. Now the Holy Spirit dwells within us and empowers us. Continually committed to Jesus as our Saviour and Lord, we are set free from the burden of our past deeds. No longer do we live in the darkness, fear of evil powers, ignorance, and meaninglessness of our former way of life. In this new freedom in Jesus, we are called to grow into the likeness of His character, communing with Him daily in prayer, feeding on His Word, meditating on it and on His providence, singing His praises, gathering together for worship, and participating in the mission of the Church. We are also called to follow Christ's example by compassionately ministering to the physical, mental, social, emotional, and spiritual needs of humanity. As we give ourselves in loving service to those around us and in witnessing to His salvation, His constant presence with us through the Spirit transforms every moment and every task into a spiritual experience. (1 Chron. 29:11; Ps. 1:1, 2; 23:4; 77:11, 12; Matt. 20:25–28; 25:31–46; Luke 10:17–20; John 20:21; Rom. 8:38, 39; 2 Cor. 3:17, 18; Gal. 5:22–25; Eph. 5:19, 20; 6:12–18; Phil. 3:7–14; Col. 1:13, 14; 2:6, 14, 15; 1 Thess. 5:16–18, 23; Heb. 10:25; James 1:27; 2 Peter 2:9; 3:18; 1 John 4:4.)[1]

1. *28 Fundamental Beliefs*, 2020, paragraph 11, https://tinyurl.com/5n7hvra.

The one major issue that seems common across the continent is a concern with church members' involvement with spiritualistic rituals. This is not a new issue in Christianity or a problem only in the Adventist Church. Many who join Christian churches come from tribal societies where African indigenous religions are woven into every aspect of life. Since community is vital in these societies, a failure to carry out a designated ritual activity in relationship to the ancestors can create severe problems for new converts. In times of illness or mental distress, the spirit world offers readily available traditional solutions. The temptation to turn to indigenous religious practices is strong. Some members are ignorant of the biblical teaching on the state of the dead and spiritualistic practices. Others know these teachings but are drawn to traditional activity under significant family pressure and look to ancestral practices for comfort. Members of indigenous societies in Asia and Central and South America experience similar conflicts.

To meet the challenges of syncretistic practices, a new belief was added

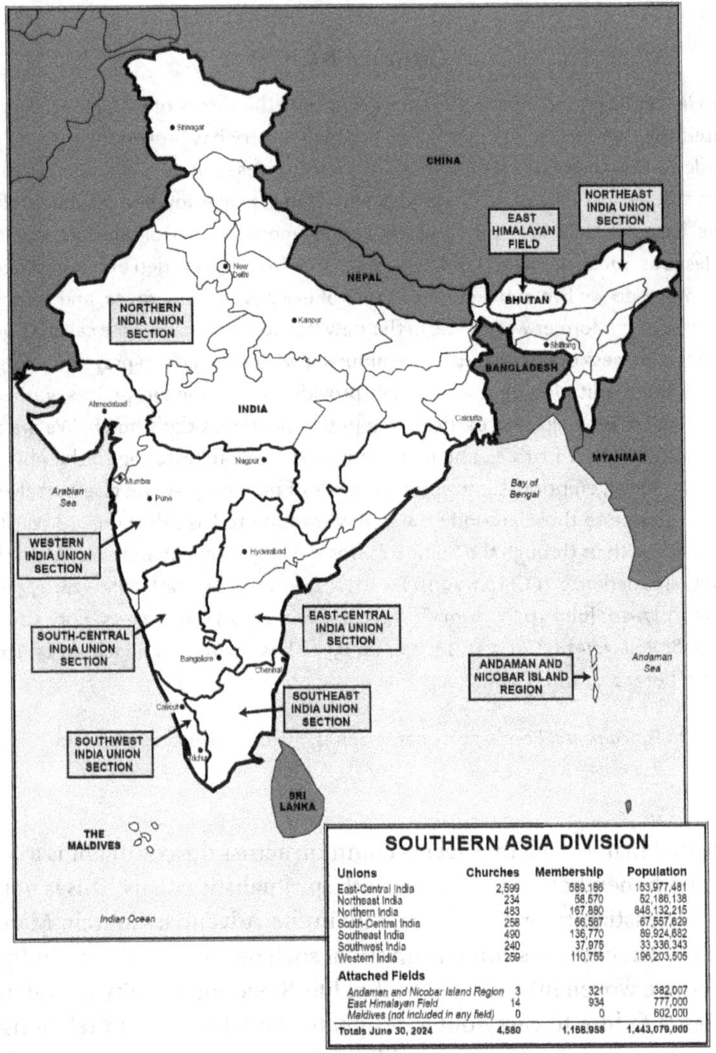

SOUTHERN ASIA DIVISION

Unions	Churches	Membership	Population
East-Central India	2,599	589,186	153,977,481
Northeast India	234	58,570	52,186,138
Northern India	483	167,880	848,132,215
South-Central India	258	66,567	67,557,629
Southeast India	490	136,770	89,924,682
Southwest India	240	37,975	33,336,343
Western India	259	110,755	196,203,505
Attached Fields			
Andaman and Nicobar Island Region	3	321	382,007
East Himalayan Field	14	934	777,000
Maldives (not included in any field)	0	0	602,000
Totals June 30, 2024	**4,580**	**1,168,958**	**1,443,079,000**

Map of India indicating the union subdivisions of the Southern Asia Division

to the official Statement of Fundamental Beliefs in 2005. Its stated topic was "Growing in Christ," and it specifically addresses the power of demonic spirits in the lives of believers. Emphasizing how Jesus triumphed over the forces of evil by his cross, the new statement points out that he subjugated demonic spirits to his will during his early ministry and broke their power. It states that Jesus's victory gives us victory over evil. We no longer need to fear evil powers because the Holy Spirit dwells within us and empowers us.

South Asia

In 1970, the church in India was tiny, both in numbers and compared to the country's population. The Statistical Report for 1970 listed 39,415 church members in a country with a population of approximately 557,000,000. That is one Seventh-day Adventist member for about every 14,144 Indians. The prospect for significant growth seemed small in a country that could be hostile to Christianity. Surprisingly, the membership doubled each of the following three decades to 87,869 in 1980, 163,384 in 1990, and 349,030 in 2000. However, between 2000 and 2010, the membership number more than quadrupled to 1,476,866. Correcting this number, the church's Statistical Report for 2020 significantly adjusts the church membership statistics by removing 491,330 members. Thus, the membership figure at the end of 2020 was 1,130,220. This shows that there is one Adventist member per 1,237 people in India.

Much of the growth in India occurred in the East-Central Section (with 578,514 members in June of 2022), encompassing the states of Andhra Pradesh and Orissa on the east coast of India. There is one Adventist for every 254 people in the general population. The rest of the Adventist membership in India is spread unevenly throughout the country. The Northern India Section has the largest population but only one Adventist for each 4,928 in the population. See the table below.

Sections (Unions)	**Population for each Adventist**
East-Central Section	254
Southeast Section	649
Northeast Section	923
Southwest Section	1,077
South-Central Section	1,113
Western Section	1,857
Northern Section	4,928

What explains these statistics? There was a major evangelistic outreach between 2000 and 2010. One part of this outreach was the deployment of Global Mission Pioneers. This innovative program began in 1990 and supported local volunteers in evangelistic outreaches to unentered areas. Global Mission Pioneers were less costly than overseas workers and had the advantage of being familiar with the language and culture.[8]

8. "Global Mission Pioneers," Seventh-day Adventist Church, accessed March 17, 2025, https://tinyurl.com/5fbz2eny.

Another factor in the evangelistic outreach was an effort to build new churches. In 1999, Maranatha International, an American volunteer organization, began a project to build churches in India. By 2020, volunteers had built two thousand church buildings in a country with 4,537 congregations and 4,788 companies. News reports tell how church buildings became centers for outreach. One of the earliest church structures Maranatha built was in Barara, Haryana, 128 miles (207 kilometers) north of New Delhi. The church building was constructed in November 1999 when the only two Adventists in the city were Pastor Sharan Masih and his wife. By 2020, the church in Barara had 400 members, and on special occasions, such as Christmas, up to 1,500 people gathered at the church, sitting inside the building and outside under tents. Five daughter congregations were established within three miles of the original church building. Fifteen church companies meet under the leadership of Pastor Masih and his wife.[9]

If this kind of outreach occurred in multiple areas, one can see how the church in India expanded rapidly after 2000. What is difficult to assess are all the other factors that attracted people to the church and why so many who did join later left. There are areas in Andhra Pradesh where Maranatha built churches, but the buildings are now abandoned with no pastor and no congregation.

East Asia

Three countries dominated the Adventist work in East Asia: the Philippines, Korea, and Indonesia. The most extensive Adventist presence is in the Philippines, the only Asian nation with a Christian heritage due to its Spanish occupation (1565 to 1898). The 2024 Statistical Report lists the membership for the Philippine church at 1,217,070, making it the largest Adventist constituency in Southeast Asia. The church's educational program has been one of the most significant factors in its remarkable growth. In 2025, the church operated ten colleges and universities in addition to the Adventist International Institute of Advanced Studies (AIIAS). At the same time, new issues emerged.

Conservative varieties of Adventism espoused by some early missionaries created challenges. A significant cultural issue dealt with marriage and divorce, as the Philippines remained the only country, besides the Vatican, to have no legal provision for divorce. Thus, Adventists are dependent upon Catholic priests to annul marriages or receive permission to move on to a new

9. Julie Z. Lee, "The Continually Growing Mission in India," *Adventist World*, November 5, 2020, https://tinyurl.com/5dz9pwsz.

relationship after abandonment. In some places, church leaders objected to the wearing of wedding rings while at the same time allowing dorms for gay students on college campuses. A 2020 survey of believers showed that while many believed in the seventh-day Sabbath and sanctuary, a majority of church members did not understand the biblical teaching that the dead rest in their graves until the resurrection. This revealed the lingering impact of syncretism and the need to implement Adventist teachings practically in the field.

Despite these challenges, Filipino Adventists remained among some of the church's most vital and devout adherents. Since one of the chief exports of the Philippines is its foreign workers, Adventism found itself spreading into new, hard-to-reach places thanks to these dedicated workers. Today, the largest Adventist presence in the Middle East is among Filipino foreign workers who have shared their faith with other immigrant workers.

The most dynamic Adventist church in Asia is in Korea, which has only had a significant Christian presence since 1883. In 2022, there were 262,261 members in Korea. Christianity has had an increasingly significant impact on Korea since 1950. Before the Korean War, the northern part of the country was the center of Christian work. Whatever Christian presence still exists in the North is entirely underground. In South Korea, Christianity, both Catholic and Protestant, surged to almost 23 percent of the population by 2021.[10] The growth of Christianity occurred in a society where only 17 percent of the population identified as Buddhist and 60 percent had no religious identity. Christianity has had a notable impact on the development of Korean society.[11]

Korean Adventism has grown in relationship to the population since 1980, from 1 in 918 (40,301 members) to 1 in 298 (260,114 members). This growth came with great vitality and originality, helped by South Korea's development into a wealthy nation. The Korean church has successfully used English-language schools as an evangelistic outreach. The 1000 Missionary Movement, founded in 1991, sought to mobilize 1,000 missionaries to give one year of service in mission work to unentered areas.[12] The movement was

10. "Korean Religion 1984–2021 (1) Status of Religion" [in Korean], Gallup, May 18, 2021, https://tinyurl.com/3fz9xrnh.

11. Donald I. Baker, "The Impact of Christianity on Modern Korea: An Overview," *Acta Koreana* 19, no. 1 (June 2016), https://tinyurl.com/yfr3khd5. And Kirsteen Kim, "Christianity's Role in the Modernization and Revitalization of Korean Society in the Twentieth Century," *International Journal of Public Theology* 4, no. 2 (2010): 212–36.

12. Morris Chit and John Wesley Taylor V, "Impact of the 1000 Missionary Movement Training Program on the Spirituality of the Trainees," *INFO* 3, no. 2 (October 2000), https://tinyurl.com/492ew8d3.

inspired by Jairyong Lee, a Korean pastor who became president of the Asia-Pacific Division, and its training facilities are in the Philippines. During the thirty years since its founding, it has trained 11,383 missionaries from sixty-four nations, serving in forty-seven global mission fields.[13] Alongside this outreach, the Korean church has taken a serious interest in overseas mission work, providing leadership and resources to places as far-flung as Bangladesh, Nepal, and Mongolia.

Sahmyook University, north of Seoul, has also seen dramatic growth. In 1980, it was a 666-student college; by 2021, it offered a complete university education to 5,332 students on its main campus. Of these students, only 14 percent were Seventh-day Adventists. The school viewed itself as a missionary school and had an intentional program to evangelize the students who had no faith or were of other faiths. However, by 2020, it faced some significant issues stemming from its rapid growth and low number of Adventist students. The number of applicants dropped. Due to secularization, it had to grapple with a loss of interest in the required religion courses.[14]

The church also has a significant presence in Indonesia, the most populous nation in Southeast Asia. In 2018, it was also one of the most actively religious nations on Earth, with 93 percent of the population claiming that religion was important in their lives.[15] Most people in the island nation are Muslims, but Christianity has spread primarily among indigenous people in Sulawesi and Sumatra and among residents of Chinese ancestry. There were 230,326 Adventist members in Indonesia in 2022.

In contrast to Korea, Adventist work in Japan has grown very slowly, from 9,373 members in 1980 to 14,977 in 2022. A similar slow growth rate has occurred in other Southeast Asian nations, where the religious background is more profoundly Muslim or Buddhist. As in Indonesia, many of those joining the Adventist Church in other countries of Southeast Asia come from tribal peoples, such as the Karen in Myanmar, or people of Chinese descent in the cities.

13. Edward Rodriguez, "1000 Missionary Movement Celebrates 30 Years of Service," *Adventist Review*, August 18, 2022, https://tinyurl.com/mvnnr5pe.

14. Kuk Heon Lee, "Sahmyook University," in *Encyclopedia of Seventh-day Adventists*, August 10, 2020, https://tinyurl.com/39u8vscu.

15. "The Age Gap in Religions Around the World," Pew Research Center, June 13, 2018, https://tinyurl.com/y3pa49cb.

China

For forty years (1950 to 1990) after the Communist Party gained control of China, the *Adventist Yearbook* reported only the last available information from China. It listed 278 churches and 21,168 church members. The South China Island Union Mission served Hong Kong, Macao, and Taiwan but had minimal contact with Adventists inside the People's Republic of China. All foreign missionaries were forced to leave China in 1950. The new Chinese government rapidly took over Adventist institutions. The church leaders were persecuted, and some were imprisoned. In 1956, David Lin (1917–2011), the secretary of the China Division, translated parts of *The Desire of Ages* and distributed copies. As a result, he was arrested and imprisoned for twenty years.

The government sought to create a single "postdenominational" Protestant church, combining all Protestants into the Three-Self Patriotic Movement (TSPM), which it controlled. In 1966, at the beginning of the Cultural Revolution, all religions were banned, and all religious institutions were dissolved. During this period, Christians in China could not practice their faith openly. However, many continued to meet in secret. A typical story from this period tells how the wife of a simple country farmer became gravely ill. An Adventist acquaintance offered to conduct a prayer service for her. The offer was accepted, and the wife was healed. She begged to know more about the God who had healed her. The Adventist family that prayed for her introduced her to the Bible and the clandestine group meeting in their home. The farmer and his wife experienced a profound conversion and became enthusiastic members of the group.

During this period, most Adventist believers retained their distinctive beliefs and practices and their loyalty to Adventism's unique identity, even though they had been forced into the Three-Self Patriotic Movement. When the government allowed churches to meet publicly again in 1976, some Adventists aligned with the Three-Self Patriotic Movement met in officially sanctioned church buildings on the Sabbath. While not formally related to the Seventh-day Adventist denomination, they identified themselves as Seventh-day Adventists. Contact between the denominational officials and Chinese Adventists occurred, but it was sporadic and secret. However, by 1991, the church felt comfortable enough to update the statement in the *Yearbook*. Referring to new data, the *Yearbook* did not list the number of churches but reported 75,000 members. By 2000, the *Yearbook* reported that 677 churches were open in China, and there were another 1,826 congregations with a total of 254,407 members. The 2023 *Yearbook* lists 1,160 churches and a membership

Exterior of the Beiguan Seventh-day Adventist Church in Shenyang, China

of 481,062. These statistics should be seen as minimal numbers since many Adventists still worship with unregistered congregations, which may not be included in these numbers.

Since 1978, Chinese Adventists have created four informal ways of relating to the state, its religious structure, and each other. All see themselves as Seventh-day Adventists, but their patterns of belief and life are different. Attempts to reconcile the factions and unite the church in China have been unsuccessful. One group, the "Old Faction," is conservative. They see themselves preserving the old Adventist traditions they received from the missionaries. They tend to be members of the older generation. The "New Faction" see themselves as reformers, having three distinct marks: an emphasis on salvation by grace, the use of a Lord's Prayer ritual in their worship services, and the use of a hymnal that contains some new translations of missionary hymns as well as some Chinese Christian songs from recent Christian authors. A third group consists of conservatives who share the same commitments to Adventist doctrines as the "Old Faction" but refuse to align with the government-sponsored Three-Self Patriotic Movement. The fourth group split off the "New Faction" but is doctrinally and liturgically close to it. They tend to be younger and emphasize their commonality with other Protestants. They also tend to dismiss what they see as the conservatives' legalism and reliance on Ellen White.[16]

One of the distinctive marks of the Chinese Seventh-day Adventist Church in the early twenty-first century was the existence of ordained female pastors. The Bible Women of the early twentieth century provided a pattern for this development. They were among the most potent local forces for advancing Christianity and Adventism. Beginning in the 1860s, Protestant missionaries found that middle- and upper-class women in China were confined behind closed doors. To reach these women, Protestant missionaries created the role of "Bible Woman." Mrs. B. Miller (1876–1945) was the Adventist missionary primarily responsible for the women's work in Shanghai and its surrounding

16. Christie Chui-Shan Chow, *Schism: Seventh-day Adventism in Post-Denominational China* (Notre Dame: University of Notre Dame Press, 2021), 21–22 and passim.

Interior of the Beiguan Seventh-day Adventist Church in Shenyang, China

provinces between 1908 and 1940. An example of her influence can be found in the woman who served as her cook and household helper when she first arrived in Shanghai. The helper was a practitioner of indigenous Chinese religion and was virtually illiterate. However, she was deeply impressed with Mrs. Miller and her work. She learned to read Chinese so that she could read the Bible. Mrs. Miller taught her how to pray and expound the Scriptures. She was baptized and eventually became a full-time Bible Woman, planting and pastoring churches around Fenshui (Fenshuizhen) in northwestern Chekiang province. It is the Bible Women and those they trained in the local villages who kept Christianity alive in the countryside while it was outlawed between 1966 and 1976.

As Adventists emerged from the underground, it was women who primarily attended church gatherings. Since most men were employed by state enterprises, they were forced to work on the Sabbath. The state had encouraged the liberation of women from conventional expectations, so women saw nothing wrong with assuming church leadership. Beginning in 1990, the Three-Self Patriotic Movement ordained Adventist women in church leadership. By 2020, some ordained women led large congregations in buildings explicitly identified as Seventh-day Adventist churches. For example, Pastor Hao Ya Jie is the female ordained lead pastor of the Beiguan Seventh-day Adventist Church in Shenyang, China.

Between 2000 and 2018, foreign religious workers were allowed to speak and even hold semipublic meetings in China. Informal groups printed Adventist literature, and many Adventists received religious training outside China. However, in 2018, the Chinese government began a process called Sinicization. Foreign religious workers were no longer allowed to speak in China. The unofficial publishing work was closed. Anyone leaving China for religious training was interrogated and intimidated. Some Christian workers were arrested and imprisoned.

The Middle East

Before World War I, a thriving Adventist Church existed among the Armenian people in the Ottoman Empire. Most were living in what is today Turkey. However, the war brought genocide against Armenians, and in the aftermath of the war, most Greeks and the remaining Armenians were forced out of Turkey. There was also a small but active Adventist presence among the Christians in Iraq. In Egypt, George Keough did innovative work among both Muslim and Coptic people between 1909 and 1928. However, until recently, there has been little successful Adventist work among the dominant Muslims in the area. This is not unique to Adventism. Christians over the ages, including Francis of Assisi, Ramon Llull, Ignatius Loyola, and Samuel Zwemer, have sought to work with Muslims with little success.

Zwemer was inspired by the Student Volunteer Movement and spent nearly forty years in the Middle East as a missionary. He visited American colleges (including Union College in 1909)[17] to recruit missionaries for Muslim outreach. Zwemer began his ministry in the Middle East with a polemical approach that sought to point out the problems of Islam and show how it was not correct, logical, or historical. He later shifted to a less confrontational approach that sought to build relationships and affirm what was good in Islam. But his efforts resulted in probably no more than twenty-five converts.[18] Some Adventist missionaries studied with Zwemer at the School for Oriental Studies in Cairo.

A further challenge for Christianity in the Middle East has been the general exodus of Christians from the area in the last thirty years. Adventists have been among those leaving.[19] In 2000, there were 775 Adventist members in Jordan, Lebanon, Syria, and Iraq. In 2022, there were only 612. It seems likely that most of the local Adventists departed during that time and that most of those listed as members were migrant workers from Africa and Asia.

Recent work by Jerald Whitehouse has encouraged Adventists to consider a new way of relating to Muslims on spiritual matters. Whitehouse served as a missionary in Libya and Lebanon from 1966 to 1973. He became interested in

17. A. N. Anderson, "Union," *Central Union Outlook* 2, no. 5 (February 6, 1912): 4.

18. John Hubers, "Samuel Zwemer and the Challenge of Islam: From Polemic to a Hint of Dialogue," *International Bulletin of Missionary Research* 28, no. 3 (July 2004): 117–21, https://doi.org/10.1177/239693930402800306; Ruth A. Tucker, *From Jerusalem to Irian Jaya: A Biographical History of Christian Missions* (Grand Rapids: Zondervan, 1983), 241.

19. Todd M. Johnson and Gina A. Zurlo, "Ongoing Exodus: Tracking the Emigration of Christians from the Middle East," *Harvard Journal of Middle Eastern Politics and Policy* 3 (2013–2014): 39–49.

a different approach to Muslim Adventist relations during that time.[20] Many Adventists working in Muslim lands followed the polemical approach that Zwemer had used in his early ministry.

The new approach was known as contextualization. It focused on building bridges from Christianity to Islam and providing culturally acceptable literature, dialogue, and worship. Those involved in contextual ministry to Muslims initiate studies of Jesus in the Qur'an, observe prayer and festival rituals with Muslims, and speak of themselves not as Christians but as followers *of ʿĪsā al-Masīḥ* (Jesus the Messiah). That is because many Muslims equate Christians with the Crusaders. Whitehouse saw his new approach as a way to assist Muslims in preparing for the return of *ʿĪsā al-Masīḥ*, since the return of Jesus is one of the fundamental beliefs of Islam.

Whitehouse was appointed the ADRA director of a country on the continent of Asia and had the opportunity to try the contextualized approach. Working with two local Adventists from a Muslim background, he developed an outreach to Muslims in the countryside. There was considerable discussion when Whitehouse first presented his plan to the Division Committee. Some were quite skeptical. However, a General Conference vice president argued it was worth a try since none of the other approaches the church had attempted with Muslims had succeeded. After his comment, the division approved Whitehouse's plan.

Spearheaded by the two former Muslim Adventists, the approach began with studies of Jesus in the Qur'an. Eventually, it led to the study of the *Injil* (the gospel and the rest of the New Testament). This method found ready acceptance in one of the country's rural provinces. Those who responded were discipled into a biblically based faith and were led to adopt the basic beliefs of Seventh-day Adventists, including the Sabbath. They were baptized but remained within their Muslim community without repudiating Islam. None officially became a member of the Seventh-day Adventist Church, leading to some angst on the part of denominational officials.

By 2024, there were more members of this unofficial group than official members of the church in that country, which remains nameless for security reasons. Church leaders gave extensive consideration to how this unique ministry could relate to the worldwide Adventist Church. They decided that the best solution was to allow independent Adventist-supporting ministries to

20. See Wolfgang Lepke, "The Story of Jerald Whitehouse," in *A Man of Passionate Reflection: A Festschrift Honoring Jerald Whitehouse*, ed. Bruce L. Bauer (Berrien Springs, MI: Dept. of World Mission, Andrews University, 2011), 19–36, https://tinyurl.com/mrx7b6ee.

assume the coordination and supervision of an expanding number of contextualizing ministries, most of which are without publicity by design.

Adventist Frontier Missions (AFM) has also initiated "tentmaking" missions to Muslim countries. While it explicitly rejected the contextualization approach, as did the denominational leadership after 2010, it also sought to begin work with Muslims by building personal relationships rather than by an argumentative approach. AFM's missions have had limited success in encouraging Muslims to become Seventh-day Adventists. Another approach has included the movement of Brazilian tentmakers to Muslim countries. Because of security concerns, not much has been published about any of these efforts.

A recurring theme in this survey of trends in the Adventist Church in the early twenty-first century is the challenge of secularism. Another theme is growth, but it is tempered with concern about the need for discipleship. A third theme is migration, with people from the Global South impacting the church in the Western world and Westernized migrants returning to impact their homeland. Undergirding all these trends is a devotion to the mission and message of the Seventh-day Adventist Church. Those involved in sharing the three angels' messages are impatient for the return of Jesus.

Questions for Discussion

1. How would you define secularism? Where have you seen its influence in the Seventh-day Adventist Church?
2. How has Adventist education influenced the church in South and Central America as well as Africa?
3. What challenges does the church face in Africa? What do you see as some of the solutions to these challenges?
4. The church faces significant problems with discipling its new members. What might be some ways of addressing these problems?
5. What might be some reasons for embracing the contextualized approach to Muslims? What might be some reasons for rejecting it?

CHAPTER 14

Opportunities and Challenges

The greatest challenge facing the Seventh-day Adventist Church remains balancing faithfulness to the mission and message of the church with adapting to a diverse and changing world. It remains to be seen how Adventism will relate to significant shifts in the world population. Other points of tension and discussion include global population shifts due to migration, changes in birthrates, competition for and the limits of natural resources, creation care, race, and the church's views on gender. Each of these calls for a balance between impatience for Christ to return and patient waiting. The church will need to discern what activity its mission calls for and what it should wait for God to accomplish.

Population and Birthrates

The 1980s witnessed a concern about a global population explosion. By the 2010s, however, it became apparent that steeply falling birthrates worldwide were significantly impacting religions worldwide, including Adventism. Such declines have coincided with greater affluence and a tendency toward secularism.[1] Total fertility rates in the United States between 2020 and 2025 have averaged 1.9 children per woman for Christian women, 1.6 for religiously unaffiliated, and 2.0 for women of other religions.[2] Such figures are probably similar in other countries in the Global North. One of the lowest birthrates in the world has been in Japan, at 1.26 (2022), with 70 percent of the people estimated to identify as nonreligious.[3] On the other side of the globe, Uruguay has a birthrate of 1.49 (2021), with 44.5 percent identifying as nonreligious and another 42.4 percent identifying as Deist or atheist. Declining birthrates in

1. See Philip Jenkins, *Fertility and Faith: The Demographic Revolution and the Transformation of World Religions* (Waco, TX: Baylor University Press, 2020).

2. "Modeling the Future of Religion in America: Methodology," Pew Research Center, September 13, 2022, https://tinyurl.com/3ec5bdfw.

3. Mari Yamaguchi, "The Nones of Japan," Associated Press, October 5, 2023, https://tinyurl.com/ywb788kr.

An Adventist Theological Continuum

A wide range of theological perspectives extends across Adventism, ranging from reactionary conservatism to progressive liberalism. This continuum can be seen in the wide range of media ministries with their online presence.

A characteristic among reactionary groups, such as Fulcrum7, Walter Veith, and ADvindicate, is that prooftexts from the Bible and Ellen White feature prominently in their publications. The publishers of *Fulcrum7* were once associated with ADvindicate but parted ways over the more liberal political views it sometimes published. Thus, Fulcrum7 has not only a religious but also a socially and politically conservative muckraking agenda. Its website states its belief that progressive liberalism has taken over Adventist educational institutions along with various administrative levels of the church. Thus, they tended to be critical of the denominational structure. Walter Veith's online lectures not only promote literal creationism but also advocate that the King James Version is the only accurate English Bible translation. He also argues that Jesuits have infiltrated Adventism. During and after the COVID-19 pandemic (beginning in 2020), Veith promoted a range of conspiracy theories that connected the pandemic to his belief that Christ would return before 2027. The website of a third conservative group, ADvindicate, states that it is theologically supportive of the denomination but sees itself as able to deal with controversial issues in a way that the official Adventist publications cannot. It strongly opposes women's ordination and accommodation for the concerns of people with LGBTQ+ orientations.

While still quite conservative but maintaining a more positive view of the organized church, Doug Batchelor of Amazing Facts and his former associate Steven Bohr of Secrets Unsealed Ministry focus more on traditional forms of evangelism and Adventist apologetics. Secrets Unsealed has a significant Spanish-language ministry. The Three Angels Broadcasting Network (3ABN) is another conservative organization. Its international programming features mainstream Adventists along with a wide range of independent ministries, such as Secrets Unsealed. Amazing Facts and 3ABN remain independent of the denomination primarily because their leadership does not wish to abide by denominational policies and regulations, which they would find quite

many nations of the globe contribute to the probability of substantial migration shifts as various people groups around the world with larger populations migrate to more available resources or compete for limited resources.

Migration has always been a major factor in world affairs. In the Bible, Abram was a migrant from Mesopotamia to Palestine. Jesus was a migrant from Judah to Egypt. Paul traveled throughout the Mediterranean region, visiting migrant churches. All of the nations in modern Europe have their limiting, especially regarding the denominational wage scale. When church leaders in the late 1990s and early 2000s were unable to bring these ministries together, the denomination formed its own official media ministry known as the Hope Channel.

The Adventist Defense League is also fully supportive of the church, though not endorsed by it. This lay-run organization's website seeks to provide high-quality responses to issues raised by former and progressive Adventists who criticize the denomination and its theological positions. They are an example of a new form of apologetics that has arisen as media ministries proliferate with the need to debunk false and misleading information. At times, online sources and their translation have helped spread ideas from one part of the world quickly to another. In Asia, in about 2013, an Adventist lay member invested sizable financial resources to translate English-language anti-Trinitarian materials into various languages across Asia. Within a very short time, anti-Trinitarian topics quickly became a significant issue of concern.

On the more progressive side of Adventism, Loma Linda Broadcasting Network has a variety of channels appealing to international audiences. It is fully supportive of the denomination and usually avoids controversial topics.

Two of the most progressive Adventist media sources include *Adventist Today* and *Spectrum*, with each providing news and opinion pieces in both print and online. Their newsfeeds often cover news items that official channels do not cover because they might embarrass the denomination. *Spectrum* is published by the Association of Adventist Forums, founded in the 1960s, to meet the needs of the growing number of graduate students attending graduate programs. Today it remains a source for progressive scholarly articles on a wide range of topics of current interest as well as a forum for art and poetry by Adventists. Both *Adventist Today* and *Spectrum* publish articles in their journals and websites that are critical of denominational decisions, and they both support full accommodation of LGBTQ+ activists' concerns. They also publish articles that attempt to reconcile scientific accounts of Earth's history with the biblical account. Theological articles they publish tend to advocate for a revision of Adventist theology to make it more relevant to the modern world.

From conservative to progressive Adventism, Adventist church members have many sources and choices from which to gather information.

roots in a significant migration of "barbarians" that occurred in the fifth and sixth centuries. All Americans of European or African descent migrated across the Atlantic. In fact, the spread of Christianity throughout the globe has come about primarily through migration.[4]

4. Jehu J. Hanciles, *Migration and the Making of Global Christianity* (Grand Rapids: Eerdmans, 2021).

These patterns of migration are especially evident in the Seventh-day Adventist Church. The pressures and challenges of migration were especially evident by 2020 as the migration of church members, including pastors and teachers, from other parts of the world supported the declining populations of church members in the Global North. This trend led to a seismic shift in denominational demographics.

In the 2020s, a growing percentage of church members in places such as England and Ontario, Canada, are of Caribbean or African descent. The historic populations of whites and blacks in these areas have been replaced mainly by immigrant groups, leading to inherent tensions between these groups due to differing cultural expectations, particularly concerning race and gender. North America has also seen significant waves of immigration from Central and South America, resulting in a substantial increase in the Spanish-speaking population, which accounts for nearly one-third of the church membership of the North American Division in the mid-2020s. These demographic changes within the church mirror global population shifts and furthermore highlight the challenges and opportunities the church faces in the modern world.

Another significant migratory shift has been in places with large numbers of Seventh-day Adventists, such as the Philippines. Many Adventists are included in the 2,300,000 overseas Filipino workers who work in many countries around the world, some in places where Adventism has had difficulty establishing a presence. Filipino Adventists serve as nurses, pastors, and teachers worldwide. Immigrant Filipino workers in Middle Eastern countries have organized immigrant churches in traditionally Muslim lands. Those countries tolerate a minimal Christian presence to satisfy the needs of their migrant workers.

The leadership of the General Conference, historically dominated by people from North America, Europe, and Australia, no longer has any significant representation from these areas at the world church headquarters. In 2024, the three executive officers consisted of one North American, Ted Wilson, as president; one person from Inter-America, Paul Douglas, as treasurer; and another from South America, Erton Köhler, as secretary. Similarly, the composition of the North American Division is made up of G. Alexander Bryant (African American), executive secretary Kyoshin Ahn (Korean), and Judy Glass as treasurer (white). Likely, the significant pool of leadership for the future of the world church will come from areas where most of the denomination's 23 million members live. Declining birthrates and immigration have radically changed the Adventist denomination worldwide. The denomination that largely began in North America among people of European heritage has become an immigrant church in Europe and North America, sustained by the movement of many different groups who have migrated from around the world.

Creation Care

From the earliest beginnings, Adventists have watched the heavens for signs of the end. Whether earthquakes or typhoons, changes in the earth or the heavens have been seen as indicators of Jesus's soon return (Rev. 11:18). As time has progressed, a burgeoning world population with limited resources, coupled with the human tendency to exploit nature, suggests difficult times ahead. The increase in temperatures brought about by the Industrial Revolution has caused global warming, which in turn has begun to melt the polar ice caps and cause sea levels to rise. These changes point to the probability of significant migrations of large numbers of people responding to drought, flooding, loss of seaside homes, and the likely political upheaval that these changes will bring. It is no wonder that scholars have noted that the Christian church of the future will have to grapple with the reality of climate change.[5]

A survey of Adventists in the American South suggests that Adventists are more aware and sensitive to creation care than most evangelical Christians.[6] This appears likely due to the Adventist emphasis upon the seventh-day Sabbath and God's creation of this earth. The Sabbath is a sacred symbol of God's creative and redemptive activity.

Adventists believe that Jesus is coming, and they value the world made new. It stands to reason that if God placed humanity as stewards of this earth, one must learn how to care for God's creation while patiently waiting for Christ to return. An additional impetus comes from an Adventist reading of Revelation, which points to a cataclysmic time right before Christ's return. When the earth is made new, it is notable that there will be "no longer any sea" (Rev. 21:1). This can reassure God's people, who at times impatiently wait for an end that will come when there will be no more rising sea levels. The logic of Adventism is that God expects those going to a new earth to first take care of the earth that they inhabit. God's people ultimately look forward to the time when the earth will be made new again (Rev. 21:5).

5. See Philip Jenkins, *Climate, Catastrophe, and Faith: How Changes in Climate Drive Religious Upheaval* (New York: Oxford University Press, 2021).

6. Robin Globus Veldman, *The Gospel of Climate Skepticism: Why Evangelical Christians Oppose Action on Climate Change* (Oakland: University of California Press, 2019).

On the other hand, there do remain some Adventists who either avoid the topic or deny that climate change even exists. Some point to conspiratorial ideas or a culture of avoidance, and still others suggest that Roman Catholic support for the mitigation of climate change is a reason why Adventists should not talk about climate change and creation care.

In 2024 the first creation care conference was held at Andrews University. It resulted in a gathering of scientists and theologians to actively discuss the implications of climate change for Adventism in the future. While conversations continue, Adventist responses are, at best, mixed, even if somewhat predisposed to care for the environment. For a world church impacted by such an important issue, the Seventh-day Adventist Church is uniquely poised to engage in continued conversations about the environment. Some historians have pointed out that the Christian church of the future will need to care deeply about the environment and speak about its rapid deterioration.

President Wilson and Samuel Saw visiting President Duterte of the Philippines on November 10, 2021

Nationalism and Secularism

A significant issue facing the Seventh-day Adventist Church in the twenty-first century is tribalism or nationalism, prioritizing one's ethnicity or politics above one's Adventist or Christian identity. This has been a long-standing problem, whether one looks at the infatuation of some Adventists with Hitler in the 1930s or the massacre of the Tutsis by the Hutus in Rwanda in 1994. In that later crisis, Adventists were on both sides of a genocide. Some surveys suggest that leaders around the global church believe that nationalism remains one of the most divisive issues in Adventism.

The quest for political favor has risen as populations of Adventists in some parts of the world have surged. Politicians are eager to exploit the Adventist population base to get elected. In 2016, Rodrigo Duterte was elected to a six-year term as president of the Philippines. His term in office was marked by nativism and anti-American rhetoric. Once, in conflict with the Roman Catholic bishops, he threatened to become a Seventh-day Adventist. This received significant attention, especially within the Adventist community. The possibility and prestige of having the head of their country join their community, despite his ignorance of its beliefs or a conversion experience, rose to fever pitch among Adventists. Ultimately, he never joined Adventism, but such aspirations did pave the way for visits by political leaders to Adventist events and, at one point, a visit by Ted Wilson and division leaders to the presidential palace.

In the 2016 American election, Adventists had a viable presidential candidate for the first time, surgeon Ben Carson (b. 1951). His candidacy briefly gained traction, but Donald J. Trump eventually overtook him. Carson then accepted a place in Trump's cabinet, becoming the highest Adventist government official in the history of the United States, even as Carson distanced himself from his Adventist background. Trump's election raised questions about the relationship between Adventists and politics in the country where Adventism began. Adventists were divided by the culture wars, especially after the election, with debates about the COVID-19 vaccine and wearing masks. Many socially and politically conservative Adventists, worried about rapid changes in the broader culture, supported Trump's bid to exclude immigrants and place conservative justices on the Supreme Court who ultimately overturned the ruling supporting abortion rights.

Intriguingly, Adventists mirrored the broader culture wars in America. In the late 1970s, abortion became a loyalty test among conservative evangelicals.

Ben Carson, a candidate for the United States presidency

In the Adventist Church, which had a more moderate position on abortion up until that point, the stance of many Adventists morphed with the culture, especially in the southern United States. In the 1970s, conservative church president Robert H. Pierson kept a notebook of controversial topics, which included abortion. His notebook suggests that the church should be careful about the topic of abortion and retain a moderate position, noting that medical personnel should be consulted when necessary. Yet, as the wider culture shifted among evangelicals, making this a test of orthodoxy, many Adventists came to see this as a vital topic. They believed that abortion should be strictly forbidden in all but the most extreme circumstances. Such changes can be seen in statements made by the denomination that shifted the church's official stance toward a more conservative viewpoint in 2019.[7]

Some church members and even leaders became dedicated to conspiracy theories such as QAnon and actively supported Trump. A group of Adventists distributing copies of Ellen White's *The Great Controversy* showed up in news coverage at major political milestones, notably on January 6, 2021. On that day, when attempts were made to disrupt the transfer of power to the newly elected Joseph Biden, copies of the book were seen being thrown into the air and into the trash afterward. Again, on July 14, 2024, at the time of an assassination attempt on Trump in his run for a second term, media coverage featured interviews with Adventists gathered once again to distribute copies of *The Great Controversy*.

Culture wars became especially pronounced in Adventist churches with the COVID-19 pandemic in 2020–2022. Many regions of the world had significant limits, whether mandating face masks or closing churches. Before the pandemic, many churches had been resistant to both an online presence and online giving. The pandemic forced them to quickly go online and adopt online giving through the AdventistGiving.org website and app. As of 2024, over 1 billion dollars were being received annually through this digital financial process. Participation in online giving grew from 10 percent of churches in North America to 99 percent within a year, requiring the expansion of personnel at the North American Division headquarters to provide infrastructure and support. Similar growth occurred throughout the world. Consistent with the broader culture, smaller churches tended to decline while larger churches grew since they could offer a wider variety of programs for an online com-

7. General Conference of Seventh-day Adventists, "Statement on the Biblical View of Unborn Life and Its Implications for Abortion," November 13, 2019, https://tinyurl.com/yc6kr793.

munity. Overall, Adventist financial contributions grew during the pandemic despite an economic recession. Many local congregations became exceptionally polarized as they either explicitly favored or rejected protective masks or vaccines.

The first twenty years of the twenty-first century saw a massive worldwide shift from voice, printed text, and video in analog format to digital communication via the Internet. This shift had a major impact on journalism, shifting it from print to online. The introduction of smart phones put the fastest computing technology at everybody's fingertips. For the first time in world history, people could instantly contact anyone around the globe at virtually no cost. Just as Adventists adopted radio and television to spread their message, Adventists have adopted the Internet as a means of evangelism. The 1990s witnessed a series of global evangelism ("Net") events that featured prominent Adventist speakers that were downloaded by satellite to various sites around the world. By the 2010s digital evangelism focused on creating online forums and a digital presence.

During the pandemic, many schools and churches pivoted to Zoom and other similar forms of technology to gather for Sabbath school, church, Pathfinders, Bible studies, or to pursue one's education. However, digital isolation created a yearning for more meaningful points of contact, and churches and schools that returned to in-person services tended to recover attendance and giving patterns sooner than those that did not. This also contributed to the development of entirely virtual churches and new methods of communicating with members by turning Bible studies, classes, and sermons into regular podcasts.

It became possible for almost anyone to disseminate their views on the Internet to audiences worldwide. Some of the most popular online pundits promulgated unusual and absurd content often amplified in new ways. Some people became confused by a strong and powerful media personality and came to believe things for which there was no evidence. At the same time, the increased proliferation of content made it more challenging than ever for one's voice to be heard amid so much noise. Online social media stars tended to garner extra views and attention because of their sensational or absurd ideas and ability to master complex algorithms to attract viewers. Some of the most salacious and sensational content often received the most views, creating an increased amount of false information and conspiracy theories. Perhaps some of the most widely watched content was produced by Adventist purveyors who made money capitalizing upon Adventist fears about Jesuit infiltrators. One particularly prominent website touted a mix of conspiracy theories with

Ted Wilson speaks at the 2015 General Conference session

politically and socially conservative messages, creating a conservative blend that was unable to separate faith and politics from one another. Since social media respects few limits, these trends have been amplified worldwide.

Gender

Historian Molly Worthen has argued that every major denomination has had to wrestle with women's ordination.[8] Often, these debates were prefaced by a discussion on spiritual formation, and how the denomination responded signaled whether it would resist or embrace change in its relationship to the larger culture.

Seeking to develop a worldwide consensus, beginning in 2010, General Conference president Ted Wilson initiated a series of measures leading to what many hoped would be the definitive decision on the part of the church. Committees were created in each of the world divisions to study the theology of ordination. Each committee was tasked with making recommendations to a General Conference committee concerning the biblical theology

8. Molly Worthen, *Apostles of Reason: The Crisis of Authority in American Evangelicalism* (New York: Oxford University Press, 2013).

of ordination related to women's ordination. Meeting between 2010 and 2014, the thirteen divisions of the world church each held their own Theology of Ordination Study Committee (TOSC) to meet and arrive at their own conclusions. Seven of the thirteen committees concluded that the textual material from the Bible and Ellen White supported the ordination of women or contained no barriers to that ordination. After the division committees met, the overall General Conference Theology of Ordination Study Committee met in June 2014. Of the ninety-five voting members, sixty-two (65 percent) supported women's ordination.

Stacked ballots ready for the vote on women's ordination

Wilson had established a process with the TOSC to discern the direction the church should go on women's ordination. However, he then chose not to follow that process to the conclusion evident in the commission's recommendations. Instead of taking the recommendation of the General Conference TOSC to the floor of the General Conference session, the steering committee merely offered a simple up-or-down motion on the issue, thereby not allowing for any mediating position(s). The motion included an affirmation that each delegate had prayerfully studied the issue of ordination in the Bible and the writings of Ellen White, as well as the reports of the study commissions. It included an affirmation that the delegate was voting for what was best for the church and the fulfillment of its mission. The delegates were then to indicate whether it was "acceptable for division executive committees, as they may deem it appropriate in their territories, to make provision for the ordination of women to the gospel ministry? Yes or No." After a lengthy discussion, during which President Wilson spoke concerning the question, the 2,363 delegates cast their ballots: 1381 voted no, and 977 voted yes.

It should be noted that none of the votes on women's ordination at General Conference sessions dealt with the actual theological issues; all merely addressed pragmatic policy issues. In this context, two unions in North America reexamined their policy of ordination in the structure of the Seventh-day Adventist Church. Administrators in the Pacific Union and the Columbia Union noted that no actual policy exists in the denomination forbidding the ordination of women. The only policies that shed light on the issue referred to ordained ministers with masculine pronouns. They also noted that the issue

Annual Council members vote on the compliance committees

of granting ordination ultimately rested at the union level. Arguing implicitly that the issue should never have been debated at the General Conference level, the Pacific Union and Columbia Union constituencies voted to adopt ordination without regard to gender. Among the first to be ordained in these unions was Sandra Roberts, who was subsequently elected by the constituents of the Southeastern California Conference as their president. In 2021, the Mid-America Union also approved an action that resulted in the ordination of women. Similar discussions have occurred in Europe and Australia, where, due to laws pertaining to the equality of men and women, the denomination has had to push for equal and full ordination status for both men and women or, in some instances, ceased to offer credentials altogether.

Wilson took the view that the North American unions that approved women for ordination were not in compliance with General Conference policy. Between 2015 and 2017, he brought items to the Annual Council each year, seeking to bring the unions into compliance. None of his proposals succeeded in accomplishing his goal. The General Conference Executive Committee proposed a set of compliance committees at the 2018 Annual Council, but ultimately, they needed more support to function and were abandoned. Some church leaders, even though they favored restricting women in pastoral ministry, did not want additional scrutiny concerning noncompliance with other church policies. For example, some regions of the world wanted to avoid drawing extra scrutiny, especially regarding financial policies and auditing. It seemed to them that the compliance committees were an example of General Conference overreach. They did not see the need to enforce uniform policies for the entire world church that could, in turn, expose themselves to noncompliance in other areas of church policy.

Even in Western countries, generally in favor of women's ordination, there was no uniform support for it. Some Adventists strongly identified with the historical fundamentalist wing of American religion not only about the role of women but also on other issues such as abortion, gun rights, and vaccines. The best example is Doug Batchelor, the Amazing Facts television ministry leader and one of the wealthiest televangelists in America. He inherited some of his wealth, but Amazing Facts sets its own pay scale, and, in 2024, all of its top administrators were reported receiving between $140,000 and $208,000 per year.[9] He criticized what he viewed as liberal-leaning theologians at the Seventh-day Adventist Theological Seminary. As a famous evangelist with a strong following, he made controversial posts on social media, including a remarkable one of a men's group toting guns, advocating a militant, muscular variety of Adventist Christianity. Supporters of Batchelor noted his traditional folk-style approach to Adventist evangelism, one that garnered consistent financial support from a global fan base.

Perhaps the most controversial topic facing the church in the early twenty-first century related to lesbian, gay, bisexual, transgender, queer, and other sexualities (LGBTQ+). The church was forced to deal with this issue, beginning with the founding of Kinship International in 1981. The 1980s and 1990s brought increasing awareness of the topic. This sparked a wide variety of responses. The official position of the denomination was that a person with a homosexual orientation should live a celibate life and not advocate for this lifestyle. Ultimately, the denomination condemned all same-sex "practices and relationships" and remained very public in its opposition to same-sex

9. "Amazing Facts," Ministry Watch, updated March 28, 2024, https://tinyurl.com/2durjsvm. As of March 2024, Amazing Facts received a score of 36 out of 100 for financial efficiency from Ministry Watch and a recommendation of "withhold giving." Its financial efficiency is in the bottom 20 percent of comparable ministries. It received a D grade for transparency for not being a member of the Evangelical Council for Financial Accountability and for not posting its audited financial statement on its website, among other things. It reported net assets of nearly $104,000,000 on the government IRS Form 990. This marks it as the third-wealthiest educational media ministry on Ministry Watch's list.

marriage.[10] In 2023, the denomination launched a new task force on human sexuality to educate church members on the topic.[11]

Church members affected by sexual abuse and violence came forward to tell their stories during the #MeToo movement that emerged in North America in 2017. When state and provincial regions removed time limits within which victims could seek legal solutions, the denomination began to face new lawsuits. In response, the church implemented new safeguards for all church employees and all adults working with children.

Tragically, in West Virginia, thirty-two plaintiffs came forward in 2017 alleging significant abuse that occurred at a self-supporting institution run by Adventist church members. Since a conference official had served on its board, a court found the denomination liable by association. The church reached a record $100,000,000 settlement with the plaintiffs, and some staff members were jailed.[12]

This lawsuit had profound implications for the denomination as it reassessed its policies and put into place new measures to help prevent further sexual abuse. New policies were implemented to ensure that church employees did not serve on boards from entities not listed in the *Seventh-day Adventist Yearbook* without administrative approval. Such policies were an attempt to limit legal exposure to the denomination from self-supporting institutions not governed by church working policy. Since these institutions were often led by people with intense personalities, they could quickly face crises and disappear, leaving the denomination on the hook for the mess left behind. While many self-supporting institutions made positive contributions, the lack of serious accountability created potential liability problems the church was no longer willing to accept.

10. "Stances of Faith on LGBTQ+ Issues: Seventh-day Adventist Church," Human Rights Campaign, accessed March 31, 2025, https://tinyurl.com/2m3bt87r, and the official position of the denomination is available at: General Conference of Seventh-day Adventists, "Seventh-day Adventist Position Statement on Homosexuality," October 3, 1999, revised October 17, 2012, https://tinyurl.com/sy6xfmzh.

11. General Conference of Seventh-day Adventists, "God's Gift: Human Sexuality," 2024, https://tinyurl.com/ycy99udw.

12. John Raby, "Lawsuit Settled over Widespread Abuse of Former Students at Shuttered West Virginia Boarding School," Associated Press, updated August 23, 2023, https://tinyurl.com/bdcs6p93.

Adventists and Culture

Since its beginning, the broader culture has impacted Adventism, yet the church has also contributed to the broader culture. Some of its contributions have been profound. Whether people worldwide realize it or not, Adventists have impacted their lives, from breakfast cereals to sophisticated medical care. Some of the longest-living people on the planet are Adventists, as featured in Blue Zones by *National Geographic* magazine. Adventist facilities are part of one of the largest health-care systems in the world, with the systems in North America grossing over 40 billion dollars annually by 2024. The AdventHealth 400 race and car (mentioned in chapter 11) demonstrate how Adventism has shifted from a movement on the margins to one in the mainstream.

Adventism has also contributed to the broader culture in some rather uncomfortable ways. During the heyday of the fundamentalist-modernist controversy, the Adventist movement shifted from simply being anti-evolution to a narrow flood chronology through the writings of George McCready Price. Some Adventists, eager to protect their system of private education, supported the second wave of the Ku Klux Klan with its racist sensibilities. And B. G. Wilkinson, in his militant opposition to liberalism, touted the idea that the King James Version of the Bible was the only inspired translation. Such ideas contributed to extreme fundamentalist rhetoric and the polarization of American religion.

Conversely, Adventists have been far more influenced by the broader culture than previously acknowledged. Adventists made every significant structural change in the denomination's history when confronted with depression and bankruptcy. For the most part, Adventists have paralleled the wider evangelical and fundamentalist trajectories, especially regarding race and gender. For a movement in which many women participated and which promoted integration and racial equality, the denomination witnessed steep reversals in both areas through the twentieth century. It is startling how closely Adventism has mirrored the broader cultures within which it has existed. At times, some Adventists have veered near syncretism as they have adapted to various cultural settings.

Today, Adventism is characterized by its many varieties, held together by shared beliefs and practices. These have been appropriated, interpreted, and adapted in various cultural settings. This can best be seen in the variety of ways the Sabbath is observed worldwide. From their very inception, Adventists have consistently emphasized the sacredness of the seventh day as a day of worship. Yet the way Adventists worship is different worldwide, and strictures about what can or should not be done during those sacred hours vary substantially between people groups. In the Batak culture on the island of Sumatra, church custom forbids members from attending funerals on Sabbath since they are daylong affairs with a variety of pagan rituals featuring unclean foods. In other societies, church members prefer funerals on Sabbath afternoons. In some parts of the world, it is forbidden to bring a water bottle inside the sanctuary. In other regions, bringing a water bottle and quietly drinking water is not considered wrong. Other examples could be shown to illustrate the complexity of Sabbath observance.

Adventists today wait patiently in the face of the dangers of wealth and poverty, relativism, and persecution. They wait impatiently for the end of injustice, inequity, racism, and paternalism. One of the greatest challenges facing Adventism is the delay of the end. Adventists have preached the soon coming of Jesus for 180 years and are in danger of seeing apocalyptic events around each corner or becoming complacent. The story and varieties of Adventism remain both diverse and complex. Adventism arose as a uniquely American movement, but even at its beginning, it was part of a global revival that arose through vigorous Bible study that brought a sense that God's moral government would judge and evaluate this world. Do Adventists today see themselves as a chosen people called to live out the kingdom of God here on this earth in preparation for the earth made new?

The Seventh-day Adventist Church has become one of the most international and diverse institutions on Earth, perhaps exceeded only by the Roman Catholic Church in scope and structure. The shift to the majority Global South was on full display at the 2025 General Conference Session. Erton C. Köhler (b. 1969) was elected president of the world church, the first Latino elected to the General Conference presidency and the first from the Global South. The 2025 leadership team was augmented by Paul H. Douglas (b. 1966), treasurer, born to Cuban parents in Jamaica, and Richard E. McEdward (b. 1966), executive secretary. McEdward was an American with extensive missionary experience, including most recently in the Middle East. The new slate of general vice presidents was one of the most representative of the world church. Köhler's celebration of differences in the church and his emphasis on the church rising powerfully for mission and on discipleship suggested new directions for the church. On the opening day of the session, the delegates voted overwhelmingly against a small minority of vociferous opponents of COVID-19 vaccines who tried several times to get the issue of vaccinations on the business agenda. One advantage of the church's broad global constituency was that a small minority of very conservative anti-vaxers caught up in American culture wars were seen as completely irrelevant to church representatives in the Global South, where vaccines are valued and recognized for saving lives.

The church's mission and message have gained a following in almost every nation. Its impact has varied, from profound cultural change in Peru, Jamaica, and Papua New Guinea to minimal influence in the Middle East. Yet, as Adventists wait for Jesus's second coming, they remain dedicated to Jesus as their Savior, to the Sabbath as the sign and experience of rest in him, and to the hope of his soon return.

In the first quarter of the twenty-first century, the Seventh-day Adventist Church finds itself caught between two perspectives on Christ's return. Some are primarily impatient with injustice, evil, and oppression in this world. Others are more impatient for Jesus's advent. The temptation for the first group is to be so caught up in fighting evil and injustice that Jesus and his return fade into the background. The other group's temptation is to work hard at hastening Jesus's return, ignoring the here and now and feeling that the Advent depends on their efforts and flawlessness. The church faces the challenge of embracing both kinds of impatience without going to extremes.

Review

1. What is Christian nationalism, and how widespread is it?
2. What have been some of the societal changes that have impacted the church? Which should be adopted, and which should be resisted?
3. How has the recent controversy over women's ordination related to the issue of women's ministry as described in previous chapters of this book?
4. How might members of the Seventh-day Adventist Church integrate its impatience with injustice and its impatience for Jesus to return?

Glossary

Cross-references to other glossary entries in bold type

Adventist Review. The main publication of the Seventh-day Adventist Church. Originally called the *Second Advent Review and Sabbath Herald* (often shortened to *Review and Herald*) and renamed, later, the *Adventist Review*, it remains the primary organ for disseminating news and inspiration within the denomination.

Adventist Youth (AY). A department of the local church focused on youth ministry, typically led by young people who engage with other young people. AY typically organizes activities within the local congregation, often on Sabbath, but at other times as well. The term is still used in some developing parts of the world but in North America tends to be passé.

Adventurers. A denominational ministry that has club chapters in the local church. The Adventurers club is open to children from preschool through grade 4 (or ages four to nine) who agree to keep the Adventurer pledge and law. In 2016, Adventurers expanded outside the North American Division and was adopted by the General Conference Youth Ministries Department. It also expanded from the original four levels (grades 1–4) to six (including preschool and kindergarten).

Babylon. The capital of the Babylonian Empire during the mid-first millennium BC. Babylon played a large role in the Old Testament as the nation that destroyed the Jerusalem temple in 586 BC and took many Jews captive. It has also become a metaphor for religious apostasy and appears, in a spiri-

Grateful acknowledgment is given to Pacific Press for permission to use material in the glossary adapted from Michael Campbell, *Pocket Dictionary for Understanding Seventh-day Adventism* (Nampa, ID: Pacific Press, 2020).

tual sense, in the book of Revelation as a symbol of corrupt powers that lead people astray.

baptismal vow. A commitment by the person being baptized to the beliefs and practices of the Seventh-day Adventist Church. In some instances, rather than reciting all twenty-eight fundamental beliefs, an Adventist minister may use the abbreviated list of thirteen affirmations at baptism and ask the person if she or he accepts them.

Bible Conference. Any large gathering devoted to Bible study. The early **Sabbatarian Adventist** pioneers met during a series of Bible Conferences from 1848 to 1850 in order to establish the theological pillars of Sabbatarian Adventist theology (Sabbath, sanctuary, second coming, spirit of prophecy, and the state of the dead). During the twentieth century, Adventists held a series of three major Bible Conferences (1919, 1952, 1974), and more recently, over the past two decades, the Biblical Research Institute has held large Bible Conferences for church leaders and scholars to discuss important theological and biblical topics.

blessed hope. A biblical reference (Titus 2:13) from the King James Version to the **second coming** of Christ.

camp meeting. A religious gathering lasting several days, typically with a number of large tents where meetings are held (although camp meetings today may or may not use tents). Camp meetings were a distinctive feature of American revivalism and became ubiquitous during the Second Great Awakening. During the Millerite revival, Joshua V. Himes had the largest tent ever made in America up to that time in order to hold large crowds. Early Seventh-day Adventists began to hold regional camp meetings around 1867–1868 to conduct evangelism and disciple church members. Ellen White spoke on temperance to an estimated ten thousand people at the Groveland, Massachusetts, camp meeting in 1876. Though they exist in North American Adventism, even to this day, camp meetings have become much less frequent than in the past.

canvassing. The act of selling literature door-to-door, popularized as a commercial enterprise during the nineteenth century. Church leaders found canvassing to be an effective way to disseminate Adventist literature. The **colporteur** work was developed early within Adventism, when George A. King proposed selling books, door-to-door, about health and Christian belief, with the hope of these contacts leading to Bible studies. That is, canvassing was, and remains today, a form of outreach to the world.

clean and unclean foods. Foods that could be eaten and foods that could not be eaten. Though the distinction between types of animals and fish and other creatures existed long before the Jewish nation did (see Gen. 7), a clear distinction between what was clean and what was unclean was spelled out in the books of Deuteronomy and Leviticus. Discussions about clean and unclean foods in early Seventh-day Adventism began in the 1870s and matured toward the turn of the century. Because the distinction between clean and unclean existed prior to the Jewish nation and even the apostle Peter continued to claim that he had not eaten any unclean thing even after Christ's death and resurrection (Acts 10:14), Seventh-day Adventists believe that members should not eat unclean food.

colporteur(s)/colporteuring. The distribution and sale of literature door-to-door. George King was the first colporteur, who sold copies of Uriah Smith's classic, *Daniel and Revelation*. See also **canvassing**.

compilation. A book compiled of excerpts from the writings of Ellen G. White. Some books were compiled during her lifetime and under her supervision, and others after her death. As a rule, when Adventists refer to a "compilation," they are referring to one of the many books compiled after her death in 1915. Official compilations are done under the auspices of the Ellen G. White Estate.

conditional immortality. With regard to **eschatology**, the position that human beings *receive* eternal life, immortality, only as a gift of grace through faith in Jesus Christ. God alone possesses immortality. Seventh-day Adventists reject the idea of an immortal soul, which is a pagan belief that has infiltrated Christianity and that bestows unconditional immortality on all humans. Those who reject God's gift of immortality will, at the end of time, face "everlasting destruction" (2 Thess. 1:9); that is, they are destroyed forever, as opposed to burning in conscious torment forever, another false belief that comes out of the immortality-of-the-soul error.

conference (organization). A group of churches in a geographic region, often (but not always) in a given state, province, or territory.

conscientious objector. Someone who refuses to bear arms during times of war. Early **Sabbatarian Adventists** wrestled with how to relate to the American Civil War, which was raging at the time the denomination formally organized (1863). Increasing calls for troops led to forced conscription. At first, conscientious objectors could buy their way out, which almost bankrupted the fledgling church. Finally, J. N. Andrews was commissioned to present the case of the Seventh-day Adventist Church, which ultimately led to formal recognition of church members as "conscientious objectors." This remained the default position of the denomination through most of the twentieth century until the Vietnam War, after which the Adventist stance changed. Today, Adventism is split between some who strongly support pacifism, including laying down arms, and others who actively serve in various militaries. The topic remains a complex and controversial one within Adventism. The most famous Adventist conscientious objector was the Medal of Honor winner Desmond Doss, whose heroics were immortalized in the 2016 Mel Gibson film *Hacksaw Ridge*.

day/year principle. The concept, firmly established in Scripture, that a day in certain Bible prophecies equals a literal year. Historicist interpreters of Bible prophecy based this principle on several Bible examples, including Numbers 14:34, Ezekiel 4:5–6, Daniel 9:24–27, and Genesis 29:27. For instance, many Bible expositors around the world during the late eighteenth and early nineteenth century, using the day-year principle, pointed to the 1,260 day/year prophecy being fulfilled around 1798, when French General Berthier took Pope Pius VI captive (where he died), effectively curtailing the influence of the papacy. It was seen as a stunning fulfillment of prophecy and more validation for the day-year principle. Seventh-day Adventists accept the day-year principle as a crucial tool for understanding prophecy and last-day events.

division (organization). A large region of the world church consisting of **unions** (which are made up of **conferences**, and conferences are made up of local churches). Each division serves as a regional headquarters for the **General Conference**, with each division president serving as a vice president of the General Conference. At present, the Seventh-day Adventist Church worldwide is composed of thirteen divisions. Divisions were established in 1918.

dress reform. A concept developed within early Adventism regarding proper dress for women. First spurred on by concern that certain forms of dress were actually unhealthy for women (some easily caught on fire in the kitchen), Adventists, gradually, during the 1860s and 1870s, encouraged principles of healthful dress so that Adventist women could express their individual tastes and preferences while, at the same time, dressing modestly and in a way that would not draw undue attention to themselves. See also **reform dress**.

elder. An appointed leader in a local church. A small group of local church elders are elected by the local church congregation to provide leadership for the church and to work closely with the church pastor. Also, the term "elder" can be used as a special designation of respect for an ordained Seventh-day Adventist minister.

eschaton, eschatology. "Eschaton" refers to the **second coming** and the end of the world; "eschatology" refers to end-time events.

foot washing. The washing of feet during the Lord's Supper as a means of following the example of Jesus Christ, who washed the feet of his disciples (John 13:1–17). Seventh-day Adventists are the largest denomination in the world who retain this practice (although a few small Baptist denominations also practice foot washing).

General Conference. An overarching body of local conferences, organized in 1863. Its purpose was to unite the interests of the developing church. Later, **unions** and **divisions** would be added. The General Conference serves as the highest entity of the worldwide Seventh-day Adventist Church. Church headquarters was originally located in Battle Creek, Michigan, and, after 1904, relocated to Takoma Park, Maryland. Since 1989, the General Conference headquarters have been in Silver Spring, Maryland.

great controversy. The concept, revealed in Scripture (and elaborated on by Ellen White), which teaches that the world is involved in a cosmic struggle between Christ, the Creator, and Satan, a fallen angel. It began with the origin of sin in heaven and ends with the final eradication of sin after the millennium. Seventh-day Adventists believe that the great controversy theme forms the overarching story, the narrative, upon which world history plays out and helps us better understand how evil can exist in a world created by a loving God. Also, the title of one of Ellen White's most influential books.

Great Disappointment. The period immediately after October 22, 1844, when Millerites expected Christ to return. When he did not, many Millerites were devastated, hence the phrase "the Great Disappointment."

health message. The Seventh-day Adventist emphasis on healthful living, both for the individual member's advantage and as a means of outreach to others. Though some early Adventists were into health reform, not until Ellen White received a comprehensive health-reform vision on June 5, 1863, about the importance of the whole person—body, mind, and spirit—including eight laws of health, did Seventh-day Adventists start really promoting "the health message."

independent ministries. Organizations whose ministry lies outside the scope of the official organization of the Seventh-day Adventist Church. These ministries are generally self-supporting. Some are very loyal to the official church and work closely with it. Others, unfortunately, are very critical of the denomination and tend to put the worst spins possible on all that the church does. Independent ministries that accept **tithe** are generally considered divisive and should be avoided.

ingathering. An annual drive, popular during the twentieth century, to raise funds for missionary work. Jasper Wayne, from Iowa, initiated the first program in 1903 when he erroneously received extra denominational periodicals and distributed them in return for a donation for missions. In 1908, the General Conference adopted the idea and renamed it "Harvest Ingathering." Today the practice is all but forgotten, at least in North America.

investigative judgment. The work of Jesus in the Most Holy Place of the heavenly **sanctuary** in preparation for the **second coming**. Initially, William Miller believed that the cleansing of the sanctuary described in Daniel 8:14 referred to this earth. After the **Great Disappointment**, **Sabbatarian Adventists** shifted their attention to the ministry of Christ in the heavenly sanctuary. Over time, early Sabbatarian Adventists connected the idea of the cleansing of the sanctuary with the pre-advent judgment. The judgment would be based on the Ten Commandments, which were contained in the ark in the Most Holy Place. Since the Sabbath was the one commandment that was being ignored by most Christians, it became the focus of the Adventist approach to the judgment. As early as 1841, Josiah Litch taught that a judgment must take place prior to Christ's return. Through the years, what became the Seventh-day Adventist Church refined the doctrine, which is explained in detail by Ellen White in *The Great Controversy*. It is also part of fundamental belief number 24.

"the last days." An expression among Adventists that refers to the time right before the soon return of Christ. This expression is often used in conjunction with the warning of Christ, found in Matthew 18, about "wars and rumors of wars" and the overall moral degradation of humanity. Some people may also reference any of the final events, such as the **time of trouble** that happens immediately before Christ's **second coming**, as being signs of "the last days."

Last Generation Theology (LGT). A concept first promulgated by E. J. Waggoner as he drifted toward pantheism during the 1890s and, through the writings of M. L. Andreasen, reached full maturity during the fundamentalist era of the 1920s and 1930s. Though a last generation will exist before Christ comes, LGT focuses on perfectionism, the idea being that when God's people are perfect, they will trigger the end-time events leading up to the **second coming**. The problems with LGT are twofold. First, it focuses the **Great Controversy** narrative on the accomplishments of human beings rather than on Jesus Christ. Second, it utilizes an unbiblical understanding of sanctification that focuses on external behavior instead of internal transformation, leading to a Christlike character. Some advocates of LGT misuse one of the most widely circulated statements by Ellen White, in which she states that "when the character of Christ shall be perfectly reproduced in his people," the end will come. Unfortunately, some do not read the rest of the paragraph or chapter in which Ellen White clearly describes true Christian perfection in terms of character rather than human achievement or works. Though many faithful and loyal Adventists adhere to LGT, it's not generally accepted by church theologians.

Latter Rain. Rain later in the agrarian cycle of the Holy Land that helped to ripen the crops for harvest. It is in contrast to the "early rain," which helped the seeds to germinate. The eschatological outpouring of the Spirit is likened to the falling of the latter rain, and it is for this added power that Christians are to send their petitions to the Lord of the harvest "in the time of the latter rain."[1] Adventists have pointed to the references to the Holy Spirit in conjunction with the final preparation of God's people for the **second coming** (Joel 2:28; Isa. 44:3).

lay activities. The work of the laity in the mission of the church. The "laity" are those in the church who are not clergy. In Seventh-day Adventist jargon, the term can be used humorously to refer to Sabbath "activities," such as taking a nap (hence the link to the word "lay," as in lying down).

mark of the beast. The mark of a beast described in Revelation 13 that comes "out of the sea" seeking to enforce false worship on the world. This is in contrast to worshiping the Creator (Rev. 4:11), a central theme in the book. Adventists believe that the seventh-day Sabbath is a symbol of loyal worship by God's peo-

1. Zech. 10:1 KJV. Ellen G. White, *Acts of the Apostles* (Mountain View, CA: Pacific Press, 1911), 54–55.

ple at the end of time and that Sunday worship is a counterfeit for God's divine command that will be linked at the end with the "mark of the beast" (Rev. 16:2). Adventists are very clear that no one today has "the mark of the beast" since they believe the issue between Sabbath keeping, as a sign of allegiance to the Creator, and Sunday keeping will be a crucial factor only in the last days.

master guide. One who has completed all the levels (or classes) of a distinct leadership curriculum. The curriculum can also be done independently to train youth ministry leaders.

one hundred forty-four thousand (144,000). The number of God's saints at the end time, who stand triumphant, undefiled, and ultimately victorious at the **second coming** (Rev. 7:4). While this number has prompted speculation, particularly as the denomination reached 144,000 church members around 1920, Adventists, including Ellen White, have traditionally maintained that this is a symbolic number consistent with the rest of the symbolism in Revelation 7.

ordinance. Within the church, a rite instituted by Christ and used as a tangible sign. Most Christians other than evangelicals prefer the term "sacrament" because they believe the rites impart actual grace (although a few Protestants also embrace this term). Adventists, like Protestants in general, embrace only two church ordinances: baptism and the combined practice of **foot washing** and the Lord's Supper (enacted in the same ceremony and so generally considered as one). Protestants furthermore believe that it is not the actual symbols that impart grace, but rather, the ordinances are effective through the Word of God and faith.

Pathfinder(s). Member(s) of a club whose purpose is to create a fun experience for Adventist young people to help them develop life skills and grow closer to Jesus. The idea of developing Pathfinder clubs was first advocated by A. W. Spalding and Harriet Hold in 1922 and officially recognized at the 1950 **General Conference** session. Pathfinders frequently participate in Pathfinder Bible Experience (PBE) and various kinds of camporees to develop their skills and earn honors. They are divided up into different classes (or levels) based on age and grade. The highest level of leadership training is **master guide**.

potluck. A fellowship gathering where church members bring various dishes to share together as a meal after the divine worship church service.

present truth. A special message given by God for his people at a particular time, especially for God's **remnant**, who are preparing for Christ's return. The idea also encompasses the notion of progressive revelation, which is that our understanding of truth must grow and deepen as we continue to study the Word of God. This understanding of present truth has led Seventh-day Adventists to reject creeds. The preamble to the statement of twenty-eight fundamental beliefs recognizes that both our articulation and our understanding of truth must never become rigid. Seventh-day Adventists believe that the three angels' messages of Revelation 14 constitute "present truth" for this time.

probation, close of. The teaching that, at a certain point in salvation history, all decisions for or against Christ shall be finalized. In Seventh-day Adventist theology, the idea is understood as follows: at the close of the **investigative judgment**, Jesus Christ concludes his priestly ministry in the **sanctuary** in heaven since all human beings have made an irrevocable choice for good or bad. Thus, the eternal destiny of all human beings has been finalized by their own choice. This is known as "the close of probation" and is an essential element in the preparation for the **second coming** of Christ.

reform dress. A specific type of dress worn by health reformers in the nineteenth century. It differed from the heavy and long dresses then in vogue, which tended to drag along the ground (and featured large hoops and tight corsets). The reform dress simplified women's clothing, making it easier for women to breathe. It was safer, too (it was less likely to catch on fire in the kitchen). Ellen White urged Adventist women in the 1860s to adopt the reform dress. A few women urged that Adventist women exclusively wear this, and only this, specific pattern of dress, even as society changed and new and healthier options for women's clothing became available. Ellen White rebuked these women, noting that it had the best form around when they first embarked upon dress reform, but that Adventist women should now be flexible. Using principles of modesty, women can choose what looks best on them without drawing unnecessary attention to themselves. In fact, Ellen White encouraged every Adventist woman to have at least one red dress. See also **dress reform**.

Two examples of the reform dress

regional conferences. Administrative units of the Seventh-day Adventist Church operated by and comprised primarily of African Americans that cover most of the territory in the continental United States, save for western states. Regional conferences were established by the General Conference in 1944–1945 in response to systematic and persistent racism against black Adventists. Initially consisting of five conferences with a membership of about 20,000, as of 2024, there were nine regional Conferences with a membership of 283,877, almost a quarter of the membership of the North American Division.

remnant. A small portion, or something remaining or left over. In Adventist theology, the term refers to God's people at the very end of time. According to Revelation 12:17, this "remnant" will be characterized by two primary characteristics: they will (1) keep all of God's commandments and (2) have the testimony of Jesus, which Revelation 19:10 defines as the **spirit of prophecy**. Adventists have identified their own church with this remnant because of two things: first, their adherence to the seventh-day Sabbath among the commandments; second, the gift of prophecy through the life and writings of Ellen G. White is, they believe, "the spirit of prophecy." At the same time, Seventh-day Adventists do not teach that they alone are saved. Instead, they see their identification as giving them a great responsibility to proclaim what they believe to the world.

Review and Herald. The main publication of the Seventh-day Adventist Church, first published under another name in 1849. From 1980 onward, the publication was renamed the *Adventist Review* and continues to be the official publication of the worldwide Seventh-day Adventist Church. In 2005, the denomination rolled out a monthly version called *Adventist World*, distributed to tithe-paying members around the globe and offered in seven languages and online in twelve languages.

revival and reformation. A major church initiative implemented at the 1973 and 2014 Annual Council sessions by the Executive Committee of the General Conference. In 1973, Robert H. Pierson called for deeply spiritual devotionals and fasting and prayer on the part of church leaders in anticipation of the Holy Spirit bringing major revival within the denomination. Similarly, church president "Ted" N. C. Wilson called for the world church to focus on Bible study and prayer in preparation for Christ's **second coming**.

Sabbatarian Adventists. A small group of disappointed believers who, after the **Great Disappointment**, began to search for new spiritual truths. This led to a series of Sabbath and Sanctuary Conferences from 1848 to 1851. This term is used for the Advent people who kept the Sabbath up until the time when the denomination officially organized as Seventh-day Adventists in 1863.

Sabbath school. A program, patterned after Sunday schools, designed on Sabbath mornings for worship and Bible study in addition to the worship service. As early as 1852, James White introduced the *Youth's Instructor* to facilitate Bible lessons, especially for young people. In 1863, Uriah Smith wrote the first series of Bible lessons for adults, which were published in the *Review and Herald*. After Goodloe Harper Bell began to publish training materials for Sabbath school leaders in 1869, there developed a more general pattern and organization of Sabbath schools throughout the denomination. The first Sabbath school songbook was titled *The Song Anchor* (1878), with songs for little children. By 1901, the Sabbath School Department became an official part of the church. Today Sabbath School and Personal Ministries is a department of the General Conference of Seventh-day Adventists.

sanctuary. The throne room of God and the center of his salvation activity for the world. "Thy way, O God, is in the sanctuary" (Ps. 77:13 KJV). The ancient Hebrew tabernacle/sanctuary was a model of the sanctuary in heaven (Heb. 8:1–5; 4:14–16; 9:11–28; 10:19–22; 1:3; 2:16, 17). The earthly sanctuary had two apartments for two ministries: the Holy Place for daily sacrifices, and the Most Holy Place, which was for the Day of Atonement once a year. These two rituals represented the sequential ministry of Christ, which began in the first apartment of the heavenly sanctuary after Christ's death on the cross (symbolized by the animal sacrifices), and then transitioned to the Most Holy Place, beginning in 1844 (Dan. 7:9–27; 8:13, 14; 9:24–27; Num. 14:34; Ezek. 4:6; Lev. 16; Rev. 14:6, 7; 20:12; 14:12; 22:12). This work by Christ our High Priest is the **investigative judgment**. At the conclusion of Christ's work in the Most Holy Place in heaven, Christ will return to claim his people as his own at the **second coming**.

sanitarium. Envisioned by John Harvey Kellogg as a place to learn how to get well and stay well. He coined the term based on the European term "sanitorium." It combined the idea of a hotel, hospital, and health resort. A sanitarium came to be a medical clinic or hospital that had a particular emphasis on natural remedies such as hydrotherapy (water treatments).

seal of God. The seventh-day Sabbath is the visible symbol of God's seal for God's people at the end of time (Rev. 7:2–3; 14:7). The Holy Spirit becomes the sealing agency that settles us into a commitment to Christ and a commitment to his truth, so that we cannot be moved (Eph. 4:30). Usually seen as being in contrast with the **mark of the beast**.

second coming. According to Bible prophecy, this is the future return of Jesus Christ. At his first coming, two thousand years ago, Christ came "to bear the sins of many." He "will appear a second time, not to bear sin, but to bring salvation to those who are waiting for him" (Heb. 9:28). Christ's return will be personal, bodily, sudden, and, ultimately, triumphant. No one knows the precise time of his return (Matt. 24:36), even though signs will indicate the time is drawing near. For Seventh-day Adventists, the second coming is the consummation of all their hopes, for it leads to the end of this sinful world and the beginning of a new existence without sin, suffering, and death.

shaking time. The time right before the **second coming** when those individuals who are not anchored in a personal relationship with Jesus and anchored in a solid confidence in Scripture leave God's people.

shut door. Belief that the **close of probation** occurred for Christians in 1844. Initially, Ellen White also accepted this position, but after an 1849 vision that portrayed Jesus shutting the door to the Holy Place as he moved to the Most Holy Place, she and other early **Sabbatarian Adventists** dropped the teaching, viewing it as an error, especially as they more fully developed the doctrine of the **investigative judgment** and embraced a worldwide mission.

sleeping in the Lord. A euphemism for death. The Bible describes death as a "sleep" (Acts 7:60) where people lose consciousness (Ps. 115:17; Eccles. 9:10) until they awake at the resurrection (Ps. 17:15). Upon death, the body returns to dust (Eccles. 3:19–20). Adventists embrace the nonimmortality of the soul.

social meeting. A specific gathering time where believers would share their testimonies. The term was used frequently by early pioneers. James White stipulated that such testimonies should not last more than two or three minutes each, and an excellent "social meeting" was when everyone in the room had several opportunities to share their faith and encourage one another in their hope in Christ's **second coming**.

Spectrum. An independent Adventist journal dedicated to reporting on Adventist beliefs and polity. The journal, founded in 1969, provides an opportunity for those who sometimes may disagree with official church policy to voice their concerns.

spirit of prophecy. The prophetic gift as manifested through the life of Ellen G. White. The term is used only once in the Bible (Rev. 19:10), where it is interpreted as one of the identifying marks of God's **remnant** church (Rev. 12:17).

Sunday law(s). Legislated Sunday observances or laws (also known as "blue laws") that were of special concern to Adventists during the nineteenth and early twentieth centuries. As early as 1858, Ellen White predicted that God's **remnant** people would be persecuted as Sabbath keepers just prior to the **second coming**. During the 1880s and 1890s, a wave of Sunday legislation brought on localized persecution. For the eleven years after 1885, over one hundred Adventists (mostly in the South) were arrested for breaking these laws. Adventists responded by actively opposing such legislation and by bringing notoriety to these cases. Ellen White supported efforts to ensure "liberty of conscience."[2] She furthermore affirmed that Sunday legislation will take place on a national level as the "last act in the drama."[3]

supporting ministry. An independent ministry that maintains a constructive and, therefore, supportive role to the official Seventh-day Adventist Church. Supporting ministries contrast with those ministries that are more critical of the church or those that are outright dissident and seek to divert **tithe** and lure away church members.

systematic benevolence. The earliest system for church giving adopted in 1859, in the wake of the 1857–1858 panic, a time of economic turmoil in the United States. At that time, when there were only a handful of ministers, several gave up ministry for other forms of employment. Consequently, the new denomination embraced this simple plan. Based on 1 Corinthians 16:2 and 2 Corinthians 9:5–7, it urged men between the ages of eighteen and sixty to give five to twenty-five cents per week; and women to give two to ten cents per week. An additional one to five cents were contributed for every one hundred dollars of property. This system was later replaced by the **tithing** plan. It was sometimes known as "Sister Betsy."

temperance. There are two primary definitions of "temperance." First is the nineteenth-century historical temperance movement that warned against the dangers of alcohol, tobacco, and other harmful substances. Second, temperance can also refer to the need for moderation and exercise of "moral power"

2. Ellen G. White, *Testimonies for the Church*, vol. 5 (Mountain View, CA: Pacific Press, 1889), 452.

3. Ellen G. White, *Christian Service* (Hagerstown, MD: Review and Herald, 1925), 50.

and the exhibiting of self-control and moderation in all things. In January 1879, Ellen White and other church leaders organized the American Health and Temperance Association with Dr. J. H. Kellogg as the first president.

Testimonies. A generic term for the prophetic writings of Ellen G. White, and more specifically, a series of counsels written to individuals, churches, and for the denomination at large that were distributed in pamphlet form and later bound into nine volumes (from 1855 to 1909).

three angels' messages. The angelic messages of Revelation 14:6–12, which Seventh-day Adventists regard as symbolic of their own message and mission to the world just prior to the **second coming**. The first angel's message (v. 6) has the "eternal gospel" to preach to all the world and includes a warning that "the hour of his judgment has come." The second (v. 8) is a warning about the fall of Babylon, which encompasses false systems of worship at the end of the world. The third (v. 9) is a warning against worshiping the beast and its image. The mission of the Seventh-day Adventist Church is to proclaim to all peoples "the everlasting gospel" in the context of the three angels' messages of Revelation 14:6–12.

time of trouble. Also known as the "time of Jacob's trouble" (Gen. 32:22–30). It is a brief period of tribulation just before the **second coming** but right after the **close of probation**. We don't know how long it will last, but it is understood to be simultaneous to the seven last plagues. Ellen White indicates that those who keep the seventh-day Sabbath faithfully will "become the special point of controversy throughout Christendom" as "religious and secular authorities" seek to enforce Sunday observance.[4]

tithe/tithing. A fundamental belief that teaches a return of tithes and offerings "for the proclamation of His gospel and the support of His Church." Such funds are used to support Adventist clergy, evangelism, and teaching the Bible in Adventist schools. See also **systematic benevolence**.

truth or "the truth." A special understanding of "truth" (or "the truth") that Seventh-day Adventists believe will help prepare people for the **second coming** of Jesus. It reflects the special role of God's people, who will be defined by their message and mission as found in the **three angels' messages** of Revelation 14. Adventists, therefore, have a special calling as a **remnant** church to stand for biblical truth right before the second coming.

4. Ellen G. White, *The Great Controversy* (Mountain View, CA: Pacific Press, 1911), 615.

union (organization). An administrative level of church organization that consists of a number of **conferences** (and possibly missions). The unions form the basic administrative building block of the denomination, and union presidents are automatically members of the **General Conference** executive committee. Many unions also serve as constituencies for Adventist colleges (with the union president often serving as board chair), accreditation, and various other aspects of administration, such as auditing services. A series of unions generally form a **division** of the world church. Unions were first instituted at the 1901 General Conference session with strong support from Ellen G. White to help create more leadership accountability and to decentralize power out of the hands of just a few.

United States in prophecy. The Seventh-day Adventist Church was a movement that began during the mid-nineteenth century, a time of hopeful optimism about the ability of human progress and democracy. Adventists, by way of contrast, shared a growing pessimism that, while America originally embraced the separation of church and state, eventually the nation would become an oppressor. Adventists point to Revelation 13:11–12, to the lamb-like beast that eventually spoke as a dragon. Because a beast represents a kingdom (Rev. 17:15), and because a lamb symbolizes Christ (John 1:29), this kingdom originates as a Christian nation embracing principles of liberty and freedom for the oppressed, along with worldwide influence (Rev. 13:12). However, this nation is later portrayed as being central to enforcing "**the mark of the beast**" upon the world, which means that America will become a religiously oppressive power. Ellen White predicts that when Protestantism combines with Roman Catholicism and spiritualism, there will be a "threefold union" that will push the United States to "repudiate every principle of its Constitution as a Protestant and republican government."[5]

veggie meat/vegemeat. Vegetarian meat substitutes. Since the late nineteenth century, Adventists have developed a whole host of analogs, most of them made of soybeans, to create "healthy" alternatives. Some popular products include Big Franks, Fri-chik, Grillers, Prosage, Stripples, and Wham.

5. White, *Testimonies for the Church*, 5:451.

Photo Credits

The authors and publisher wish to express gratitude to several organizations for the use of photographs in this book. The photo on p. 109 is courtesy of the Archives of the Student Volunteer Movement for Foreign Missions (RG 42), Special Collections, Yale Divinity School Library. Photos on pp. 17, 43, 53, and 138 are courtesy of the Center for Adventist Research. Photos on pp. 38 (bottom), 57, 102, 104 (top), 121 (top), 132, and 144 are courtesy of the Ellen G. White Estate, Inc. Photos on pp. 14, 18–38, 40, 47, 59, 61–69, 91–97, 101, 103, 104 (bottom), 106, 111 (top), 112, 114 (right), 116, 121–31, 138, 151–52, 156, 175–83, 204–19, 239, 249–56, and 272–93 are courtesy of the General Conference Archives. The photo on p. 41 is courtesy of the Adventist Digital Library. The photo on p. 60 is courtesy of the Historical Archives of Adventism in Europe, Collonges-sous-Salève section (France), Ertzberger family collection. The photo on p. 170 is courtesy of the Historical Archives of Seventh-day Adventists in Europe. The photo on p. 105 is courtesy of the Hoover Institution Library & Archives, Image 155, Album D, Francis E. Stafford photographs. The photo on p. 108 is courtesy of the Library of Congress, Geography and Map Division. Photos on pp. 140, 150, and 186–93 are courtesy of the North American Division of Seventh-day Adventists Office of Archives, Statistics, and Research. The photo on p. 154 is courtesy of the Union Adventist University Archives, Lora McMahon King Heritage. The photo on p. 114 is by Frederick Gutekunst. The photo on p. 225 is by Sydney Allen. The photos on pp. 262–63 are by Edward Martin Allen.

Bibliography

"About Three-in-Ten U.S. Adults Are Now Religiously Unaffiliated." Pew Research Center, December 14, 2021. https://tinyurl.com/yfknjurf.

"The Age Gap in Religions Around the World." Pew Research Center, June 13, 2018. https://tinyurl.com/y3pa49cb.

"Amazing Facts." Ministry Watch, updated March 28, 2024. https://tinyurl.com/2durjsvm.

Anderson, A. N. "Union." *Central Union Outlook* 2, no. 5 (February 6, 1912): 4.

Anderson, Eric, ed. *Reclaiming the Prophet.* Nampa, ID: Pacific Press, 2025.

Ashworth, Warren Sidney. "Edward Alexander Sutherland and Seventh-day Adventist Educational Reform: The Denominational Years, 1890–1904." PhD diss., Andrews University, 1986.

Baker, Alonzo L. "The San Francisco Evolution Debates." *Adventist Heritage* 2, no. 2 (Winter 1975): 23–32.

Baker, Delbert. *The Unknown Prophet.* Washington, DC: Review and Herald, 1987.

Baker, Donald I. "The Impact of Christianity on Modern Korea: An Overview." *Acta Koreana* 19, no. 1 (June 2016). https://tinyurl.com/yfr3khd5.

Barkun, Michael. *Crucible of the Millennium: The Burned-Over District of New York in the 1840s.* Syracuse, NY: Syracuse University Press, 1986.

Bates, Joseph. *The Sabbath, a Perpetual Sign.* New Bedford, MA: Benjamin Lindsey, 1847.

Bates, Joseph, J. H. Waggoner, and M. E. Cornell. "Address." *Review and Herald* 7, no. 10 (December 4, 1855): 78–79.

Bebbington, David. *The Evangelical Quadrilateral.* Vol. 1. Waco, TX: Baylor University Press, 2021.

Beecher, Charles. *The Bible a Sufficient Creed.* Boston, 1846. https://tinyurl.com/5enf5wyy.

Blaich, Roland. "Render unto Caesar: German Adventists and the Nazi State." *Adventist Today* 33, no. 1 (Winter 2025): 8–11.

———. "Selling Nazi Germany Abroad: The Case of Hulda Jost." *Journal of Church and State* 35, no. 4 (Autumn 1993): 807–30.

Bliss, Sylvester, and Apollos Hale. *Memoirs of William Miller, Generally Known as a Lecturer on the Prophecies, and the Second Coming of Christ.* Boston: J. V. Himes, 1853.

Branson, W. H. "A Great Forward Movement." *Review and Herald* 107, no. 59 (November 27, 1930): 4.

———. "Loyalty in an Age of Doubt." *Ministry* 6, no. 10 (October 1933): 3.

Brazilian White Center–UNASP. "Belz, Guilherme (Wilhelm) (1835–1912)." In *Encyclopedia of Seventh-day Adventists,* January 29, 2020. https://tinyurl.com/3mjmnw2r.

Brinsmead, Robert D. "A Review of the Awakening Message, Part 1." Current Theological Issues Reviewed. Fallbrook, CA: Present Truth, 1972.

Burke, Peter. *Sarpi: History of Benefices and Selections from History of the Council of Trent.* New York: Washington Square Press, 1967.

Burton, Kevin M. "God's Last Choice: Overcoming Ellen White's Gender and Women in Ministry During the Fundamentalist Era." *Spectrum* 45, no. 2 (Summer 2017): 148–76.

"Business Proceedings of B.C. Conference." *Review and Herald* 16, no. 21 (October 9, 1860): 161ff.; 16, no. 22 (October 16, 1860): 169ff.; and 16, no. 23 (October 23, 1860): 177ff.

"By a Letter Just Received." *Home Missionary* 6, no. 5 (May 1894): 110–11.

Campbell, Heidi. "Women in Adventist History." In *The Oxford Handbook of Seventh-day Adventism,* edited by Michael W. Campbell, Christie Chui-Shan Chow, David F. Holland, Denis Kaiser, and Nicholas Patrick Miller, 493–509. New York: Oxford University Press, 2024.

Chadwick, L. C. "West Africa." *Review and Herald* 71, no. 1 (January 2, 1894): 16.

Chism, Ashlee. "Adventists and the City/Country Living." In *Encyclopedia of Seventh-day Adventists,* January 3, 2024. https://tinyurl.com/9nmdttrf.

Chit, Morris, and John Wesley Taylor V. "Impact of the 1000 Missionary Movement Training Program on the Spirituality of the Trainees." *INFO* 3, no. 2 (October 2000). https://tinyurl.com/492ew8d3.

Chow, Christie Chui-Shan. *Schism: Seventh-day Adventism in Post-Denominational China.* Notre Dame: University of Notre Dame Press, 2021.

Coles, L. B. *Philosophy of Health: Natural Principles of Health and Cure: or, Health and Cure Without Drugs; also, the Moral Bearings of Erroneous Appetites.* Boston: Ticknor, Reed & Fields, 1854.

"Consensus Statement: Christ in the Heavenly Sanctuary." *Ministry* 53, no. 10 (October 1980): 16–19.

Crisler, Clarence C. "The Death of Sister White." *Pacific Union Recorder* 14, no. 50 (July 22, 1915): 1.

Crocombe, Jeff. "'A Feast of Reason': The Roots of William Miller's Biblical Interpretation and Its Influence on the Seventh-day Adventist Church." PhD diss., University of Queensland, 2011.

Damsteegt, P. Gerard. *Foundations of the Seventh-day Adventist Message and Mission*. Grand Rapids: Eerdmans, 1977.

Davidson, Richard. "The Meaning of Nisdaq in Daniel 8:14." *Journal of the Adventist Theological Society* 7, no. 1 (Spring 1996): 107–19.

Doukhan, J. B., ed. *Thinking in the Shadow of Hell: The Impact of the Holocaust on Theology and Jewish-Christian Relations*. Berrien Springs, MI: Andrews University Press, 2002.

Ferch, Arthur J. *Towards Righteousness by Faith: 1888 in Retrospect*. Wahroonga, NSW, Australia: South Pacific Division of Seventh-day Adventists; Warburton, Vic., Australia: Signs Publishing Co., 1989.

"Flashes of Oregon Events." *Roseburg (OR) News Review*, April 30, 1936, 1.

Fortin, Denis. *G. I. Butler: An Honest but Misunderstood Church Leader*. Nampa, ID: Pacific Press, 2023.

Friend, Henry C. "Abraham Lincoln and the Court Martial of Surgeon General William A. Hammond." *Commercial Law Journal*, March 1957, 71–78.

Froom, LeRoy Edwin. *The Conditionalist Faith of Our Fathers: The Conflict of the Ages over the Nature and Destiny of Man*. Washington, DC: Review and Herald, 1966.

———. "Our Earliest and Latest Bible Conference." *Ministry* 25, no. 10 (October 1952): 4ff.

Furay, Conal, and Michael J. Salevouris. *The Methods and Skills of History: A Practical Guide*. 2nd ed. Wheeling, IL: Harlan Davidson, 2009.

General Conference of Seventh-day Adventists. "God's Gift: Human Sexuality." 2024. https://tinyurl.com/ycy99udw.

———. *Our Firm Foundation; A Report of the Seventh-day Adventist Bible Conference Held September 1–13, 1952, in the Sligo Seventh-day Adventist Church, Takoma Park, Maryland*. Washington, DC: Review and Herald Publishing Association, 1953.

———. "Seventh-day Adventist Position Statement on Homosexuality." October 3, 1999, revised October 17, 2012. https://tinyurl.com/sy6xfmzh.

———. "Statement on the Biblical View of Unborn Life and Its Implications for Abortion." November 13, 2019. https://tinyurl.com/yc6kr793.

General Conference Proceedings. *Review and Herald* 60, no. 46 (November 20, 1883): 733.

Geraty, L. T. "Adventists and Archaeology." In *The Oxford Handbook of Seventh-day Adventism*, 337–51. New York: Oxford University Press, 2024.

Gibson, L. James, and H. M. Rasi. *Understanding Creation: Answers to Questions on Faith and Science*. Nampa, ID: Pacific Press Publishing Association, 2011.

"Global Mission Pioneers." AdventistMission.org. Accessed March 17, 2025. https://tinyurl.com/5fbz2eny.

Graybill, Ron. *Mission to Black America*. Mountain View, CA: Pacific Press, 1971.

Greenleaf, Floyd. *In Passion for the World: A History of Seventh-day Adventist Education*. Nampa, ID: Pacific Press, 2005.

Hacker, J. David. "Decennial Life Tables for the White Population of the United States, 1790–1900." National Library of Medicine, April 2010. https://tinyurl.com/awzw5eyw.

Halliwell, Leo B., and Jessie Halliwell. *Light in the Jungle: The Story of Leo and Jessie Halliwell's Mission Along the Amazon*. Abridged ed. Mountain View, CA: Pacific Press Publishing Association, 1959.

Hanciles, Jehu J. *Migration and the Making of Global Christianity*. Grand Rapids: Eerdmans, 2021.

Haskell, Stephen N. "South Africa. A Visit Among the Churches." *Review and Herald* 71, no. 51 (December 25, 1894): 810.

Heald, B. M. "Radio Possibilities." *Review and Herald* 101, no. 36 (September 4, 1924): 13.

Holifield, E. Brooks. *Theology in America: Christian Thought from the Age of the Puritans to the Civil War*. New Haven: Yale University Press, 2003.

Horn, Siegfried H. "The Basic Date of the 2300-Year Period Confirmed by New Discoveries." *Review and Herald* 130, no. 18 (April 30, 1953): 8–9.

———. "The Old Testament Text in Antiquity." *Ministry* 60, no. 11 (November 1987): 4–8.

Howell, Warren E. "Progress of Our School Work." *Review and Herald* 96, no. 31 (July 31, 1919): 22.

Hubers, John. "Samuel Zwemer and the Challenge of Islam: From Polemic to a Hint of Dialogue." *International Bulletin of Missionary Research* 28, no. 3 (July 2004): 117–21. https://doi.org/10.1177/239693930402800306.

Hunt, William C., and Edwin M. Bliss. *Religious Bodies: 1916*. Washington, DC: Government Printing Office, 1919. https://tinyurl.com/mt7ysxbf.

"In U.S., Decline of Christianity Continues at Rapid Pace." Pew Research Center, October 17, 2019. https://tinyurl.com/ypxk9m4z.

Jenkins, Philip. *Climate, Catastrophe, and Faith: How Changes in Climate Drive Religious Upheaval*. New York: Oxford University Press, 2021.

———. *Fertility and Faith: The Demographic Revolution and the Transformation of World Religions*. Waco, TX: Baylor University Press, 2020.

Johnson, Todd M., and Gina A. Zurlo. "Ongoing Exodus: Tracking the Emigration of Christians from the Middle East." *Harvard Journal of Middle Eastern Politics and Policy* 3 (2013–2014): 39–49.

Jones, Jeffrey M. "U.S. Church Membership Falls Below Majority for First Time." Gallup, March 29, 2021. https://tinyurl.com/mr3d5j7u.

Jones, R. Clifford. "James Kemuel Humphrey and the Emergence of the United Sabbath-Day Adventists." *Andrews University Seminary Studies* 41, no. 2 (2003): 255–73.

Jones-Gray, Meredith. *As We Set Forth: Battle Creek College & Emmanuel Missionary College*. Berrien Springs, MI: Andrews University, 2002.

———. *Forward in Faith: Andrews University, 1960–1990*. Berrien Springs, MI: Andrews University, 2024.

[Kellogg, John Harvey?] *The Battle Creek Idea*. N.p.: n.d., ca. 1907. https://tinyurl.com/2v799fwu.

Kelly, David. "George Vandeman; TV Evangelist Made Pioneering Broadcasts to Soviet Union." *Los Angeles Times*, November 4, 2000. https://tinyurl.com/yc57htb8.

Kern, M. E. "The Secretary's Report." *Review and Herald* 115, no. 24 (May 31, 1936): 59–61.

Kim, Kirsteen. "Christianity's Role in the Modernization and Revitalization of Korean Society in the Twentieth-Century." *International Journal of Public Theology* 4, no. 2 (2010): 212–36.

Knight, George R. *Early Adventist Educators*. Berrien Springs, MI: Andrews University Press, 1983.

———. "Harbor Springs, Michigan." In *The Ellen G. White Encyclopedia*, edited by Denis Fortin and Jerry Moon, 856. Hagerstown, MD: Review and Herald, 2013.

———. *A Search for Identity: The Development of Seventh-day Adventist Beliefs*. Hagerstown, MD: Review and Herald Publishing Association, 2000.

———. "Spiritual Revival and Educational Expansion: Between 1890 and 1900 the Number of Church Schools Jumped from 13 to 246. Why?" *Adventist Review* 161, no. 13 (March 29, 1987): 8–11.

———. *A User-Friendly Guide to the 1888 Message*. Hagerstown, MD: Review and Herald Publishing Association, 1998.

———. "Viewpoints." In *Seventh-day Adventists Answer Questions on Doctrine*, annotated ed. Berrien Springs, MI: Andrews University Press, 2003.

———. *William Miller and the Rise of Adventism*. Nampa, ID: Pacific Press, 2010.

Knight, George R., and Gerald Wheeler. *Organizing to Beat the Devil: The Development of Adventist Church Structure*. Hagerstown, MD: Review and Herald Publishing Association, 2001.

"Korean Religion 1984–2021 (1) Status of Religion." [In Korean.] Gallup, May 18, 2021. https://tinyurl.com/3fz9xrnh.

Land, Gary. *Teaching History: A Seventh-day Adventist Approach*. Berrien Springs, MI: Andrews University Press, 2000.

Lee, Julie Z. "The Continually Growing Mission in India." *Adventist World*, November 5, 2020. https://tinyurl.com/5dz9pwsz.

Lee, Kuk Heon. "Sahmyook University." In *Encyclopedia of Seventh-day Adventists*, August 10, 2020. https://tinyurl.com/39u8vscu.

Lepke, Wolfgang. "The Story of Jerald Whitehouse." In *A Man of Passionate Reflection: A Festschrift Honoring Jerald Whitehouse*, edited by Bruce L. Bauer, 19–36. Berrien Springs, MI: Dept. of World Mission, Andrews University, 2011. https://tinyurl.com/mrx7b6ee.

Lindsay, Allan G. "Goodloe Harper Bell: Pioneer Seventh-day Adventist Christian Educator." 1982. Digital Commons @ Andrews University 1982-01-01T08:00:00Z.

Lipka, Michael. "The Most and Least Racially Diverse U.S. Religious Groups." Pew Research Center, July 27, 2015. https://tinyurl.com/4whhndan.

———. "Why America's 'Nones' Left Religion Behind." Pew Research Center, August 24, 2016. https://tinyurl.com/mv2msydh.

Lloyd, Trevor. "The Untold Story of Glacier View." *Spectrum*, March 25, 2023. https://tinyurl.com/zwp4paje.

Loconte, Joe. *The End of Illusions: Religious Leaders Confront Hitler's Gathering Storm*. Lanham, MD: Rowman & Littlefield, 2004.

London, Samule G., Jr. *Seventh-day Adventists and the Civil Rights Movement*. Jackson: University Press of Mississippi, 2009.

Loughborough, J. N. *The Church: Its Organization, Order, and Discipline*. Washington, DC: Review and Herald, 1907.

———. "Image of the Beast." *Review and Herald* 17, no. 9 (January 15, 1861): 69.

"Luther J. Burgess." *Pacific Union Recorder* 45, no. 48 (July 3, 1946): 6.

Mabat, Yael. *Sacrifice and Regeneration: Seventh-day Adventism and Religious Transformation in the Andes*. Lincoln: University of Nebraska Press, 2022.

MacGuire, Mead. "We Need Victory." *Ministry* 1, no. 1 (January 1928): 9–10.

Magan, P. T. "The Educational Conference and Educational Reform." *Review and Herald* 78, no. 32 (August 6, 1901): 508.

Marsden, George M. *Fundamentalism and American Culture*. 2nd ed. Oxford: Oxford University Press, 2006.

Marshall, Joey. "The World's Most Committed Christians Live in Africa, Latin America—and the U.S." Pew Research Center, August 22, 2018. https://tinyurl.com/bdcm7ffv.

McChesney, Andrew. "Cero Church." *Mission 360°* 11, no. 4 (January 2024): 13.

McFarland, Ken, and W. Augustus Cheatham. *Railway to the Moon: The Impossible Dream*. Boise, ID: Pacific Press Publishing Association, 2005.

McKay, Donald W. "Two Decades of TV Progress: *Faith for Today* Celebrates Its Twentieth Birthday on May 21." *Ministry* 43, no. 5 (May 1970): 3–6.

"Meeting Hears Hitler Praised." *Detroit Free Press*, April 11, 1936, 5. https://tinyurl.com/34ehj385.

"The Message by Radio." *Review and Herald* 101, no. 48 (November 27, 1924): 19.

"Modeling the Future of Religion in America." Pew Research Center, September 13, 2022. https://tinyurl.com/muyazp6c.

"Modeling the Future of Religion in America: Methodology." Pew Research Center, September 13, 2022. https://tinyurl.com/3ec5bdfw.

Morgan, Douglas. *Adventism and the American Republic: The Public Involvement of a Major Apocalyptic Movement*. Knoxville: University of Tennessee Press, 2001.

———. *Change Agents: The Lay Movement That Challenged the System and Turned Adventism Toward Racial Justice*. Westlake Village, CA: Oak & Acorn, 2020.

———. "Civil War." In *The Ellen G. White Encyclopedia*, 718–21. Hagerstown, MD: Review and Herald, 2013.

———. "Sheafe, Lewis Charles (1859–1938)." In *Encyclopedia of Seventh-day Adventists*, June 1, 2022. https://tinyurl.com/2p8xaprm.

Moskala, Jiří, and John Peckham, eds. *God's Character and the Last Generation*. Nampa, ID: Pacific Press Publishing Association, 2018.

Mott, Linn. "Not Waiting for Godot: The History of the Academy of Certified Archivists and the Professionalization of the Archival Field." *American Archivist* 78, no. 1 (2015): 96–132. https://doi.org/10.17723/0360-9081.78.1.96.

"Mrs. Georgia Burgess." *Eastern Tidings* 43, no. 20 (October 15, 1948): 6.

Mustard, Andrew Gordon. *James White and SDA Organization: Historical Development, 1844–1881*. Berrien Springs, MI: Andrews University Press, 1987.

Nam, Juhyeok. "Reactions to the Seventh-day Adventist Evangelical Conferences and Questions on Doctrine 1955–1971." PhD diss., Andrews University, 2005.

Neff, Merlin L. "CRASH! Crash! Goes the Stock Market." *Signs of the Times* 56, no. 48 (December 3, 1929): 1–2.

Nichol, Francis D. "The Bible Conference." *Review and Herald* 129, no. 35 (August 28, 1952): 1ff.

———. "For Such a Time as This." *Review and Herald* 111, no. 27 (July 5, 1934): 4–5.

———. "The Growth of the Millerite Legend." *Church History* 21, no. 4 (December 1952): 296–313.

———. *The Midnight Cry: A Defense of the Character and Conduct of William*

Miller and the Millerites, Who Mistakenly Believed That the Second Coming of Christ Would Take Place in the Year 1844. Washington, DC: Review and Herald, 1944.

Nix, James R. *Early Advent Singing: A Collection of 52 Early Adventist Hymns with Illustrating Stories*. Hagerstown, MD: Review and Herald, 2000.

Nowak, Karel, and ANN Staff. "Spain: Romanian President Attends Adventist Church in Madrid." Adventist News Network, October 27, 2008. https://tinyurl.com/e4pur74m.

Numbers, Ronald L. *The Creationists*. Berkeley: University of California Press, 1992.

———. *Prophetess of Health: A Study of Ellen G. White*. 3rd ed. Grand Rapids: Eerdmans, 2008.

Oh Man Kyu. "Korea." In *Light Dawns over Asia*, edited by Gil G. Fernandez, 63–91. Silang, Cavite, Philippines: AIIAS Publications, 1990.

Oliveira, Kevin Vinicius Felix, and Clodoaldo Tavares. "Snow, Samuel Sheffield (1806–1890)." In *Encyclopedia of Seventh-day Adventists*, April 7, 2022. https://tinyurl.com/4e77yess.

Oliver, Barry David. *SDA Organizational Structure: Past, Present, and Future*. Berrien Springs, MI: Andrews University Press, 1989.

Osei-Bonsu, Robert. "Sabbath Observance Among the Akan's of Ghana and Its Impact on the Growth of the Seventh-day Adventist Church in Ghana." *Asia-Africa Journal of Mission and Ministry* 7, no. 3 (2013): 3–26. https://tinyurl.com/4vs529cd.

Osorio, Fernando. "In the Inca Union." *Review and Herald* 95, no. 52 (December 26, 1918): 23.

Ottschofski, Hannele. "The Problem of Women's Ordination, Part 1: The Church in Finland Led the Way." *Adventist Today*, December 1, 2019. https://tinyurl.com/nh49rhfv.

Owusu-Mensa, Kofi. *Saturday God and Adventism in Ghana*. Ghana: Advent Press, 2023.

"Praise Bestowed on Hitler's Rule." *Battle Creek Enquirer*, October 22, 1933, 5.

Prescott, W. W. "Report of the Educational Secretary." *Review and Herald Extra, Daily Bulletin of the General Conference* 5, no. 15 (February 23, 1893): 350.

Price, George McCready, and Joseph McCabe. *Is Evolution True? Verbatim Report of Debate Between George McCready Price and Joseph McCabe Held at the Queen's Hall, Langham Place, London, W., on September 6, 1925. Rev. by Both Disputants*. London: Watts, 1925.

"Proceedings of the Eleventh Annual Meeting of the General Conference of S. D. Adventists." *Review and Herald* 41, no. 13 (March 11, 1873): 108.

Raby, John. "Lawsuit Settled over Widespread Abuse of Former Students at Shuttered West Virginia Boarding School." Associated Press, updated August 23, 2023. https://tinyurl.com/bdcs6p93.

"Raise Large Sum for Adventists Schools: State Meetings to Come to Close at Park This Evening." *Fresno Morning Republican*, May 9, 1915, 32.

Ramik, Vincent. "The Ramik Report: Memorandum of Law Literary Property Rights 1790–1915." Ellen G. White Estate, August 14, 1981. https://tinyurl.com/8sc5rn4x.

———. "There Simply Is No Case." Interview with Vincent Ramik. *Adventist Review* 158, no. 38 (September 9, 1981): 4–6.

Reid, George W. *A Sound of Trumpets: Americans, Adventists, and Health Reform*. Washington, DC: Review and Herald Publishing Association, 1982.

"Report of the 1919 Bible Conference." Office of Archives, Statistics, and Research. Accessed March 18, 2025. https://tinyurl.com/yc2twt7n.

Robert, Dana L. *Occupy Until I Come*. Grand Rapids: Eerdmans, 2003.

Robinson, Virgil. "Ellen G. White: Who Was She? Part 2." *Signs of the Times* 98, no. 11 (November 1971): 10–13, 32.

Rock, Calvin B. *Protest and Progress: Black Seventh-day Adventists and the Push for Parity*. Berrien Springs, MI: Andrews University Press, 2018.

Rodriguez, Edward. "1000 Missionary Movement Celebrates 30 Years of Service." *Adventist Review*, August 18, 2022. https://tinyurl.com/mvnnr5pe.

Roth, Ariel A., and L. James Gibson. "Geoscience Research Institute." In *Encyclopedia of Seventh-day Adventists*, May 10, 2022. https://tinyurl.com/3w644z6b.

Rowe, David L. *God's Strange Work: William Miller and the End of the World*. Grand Rapids: Eerdmans, 2008.

Ruud, Niq. "George McCready Price and Seventh-day Adventism's Influence on the Rise of Modern Creationism." *Church History and Religious Culture* 104, no. 1 (2024): 118–30. doi: https://doi.org/10.1163/18712428-bja10066.

Schubert, Walter. "Addresses Given at the S. D. A. Bible Conference, Takoma Park, Maryland, September 11, 12, 1952: Evangelization of Apostolic Roman Catholics." Translated from Spanish by Leona Running. Washington, DC: Ministerial Association, 1952.

Schuberth, H. F. "Central European Division." *Review and Herald* 107, no. 28 (June 5, 1930): 104–5.

Schwarz, Richard W., and General Conference of Seventh-day Adventists Department of Education. *Light Bearers to the Remnant: Denominational History Textbook for Seventh-day Adventist College Classes*. Mountain View, CA: Pacific Press Publishing Association, 1979.

"The S. D. A. School." *Review and Herald* 39, no. 26 (June 11, 1872): 204.

Shenk, W. R. "Rufus Anderson and Henry Venn: A Special Relationship?" *International Bulletin of Missionary Research* 5, no. 4 (October 1981): 168–72. https://tinyurl.com/27rr8wyy.

Sire, James W. T*he Universe Next Door: A Basic Worldview Catalog.* 5th ed. Downers Grove, IL: InterVarsity Press, 2009.

[Smith, Uriah.] "Our Righteousness." *Review and Herald* 66, no. 24 (June 11, 1889): 376.

Spalding, Arthur W. *Christ's Last Legion.* Washington, DC: Review and Herald, 1949.

———. *Footsteps of the Pioneers.* Washington, DC: Review and Herald, 1947.

Spence, Martha. "Camp Meeting Near Rochester." *Midnight Cry!*, August 1, 1844, 22.

Spicer, William A. *The Spirit of Prophecy in the Advent Movement.* Washington, DC: Review and Herald, 1937.

Spies, F. W. "Brazilian Union Conference." *Review and Herald* 97, no. 39 (September 23, 1920): 12.

Sprengel, Merton E. "The Dark Day Plus 200." *Review and Herald* 157, no. 26 (May 22, 1980): 5–8.

———. "1780 Accounts of the Dark Day." *Review and Herald* 157, no. 28 (June 3, 1980): 11–14.

———. "Seventh-day Adventist Views on the Dark Day." *Review and Herald* 157, no. 27 (May 29, 1980): 9–12.

Stanley, Brian. *The Global Diffusion of Evangelicalism: The Age of Billy Graham and John Stott.* Downers Grove, IL: IVP Academic, 2013.

"The State of African Americans in the South." Digital History. Accessed March 18, 2025. https://tinyurl.com/yn7n6mmh.

States, George O. "Lessons from Past Experiences—No. 22." *Review and Herald,* 85, no. 5 (January 30, 1908): 11.

Teel, Charles, Jr. "Revolutionary Missionaries in Peru: Fernando and Ana Stahl." *Spectrum* 18, no. 3 (February 1988): 50–52.

Thottam, Jyoti. "Opinion Today." *New York Times*, January 22, 2024. https://tinyurl.com/3hj6e4y7.

Timm, Alberto Ronald. "The Sanctuary and the Three Angels' Messages 1844–1863: Integrating Factors in the Development of Seventh-day Adventist Doctrines." PhD diss., Andrews University, 1995. https://dx.doi.org/10.32597/dissertations/155/.

Tooley, Mark David. *Methodism and Politics in the 20th Century from William McKinley to 9/11.* Fort Valley, GA: Bristol House, 2011.

Tucker, R. A. *From Jerusalem to Irian Jaya: A Biographical History of Christian Missions.* Grand Rapids: Zondervan, 1983.

Unruh, T. E. "The Seventh-day Adventist Evangelical Conferences of 1955–1956." *Adventist Heritage* 4, no. 2 (Winter 1977): 35–46.

Valentine, Gilbert M. "Adventist-Evangelical Conferences, 1955–1956." In *Encyclopedia of Seventh-day Adventists*, December 4, 2023. https://tinyurl.com/5pxjead8.

———. *Ostriches and Canaries*. Westlake Village, CA: Oak & Acorn, 2022.

———. "Palmdale Conference (1976)." In *Encyclopedia of Seventh-day Adventists*, January 29, 2020. https://tinyurl.com/2mm8b8ka.

Vande Vere, Emmet K. *The Wisdom Seekers: The Intriguing Story of the Men and Women Who Made the First Institution for Higher Learning Among Seventh-day Adventists*. Nashville: Southern Publishing Association, 1972.

Veldman, Robin Globus. *The Gospel of Climate Skepticism: Why Evangelical Christians Oppose Action on Climate Change*. Oakland: University of California Press, 2019.

Veltman, Fred. "The *Desire of Ages* Project: The Conclusions." *Ministry* 63, no. 12 (December 1990): 11–15.

———. "The *Desire of Ages* Project: The Data." *Ministry* 63, no. 10 (October 1990): 4–7.

———. "Life of Christ Research Project." Office of Archives, Statistics, and Research. Accessed March 18, 2025. https://tinyurl.com/bdcwr7w4.

W[aggoner], [E. J.]. "Comments on Galatians 3. No. 9." *Signs of the Times* 12, no. 34 (September 2, 1886): 534 [7].

Waggoner, J. H. "Present Truth." *Review and Herald* 28, no. 10 (August 7, 1866): 77.

Weber, Timothy P. *Living in the Shadow of the Second Coming: American Premillennialism, 1875*. Chicago: University of Chicago Press, 1987.

Weeks, Howard B. *Adventist Evangelism in the Twentieth Century*. Washington, DC: Review & Herald Publishing Association, 1969.

Wheeler, Gerald. "The Historical Basis of Adventist Standards." *Ministry* 62, no. 11 (October 1989): 10–11.

———. *James White: Innovator and Overcomer*. Hagerstown, MD: Review and Herald Publishing Association, 2003.

Whidden, Woodrow W. *E. J. Waggoner: From the Physician of Good News to the Agent of Division*. Hagerstown, MD: Review and Herald Publishing Association, 2008.

White, Ellen G. "Christ Prayed for Unity Among His Disciples." *Review and Herald* 67, no. 10 (March 11, 1890): 1–2.

———. "Communication from Sister White." *Review and Herald* 7, no. 15 (January 10, 1856): 118.

———. *Counsels on Diet and Foods*. Washington, DC: Review and Herald, 1938.

———. *Counsels to Parents, Teachers, and Students*. Mountain View, CA: Pacific Press, 1913.

———. *Daughters of God.* Hagerstown, MD: Review and Herald Publishing Association, 1998.

———. *Desire of Ages.* Mountain View, CA: Pacific Press, 1898.

———. *Early Writings.* Washington, DC: Review and Herald, 1882.

———. *Education.* Mountain View, CA: Pacific Press, 1903.

———. *Life Sketches of Ellen G. White.* Mountain View, CA: Pacific Press, 1915.

———. *The Ministry of Healing.* Mountain View, CA: Pacific Press, 1905.

———. *The Ministry of Health and Healing.* Nampa, ID: Pacific Press, 2004.

———. *Testimonies for the Church.* Vol. 1. Mountain View, CA: Pacific Press, 1885.

———. *Testimonies for the Church.* Vol. 5. Mountain View, CA: Pacific Press, 1889.

———. *Testimonies for the Church.* Vol. 9. Mountain View, CA: Pacific Press, 1909.

[White, James.] "DOINGS OF THE BATTLE CREEK CONFERENCE October 5 & 6, 1861." *Review and Herald* 18, no. 19 (October 8, 1861): 148.

———. "Gospel Order." *Review and Herald* 4, no. 22 (December 6, 1853): 173.

———. "Spiritual Gifts." In *Spiritual Gifts*, vol. 3, by E. G. White, 9–31. Battle Creek, MI: Seventh-day Adventist Publishing Association, 1864.

———. "Time to Commence the Sabbath." *Review and Herald* 31, no. 11 (February 25, 1868): 168.

———. "Yearly Meetings." *Review and Herald* 14, no. 9 (July 21, 1859): 68.

White, William C. "General Session on April 9, 1903." *General Conference Bulletin* 5, no. 10 (April 10, 1903): 158.

Wilcox, F. M. "Impressions and Dreams." *Review and Herald* 100, no. 7 (February 15, 1923): 7.

Williams, W. H. "Hold Our Mission Lines—This Our Watchword." *Review and Herald* 110, no. 25 (June 22, 1933): 1.

Wilson, Brian C. *Dr. John Harvey Kellogg and the Religion of Biologic Living.* Bloomington: Indiana University Press, 2014.

Worthen, Molly. *Apostles of Reason: The Crisis of Authority in American Evangelicalism.* New York: Oxford University Press, 2013.

Yamaguchi, Mari. "The Nones of Japan." Associated Press, October 5, 2023. https://tinyurl.com/ywb788kr.

Youngberg, Norma R., and Gerald H. Minchin, *Under Sealed Orders: The Story of Gus Youngberg.* Mountain View, CA: Pacific Press, 1970.

Zurlo, Gina A. "A Demographic Profile of Christianity in Sub-Saharan Africa." In *Christianity in Sub-Saharan Africa*, edited by Kenneth R. Ross, J. Kwabena Asamoah-Gyadu, and Todd M. Johnson, 3–18. Edinburgh: Edinburgh University Press, 2017. https://tinyurl.com/37skt2t9.

Index

INDEX